◀ ◀ ◀ ◀ ◀ ◀ ◀ ◀ ◀ ◀ ◀ ◀ ◀ ◀ STATES OF MEMORY

POLITICS, HISTORY, & CULTURE
A Series from the International Institute
at the University of Michigan

SERIES EDITORS
Julia Adams and George Steinmetz

SERIES EDITORIAL ADVISORY BOARD
Fernando Coronil, Geoff Eley, Fatma Muge Gocek,
Nancy Rose Hunt, Webb Keane, David Laitin, Julie
Skurski, Margaret Somers, Ann Laura Stoler,
Katherine Verdery, Elizabeth Wingrove

Sponsored by the International Institute at the University of Michigan and published by Duke University Press, this series is centered around cultural and historical studies of power, politics, and the state—a field that cuts across the disciplines of history, sociology, anthropology, political science, and cultural studies. The focus on the relationship between state and culture refers both to a methodological approach—the study of politics and the state using culturalist methods—and to a substantive approach that treats signifying practices as an essential dimension of politics. The dialectic of politics, culture, and history figures prominently in all the books selected for the series.

A complete list of titles appears at the end of this book.

CONTINUITIES, CONFLICTS,

AND TRANSFORMATIONS IN

NATIONAL RETROSPECTION

Edited by Jeffrey K. Olick

DUKE UNIVERSITY PRESS

DURHAM AND LONDON 2003

◀ ◀ ◀ ◀ ◀ ◀ ◀ ◀ ◀ ◀ STATES OF MEMORY

Designed by Rebecca M. Giménez
Typeset in Scala by Keystone
Typesetting · Library of Congress
Cataloging-in-Publication Data
appear on the last printed page of
this book. Acknowledgments for the
use of copyrighted material appear
on page 355, which constitutes an
extension of the copyright page.

◀ ◀ ◀ CONTENTS

◄ ◄ ◄ ◄ ◄ ◄ ◄ ◄ ◄ ◄ ◄ ◄ ◄   ACKNOWLEDGMENTS

This book had its origins in two sessions on collective memory at the 1996 meeting of the Social Science History Association, and subsequently as a special issue of *Social Science History* (volume 22, #4, 1998). Paula Baker, then editor of *Social Science History*, was instrumental in enabling the transformation of the sessions into the journal special issue, and offered excellent advice, organizational skill, and moral support throughout the process. Amir Weiner, Priscilla Ferguson, and Daniel Levy provided help and advice along the way. I thank Danny especially for his generosity of spirit and intellectual sustenance.

Introduction

◀ ◀ ◀ ◀ ◀ ◀ ◀ ◀ ◀ ◀ ◀ ◀ ◀ ◀   J E F F R E Y K . O L I C K

Since at least the nineteenth century, scholars and politicians alike have recognized the fundamental connection between memory and the nation. While political elites invented and propagated legitimating traditions, historians objectified the nation as a unitary entity with a linear descent. At the same time, critics like Renan pointed out that forgetting is at the heart of national self-understanding—forgetting alternative possible stories and alternate possible identifications—while Nietzsche bemoaned the proliferation of "monumental" history. The First World War seemed to many good enough reason to abandon nationalist chauvinism, but for others a myth of the war experience "provided the nation with a new depth of religious feeling, putting at its disposal ever-present saints and martyrs, places of worship, and a heritage to emulate" (Mosse 1990). And the anemic internationalism of the 1920s was just that—inter-nationalism rather than postnationalism, based on a nebulous and misunderstood notion of "self-determination"—where the burning memory of stabs in the back and imposed settlements fanned old antipathies to new heights. Memory has long been the handmaiden of nationalist zeal, history its high counsel. Even those like Nietzsche and Renan who critiqued memory's ambitions understood its centrality.

Recent theorists of nationalism, however, have challenged both national memory and historiographical nationalism by historicizing the nation as an identitarian as well as political form. As Benedict Anderson (1991: 5) puts it, there is a paradox in "the objective modernity of nations in the [non-nationalist] historian's eye vs. their subjective antiquity in the eyes of nationalists." According to Anderson, the nation is the only candidate to make up for the missing existential securities lost with the decline of the religious world view resulting from the accelerated rhythms of life under print-capitalism. Anderson argues that a massive transformation of temporal perceptions and an associated rise of interest in the past thus made it possible, even necessary, "to think the nation" in the eighteenth and nineteenth centuries. Nationalism, as Anthony Smith (1986) puts it, in the process became "a surrogate religion which aims to overcome the sense of futility engendered by the removal of any vision of an existence after death, by linking individuals to persisting communities whose generations form indissoluble links in a chain of memories and identities."

Theorists of postmodernity, however, have focused not on the rise of the memory-nation but on its demise in recent years. This is not old-style modernization theory, which sees nationalism as an intermediate stage in a progression from enchanted to disenchanted world views, though it does occasionally reverberate teleological overtones. Rather, these authors have problematized the role of memory as one component in a complex and shifting amalgam of perceptions that form the pervasive and permanent, though ever-changing, historicity of the world. There are no identities, national or otherwise, that are not constituted and challenged in time and with histories, but nations have had a special place in the history of memory and identity and in the history of their relations. Memory and the nation have a peculiar synergy. Even when other identities compete with or supplant the national in postmodernity, they draw on—and are increasingly nostalgic for—the uniquely powerful forms of memory generated in the crucible of the nation-state.

According to Pierre Nora (1992)—the preeminent figure in recent discussions of the memory-nation nexus—the memory-nation in its ascendancy relied on national historical narratives to provide continuity through identity. In the nineteenth century, Nora argues, the nation as a foundation of identity eroded as the state ceded power to society. The nation itself, earlier shored up by memory, now appears as a mere "memory trace." Nora thus sees the nation-state as declining in salience, the last incarnation of the unification of memory and history, a form in which history could provide the social cohesion memory no longer could. But history too has now lost its temporary ability to transmit values with pedagogical authority (Wood 1994). We are left with a proliferation of different memories; the remains of unitary history are but residues scattered throughout the social landscape.

"We speak so much of memory," Nora writes, "because there is so little of it left." Where premodern societies lived within the continuous past, contemporary societies have separated memory from the continuity of social reproduction; memory is now a matter of explicit signs, not of implicit meanings. Our only recourse has been to represent and invent what we can no longer spontaneously experience. The memory-nation of the late-nineteenth century was never really up to the task, though it managed for a while because it used the past to project a unitary future. Now, since the end of the twentieth century, we experience a memory boom in which novelty is associated with new versions of the past rather than with the future. In contrast to the historical fever to legitimize the nation-state that Nietzsche derided, "the mnemonic convulsions of our culture," Andreas Huyssen (1995) writes, "seem chaotic, fragmentary, and free-floating."

But theorists of postmodernity are divided as to whether this is a case of total loss. Nora's grand project to catalogue all of the "sites of memory" in French society has been labeled by some critics a neonationalist fantasy (Englund 1992). Patrick Hutton (1993) has characterized it as a call not to celebrate the past but to celebrate our celebrations of the past; Hutton refers to Nora's project as the attempt to autopsy the past's remains. On the other hand, many others are relieved by the refutation of nationalist grand narratives. Jonathan Boyarin (1994), for instance, points out that statist ideologies "involve a particularly potent manipulation of dimensionalities of space and time, invoking rhetorically fixed national identities to legitimate their monopoly on administrative control." Prasenjit Duara (1995) writes that the relationship between linear historicity and the nation-state is repressive: "National history secures for the contested and contingent nation the false unity of a self-same, national subject evolving through time" enabling "conquests of Historical [sic] awareness

over other, 'nonprogressive' modes of time." Huyssen (1995) sees in recent positions "a welcome critique of compromised teleological notions of
history rather than being simply anti-historical, relativistic, or subjective."

◀ ◀ ◀

At a more mundane level, it is clear that questions of memory and its
relation to national and other identities have moved to the center of a
variety of intellectual agendas in the past ten to twenty years (see Olick
and Robbins 1998). Scholars from a wide range of disciplines and with
diverse area specialties have begun to examine aspects of social memory.
Sources of this scholarly interest include a revival in cultural sociology
(Crane 1994) and the sociology of knowledge (Swidler and Arditi 1994),
the turn first to social and then to cultural history and the associated
questioning of historiography's epistemological privilege (Hutton 1993),
as well as multiculturalism's interest in unrecorded histories as sources
for alternative narratives and identities. Scholarly interest in memory,
however, has largely followed political developments, including the increase of redress claims, the rise of identity politics, a politics of victimization and regret, an increased willingness of governments to acknowledge
wrongdoing, as well as the breakdown of repressive regimes that have left
difficult legacies behind—all part of the decline of the memory-nation
as an unchallengeable hegemonic force. It is possible to trace some of
this, as I do in my paper in this volume, to the universal impact of the
Holocaust, to principles of justice developed for the Nuremberg tribunals,
as well as to German and other struggles with this legacy. But as the
theories outlined above demonstrate, there is something more broadly
existential and epochal going on here.

One problem with the diverse landscape of scholarship on memory,
and particularly on the memory-nation connection, is that it has often
opted for one extreme or the other: either epochal generalizations of the
sort outlined above that move in the rarefied atmosphere of general theory and macro-history; or parochial case studies that may appreciate the
uniqueness of particular moments in particular places but often miss
what is general or comparable in the cases. A common syndrome is the
attempt to address through a few references in a first chapter other cases
that are rarely examined again in the rest of the work. From the other side,
there is the temptation to level unique cases as mere instantiations of a

trend that occurs above or beyond the memory work done in particular times and places, the subjectless history of theoretical eschatology.

The papers presented here seek, in their own ways, to remedy the infelicitous choice between parochialism and generalism in the analysis of the memory-nation nexus. As I've written elsewhere (Olick and Robbins 1998), social memory studies is a "non-paradigmatic, transdisciplinary, centerless enterprise." In other words, despite an enormous efflorescence of interest in social remembering—and particularly in the memory-nation nexus—surprisingly slow headway has been made conceptually and methodologically, and unfortunately little cross-case discourse has developed. The authors here are unusual in that they are immersed in their particular cases as well as fundamentally interested in methodology and cross-case connections. Their papers provide illustrative case studies that contribute to middle-level theory—not as an alternative to either particular or grand approaches, but as part of an integrated program that includes elements of each, where the general and the particular, epochal and eventful, inform each other iteratively in scholarship as they do in life.

The first major issue with which each must come to terms is methodological: How do we approach a phenomenon—or set of phenomena—at once so general and particular? What mechanisms and patterns are common across cases, how are distinct cases connected, and how do we discover or theorize these commonalities and connections without hypostatizing or reifying them? Given the origins of the concept of collective memory in the crucible of statist agendas, unfortunately, scholars of the memory-nation nexus have inherited reductionist tendencies. Regarding nationalism, for instance, Rogers Brubaker has demonstrated that scholars mistakenly begin by trying to define what a nation is because they see nations as entities. In the process, Brubaker argues, they risk adopting "categories of practice as categories of analysis." Nationalists work hard, that is, to reify the term (nation) on which they base their claims. But nations are not entities that develop; they are practices that occur, institutional arrangements that are continually enacted and reenacted. Scholars must therefore be careful to "decouple the study of nationhood and nationness from the study of nations as substantial entities"; they need to study the reifications of nationalists without certifying them ontologically.

Brubaker notes in regard to nationalism research that "one might think this sociologically naive view has no place in recent scholarship."

But the situation is even more dire in the literature on collective memory, where the very term substantializes what is in fact a fluid process. Where *remembering* is a quintessentially relational phenomenon (what is it if not relating?), *memory* is a grossly substantialist metaphor, implying cold storage rather than hot use. This is to say nothing of "collective," which often implies all the problems Simmel found with "society" when he replaced it with "sociation," in addition to the standard anti-Durkheimian critique of an assumed unity. How, then, are we to approach collective memory without adopting the bogus naturalism of memory makers or the misleading substantialism of an outdated social science?

The literature on "collective memory" has provided two polar options: either treat collective memory as the lowest common denominator or normal distribution of what individuals in a collectivity remember, or see "the collective memory" as a "social fact sui generis," a matter of collective representations that are the properties of the "collective consciousness," which is itself ontologically distinct from any aggregate of individual consciousness.[1] Maurice Halbwachs—the seminal figure in this field—often sounds like a true Durkheimian in the latter vein (which makes sense, given that he was Durkheim's student), but he also provides the seeds of a "third way." All remembering, Halbwachs argues, takes place in group settings and is a matter of social interaction. In this way, it does not make sense at the limit to distinguish sharply between individual and social memory. Furthermore, highlighting this interactive setting helps avoid hypostatizing memory. Rather, it is to grasp the processual aspects of *remembering*, not the static aspects of *memory*. Halbwachs hints at these moves, though his vocabulary remains distinctly classical.

In more contemporary language, it makes sense to refer to mnemonic "practices" rather than treating "the collective memory" as a "social fact sui generis" in the Durkheimian sense, or reducing it to mere properties of cognitive atoms. A genuinely processual scholarship—which, as I discuss at the end of this introduction, is the hallmark of a new historicism in the social sciences—thus avoids the substantialist temptations by viewing social remembering as the ideological projects and practices of actors in settings. People, alone or together, remember, recollect, commemorate, etc. These various mnemonic practices, however, create only the appearance of substance rather than an actual entity scholars should treat as (the?) collective memory. Actors make claims on behalf of memory, assert what they think it is and what they want to have as parts of it; scholars study remembering and the variety of other practices associated with it (e.g., commemoration, museification, heroization, etc.) but avoid taking claims made on behalf of and in terms of collective memory as indicators of a substantial entity—"the collective memory." The scholar's job, again, is to chart the uses of the claim, not to participate in its ontological transubstantiation from concept into reality.

This point may seem easily assimilable to standard "constructionist" positions in the interpretive social sciences, which emphasize the ways in which taken-for-granted categories of thought and action are really the products of the interested activities of particular actors rather than features of nature. Social constructionism, of course, is a much maligned position, but not always for the right reasons. Critics charge constructionists with idealism, with the assertion that "social reality" is merely the emanation of the minds of social actors. But few constructionists truly go that far. The constructionist challenge is to highlight the active involvement of people in making the social world around them. The real problem with constructionism is thus not idealism. Instead, it is a tendency toward voluntarism: Constructionists often move too easily from W. I. Thomas's famous dictum that "situations defined as real are real in their consequences" *not* to the belief that situations *defined* as real *are* real, but to the belief that all one has to do to create an identity is "imagine" it.

The papers that follow here are more careful. They show how memory-makers don't always succeed in creating the images they want and in having them understood in the ways they intended. Social actors are often caught in webs of meaning they themselves participate in creating, though not in ways they necessarily could have predicted. While these papers do not respond explicitly to a methodological manifesto (mine or someone else's) for social memory studies, taken together they advance our understanding of mnemonic nationalism and national mnemonics in this way. Noting that memory is supposed to underwrite identity by establishing permanence and continuity in the face of rampant change, these papers ask what happens when the conditions of memory itself change dramatically. These papers examine cases in which national memory is in flux, and thus they problematize the idea of collective memory as they study claims made on its behalf.

Almost all the authors, for instance, highlight that memory itself has a history; not only do particular memories change, but the very faculty of memory—its place in social relations and the forms it imposes—changes over time. Additionally, memory is never unitary, no matter how hard various powers strive to make it so. There are always subnarratives, transitional periods, and contests over dominance. One tendency in the literature on social memory has been to treat this contestation and struggle for dominance as memory's purpose, that is, to see memory in instrumentalist terms (Olick and Robbins 1998). All of the papers here, however, resist this instrumentalist position without dismissing its insights. As Francesca Polletta argues, for instance, the political stakes in memory are not always clear. Part of the struggle over the past is not to achieve already constituted interests but to constitute those interests in the first place. As Lyn Spillman demonstrates, the pursuit of interests always works in combination with the multivalent meanings that the past allows; neither the "inherent meanings" of the past nor pure exigency in the present can explain why some pasts endure while others die out. Memory's salience at any given point in time, moreover, depends not only on its meanings and their manipulations but, as I and others demonstrate, on the complex trajectories memory forms over time. As Spillman sums it up, memory is consequential but in paradoxical ways.

Additionally, all of the papers here problematize, to one degree or another, conventional distinctions between history and memory as differences between truth and subjectivity. Instead, the papers argue that history and memory are varieties of historical consciousness. While such an approach can lead to an unproductive relativism, these papers pursue arguments that strive merely to show how claims of truth and meaning are accomplished, rather than to judge such claims. As Fred Corney argues, only in this way can scholarship on memory avoid participating in its reification.

Another, perhaps more substantive, similarity in these papers is the way in which many of them highlight the struggle for some kind of "normalization" of memory. Each of the societies discussed in these papers produces ideas of what a normal past should look like, and uses those images as ideals to strive for or denied rights to long for. These images include claims for the genuineness of revolution (imperial France, fascist Italy, communist Russia, Maoist China), of inclusiveness (United States, Australia), of innocence or ignorance (Germany, Japan, Spain), and of inevitability (Israel). In each case, there are voices and data that deny those claims. Given the seeming pervasiveness of such narrative foils, we might wonder if images of normalcy serve some formal as well as substantive purposes, such as giving identitarian myths—and the programs they motivate—dramatic shape. Just as there are many reasons why cases cannot be normal, moreover, there are many definitions of normalcy. The question is how images of normalcy work within and are produced by particular societies; normalcy is as much an endogenous feature of collectivities as it is an external standard. What are the rules of normalization, and how do these change over time and vary across cases?[2]

◀ ◀ ◀

Each of these issues, of course, takes on unique contours in the different cases. In his study of the myth of the October Revolution, Fred Corney highlights the ways in which the same discourse of revolution that underlies political rhetoric has blinded scholarly analysis. Both discourses debate whether the events of 1917 were a "true" revolution. Such a focus on truth or authenticity, in this case and in general, Corney argues, "is not conducive to a reexamination by scholars of their own conceptions, desires or prejudices." The scholarly and public discourses both employ wooden distinctions between society and state as binary opposites rather than as ongoing cultural constructions. The persistence of such reifications leads scholars after 1989 to search for an "authentic" memory that was repressed by previous political agendas. Such an approach hides the ways in which public and private interpenetrate; there is no pristine memory. Nor is there a primal "event" against which memories can be judged: the October revolution, Corney argues, was above all a remembered event, an event constituted as cultural memory. "Any critical reconceptualization of October," he argues, "must begin from a critical awareness of this process of construction."

Simonetta Falasca Zamponi also focuses on a myth of revolution, this time in the case of Italian fascism. Falasca Zamponi's major contribution here is to situate this myth as a solution to the more general epochal condition of memory, brilliantly theorized by Walter Benjamin as being in a perpetual state of crisis deriving from the lost conditions of authenticity and meaning before time became "empty and homogenous." The fascist solution, Falasca Zamponi argues, was an attempt to resacralize the world by bringing back the aura of tradition through manipulation of exactly those technical means that had led to the problematic desacralization in the first place. Fascism's aesthetic politics, she argues, repossessed the rituals and cults that the modern era had promised to crush. In this process, a myth of revolution was central, for it provided the needed sense of continuity by "naturalizing" the fascist regime as an outcome of a long teleological process. "Memory," she argues, "worked as a sealing agent of national consciousness through a normalizing process that linked fascism to the sacred past."

In his study of the Paris Commune, Matt K. Matsuda illuminates how the epochal and the particular unite in one potent symbolic gesture: toppling the Vendome Column. Symbolic gestures, Matsuda demonstrates, are consequential not only because we lose control over their meanings the moment we enact them, but also because they are inextricable links in elaborate systems of meaning. No such gesture can be understood in isolation because it ramifies through a complex and often tightly knit terrain of meanings. But the toppling of the Vendome Column is a perspicuous event not only because of its pivotal political importance but also because of its comment on the epochal significance of the kind of commemoration the column embodied. In attacking this central symbol of the imperial world, revolutionary actors attacked not just the Empire, but the Imperial form of mnemonic legitimation. Resistance against a particular memory thus became resistance against a particular *kind* of memory, a stage in the transformation of the memory-nation nexus.

Papers by Paloma Aguilar, Tong Zhang and Barry Schwartz, Lyn Spillman, and Francesca Polletta focus more closely than Corney, Falasca Zamponi, and Matsuda on the domestic rather than epochal contours of official memory, though they share the focus on memory not as a vessel of truth or mirror of interests but as a process of meaning construction. In perhaps the most classically social-scientific of the papers in this volume, Paloma Aguilar analyzes the memory of the Spanish Civil War, emphasizing the different roles different versions of that memory played in different regions. Noting these differences, of course, destabilizes the very notion of a national memory. On what basis can we identify such a unified entity? Some basic facts may be shared in different populations, but these same facts have widely differing moral and identitarian consequences depending on location, interest, experience, and attitude. Moreover, the ability of national elites to support an integrative identitarian program depends on their abilities to negotiate and accommodate these different positions. In Spain, this created an environment of mnemonic accomodationism. A unifying agenda could succeed only insofar as it did not exacerbate powerful differences. But in some ways, even this strategy could not succeed because accomodationist attempts ultimately could not circumvent Spain's "plurinational" structure.

Lyn Spillman undertakes a rich comparison of centennial and bicentennial celebrations in the United States and Australia. Her explicit goal is to theorize why memories differ not regionally but over time—why some memories at a national level persist while others fade. Here Spillman develops a productive combination of "instrumentalist" and "essentialist" approaches. The former sees the past as a malleable resource in the present, subject to the vicissitudes of contemporary usefulness and power. Spillman demonstrates through her cases that such an approach cannot account for the differential persistence of similar founding moments. Her answer is that differences of persistence are the results not of the inherent meaning of past events or of present exigency alone but of the combination of meaning and exigency, in which the degree of the past's meaningful multivalence increases its likelihood of survival. In the cases she analyzes, the crucial difference lay in their openness to oppositional politics: where they were open, they persisted; where they were not, they lost salience as oppositional consciousness gained power.

Tong Zhang and Barry Schwartz address similar issues, though in their case tracing the career of a reputation—that of Confucius—through a particular transformative event—the Cultural Revolution in Maoist China. Like Matsuda, they highlight the complexity of a cultural system, demonstrating the cultural logics of memory: "The communist establishment," they demonstrate, " . . . was simultaneously drawn to Confucius because his memory legitimated its hegemony and repelled by Confucius because his ideals opposed its revolution." "The regime's reinterpretation of Confucius," they argue, "was required by the logic of its new political cause, but the significance of that new interpretation cannot be reduced to the political interests it served." The solution, they contend, was not to alter the image of Confucius but to develop a new form of appropriation: "critical inheritance." The important generalizable point here is that the malleability of memory is neither a given nor even something that varies

quantitatively: malleability changes qualitatively—it is sometimes a matter of alteration, sometimes a matter of selection, and sometimes one of
inflection. Malleability, moreover, is in the context as well as in the image.
While one might be concerned with the characterization here of China as
a "backward" society, the sociological insights about memory—the emphasis on the social context not only of memories but of the conditions for
transforming them—are key and durable.

Francesca Polletta's paper on the memory of Martin Luther King Jr.
in the U.S. Congress shows at an even closer level the problems with
straightforward instrumentalist accounts: she demonstrates how difficult
it is for actors, and by extension for analysts, to know what the different
interests are in battles over the past. She argues that interests are defined
in the course of struggles over the past, not prior to them, by showing how
black legislators negotiated the perils of their liminal position between
legitimate authority and oppositional challenge. The general lesson from
this case, she argues, is that states are not monolithic entities but comprise numerous actors with overlapping, competing, and changing constituencies. Her analysis highlights the unique problems that commemorating dissent can pose for "open" societies. Such challenges, Polletta
writes, show how cultural conventions of commemoration are neither
unchanging nor universal but rather the products of ongoing struggle.

Papers by Ram, Olick, and Gluck show how memory contestation is
not just the product of social contestation but is part of official narratives
themselves. In his study of the recent (and ongoing) Israeli historians'
dispute, Ram shows how collectivities are involved in a constant process
of selection among various narrative options. This process, however, has
become even more problematic in recent years. Ram situates the new
Israeli critical discourse within developments in academic historiography
toward a questioning of history's epistemological claim, and also within
broader epochal shifts toward a postmodern society rife with tensions
between the global and the local. Following Nora and the other epochal
theorists discussed earlier in this introduction, Ram argues that Israel is
facing the declining salience of the unitary memory-nation, a "scrambling
of the unilinear and teleological national metanarrative by a variety of
supra-narratives, subnarratives, backlash narratives, and subsidiary narratives." Historical revision, as is occurring in Israel, is now a worldwide
phenomenon and sheds as much light on the present as on the past.

My own paper on official memory in Germany since 1989 shares many of the themes discussed in the other papers. I simultaneously situate the German case in the more general context of the politics of regret and trace that mood to the history of the German case. Like the others, I resist purely instrumentalist approaches, arguing that it is essential to appreciate how memory is path-dependent as well as instrumental and meaningful. The German case is an especially interesting demonstration of these processes in part because memory has been such an explicit presence in public discourse there for so many years. There is much to be learned, I argue, from how German leaders have negotiated their desire for "normalization" through the related strategies of relativization and ritualization. If history is any indicator, we should see these strategies adapted and adopted elsewhere as well. The lesson for the theory of memory is that whether the past passes away or not depends not only on its meanings and its contexts, but also on its forms and commemorative trajectory.

In a particularly important paper for understanding the epochal contours of memory, Carol Gluck focuses on the "end" of the "postwar" in Japan. The "postwar" is such a perspicuous concept for analysis because it embodies a central modern narrative desire—the desire to move beyond a bad past to a good future. Nevertheless, as Gluck argues, "the discursive solidity of modernity, of course, was a mirage." Japan experienced multiple postwars deriving from multiple and, in important ways, incompatible narrative frameworks, and thus ended these postwars at diverse times and places and in diverse ways. This multiplicity, Gluck argues, "rendered different fractal patterns of . . . [Japan's] late modernity, itself understood as a belated opportunity to remedy the defects of an earlier phase of the process of becoming modern." The ends of Japanese postwars, in this way, imply the end of a particular conception of the modern, one in which memory can be reconciled with past understandings, contemporary desires, and future ambitions. Situating the memory of the Second World War within the memory of earlier periods of Japanese history and within global narratives of progress reveals what Gluck calls "conceptual insufficiencies" for facing an end of one thing without it indicating a direction for the next. It may have been a great gesture to topple imperial legitimation along with the Vendome Column as Matsuda discusses, but with the loss of the Utopian vision inherent in that gesture we no longer quite know what to hope for. And as Nora, Anderson, Smith, and the other

theorists of nationalism cited above argue, national memory and commemoration are fundamentally hopeful practices. Gluck's paper develops
the dark side of these transformations.

Finally, from a rather different vantage point, Eviatar Zerubavel reveals
some features of national commemoration that are not obvious with either theoretical or case study approaches. In particular, Zerubavel illuminates the ways in which national calendars serve as cognitive maps
organizing structures of national identification. While there appear to be
a number of competing narrative structures for the "postwar," differing
interest positions on commemorative issues in different countries, diverse ideas of historical normalcy, and so on, there are some remarkable consistencies across cases in both the forms and contents of temporal mapping through national calendars. Indeed, Zerubavel argues that
"even what may at first glance seem nation-specific is usually but an
exemplar of some *trans*national commemorative pattern." The important
result here is that there is something specific and unique about national
commemoration as a form. Even as modernity becomes less certain and
the meanings of the past seem to multiply and become less secure, the
basic institutional structure remains fairly constant. Certainly, there has
been some innovation in national liturgies as well as in the interpretation
of established dates, but calendars as cognitive maps make powerful institutional sources of stability. Zerubavel thus identifies a powerful mech-
anism of commemorative consistency as well as an important set of characteristics of national commemoration per se.

◄ ◄ ◄

Taken together, the papers assembled here draw on and contribute to a
growing consolidation of social memory studies, one that includes an
interest in general epochal theory and the expert knowledge of area spe-
cialism. They show as well how theories of memory, theories of nationalism, and case studies are all involved in the same analytical project and are
each necessary to its fulfillment. The papers do this, moreover, while
avoiding the twin pitfalls of reification and voluntarism common in these
enterprises. They emphasize the ongoing processes of social construction
without ignoring instrumental, institutional, and historical claims. The
book's title—attractive for the double meaning of states—may thus appear
somewhat misleading: the memory discussed here is never static.

Theorists like Brubaker, among many others, have lately argued that historical social science has paradoxically been less genuinely historical than earlier models—turning more to data from the past but starting with unhistorical, static, substantialist, and otherwise discreditable concepts. A recent volume of essays on the so-called historic turn in the human sciences (McDonald 1996), for instance, argues that the social scientific turn to history, while salutary, has largely failed to historicize its own concepts. The approach to memory in national contexts developed here seems to be just the kind of historicizing project demanded, and the essays here are thus part of a broader transformation in historical social science. In what ways?

First, memory is the central faculty of our being in time; it is the negotiation of past and present through which we define our individual and collective selves. Memory should thus be a central topic for historical sociology. But second, the kind of approach developed in these essays, one that resists reification and instrumentalism, is crucial to the interrogation of categories of analysis that "processualists" (Brubaker 1996), "relationists" (Emirbayer 1997), and "temporalists" (Abbott 1988; 1990; 1994; Somers 1996; and Sewell 1996) have called for. Neither the nation nor memory is "natural," nor are their relations straightforward. Social memory studies of this kind thus mark a major transformation in the historical social sciences just as they interrogate major transformations in the social world as we assumed it was. To do this well, we need the approaches developed in these papers as well as the conversation that emerges out of juxtaposing them here.

NOTES

1. See Olick (1999) for a review of these two approaches.
2. See the special issue of *Sozialer Sinn* (vol. 2, 2001) on normalization.

REFERENCES

Abbott, A. 1988. "Transcending General Linear Reality." *Sociological Theory* 6: 169–86.
———. 1990. "Conceptions of Time and Events in Social Science Methods: Causal and Narrative Approaches." *Historical Methods* 23 (4): 140–150.
———. 1994. "History and Sociology: The Lost Synthesis." In Eric Monkkonen, ed.,

Engaging the Past: The Uses of History Across the Social Sciences. Durham, N.C.: Duke University Press.

Anderson, B. 1991. *Imagined Communities: Reflections on the Origins and Spread of Nationalism*. 2d ed. London: Verso.

Boyarin, J., ed. 1994. *Remapping Memory: The Politics of TimeSpace*. Minneapolis: University of Minnesota Press.

Brubaker, R. 1996. *Nationalism Reframed: Nationhood and the National Question in the New Europe*. New York: Cambridge University Press.

Crane, D., ed. 1994. *The Sociology of Culture: Emerging Theoretical Perspectives*. Oxford: Blackwell.

Duara, P. 1995. *Rescuing History from the Nation: Questioning Narratives of Modern China*. Chicago: University of Chicago Press.

Emirbayer, M. 1997. "Manifesto for a Relational Sociology." *American Sociological Review* 103, 2, Sept., 281–317.

Englund, S. 1992. "The Ghost of Nation Past." *Journal of Modern History* 64 (June): 299–320.

Hutton, P. 1993. *History as an Art of Memory*. Hanover, N.H.: University Press of New England.

Huyssen, A. 1995. *Twilight Memories: Marking Time in a Culture of Amnesia*. New York: Routledge.

Mosse, G. 1990. *Fallen Soldiers: Reshaping the Memory of the World Wars*. New York: Oxford University Press.

Nora, P., ed. 1992. *Les Lieux de mémoire*. 7 vols. *Les France, La République, Lé Nation* . . . Paris: Gallimard.

Olick, J. K. 1999. "Collective Memory: The Two Cultures." *Sociological Theory* 17, no. 3: 333–48.

Olick, J., and J. Robbins. 1998. "Social Memory Studies: From 'Collective Memory' to the Historical Sociology of Mnemonic Practices." *Annual Review of Sociology* 24: 105–40.

Sewell, W. H. Jr. 1996. "Three Temporalities: Toward an Eventful Sociology." In Terrence J. McDonald, ed., *The Historic Turn in the Human Sciences*. Ann Arbor: University of Michigan Press.

Smith, A. 1986. *The Ethnic Origins of Nations*. Oxford: Basil Blackwell.

Somers, M. 1996. "Where is Sociology After the Historic Turn? Knowledge Cultures, Narrativity, and Historical Epistemologies." In Terrence J. McDonald, ed., *The Historic Turn in the Human Sciences*. Ann Arbor: University of Michigan Press.

Swidler, A., and J. Arditi. 1994. "The New Sociology of Knowledge." *Annual Review of Sociology* 20: 305–29.

Wood, N. 1994. "Memory's Remains: *Les Lieux de Mémoire*." *History and Memory* 6, no. 1: 123–50.

Rethinking a Great Event:

The October Revolution

as Memory Project

◀ ◀ ◀ ◀ ◀ ◀ ◀ ◀ ◀ ◀ ◀   FREDERICK C. CORNEY

What if that discourse about [the French Revolution as] a radical break reflects no more than the illusion of change? . . . Unless the historian comes to grips with it, he is bound to execrate or to celebrate, both of which are ways of commemorating.—François Furet, *Interpreting the French Revolution*

Insofar as we yield without struggle to an external suggestion, we believe we are free in our thought and feelings. Therefore most social influences we obey usually remain unperceived.—Maurice Halbwachs, *The Collective Memory*

Even under the increasingly more open conditions of glasnost and after, the October Revolution has proven difficult for Western, Soviet, and post-Soviet historians to reconceptualize. In this essay I shall examine the reasons behind this difficulty and suggest where a reconceptualization of October might fruitfully be sought. Rethinking October from the perspective of recent research into the construction of historical or collective memory, I will argue, affords unique insights into exactly why October has proven so enduring. Focusing on the October Revolution as the crucial element in the primarily Bolshevik efforts to establish and enshrine the legitimacy of the new Soviet state during the first decade after October

1917 problematizes the event in a way that traditional approaches, deeply implicated in this issue of (il)legitimacy, are unable to do.[1]

In early 1995, the right-wing Liberal Democratic Party's (LDPR) faction in the Russian parliament (Duma) tabled a draft law entitled "On Recognizing as Illegal the Coup d'État [*gosudarstvennyi perevorot*] in Russia on 7 November (25 October) 1917." In March, Pavel Volobuev (1995: 3), a prominent historian, criticized the draft in a letter to *Pravda*. He drew an analogy between this act and the actions of the Chamber of Deputies in Bourbon France in 1815 that launched "malicious attacks and slander against the revolution and its activists" in an attempt to "extirpate from the popular consciousness any memory of the revolution." The failure of this attempt, he noted, was evident in the continued celebration by Frenchmen of 14 July, "the day of the start of one of the greatest (but also bloodiest) revolutions," as a national holiday. Volobuev warned that in its wake such a law could bring other laws abolishing all decrees taken by the Soviet government from 7 November 1917 to 5 December 1936. He sarcastically urged the LDPR to take the bull by the horns and propose a draft law recognizing the February Revolution as a coup d'état as well. In closing, he warned the authors of the draft law that "any disrespect for the history of the Fatherland, especially for its great pages, will sooner or later be avenged."

The draft law and Volobuev's response to it were interesting for what they revealed about the terms of the protracted debate about the Soviet past across the preceding decade. The LDPR had attacked the legitimacy of October by denying its right to be termed "revolution." Volobuev defended its legitimacy in a familiar Soviet-era invocation of October's place in a broader (French) revolutionary tradition, its place in individual and historical memory and in the national identity of Soviet Russia. As Martin Malia (1992: 9) has noted with regard to the question of whether October was a genuine workers' revolution or an armed insurrection by a political clique, such debates were really about the "legitimacy of the Soviet regime." Furthermore, since October has frequently been the conscious or unconscious telos of many historians' works, defining both the choice of and justification for the subjects studied, it is difficult to overestimate the significance of the issue of (il)legitimacy.

Still, this issue remains largely unquestioned in the many Western studies of glasnost-inspired revisions of the Soviet past. Such studies contrast the tentative modifications to the history of the October Revolution during the first years of glasnost against the "frank reassessment of the Revolution" (Marsh 1995: 147) that has purportedly occurred during the 1990s.[2] As evidence of such changes, Western scholars (Marsh 1995: chap. 9; Davies 1989; Nove 1989) point to the (re)publication of early sources critical of October, the appearance in the academic and popular press of less caricatured representations of those individuals or groups who opposed the Bolsheviks early on, or the "return" of those Bolsheviks who came to oppose party policies during the course of the 1920s. Similarly, in these first years of glasnost, Soviet historians ("Izuchenie" 1987: 52) identified the kinds of "new themes and trends" needed for a reappraisal of October, singling out the role of the intelligentsia, the urban middle classes, the antidemocratic regimes on White Guard territory, the "revolutionary creativity of the masses," and so on. Discussion of the viability of various "alternatives" to the October Revolution was widely welcomed as evidence of this reappraisal (Mogil'nitskii 1989; Shister 1990; Rogovin 1992; Butenko 1990; Frankel 1992: 3–13). Even for those historians who raised doubts about the traditional Soviet picture of a united Bolshevik Party under Lenin, faithfully supported by the masses and in firm control of the revolutionary timetable, October qua revolution remained beyond the limits of disbelief (Startsev 1987). Quite the contrary, the 70th anniversary of October 1917 brought to the pages of academic journals renewed pledges of faith from Mikhail Gorbachev in a landmark speech on this occasion, casting the present upheavals in Soviet society as a continuation of the October Revolution ("Oktiabr'" 1987; see also Iotov 1987). As the Soviet historian V. M. Selunskaia ("Izuchenie" 1987: 60) wrote at that time: "The October Revolution is the primary event of the twentieth century. Soviet historiography must preserve this fact in the historical memory of the peoples, reconstructing an ever more complete, adequate, and objectively truthful image of the first victorious socialist revolution in all its complexity and contradictoriness."

Yet as R. W. Davies (1997: 11–12) has shown, by the turn of the decade the early modifications to the official interpretation of October produced not a reevaluation of October but rather a wholesale condemnation of it by several erstwhile defenders of orthodox Leninist positions. This rejection of the Soviet past by indigenous historians was endorsed by prominent Western historians as a vindication of their own approaches (Conquest 1990, 1992; Pipes 1994; for a critique of this tendency, see Kenez 1991, 1995). The failed coup of August 1991 was followed by the removal of many symbols of Communism, indeed by a "new orthodoxy" of anti-Communism, although in 1991 October could still find its public defenders as a "genuinely popular revolution" (Davies 1997: 41, 47). Davies (1997: 11) cited a more typical sentiment expressed in April 1990 by a Soviet historian who insisted that the "true history" of the Soviet period could be written only if the "path on which Russia had embarked in October 1917 was recognized to be illegitimate."

In this atmosphere, the 73rd anniversary of the October Revolution became in the pages of *Pravda* a rearguard defense of the holiday against suggestions from certain quarters that the birth of the Soviet state should no longer be celebrated.[3] Articles welcomed the new political thinking "free of the myths and dogmas of the age of barracks communism" but cautioned against attempts "to negate the great and the valuable in our historical heritage."[4] Two noted historians wrote in support of the holiday and against the "present noisy campaigns against Lenin, Bolshevism and the October Revolution, indeed against Soviet power itself."[5] Editorials insistently chronicled the crowds of people who, despite the harsh conditions of life, turned out "in support of October" not only in Moscow but all over the country.[6] Personal pledges of support for the October Revolution were featured.[7] A year later, one newspaper published quotations ranging from a traditional embrace of October as the "stellar hour of the peoples of Russia" to a condemnation of it as a "very important event which had exclusively negative effects on the fate of Russia and all the rest of the world."[8]

The formal denunciation of the Communist past peaked with Boris Yeltsin's dissolution of the Supreme Soviet in the fall of 1993 and his pledge in November to do away with the "vestiges of the Communist and Soviet past" (Davies 1997: 59). This process was still incomplete four years later. On succeeding anniversaries of October, *Pravda* continued, although less and less defiantly, to be a beleaguered voice in support of the holiday. On what would, under the Soviet state, have been a gala celebration of October, the 75th anniversary was marked by a banner headline in *Pravda* noting that a ceremonial meeting devoted to this anniversary of the Great October Socialist Revolution had *not* taken place, and by articles that imagined how the centenary of October would look back at 1992 as a time when Russia was "the center of world anti-Communism."[9] Subsequent anniversaries were marked on the pages of *Pravda*, and scarcely anywhere else, by complaints about the lack of festive crowds on the streets and the threatening presence of security forces, and by ever more frequent evocations of nostalgia for the unity and comradeship of earlier anniversary celebrations.[10]

The reexamination of the Soviet past ushered in by glasnost and reflected in these changing commemorative efforts has been regarded, in the West and in the USSR, as essentially a *political* problem. Soviet historians' and others' conscious use of the October Revolution as a tool of political legitimization of the Soviet state has long been recognized (Bonwetsch 1976). Few would deny that Soviet historians wrote within political constraints that produced some of the driest and most formulaic writing on Soviet history, particularly on the October Revolution and the Bolshevik Party (Von Hagen 1992; Enteen 1989a, 1989b). Soviet academicians themselves criticized the "tremendous ideological and political bias" (Sakharov 1993: 191) that marked Soviet historical scholarship, or they explicitly blamed the "politicization" of history in the 1920s and 1930s for "monstrous aberrations" in Soviet society ("Istoricheskaia nauka" 1990: 75). Increasingly, they self-consciously rejected their earlier "politicized" approaches to their history, now championing the filling in of the "blank spots" (*belye piatna*) in their past, in an attempt to "complete" the historical record. Consciously "removing" themselves from their histories, glasnost-era historians embraced the illusion that historians merely provide the mouthpiece through which history speaks, through which documents relate past events.

Western scholars have long contrasted traditional Soviet scholarship against their own supposedly more objective and dispassionate accounts of the Soviet past. Just as, 30 years before, Robert V. Daniels's (1967: ix) study of October sought the "historical truth about the October Revolution," so Edward Acton's (1990: 209) recent "rethinking" looked to newly accessible archives to spur the effort "to recover the real drama of 1917 from the myths that it inspired." Both sides of the divide shared the same goal: a more truthful and complete record of the October Revolution, a goal that they believed could be attained under more judicious political conditions. That many researchers believe this record can be found in the Soviet archives is shown by the "archival gold rush" (Von Hagen 1993: 99–100) many have engaged in since the late 1980s. This focus on the political, pivoting on the issue of October's (il)legitimacy, has reduced Soviet historiography in the West and increasingly in Russia to what David Joravsky (1994: 851) has called a "good guy–bad guy melodrama."

OCTOBER REIFIED

Such reappraisals, to invoke François Furet's (1981: 17) conclusions from his study of the French Revolution, continue to execrate or celebrate October, thereby commemorating it. They in effect maintain its reified status and obstruct any deeper analysis of its historical and cultural genesis as a foundation event and its very real political and social function as such within early Soviet society. "Reification," Richard Handler (1994: 27) points out with reference to such terms as *nation, culture, tradition,* and *identity,* is "an epistemological problem not easily vanquished, for it pervades the rhetorical and conceptual apparatus of our scientific world view." His words apply equally well to the concept of revolution and to such related concepts as state and society. From the moment they took power in October 1917, the Bolsheviks deployed enormous resources to cast the takeover as a bona fide revolution, while their opponents were equally insistent on casting it as an illegitimate coup by a clique of adventurers (and "outsiders"). Generally, however, there was little disagreement about what constituted revolution, merely that this event did not merit the term.

It should not be surprising, given the conscious process of reification and mythicization of the October Revolution that took place within the USSR, that the event was for decades beyond question, certainly politically and perhaps emotionally, for many Soviet historians. More interesting is that revolution writ large shaped the debate among Western historians too. A denial of the very applicability of the term to the events of October 1917 was implicit in those scholars (Schapiro 1970; Daniels 1967;

Wolfe 1961) who, influenced by the totalitarian theories of the 1950s, sought the motive forces of the October overthrow in the program and resolutions of the Bolshevik Party and the actions and ideologies of its leaders, particularly Lenin. Guided by similar assumptions, other scholars (Brovkin 1987; Broido 1987; Radkey 1958, 1961) have sought explanations of October in the "failures" of other parties or individuals rather than in the "successes" of the Bolsheviks.

Those Western scholars who cut their political teeth during the social activism of the 1960s faulted political historians for paying too much attention to the state and the party and underestimating what Ronald Suny (1983: 32) calls the "more fundamental social and economic structures and conflicts in Russian society." For them, the October takeover was not a political coup by "outsiders" confined largely to Petrograd and Moscow but a countrywide, socially anchored revolution. These scholars attempted to identify the social legitimacy of the October Revolution through an examination of the role it played in one or another social or political group. Some (Haimson 1964, 1965, 1988) sought the causes of the revolution in the polarizing rifts among various classes from the turn of the century onward. The Bolshevik Party was no longer studied as the dominion of a handful of politicians, but as an organization integral to society, or at least to the working class (Rabinowitch 1968, 1978; Service 1979). The part played by the working class, and to a lesser degree by other social groups, in bringing about the revolution "from below" became a major focus of Western research (Kaiser 1987; Gill 1979; Suny 1972; Pethybridge 1972). Driven by similar conceptions, others (Wildman 1967; Bonnell 1983; Lane 1969) sought the longer-term "roots" of the revolution, again especially within the working class.

In a sense, October's affirmers and deniers were motivated by the same desire, namely, to save society from the state. Those who celebrated it as a revolution regarded it as a perhaps destructive but ultimately empowering force, providing voices to the silent masses. One such study aimed to show the "unheroic side of the Russian Revolution, of the ordinary men and women whose participation was essential to the revolution's outcome" (Koenker 1981: 3; Smith 1983; Mandel 1983, 1984; Pethybridge 1964). Those who regarded it as a "classic coup d'état" contrasted it with "genuine revolutions, [which] of course, are not scheduled and cannot be betrayed" (Pipes 1993: 498; see also Pipes 1992). In this view, Bolshevik power, illegitimately gained, could be maintained only through force, and in the final analysis only at society's expense.[11]

Such views share the conception of state and society as binary opposites, fostering a belief among many scholars that society's "true" voices were to be found in opposition to the given political regime (or state) (Mel'gunov 1953: 7; Schapiro 1977; Bettelheim 1976). This was considered particularly fitting in the case of the socialist or postsocialist states, "unauthorized representations of the past [being] the . . . windows through which we seek to understand socialist systems" (Watson 1994: 2). State institutions and policies were believed to impose an "official," largely sterile culture on a population by any means necessary. The illegitimate nature of the Soviet regime could be revealed, it was argued, by drawing back the "veil" of official culture, as historians claimed to divine the "genuine" thoughts of the people in the street, to hear what they "really" believed when not parroting the official line for personal gain or physical survival.

Recent studies, beginning to draw on Furet's insights (see, for example, Suny 1994), have attempted to understand the Soviet system not as a polarized, dichotomous entity but rather as a broad cultural and political project that provided individuals and groups with a wide variety of opportunities to create places for themselves within this system. In his study of the culture of the city of Magnitogorsk during the 1930s, Stephen Kotkin (1995: 22) proposes a shift in focus from "what the party and its programs *prevented* to what they *made possible*, intentionally and unintentionally." Kotkin's (1991) focus on the importance of language in the revolutionary exercise of power, as well as on the institutionalization of the very categories by which individuals in this new state conceived of themselves as part of this new state, has profound implications for the study of October. For the October Revolution was most enduringly a linguistic and institutional battle, the spoils of which would be the opportunity to recast the political, social, and cultural terrain of the former Russian Empire in profound ways. Sheila Fitzpatrick (1993) has called the process engaged in by the Bolsheviks after October 1917 a "reclassing" of society, involving not only the ascription of class categories but also the framing and construction of the bodies of information on which historians would draw for their analyses of this society.

For the most part, this institutional and linguistic battle for October was fought within the context of "commemorating" it. Early on, the Bolsheviks argued that the underground existence and conspiratorial nature of their party, and the destruction of much documentation during the civil war period, ensured that written sources on October were scant. As the Marxist historian Mikhail Pokrovskii (Deviataia konferentsiia 1972: 102) told a party gathering in 1920, the party's "archives" had been "carried in the pockets of secretaries and destroyed tens of times over." It was widely agreed from the very beginning by Bolshevik leaders that personal and group reminiscences about October would inevitably play a major role in preserving it (Ko vsem chlenam partii 1920). These reminiscences would form the basis of the new revolutionary "archive."

The October Revolution, then, was above all a *remembered* event, an event constituted as cultural and historical memory intended to legitimize the young Soviet regime. It is precisely in this process of linguistic, historical, and cultural constitution (and the power relationships it reveals) that several scholars have found a fruitful focus for their research (e.g., Foucault 1980; Hall 1982). Some have drawn upon the recently discovered theories of the sociologist Maurice Halbwachs (1925, 1980) on collective memory. His argument that people remember only within certain social groups or frameworks and that memories, and therefore thought, cannot be constituted outside of them has shifted the focus of study from the event itself to the *process* of remembering the event, taking into special account the structuring of the groups in which memories are articulated.[12] Ignoring this process can only reinforce the reification of the event; indeed, reification requires that this process of constitution recede into the background (De Certeau 1986: 203).

To date, scholars of early Soviet history have rarely treated the role of remembrance and commemoration problematically (a notable exception is Von Geldern 1993). For these scholars, glasnost represents the retrieval of suppressed historical memory. Memory is treated as a passive or brutalized victim of the manipulations and distortions of Communist ideology extending back to the late 1920s, even earlier in some cases. With "historical truth . . . on the march," goes a common sentiment, the historians' task becomes the "historical return of memory" (Coquin 1989: 21,

24; see also Brossat and Combe 1990; Merridale 1996). In this approach, both individual and collective memory would seem to exist outside the narrative or discourse, while "real" memories of events are somehow preserved in suppressed form beneath the "official" memory. For these researchers, "unofficial" memory serves as society's moral firewall against the encroachments of the state: "Wherever memory is impoverished, culture is also impoverished in its most vital foundations, and with it morality as well in all its manifestations, from politics to daily life" (Pamiat' 1976: v). The recovery of memory is crucial, in Geoffrey Hosking's (1989: 118) view, "and by that I mean real memory, not the mythologized substitute." Such views are offered as yet one more proof of the deeply illegitimate nature of the system, best captured in Malia's (1994: 270, 314) indictment of the entire system as being held together by a socialist "Myth-Lie."

These views do not do justice to the breadth and power of the October memory project. Its power derived from its makers' invocation, both conscious and unconscious, of certain conventions that rendered the process of construction embedded within it commonsensical or beyond question. For the makers themselves, these conventions were "natural" ways of telling their story and of persuading others of its relevance to their daily lives. Power in Bolshevik hands of course meant the power of the bullet, and this has been well and rightly documented in the historiography. It also, however, meant narrative power—that is, the power of the story and hence the power of language, without which the bullet would have little meaning, and archival and institutional power, without which the story would have little authenticity. "The action of a rioter in picking up a stone," observed Keith Baker (1990: 13, 41) in his study of the French Revolution as meaning-making process, "can no more be understood apart from the symbolic field that gives it meaning than the action of a priest in picking up a sacramental vessel." This process, he noted, occurred simultaneously at various levels, including the archival, symbolic, and political levels, and involved veritable "ideological arsenals." (On the selective and constitutive role of archives, for example, in institutionalizing a major narrative, see Trouillot 1995: 52–53.) The potency of the narrative form, its pretensions to be the communication of past reality, and the conscious and unconscious elements of the processes of storytelling have received deserved scholarly attention of late (White 1987; Kozicki and Canary 1978; Harlan 1989). Moreover, the Bolshevik story of October derived much power from its invocation as a story already told. Indeed, the Bolsheviks and other revolutionaries intentionally told their story as the telos of a venerable, transcendent revolutionary tradition dating back to the French Revolution, a tradition that was invoked and reinvoked, vainly throughout the nineteenth century, most promisingly in the form of the Paris Commune of 1871, and as apotheosis in October 1917.

The Bolsheviks were also informed by traditional notions about what it actually meant to "remember" a past event and by a belief that if individuals were not very quickly caused to fix the memory of the October Revolution in their minds, it, and its significance, would dissipate. They immediately set about "recording" it while it was still "fresh" in people's minds. They courted "eyewitnesses" and "participants" in particular because they believed that these people represented the most reliable criterion of the authenticity of the narrative. As one scholar notes (Lass 1994: 91), the eyewitness is traditionally regarded as "history's most valued source. . . . An individual's narration is valued because it authenticates what it provides: the what and how of past events. The witness's eye is also the eye of memory." The elastic nature of this term is revealed by the explanatory note (Ko vsem chlenam partii 1920: 9) to a questionnaire on the October Revolution: "Anyone who was in Russia in the past three years has had the chance of either observing or even taking part in the events that have occurred."

Within days of the takeover, the government newspaper, *Izvestiia*, carried a notice on its front page calling on all "comrade participants of the October overthrow" to send articles, reminiscences, poems, and "materials related to the October Revolution" for a special jubilee issue.[13] Various announcements were made of intentions to publish ambitious and costly collections of reminiscences on the October days.[14] The Union of Soviet Journalists even appealed on the radio and in the press to foreign comrades from "Communist and revolutionary socialist parties and groups, and also to the writers, scholars and philosophers affiliated with them," for their opinions about the Russian Revolution. These foreign comrades were asked whether they believed that the October overthrow had laid the basis for a world socialist revolution, what response it evoked in the proletariat of the respective country, and which of the measures of Soviet power the respondents regarded as "positive" and which as "mistaken."[15]

These early piecemeal efforts soon gave way during the 1920s to far more organized and institutionalized attempts to ground the new Soviet state in an accumulation of evidence of its legitimacy. Institutionally, this took the form of a panoply of complementary organizations. In October 1918, a Socialist Academy of the Social Sciences was set up to coordinate the production of Marxist publications, enlist prominent Marxists from abroad, and train specialists in a Marxist approach to the writing of history. The Scientific Society of Marxists followed in December 1920, the Institute of Red Professors in February 1921, and the Scientific Research Institute in 1922. In May 1924, the Institute of Lenin was ceremonially opened. These organizations were essentially information-producing bodies, and the information they produced was stored in a centralized network of new archives, an institutional sanction of the authenticity of the materials contained therein.

Within this context, the explicit efforts to construct October as part of historical memory also took on institutional form. The Bolshevik Party set up institutions to "record" personal and group reminiscences of October, including, among many, the Commission on the History of the October Revolution and the Communist Party (Istpart for short) (1920–28), the Commission on the Twentieth Anniversary of 1905 (1924–25), and the Commission on the Tenth Anniversary of October (1926–27). The October Revolution was also a primary focus of other organizations of this kind set up in the early 1920s, such as the Commission on the History of the Trade Union Movement, the Commission on the History of the Youth and Communist Movement, the Society of Former Political Prisoners and Exiles, and the Society of Old Bolsheviks. All were devoted in one way or another to producing cumulative "evidence" of the October Revolution. As the charter of Istpart stated (Ko vsem chlenam partii 1920: 7), "Our attitude to the documents of the revolution must be as active as our attitude to the events of the revolution."

These efforts were reinforced in turn by the accumulation of visual "evidence": renamed streets and squares all over the country; new statues and plaques appropriately inscribed; decorated buildings and squares on the anniversaries of October; carefully choreographed processions that lit-

erally mapped the Stages of the Revolution onto the cities for the participants; photographs of the "seminal" revolutionary events (broadly conceived) and their leaders in newspapers and journals; museums intended
to provide a coherent visual representation of the narrative of the October
Revolution; films commissioned from famous directors to "record" the
evolution in the most dramatic terms possible (most notably, of course,
Sergei Eisenstein's *Battleship Potemkin* and *October*). "Thousands of men
and even many women," Hunt (1984: 221) has written about the French
Revolution, "gained firsthand experience in the political arena: they talked,
read, and listened in new ways; they voted; they joined new organizations;
and they marched for their political goals. Revolution became a tradition."
In the case of the October Revolution, thousands of men and women
remembered it. As Albert Rhys Williams (1921: 197), one of the corps of
foreigners in Petrograd, had already recognized in 1918, "the Revolution
was an insistent fact assailing us in eye and ear with banners and battle-
cries, parades and assemblages."

ISTPART AND THE FRAMING OF MEMORY

In order to highlight some of the motivations and assumptions that informed this memory project, I will address in a little more detail the
commemorative efforts of the most ambitious of these institutions, Istpart (for an institutional history, see Holmes and Burgess 1982; Burgess
1981). For this project was not about "recovering" historical memory but
rather about framing it in the very process of elicitation. Istpart comprised
a network of central and local bureaus, later to be supported by organized
groups of individuals (*gruppy sodeistviia Istpartu*) at the local level; it organized central and local conferences of its members to coordinate activities; it instituted a variety of venues and methods at which individual or
group memories of October could be elicited from the often semiliterate
or illiterate population, most notably the questionnaire (*anketa*) and the
evenings of reminiscences (*vechera vospominanii*).

Through Istpart, the Bolsheviks and other revolutionaries told their
story of October in ways that allowed individuals and groups to write
themselves into this history. For many during the 1920s, October became
both the expression and proof of their own identity. In general, Bolshevik
power, in terms of the success of the Bolshevik metanarrative of the past,

meant an ability to make October part of the personal and collective experience of large parts of the population. As Toews (1987: 884) observes, "Even in the most authoritarian and closed homogeneous cultures," the general population is never merely passively adopting the narrative: "Meanings are never simply inscribed on the minds and bodies of those to whom they are directed or on whom they are 'imposed' but are always reinscribed in the act of reception."

This memory project was first and foremost defined by an awareness by those responsible for it of the power of representation—not surprising, considering that for much of their existence up to 1917 political parties had been engaged in propaganda battles over competing representations of each other. Instructions from Istpart on the kind of materials to collect noted that "[our enemies] will try with all their power . . . to reinterpret the Proletarian Revolution in their own class interests."[16] Speaking at the Ninth Party Conference in September 1920, the head of Istpart, M. S. Ol'minskii (Deviataia konferentsiia 1972: 100), argued that "this archival matter . . . should in no way be entrusted to our political enemies in this area." Pokrovskii (Deviataia konferentsiia 1972: 101–2) noted that opposing political leaders were publishing "volume after volume on the history of the revolution" and that "we have nothing yet in this area." He described the collection of materials on the revolution as a "battle," which, if lost, would mean that "our children would learn the history of the revolution from White Guard pamphlets." A year later, Ol'minskii (Protokoly 1933: 135) countenanced the disturbing eventuality that in the near future, if nothing were done about the history of October, young Communists would be asking: "And what is the February Revolution? And what is the October Revolution?"

The process could not, then, be left to chance or given over to the wrong hands. In 1920, Ol'minskii (Deviataia konferentsiia 1972: 98) pointed out that there were "many living people who could with their eyewitness testimonies reconstruct the past, who could write their memoirs." Istpart was not merely about gathering materials, he wrote (Iz epokhi 1921: 3) elsewhere, but about "creating the literature of memoirs (reminiscences)." The power of these reminiscences would reside in their being anchored by the individual as part of his or her own emotional and psychological past. "The conditions of everyday life," wrote one author (Slonimskii 1919: 1), "must frame those memoirs which will be written."

Ol'minskii (Deviataia konferentsiia 1972: 99) considered this dimension crucial to the form of the questionnaires that were sent out to party members eliciting their reminiscences: "It is desirable, comrades, that you not take a pro forma attitude to this, . . . but on the contrary that each time you recall in as much detail as possible not only the content of the resolutions, decrees and leaflets, but also the psychological, daily peculiarities of the moment."

Ol'minskii's comment about "creating" the reminiscences should be understood in this context. He shared the belief with revolutionaries in general that if the right questions could only be asked of the right people in the right places, the revolutionary movement would give up its story. Asking the right questions meant helping those involved at the grassroots level to understand the significance of their individual actions: in short, to understand that they were part of that movement. From the beginning, officials intended to *locate* the past; grassroots circles (*kruzhki sodeistvii*) would assist the local Istpart branches in this. These circles would draw in the oldest members of the party and "direct participants in the revolutionary events, if possible from various localities" (Afonin 1920: 1). "Surely we just *know* about our revolution," Istpart wrote (Ko vsem chlenam partii 1920: 4). "Everybody remembers what they have seen around themselves in the corner of Russia where fate tossed him for the past three years."

Enthusiasm for the use of personal reminiscences to provide the continuity, coherence, and color of the recent past was tempered by a general mistrust of the vagaries of memory. Personal memory was regarded as naturally flawed, first because people forgot things, and second because people lacked the perspective to realize the significance of certain "memorable" events. Ol'minskii (Deviataia konferentsiia 1972: 99) drew an analogy with legal cases, in which "all witnesses talk nonsense willy-nilly, and so the perspective is distorted." These problems were not helped by the sheer logistics of eliciting information from large numbers of often illiterate contemporaries.

The methods employed by Istpart to compensate for these weaknesses in the reminiscences and provide them with the necessary "perspective" were instrumental in shaping the reminiscences they elicited. "Through corroboration, the truth can be revealed," Ol'minskii said (Deviataia konferentsiia 1972: 99). "Everywhere there are mistakes, everywhere there are also crumbs of truth." Local bureaus were instructed to register and question old party activists and to urge them to write down their reminiscences. These reminiscences were to be reviewed by the bureau members, and gaps were to be supplemented by questioning the author. Where the reminiscences were given orally, local bureau workers were to write them down.[17] Other instructions pointed out that the unreliability of personal memory rendered it quite acceptable when writing one's reminiscences to cross-check by consulting documents, newspaper articles, or books (Iz epokhi 1921: 4). Istpart requested that it be sent any documents used by the respondents to "supplement, corroborate or reinforce" their information (Ko vsem chlenam partii 1920: 9). This was felt to be especially necessary when making use of tsarist police materials, which had to be verified against the memories of "old party comrades."[18] Clearly, any reminiscences thus produced would be artifacts not only of the individual but of the broader culture of the time.

Machiavellian design should not be automatically read into these instructions. Istpart leaders regarded the past as a picture that had to be reconstructed piece by piece: "Scattered and fragmentary when taken separately, they [i.e., personal reminiscences], in their totality, must supplement each other and make possible a complete compendium of information and an illustration of party life at different times and in various regions."[19] This belief in the need for corroboration and verification of the "facts" of the reminiscences, however, made them far more than the "simple" recollections of participants or contemporaries of the events in question. It not only brought into the framing of the reminiscences the already published and accepted "facts" of October but also prompted the creation of a network of group venues that was crucial to the construction of October as an integral part of the historical memory.

Istpart shaped the memory of the October Revolution in fundamental ways. First, efforts were made from the very beginning of the project to ensure that materials were organized so as to convey the coherence and consequentiality of the October Revolution. The work plans of local Istpart bureaus were defined by a broad narrative supplied by the central Istpart. Assigned to the Petrograd bureau, Nevskii in late 1921 called for a "completely rational plan" of work and proposed for the bureau a very structured plan of publications carried out "under the constant guidance of the [bureau's] chairman."[20] For the purposes of this essay, the actual shape of the narrative is less important than its flexibility. This grand narrative was flexible enough to allow local bureaus and party committees to incorporate local events into it.[21] It allowed local bureaus to work on any period of the last two decades and still remain within and hence corroborate the narrative. Each local bureau, therefore, collected its local materials according to a predetermined template. Indeed, it was not rare for local bureaus to complain of the lack of any guidance of their work as an explanation for their inaction during the difficult, chaotic first years of the Soviet republic.[22]

Second, Istpart provided organized and structured venues at which local groups and individuals could write themselves into this narrative. The most successful of these was the evening of reminiscences. One of the very first evenings of reminiscences was held on 7 November 1920, when individuals were brought together to reminisce about the "October days of 1917 in Petrograd."[23] Access was limited to 30 people, who were warned not to miss the evening. The participants were asked beforehand to write down the most important things they did at that time on a piece of paper to be given to an Istpart member before the evening began. They were also instructed to write down things that occurred to them in the course of the evening. Other themes fed into the October narrative in less direct ways. The Moscow bureau of Istpart brought together "groups of comrades who took part in the party organizations at the same time and in the same plant, or at various periods in one plant," to help produce a "complete picture of the party organization at the plant."[24] These meetings were carefully prepared beforehand; indeed, preparatory meetings were generally held so that, as the head of the Moscow bureau put it, "the reminiscers come completely prepared for a particular subject."[25] The Orenburg bureau even held an instructional conference in December 1925 with leaders of the evenings of reminiscences about how to conduct them, providing them with questions relating to the past.[26]

The dynamic of these evenings was crucial to the eventual shape of their product. At an evening of reminiscences on the occasion of the ninth anniversary of the October Revolution in the Vasileostrov district of Leningrad, the chair acted as guardian of the narrative, attempting to keep the reminiscers on the track of the chosen subject.[27] He sacralized the gathering by having all present stand "to honor the memory of the fallen fighters of the revolution." He announced that a presidium, against which there would be no objections, had been chosen to conduct the evening. Comrade

Kudelli, a prominent member of the Leningrad bureau, then arose to expound at length on the need for "perspective" on the part of those reminiscers who had been selected because of their active participation in the revolutionary events. She reminded them "how gradually the revolution in Leningrad had developed in general and how the October overthrow had come to a head." So that their reminiscences would not be "too diffuse," therefore, Kudelli ran down a list of the "stages" of the October Revolution experienced in the course of 1917: Lenin's arrival in Petrograd, stressing the way Lenin encouraged party members to be steadfast in not supporting the provisional government; the revolutionary processions of 21 and 22 April 1917 over Miliukov's pledge to continue Russia's part in the war, stressing the response to the workers of the "armed bourgeoisie"; the "revolutionary awakening" in the plants and factories, stressing the growing persecution of the Bolsheviks; and so on. Finally, Kudelli made sure to mention by name individual leading Bolsheviks who had believed in early October that Lenin's call for an uprising was premature and who left the Central Committee as a result. "If we can focus our attention on these stages," Kudelli told them, "we will be able to present a clear picture."

Within the confines of these guidelines, individuals' reminiscences of October were revealing. One speaker used the guidelines to legitimize his criticism of certain Bolshevik leaders' present-day behavior by reminiscing about their earlier vacillations during the October days. He expressed concern that the same "disease" had now reappeared in these comrades nine years later. What kind of reminiscing was this speaker engaging in, exactly? He was invoking his personal memories of the October overthrow in the service of the present needs of the party and thus his own personal needs. He not only relied on memory but also read out sections from the Central Committee resolution on the armed uprising and quotations from Lenin condemning the vacillators who had opposed the resolution. Most significantly, his reminiscences of leading Bolsheviks during the October Revolution were viewed through the prism of his own behavior at the time. He contrasted the uncertain behavior of Bolsheviks like Grigorii Zinoviev, one of the "vacillators," with the steadfast behavior of "advanced fighters" like him—"small screws in our greatest machine, the Leninist Party." His recollection that "comrade Zinoviev's declaration [against an armed uprising] was like an exploding bombshell for us" was a product of the entire October-writing process to which he had been exposed. This process now provided all reminiscers with a clear social and political language in which to articulate their own tales of personal political activism during October. Another reminiscer remembered that his factory's poor showing during the revolution was due to its being made up of the "peasant element" as well as small shopkeepers who were hiding from the war. The few Bolsheviks in this plant, which was dominated by Socialist Revolutionaries (s rs) and Mensheviks, had to work under conditions of persecution and hostility from the plant management and, in particular, from many female workers.

Some reminiscers wrote themselves into October in an unmistakably direct fashion, brandishing their credentials by publicly boasting their personal roles. One such participant even added that he had visited Lenin in Finland. He placed himself in one of the major moments Kudelli had listed, namely, the Finland Station on 16 April 1917 to meet Lenin, and could of course not fail to be appropriately moved by the moment: "We stood to one side, far from him, but I heard him say 'Up with the Socialist Republic' and in these words it was necessary to understand that the revolution was continuing and preparing itself for 25 October." This personal epiphany should not be taken literally to signify his thoughts in mid-October 1917; neither, however, should it be dismissed merely as cynical self-aggrandizement. It is the very essence of personal memories of such events, which acquire their greatest significance in the individual autobiography. These evenings were not merely about recalling the past; they were about remembering and experiencing it as a function of the present. Within the multiple frameworks presented by the chair and narrator, the very site of the evening, and the political and social context within which it took place, not to mention the entire meaning-making process since 1917, the individual reminiscers located their autobiographies firmly within the revolutionary narrative, thereby affirming the narrative in the process. "Memory makes us," Elisabeth Tonkin (1992: 97) writes, "[and] we make memory."

◄ ◄ ◄

This kind of examination of the linguistic, institutional, and cultural constitution of October as revolution problematizes the event itself in a way that previous reappraisals have been unable to do. It eschews the long-standing argument over the legitimacy or illegitimacy of October—

namely, whether it constitutes revolution or conspiracy—and also by extension the argument over the legitimacy or illegitimacy of Soviet Russia in general. Rather, it focuses on the constitution of October as revolution and its *legitimizing function* vis-à-vis the Soviet state. For the first decade after October 1917, this process took the form of a veritable memory project, namely, a concerted and organized effort mainly by the Bolsheviks to render the revolutionary narrative the defining element of a new historical memory for the Soviet polity. All "evidence" of the revolution—whether written, archival, visual, or symbolic—produced in this project should be examined within this context. The October Revolution did not first occur, only later to be written about. It occurred in the process of writing. It was not first experienced by contemporaries, only later to be remembered. It was experienced (i.e., "understood") by them in the process of remembering. Herein lay the power of the process.

NOTES

The research for this article was made possible in part by the International Research and Exchanges Board (IREX), the Fulbright-Hays program, and the Harriman Institute of Columbia University. The author would like to thank the anonymous referees of *Social Science History* for their helpful comments on an earlier version. All translations in the article are the author's.
1. Many of the themes in this article are dealt with more extensively in my dissertation (Corney 1997).
2. For articles that claim to raise new questions about the history of the Bolshevik Party and the October Revolution in particular, see Raleigh 1989: parts 2 and 3. A generally upbeat look at recent reexaminations of the received categories of Soviet history nonetheless cautioned against the lack of original research into the 1917 revolutions (Orlovsky 1990).
3. "Zaiavlenie Sekretariata Tsentral'nogo Komiteta KPSS o 73-i godovshchine Velikoi Oktiabr'skoi sotsialisticheskoi revoliutsii," *Pravda* 278, 5 October 1990: 1; "Zachem vinit' Oktiabr'?" *Pravda* 312, 8 November 1990: 5.
4. V. Sogrin, "Ne pogoniat' istoriiu," *Pravda* 106, 16 April 1990: 1.
5. P. Volobuev and G. Ioffe, "Ne otrekaiutsia, liubia . . . ," *Pravda* 296, 23 October 1990: 1.
6. "Reportazh o voennom parade i manifestatsiiakh v Moskve," *Pravda* 312, 8 November 1990: 1, "Reportazh korrespondentov 'Pravdy' o torzhestvakh v strane," ibid.
7. See, for example, "Oktiabr' v moei sud'be," *Pravda* 312, 8 November 1990: 3–4.
8. "Tak chto zhe proizoshlo v oktiabre 17-go? . . . ," *Literaturnaia gazeta* 44 (5370), 6 November 1991: 1.

9. *Pravda* 162, 6 November 1992: 1; "Sotsializm vyderzhal ekzamen istorii," ibid. See also "Revoliutsiia sovershilas'!" *Pravda* 163, 7 November 1992.

10. See, for example, "Pust' ne paradom etot den' otmechen . . . ," *Pravda* 196, 6 November 1993: 1; "Vek ozaren revoliutsiei," ibid.; "Prazdnik v kol'tse OMONa," *Pravda* 197, 9 November 1993: 1; "Etot den' ostaetsia s nami," *Pravda* 206, 5 November 1994: 1; "Znamena Oktiabria nad Otchiznoi," *Pravda* 207, 9 November 1994: 1; "S veroi i nadezhdoi," ibid.: 2; "My—ne raby, raby—ne my," *Pravda* 201, 4 November 1995: 1; "I vnov' Oktiabr' stuchitsia v dver'," *Pravda* 202, 9 November 1995: 1.

11. On this idea, see the remarks by Malia (1991). Pipes's (1993: 501) attitude toward the Russian people (*narod*) involves a complex mix of exoneration and condemnation. They are represented both as hapless victims of a crime perpetrated by a small group of fanatical social, political, and cultural "outsiders" and as complicitous parties in their own fate; because Bolshevik "*practices* were indigenous" to Russia, "Marxism fell on a soil devoid of traditions of self-rule, observance of law, and respect for private property." In a telling representation of "the people," Pipes (1990) dedicates his study of early Bolshevik Russia to "the Victims."

12. Roger Bastide (1970: 91) has termed this creation of memories within groups always a "structured communion." A psychologist and contemporary of Halbwachs, Frederick C. Bartlett (1964: 205), described the process of remembering as "the struggle to get somewhere, the varying play of doubt, hesitation, satisfaction and the like, and the eventual building up of the complete story accompanied by the more and more confident advance in a certain direction. In fact, . . . remembering appears to be far more decisively an affair of construction rather than one of mere reproduction." He referred to the process of remembering as an "effort after meaning." More recently, the complex relationship between experience and memory has been superbly examined by Bruner (1990).

13. "K Oktiabr'skoi godovshchine," *Izvestiia* 239, 1 November 1918: 1.

14. The publishing department of the Moscow Soviet envisaged print runs of 50,000 copies for one such collection, at a cost of 400,000 rubles ("K prazdnovaniiu godovshchiny Oktiabr'skoi revoliutsii. Iubileinye izdaniia," *Izvestiia* 240, 2 November 1918: 6). Similar plans for jubilee publications were made in the provinces (see "Provintsiia. K godovshchine oktiabr'skoi revoliutsii," *Pravda* 237, 1 November 1918: 4).

15. "K tekushchemu momentu," *Izvestiia* 235, 27 October 1918: 6.

16. "Instruktsiia po sboru materialov dlia Istparta," Rossiiskii Tsentr Khraneniia i Izucheniia Dokumentov Noveishei Istorii (former Central Party Archive, hereafter cited as RTsKhIDNI), f. 70, op. 2, d. 5, l. 22.

17. "Instruktsiia dlia raboty mestnykh Biuro Istparta, 1920–1921," RTsKhIDNI, f. 70, op. 2, ed. khr. 1, l. 1.

18. Letter from Central Istpart to Head of Petrograd Istpart, RTsKhIDNI, f. 70, op. 2, ed. khr. 206, l. 97.

19. N. Baturin, "Neotlozhnaia zadacha," *Petrogradskaia pravda* 253, 11 November 1920: 1.

20. "Protokol zasedaniia Petrogradskogo biuro komissii po izucheniiu istorii partii i Oktiabr'skoi revoliutsii. 5 noiabria 19[21]g.," RTsKhIDNI, f. 70, op. 2, ed. khr. 206, l. 37.

21. For an example of how the grand narrative could accommodate a local narrative, see the periodization of the revolutionary movement offered by the Irkutsk bureau of Istpart in early 1923 ("Otchet Gubbiuro Istparta Irkutskogo Gubkoma R.K.P.," RTsKhIDNI, f. 70, op. 2, ed. khr. 5, l. 21).

22. See, for example, RTsKhIDNI, f. 17, op. 84, ed. khr. 539, l. 27; "Doklad o rabote Tverskogo Gubbiuro Istparta s oktiabria 1922 g. po aprel' 23 g.," RTsKhIDNI, f. 70, op. 2, ed. khr. 5, l. 11.

23. RTsKhIDNI, f. 70, op. 1, ed. khr. 17, l. 30.

24. "Ot gubernskogo biuro komissii Oktiabr'skoi revolutsii i RKP (Istparta) pri MK RKP," RTsKhIDNI, f. 70, op. 2, ed. khr. 216, l. 42.

25. *Biulleten' Istparta* 2, 1924: 11.

26. "Pis'mo 3-e. Istpart k 1905 godu," RTsKhIDNI, f. 70, op. 2, ed. khr. 248, l. 8.

27. "Stenograficheskii otchet vechera vospominanii ko dniu 9-oi godovshchiny Oktiabr'skoi Revoliutsii (Vasileostrovskii raikom, 30-go oktiabria 1926 goda)," Tsentral'nyi Gosudarstvennyi Arkhiv Istoriko-politicheskikh dokumentov (S. Petersburg) (former Leningrad Party Archive), f. 4000, op. 6, d. 43, l. 1–40.

REFERENCES

Acton, E. 1990. *Rethinking the Russian Revolution*. London: Edward Arnold.

Afonin, A. 1920. "K voprosu ob izuchenii R.K.P. i Oktiabr'skoi Revoliutsii." *Petrogradskaia pravda* 240, 26 October: 1.

Baker, K. M. 1990. *Inventing the French Revolution*. Cambridge: Cambridge University Press.

Bartlett, F. C. 1964. *Remembering: A Study in Experimental and Social Psychology*. Cambridge: Cambridge University Press.

Bastide, R. (1970) "Mémoire collective et sociologie du bricolage." *L'Année sociologique* 3d ser., 21: 65–108.

Bettelheim, C. 1976. *Class Struggles in the USSR: First Period, 1917–1923*. New York: Monthly Review Press.

Bonnell, V. E. 1983. *Roots of Rebellion: Workers' Politics and Organizations in St. Petersburg and Moscow, 1900–1914*. Berkeley: University of California Press.

Bonwetsch, B. 1976. "Oktoberrevolution: Legitimationsprobleme der sowjetischen Geschichtswissenschaft." *Politische Vierteljahresschrift* 2: 149–85.

Broido, V. 1987. *Lenin and the Mensheviks: The Persecution of Socialists under Bolshevism*. Aldershot, Eng.: Gower/Maurice Temple Smith.

Brossat, A., and S. Combe, eds. 1990. *A l'Est, la mémoire retrouvée*. Paris: Éditions la Découverte.

Brovkin, V. N. 1987. *The Mensheviks after October: Socialist Opposition and the Rise of the Bolshevik Dictatorship*. Ithaca, N.Y.: Cornell University Press.

Bruner, J. 1990. *Acts of Meaning*. Cambridge: Harvard University Press.

Burgess, W. F. 1981. "The Istpart Commission: The Historical Department of the Russian Communist Party Central Committee, 1920–1928." Ph.D. diss., Yale University.

Butenko, A. 1990. "Byl li neizbezhen Oktiabr'?" *Pravda* 298, 25 October.

Conquest, R. 1990. "I Told You So." *Encounter* 2: 24–26.

——. 1992. "The Party in the Dock." *Times Literary Supplement*, 6 November: 7.

Coquin, F.-X. 1989. "Comments on the Current 'Ferment' and Revision of History in the Soviet Union: Stakes, Limits, Outlook," in Takayuki Ito, ed., *Facing Up to the Past: Soviet Historiography under Perestroika*. Sapporo, Japan: Slavic Research Center, Hokkaido University: 21–32.

Corney, F. C. 1997. "Writing October: History, Memory, Identity, and the Construction of the Bolshevik Revolution, 1917–1927." Ph.D. diss., Columbia University.

Daniels, R. V. 1967. *Red October: The Bolshevik Revolution of 1917*. Boston: Beacon Press.

Davies, R. W. 1989. *Soviet History in the Gorbachev Revolution*. Bloomington: Indiana University Press.

——. 1997. *Soviet History in the Yeltsin Era*. Basingstoke, Eng.: Macmillan.

de Certeau, M. 1986. *Heterologies: Discourse on the Other*. Minneapolis: University of Minnesota Press.

Deviataia Konferentsiia RKP(b). Sentiabr' 1920 goda. Protokoly (1972) Moscow.

Enteen, G. M. 1989a. "Problems of CPSU Historiography." *Problems of Communism* 5: 72–80.

——. 1989b. "The Stalinist Conception of Communist Party History." *Studies in Soviet Thought* 37: 259–74.

Fitzpatrick, S. 1993. "Ascribing Class: The Construction of Social Identity in Soviet Russia." *Journal of Modern History* 65: 745–70.

Foucault, M. 1980. *Power/Knowledge: Selected Interviews and Other Writings, 1972–1977*. New York: Pantheon Books.

Frankel, I. J. 1992. "1917: The problem of Alternatives," in Edith Rogovin Frankel, Jonathan Frankel, and Baruch Knei-Paz, eds., *Revolutionary Russia: Reassessments of 1917*. Cambridge: Cambridge University Press: 3–13.

Furet, F. 1981. *Interpreting the French Revolution*. Cambridge and Paris: Cambridge University Press and Maison des Sciences de l'Homme.

Gill, G. J. 1979. *Peasants and Government in the Russian Revolution*. London: Macmillan.

Haimson, L. 1964. "The Problem of Social Stability in Urban Russia, 1905–1917." *Slavic Review* 23: 619–42.

——. 1965. "The Problem of Social Stability in Urban Russia, 1905–1917." *Slavic Review* 24: 1–22.

——. 1988. "The Problem of Social Identities in Early Twentieth Century Russia." *Slavic Review* 47: 1–20.

Halbwachs, M. 1925. *Les cadres sociaux de la mémoire*. Paris: Librairie Félix Alcan.

——. 1980. *The Collective Memory*. New York: Harper & Row.

Hall, S. 1981. "The Rediscovery of 'Ideology': Return of the Repressed in Media Studies," in Michael Gurevitch, Tony Bennett, James Curran, and Janet Woollacott, eds., *Culture, Society and the Media*. London and New York: Methuen: 56–90.

Handler, R. 1994. "Is 'Identity' a Useful Cross-cultural Concept?" in John R. Gillis, ed., *Commemorations: The Politics of National Identity*. Princeton, N.J.: Princeton University Press, 27–40.

Harlan, D. 1989. "Intellectual History and the Return of Literature." *American Historical Review* 3: 581–609.

Holmes, L. E., and W. Burgess. 1982. "Scholarly Voice or Political Echo?: Soviet Party History in the 1920s." *Russian History/Histoire Russe* 9, parts 2–3: 378–98.

Hosking, G. A. 1989. "Memory in a Totalitarian Society: The Case of the Soviet Union," in Thomas Butler, ed., *Memory: History, Culture and the Mind*. Oxford: Basil Blackwell: 115–30.

Hunt, L. 1984. *Politics, Culture, and Class in the French Revolution*. Berkeley: University of California Press.

Iotov, I. 1987. "Vernost' Oktiabriu, vernost' proletarskomu internatsionalizmu." *Voprosy istorii KPSS* 11: 12–25.

"Istoricheskaia nauka v 20-30-e gody." 1990. *Istoriia i istoriki*. Moscow: Nauka.

Iz epokhi "Zvezdy" i "Pravdy" (1911–1914 gg.) 1921. Moscow.

"Izuchenie istorii velikogo oktiabria. Itogi i perspektivy." 1987. *Voprosy istorii* 6: 51–72.

Joravsky, D. 1994. "Communism in Historical Perspective." *American Historical Review* 3: 837–57.

Kaiser, D. H., ed. 1987. *The Workers' Revolution in Russia, 1917: The View from Below*. Cambridge: Cambridge University Press.

Kenez, P. 1991. "The Prosecution of Soviet History: A Critique of Richard Pipes' *The Russian Revolution*." *Russian Review* 3: 345–51.

——. 1995. "The Prosecution of Soviet History, Volume 2." *Russian Review* 2: 265–69.

Koenker, D. 1981. *Moscow Workers and the 1917 Revolution*. Princeton, N.J.: Princeton University Press.

Kotkin, S. 1991. "One Hand Clapping: Russian Workers and 1917." *Labor History* 4: 604–20.

——. 1995. *Magnetic Mountain: Stalinism as a Civilization*. Berkeley: University of California Press.

Ko vsem chlenam partii. 1920. Moscow.

Kozicki, H., and R. H. Canary, eds. 1978. *The Writing of History: Literary Form and Historical Understanding*. Madison: University of Wisconsin Press.

Lane, D. 1969. *The Roots of Russian Communism: A Social and Historical Study of Russian Social Democracy, 1898–1907*. Assen, The Netherlands: Van Gorcum & Comp.

Lass, A. 1994. "From Memory to History: The Events of November 17 Dis/membered," in Rubie S. Watson, ed., *Memory, History, and Opposition under State Socialism*. Santa Fe: School of American Research Press: 87–104.

Malia, M. 1991. "The Hunt for the True October." *Commentary* 4: 24–25.

——. 1992. "Why Amalrik was Right." *Times Literary Supplement*, 6 November.

——. 1994. *The Soviet Tragedy: A History of Socialism in Russia, 1917–1991.* New York: Free Press, 1994.

Mandel, D. 1983. *The Petrograd Workers and the Fall of the Old Regime.* Basingstoke, Eng.: Macmillan.

——. 1984. *The Petrograd Workers and the Soviet Seizure of Power.* Basingstroke, Eng.: Macmillan.

Marsh, R. 1995. *History and Literature in Contemporary Russia.* New York: New York University Press.

Mel'gunov, S. P. 1953. *Kak bol'sheviki zakhvatili vlast': Oktiabr'skii perevorot 1917 goda.* Paris: Editions "La Renaissance."

Merridale, C. 1996. "Death and Memory in Modern Russia." *History Workshop Journal* 42: 1–18.

Mogil'nitskii, B. G. 1989. "Al'ternativnost' v istorii sovetskogo obshchestva." *Voprosy istorii* 11: 3–16.

Nove, A. 1989. *Glasnost' in Action: Cultural Renaissance in Russia.* Boston: Unwin Hyman.

"Oktiabr' i perestroika: Revoliutsiia prodolzhaetsia." 1987. *Kommunist* 17: 3–40.

Orlovsky, D. T. 1990. "The New Soviet History." *Journal of Modern History* 62: 831–50.

Pamiat'. Istoricheskii sbornik. 1976. Vol. 1. Moscow. New York: Khronika Press.

Pethybridge, R. 1964. *Witnesses to the Russian Revolution.* London: Allen & Unwin.

——. 1972. *The Spread of the Russian Revolution: Essays on 1917.* London: St. Martin's Press.

Pipes, R. 1990. *The Russian Revolution.* New York: Vintage Books.

——. 1992. "Seventy-five Years On: The Great October Revolution as a Clandestine Coup d'état." *Times Literary Supplement,* 6 November: 3–4.

——. 1993. *Russia under the Bolshevik Regime.* New York: Knopf.

——. 1994. "Did the Russian Revolution Have to Happen?" *American Scholar:* 215–38.

Protokoly X S"ezda RKP(b). 1933. Moscow.

Rabinowitch, A. 1968. *Prelude to Revolution: The Petrograd Bolsheviks and the July 1917 Uprising.* Bloomington: Indiana University Press.

——. 1978. *The Bolsheviks Come to Power: The Revolution of 1917 in Petrograd.* New York: W. W. Norton.

Radkey, O. 1958. *The Agrarian Foes of Bolshevism: Promise and Default of the Russian Socialist Revolutionaries, February to October 1917.* New York: Columbia University Press.

——. 1961. *The Sickle under the Hammer: The Russian Socialist Revolutionaries in the First Months of Soviet Rule.* New York: Columbia University Press.

Raleigh, D. J., ed. 1989. *Soviet Historians and Perestroika: The First Phase.* London: M. E. Sharpe.

Rogovin, V. 1992. *Byla li al'ternativa? "Trotskizm": Vzgliad cherez gody.* Moscow: Terra.

Sakharov, A. N. 1993. "Soviet Historiography: Modern Trends," in Henry Kozicki, ed., *Western and Russian Historiography: Recent Views.* New York: St. Martin's Press: 191–205.

Schapiro, L. 1970. *The Communist Party of the Soviet Union*. Norfolk, Eng.: University Paperbacks.

——. 1977. *The Origin of the Communist Autocracy: Political Opposition in the Soviet State, First Phase, 1917–1922*. Cambridge: Harvard University Press.

Service, R. 1979. *The Bolshevik Party in Revolution, 1917–1923: A Study in Organizational Change*. New York: Harper & Row.

Shister, G. A. 1990. "Byla li al'ternativa vooruzhennomu vosstaniiu?" *Istoriia SSSR* 4: 134–45.

Slonimskii, M. 1919. "Materialy dlia istorii russkoi revoliutsii." *Zhizn' iskusstva* 291, 13 November: 1.

Smith, S. A. 1983. *Red Petrograd: Revolution in the Factories, 1917–18*. Cambridge: Cambridge University Press.

Startsev, V. I. 1987. "Vopros o vlasti v oktiabr'skie dni 1917 goda." *Istoriia SSSR* 5: 36–55.

Suny, R. G. 1972. *The Baku Commune, 1917–1918: Class and Nationality in the Russian Revolution*. Princeton, N.J.: Princeton University Press.

——. 1983. "Toward a Social History of the October Revolution." American Historical Review 1: 31–52.

——. 1994. "Revision and Retreat in the Historiography of 1917: Social History and its Critics." *Russian Review* 2: 165–82.

Toews, J. 1987. "Intellectual History after the Linguistic Turn: The Autonomy of Meaning and the Irreducibility of Experience." *American Historical Review* 4: 879–907.

Tonkin, E. 1992. *Narrating Our Pasts: The Social Construction of Oral History*. Cambridge: Cambridge University Press.

Trouillot, M.-R. 1995. *Silencing the Past: Power and the Production of History*. Boston: Beacon Press.

Volobuev, P. 1995. "Chetyre professora reshili otmenit' revoliutsiiu." *Pravda* 47, 15 March.

Von Geldern, J. 1993. *Bolshevik Festivals, 1917–1920*. Berkeley: University of California Press.

Von Hagen, M. 1992. "The Stalin Debate and the Reformulation of the Soviet Past." Harriman Institute Forum 7: 1–12.

——. 1993. "The Archival Gold Rush and Historical Agendas in the Post-Soviet Era." *Slavic Review* 1: 96–100.

Watson, R. S., ed. 1994. "An Introduction." In Rubie S. Watson, ed., *Memory, History, and Opposition under State Socialism*. Santa Fe: School of American Research Press: 1–20.

White, H. 1987. *The Content of the Form: Narrative Discourse and Historical Representation*. Baltimore: Johns Hopkins University Press.

Wildman, A. K. 1967. *The Making of a Workers' Revolution: Russian Social Democracy, 1891–1903*. Chicago: University of Chicago Press.

Williams, A. R. 1921. *Through the Russian Revolution*. New York: Boni and Liveright.

Wolfe, B. D. 1961. *Three Who Made a Revolution*. New York: Dial Press.

Of Storytellers and Master

Narratives: Modernity, Memory,

and History in Fascist Italy

◀ ◀ ◀ ◀ ◀ ◀ ◀ ◀ SIMONETTA FALASCA ZAMPONI

In his 1936 essay on Nikolai Leskov—"The Storyteller"—Walter Benjamin (1969) lamented the destruction of collective memory that was taking place with the passage from community to society. In the transformed structure of modern life, claimed Benjamin, our ability to exchange experiences has diminished, and along with it, a collective sense of meaning. While tradition collapses under the irresistible force of the development of economic production, human perception also appears to be affected and penetrated by a logic of rationalization. This logic tends to annul more than past traditions and their meaning as vehicles for communal understanding; it also undermines the capacity for experience in general. In the modern world of machines and automatons, Benjamin feared, tradition was irreparably lost. With it there also vanished the remnants of collective dreams and aspirations that in the past had formed the humus of people's redemptive path toward a meaningful and fulfilled life.[1]

The figure of the storyteller, of which Leskov represented a late example, occupies a prominent role in Benjamin's reflections on the disintegration of experience and the role of memory in modernity. The storyteller, Benjamin says, constituted the catalyst of an experiential world embedded in tradition. As possessors of the art of storytelling, peasants and seamen originally provided tales of local past customs and faraway places. In the Middle Ages, instead, the artisanal trading class—a combination of resident craftsmen and journeymen—took up the role of storytellers. Practical advice and wisdom characterized their art and were transmitted and received as inherently and intrinsically social. In general, stories were a common property and linked generations together. Sprouting directly from oral tradition, stories contained and passed on the traces of a shared past. At the basis of storytelling, Benjamin concluded, there is the reality of the communicability of experience, a universal accountability of meaning—the immanence of meaning to life.

Benjamin believed that in modern times material conditions of existence fragment and personalize experience and deprive it of a coherent meaning. As is evident in the genre of the novel, which depends not on oral tradition but on the printed book, the modern individual takes himself or herself up as the center of both creation and reception.[2] In a world where the artisanal mode of production comes to be replaced by the capitalist laws of competition and individual achievement, the isolated and solitary novelist produces a book that is then read by an equally solitary reader. No exchange of counsel can take place between the writers and their audience because, unlike the story, the book reinterprets experience as a momentary and individual questioning of the meaning of life—a meaning that now needs to be looked for and constructed.[3] In this situation, one's own relation to the past is transformed. The listener to the storyteller had an interest in memorizing what he was told; memory, Benjamin wrote, "is the epic faculty par excellence," and "Mnemosyne, the rememberer, was the Muse of the epic art among the Greeks." Memory is connected to the telling and retelling of a story and "creates the chain of tradition which passes a happening on from generation to generation" (Benjamin 1969: 97, 98). In the novel, on the other hand, memory is not supported by familiar continuity; it is artificially made. The question of the past becomes displaced and problematized, and time is separated from meaning. Memory is now supposed to create a meaning of the past.

The notions of tradition, memory, past, and experience running through the Leskov essay constitute the central components of Benjamin's theory of the modern and his critique of the concept of time as signifying progress. An original contribution to Max Weber's thesis on the disenchantment of the world, Benjamin's conception of cultural modernity emphasizes the collapse of the communal bases of meaning in the new high capitalist society.[4] Benjamin argues that the passage from tradition to modernity—from community to society—occurs on the ruins of the disintegrated nature of experience and the individualizing process of memory. He also alerts us to what he believes are the consequences of such fundamental and dramatic changes.[5] Before industrialization, Benjamin claims, collective past and individual past shared a common ground. Ritual ceremonies in festive days sanctioned the unity of these two kinds of memory and reaffirmed them along with the integrated character of the community. But when there is no community and no collective past, Benjamin wondered, what becomes of remembering? What happens to experience when intersubjective meaning is lost? And what is the fate of a community when collective memory supposedly dries up? These questions underlie Benjamin's reflections on the relationship between past and present and his search for a redemptive philosophy of history. With these questions, Benjamin interrogated the nature of the moderns' relationship to the past, the link between the individual and the collective, the symbiotic exchange between identity and representation, and the role of narratives as cultural and political unifiers. Far from invoking a return to the past,[6] Benjamin problematized the consequences of a manufacturing of "aura" in the secularized age that bears the imprint of modernity. In the wake of fascism's rise, he warned against what others have called the "invention of tradition," fake rituals, an artificial restoration of memory.[7]

In this essay I examine the Italian fascists' mythical appropriation of the past by drawing on Walter Benjamin's theory of memory and tradition. Whether or not one accepts Benjamin's interpretation of modernity as lacking meaning or shares his highly idealized depiction of communities, Benjamin's emphasis on the centrality of the memory question in modern times is crucial to the argument developed in this essay for at least two reasons. First, by directing attention to the peculiar "crisis" of memory that has affected the modern age, Benjamin shows the general importance of "historicizing memory" and, therefore, of situating fascism's attitude toward the past within a specific cultural-historical context. As Richard Terdiman (1993: 3) writes, "Every culture remembers its past," but memory is not an unchanging, universal category. "Even memory has a history" (ibid.), and how remembrance occurs in each culture varies according to the categories of space and time.[8]

The second point is logically connected to the first: Benjamin's analysis leads one to interrogate the sociopolitical consequences that a remapping of memory entails for modern society in general, and for fascism in particular. The question is: How did the modern crisis of representation Benjamin alludes to affect fascism's relationship to the past, its appeal to national community, and its mythical solicitations to collective imagination? It is my contention that the answer to this quandary, and the whole discussion of the relationship between fascism, memory, and modernity, rests on the premise that the Italian fascist regime, notwithstanding its hybridity, was a modern phenomenon. It thus needs to be analyzed within the milieu in which modern memory thrived.

The goal of this article is to show how fascism epitomized in a peculiarly contradictory and destructive manner the moderns' reaction to the "perceived" sense of the end of an era, as Benjamin described it—a controversial attempt to ride the train of change while revitalizing communal roots believed to be eroding. How did the fascists confront the emergent opposition between community and society? How did they face the dilemma of choosing between tradition and modernity? How did they bridge the gap between past and present/future? What and how did they remember? And how did they tell their stories?

Following the thread of memory and its political implications, I explore the above questions within the larger frame of the relationship between historical representations, narratives, and political identities. I argue that the historical division, established in the nineteenth century, between memory and history engulfed the fascist movement and overlapped with, at the same time that it expressed, other critical dichotomies that vexed Mussolini and his adepts. The dualisms of community and society, tradition and modernity, and, at a more meta level, sacred and profane, confronted fascism with difficult dilemmas and elicited responses that ultimately exposed fascism's cultural incongruities and fallacies.

On the one hand, Mussolini believed that in order to build a national cohesive whole in Italy, fascism needed to revamp a disintegrated communal spirit, reanimate political emotions, and resuscitate tradition. On the other hand, by subscribing to the theory of the collapse of tradition, the bureaucratization of existence, and the disintegration of collective meaning in modernity, fascism left itself with no alternative solution for fulfilling its goals than to rely on constructed memory. The regime invoked authenticity against the fabricated nature of modern relations. Yet the community it strove to implement could not but be a construction, since according to its own analysis it did not exist as a spontaneous entity and remained to be built. Fascism claimed to be a novel phenomenon, a movement in the making. However, if it needed some form of past to legitimate its role as national coagulator, that past, again, could not but be a construction. In order to create a meaning of the past, fascism needed to forge memory; it needed to tell a story that resonated with all Italians, unified the polity, and established a national conscience. That story, incidentally, came to coincide with history, that is, the supposedly detached, objective account of the past. Memory and history, like other dualisms in fascism, were combined and began to run a parallel course.

I do not mean to argue that fascism's memory and/or history, although mythological and constructed, was a cynical or merely manipulative tool in the hands of party leaders and ideologues. My argument is, rather, that memory/history became a cognitive, formative means in the process of fascism's own self-understanding and definition—a cultural place to stage and rehearse beliefs, claims, and myths. The regime's recourse to memory was part and parcel of fascism's permanent search for identity—a search that, as I explain elsewhere, took place simultaneously with the efforts to build a national consciousness. The fascist myths of the revolution and of Rome that I am going to examine in this essay exemplify the performative role memory played in fascism's *Bildung* and in the shaping of its national tale. The cases of the revolution and Rome also show the interlocking operation through which memory and history worked in fascism to naturalize cultural constructs and reify already existing myths. Indeed, I wish to emphasize that fascist memory did not invent myths. In contrast, it endowed myths with the sort of meaning and form (to use Barthes's semiotic language) that, by "giving an historical intention a natural justification, and making contingency appear eternal" (Barthes 1972: 142), became a normalized blueprint for the whole nation.

The core of this essay illustrates through the examples of the myths of Rome and of the fascist revolution the intricate, idiosyncratic process through which the fascist regime elaborated its naturalized claim of representing and unifying the Italian nation. Before delving into the heart of the matter, though, we need to further define modernity's "memory crisis" and to situate fascism's position vis-à-vis the controversial role played by history as modern memory's alter ego. To this end, I briefly discuss Maurice Halbwachs, the father of collective memory studies, as representative of the modern era's ambiguous relationship to the past. The discussion of Halbwachs provides a suggestive introduction to the dilemmas fascism faced vis-à-vis modern memory.

MEMORY AND HISTORY

In the nineteenth century, remembering underwent a particularly dramatic and agonizing turn that problematized the epoch's entire relationship to the past, extending well into the twentieth century. Novels such as Alfred De Musset's and Marcel Proust's, treatises such as Henri Bergson's *Matière et mémoire*, psychiatric studies, and psychology manuals testify to the epoch's suddenly growing interest in the past—a past that came to be conceived as estranged and irretrievable, hard to access and understand. Structural changes of enormous proportions, including modifications in production and labor conditions and in demographic distribution, seemed to shatter traditions and sever people's organic links to their communities. Whether or not they were based on reality, ideal conceptions of precapitalist times influenced intellectual interpretations of the present as both reflecting a loss of meaning and fostering abstract social relations. Conscious attempts to reconstruct the past substituted for what was believed to be the natural flow connecting past and present in traditional forms of social existence. These attempts at reconstruction were in turn considered proof of the changes in the structure of memory—a signal of memory's increasing difficulty in recapturing the past.

The study of memory's dysfunctions (Roth 1989: 64; 1991) that developed at this time also called into question memory's role. Disturbances such as amnesia (what the French called *maladies de la mémoire*) proved that memory was an individualized, psychologized operation susceptible to deformations and manipulation, forgetting and emotions. An entire reimagining of memory suggested the definite and incontrovertible flaws of relying on subjective experiences to recapture the past. The perception of a cultural crisis challenged the understanding of one's own individual identity, as it interrogated the knowledge of one's place in history. At the beginning of the twentieth century, several epistemological questions led to the reconsideration of historical studies: for example, What is our past?

How do we know our past? Does the past define our collective identity? How do we relate to the past? Do we share memories? Are memories the same as history? Memory, it was argued, conveys a representation of the past and its social practices; history is the knowledge of the past. Memory is composed of myths and constructions; history is an objectified report on the past. A scientific, positivist approach characterized history's claims to knowledge, a self-proclaimed distance from individual memory that was heightened by the investigation of individual memory's dysfunctions. The professionalization of history, many argue, occurred within the frame of memory's problematized status. The unreliability of individual memory that the epoch had declared encumbered history with the task of documenting and preserving the knowledge of the past.

Although memory and history occupied the same discursive space, they came to be considered antipodes rather than complements. This is evident in the work of the French sociologist Maurice Halbwachs, who, in his 1925 book (1992 [1925]), was the first to provide a social frame for the study of memory, against the psychologizing trend typical of the era. Halbwachs's attempt to rehabilitate a controversial and besieged memory offered an original formulation of the role of collectivities vis-à-vis the past. It also privileged memory's role in society over history's. Yet Halbwachs ended up somewhat paradoxically declaring memory's failure in the face of historical science's superior certainties, thus subscribing to the era's dichotomous schema, which opposed history to memory.

According to Halbwachs, collective memory ensured the mediation between past and present through the continuous feeding of ceremonies and symbolic rituals that founded and strengthened the social character of commonly lived experience. Remembering, Halbwachs claimed, takes place in a collective context; hence, "there are several memories" (1980 [1925]: 83), just as there are several groups, and each collective memory is subject to the fluidity of group composition over time. Memory, Halbwachs insisted, is always socially constructed and does not look for impartiality; memory represents. Contemporary concerns shape the construction of the past and create it according to present interests and beliefs.[9] In this sense, Halbwachs argued, a conception of history as universal, encompassing knowledge contrasts with the plurality of memories, the heterogeneity of reminiscences. History ultimately supersedes memory—a memory that is liable, porous, and distorting.

Embedded in a positivist tradition that sought to uncover universal social laws, Halbwachs enforced the separation of history and memory as modes of knowledge and compartmentalized their functions. History, he indeed claimed, was not based on memory, and it was a mistake to try to compare the two. "The collective memory is not the same as formal history, and 'historical memory' is a rather unfortunate expression because it connects two terms opposed in more than one aspect." In fact, he continued, "general history starts only when tradition ends and the social memory is fading or breaking up" (1980 [1925]: 78). Almost echoing Benjamin, Halbwachs endowed memory with a living soul—an organic link that connected the members of a group. In contrast, history, as a "record of events" (ibid.: 83), constituted for him an erudite enterprise charged with the preservation of facts, the chronicled account of a nation's deeds. History was in essence national history and avoided the perils of subjective experience.

Within this context, Halbwachs's position regarding the status of history and memory clearly evidences the different meanings and stakes the two concepts came to embody and play out in the early twentieth century. The epoch's struggle to make sense of the emergent oppositions between community and society, tradition and modernity, past and present was reinscribed in Halbwachs's sociological discussion of collective memory. But the era's misrecognition of the epistemological issues that generally afflict history and link it to memory also reemerged in Halbwachs's original account of the social character of remembrance.

Although Halbwachs acknowledged the historical rise of professional history at the specific moment when tradition supposedly ended, he still treated not only history but also memory as timeless categories with essentially invariant roles. In Halbwachs the question of the function of social ties, upon which memory is based, overcomes the question of the nature of these ties, their content. But a consideration of functions without content, I want to argue, has the effect of freezing historical development and presenting it as univocal and linear. This in turn leads one to discount the issues of which past ends up becoming history, and how it does so. For, as many scholars argue, history is a selective representation of the past, a narrativized interpretation of events.[10] History does not merely reproduce facts; rather, it constructs their meaning by framing them within a cultural tradition that is intersubjectively shared. In sum, history resorts to discursive forms that are in themselves carriers of ideological and political implications (White 1987: ix). From this perspective, one could say that history is not very different from what Halbwachs defines as collective memory. They are both based on a common cultural tradition that supports and facilitates the communication between members of a group. And they both rely on narrative discourse as the mode through which people establish mutual understanding within a collectivity. Failure to recognize the affinity between history and memory leads to naturalizing the process of remembrance and to discounting, in the permeability of memory, the diverse interventions that determine whose concerns come to be represented each time.

It is my contention that fascism's attempt to create a tradition of memory in the fascist state exemplifies the consequences of the epistemological confusion affecting the status of memory at the turn of the century. Fully embedded in the contradictions of modernity, and facing the same dilemmas that underlay Halbwachs's theorizing, fascism resolved the apparent opposition between memory and history (as well as the ones between sacred and profane, organic and constructed, and so on) by simultaneously maintaining and erasing their supposed difference.[11] The fascist regime could not sacrifice memory to the altar of history, nor could it give up tradition for the sake of modernity. Rather, as we are going to see, fascism exalted memory's sacredness, while positing the authenticity of history. It glorified historical accuracy, while invoking memory's saintly character. To be sure, fascism's overlap of memory and history did not stand on the recognition that memory and history shared a common interpretive basis. In this sense, fascism's approach was not different from Halbwachs's. However, contrary to Halbwachs, fascism co-opted memory into sharing history's "objective" foundation. In so doing, the fascist regime reinforced the naturalization of the past that always results from ignoring the constructed nature of any form of remembrance.

The discussion to follow will closely analyze fascism's operation of creating a national tale through the weaving of history and memory. My argument is that the concepts of community and the sacred (with their opposites, society and the profane) provide interpretive frames for understanding fascism's selective process of remembrance with regard both to the origins of the fascist movement and to fascism's historical reconnection with the past.

Mussolini founded the Italian fascist movement on 23 March 1919 with the name *Fasci Italiani di Combattimento* (Italian Fasces of Combat). Born out of the war experience, the Fasces expressed the sentiments of many youth who felt that the ideals and values that had inspired the war needed to be maintained in the new postconflict reality. The sacrifice of millions in the trenches should not be annulled by the return to an unaltered "bourgeois" existence; one could make sense of the slaughter only if, in its honor, the instrumental petty logic dominating civilian life was reversed and replaced with a spiritualized approach.

By proclaiming itself the spokesperson for World War I veterans, the fascist movement took charge of the massacre's legacy and appropriated its mandate to reform the cynical structure of modern Italian society. Mussolini officially adopted and amplified the values of heroism, struggle, and sacrifice that emerged from the world conflict. These values became the core of fascism's belief in war as regeneration, its version of violence as the awakening of the dormant forces of good, and the return of the ideal and faith. Mussolini insisted that the soldiers' death called out for social changes that would bring about a new order in Italy. The political establishment especially, with its petty politicking and practices of corruption and clientelism, epitomized for the fascists the degenerate, superficial character of the bourgeois, bureaucratized world. But the fascists found the same deep distance from people's sentiments and passions in the lifeless nature of parliamentary institutions, where conflict, according to them, was just a fiction—a staged rehearsal of pacified, fake violence that in the name of representation obliterated the flame of passions (Galli 1982).

Fascism's critique of the status quo attacked the modern version of politics and proposed to replace it with novel forms that solicited, and counted on, communal emotions and participation. Democracy, as Mussolini (1934–39: 2:335) stated, had "deprived people's life of 'style.'" Fascism, however, "brings back 'style' in people's lives: that is a line of conduct, that is the color, the strength, the picturesque, the unexpected, the mystical; in sum, all that counts in the soul of the multitudes" (this translation and all others in this essay are mine). Ritualistic and symbolic practices would substitute for speeches and voting; a sacral link would connect leader and led. A supposedly spiritual reality needed to surpass the materialistic society of the postwar era in order to mend Italy's moral crisis. Mussolini believed, following Georges Sorel, that permanent struggle would save the world from barbarism. This struggle, however, had to be antiutilitarian and inspired by myths, rather than interests. Only under these conditions would violence be able to generate new moral values (Mussolini 1951–63: 2:68). Thus, Mussolini affirmed in 1920 (ibid.: 15:216–17): "Struggle is at the origin of everything because life is full of contrasts. . . . The day when there is no fight will be a day of sadness, it will be the end, the ruin." He continued to hold this perspective in later years, when he maintained that the result of the fascists' battles was less important than the actual embracing of fight (1934–39: 2:54). Or, as he said (ibid.: 1:24), borrowing the poet Giosuè Carducci's image: "We must act, move, fight, and if it is necessary, die. . . . It is blood that moves history's wheel." Violence was sacred, and sacred were those who promoted it.

Within this interpretive frame, the war as communal experience and unselfish dedication was elevated by the fascists to a high, spiritual status. The war inspired and consecrated fascism's present struggle to establish new ideals and morals, and it remained a constant point of symbolic reference for Mussolini's movement. Blood as the symbol of the soldiers' sacrifice—one's own dedication to others—also became a central signifier of the purity and sanctity of the fascist cause. In an overt reconnection to Catholic themes, fascism even designated as martyrs those of its members who died during the fights with socialists in the first years of the movement; those dead acquired a saintly halo through their actions. As Mussolini proclaimed in 1922 (1934–39: 2:328), after his followers destroyed the headquarters of the socialist newspaper *Avanti!* in Milan: "Our friends have been heroes, their gesture has been warlike. Their violence has been saintly and moral." Fascism's self-construction and representation as a lay religion drew from the themes of blood and martyrdom. "No party in Italy, no movement in recent Italian history can be compared to Fascism," Mussolini wrote (1934–39: 2:233) on 20 January 1922. "No ideal has, like the fascist one, been consecrated by the blood of so many youths."

Once it took power at the end of October 1922, fascism wove the themes of blood and martyrdom into an official narrative that, on the one hand, glorified fascism's role in the spiritualization of Italy and its reconstruction as a community. On the other hand, it helped to establish the regime's interpretation of its own beginning, the constructed and ceaselessly reiterated memory of the movement's origins. Blood, via the myth of violence, became the link between World War I and fascism's takeover of power—its "revolution." The March on Rome and its framing within fascism's history most effectively show this trend. As a matter of fact, the march, which supposedly established Mussolini in power, presents a complicated, multifaceted interpretive case that demonstrates the consequentiality of fascism's constructed memory of the revolution, its creative use of representation.

As I said above, the fascists adopted the word *revolution* to refer to Mussolini's establishment at the head of government. This use of the term, however, did not come naturally. Mussolini made a deliberate choice when invoking the word, and he was well aware of its problematic, controversial meaning. What normally defines a revolution? Is it violence, and if so, to what degree? Or is it radical change, whether bloody or not? The dilemma confronted fascism because violence, at least in its physical sense, was very minimal during the events of the March on Rome. And there were no immediate changes in the political system following the march. Furthermore, as some argue (Repaci 1972; Falasca Zamponi 1997), in practice the march never took place. The image of a military-style assault that the word *march* evokes is fictive in the case of fascism, a misleading myth that a short history of the march easily unveils.

In mid-October 1922, Mussolini and other leaders of the fascist movement planned and threatened an insurrection in Rome as a challenge to the current government. The plan envisaged the mobilization of fascist columns, originating from different parts of Italy, for the accomplishment of two simultaneous tasks: to occupy public offices in major cities and to join other fascist forces located in concentration points around Rome. The final move consisted in converging on the capital on 28 October, while negotiations were held with the government for the satisfaction of Mussolini's demands. The Duce was requesting at least five cabinets for his coalition, although he probably preferred to gain the prime ministry for himself. Behind-the-scenes maneuvers aimed at avoiding the insurrection intensified during 26 and 27 October. In effect, in a most secretive counterplan, Mussolini was hoping for a nonviolent solution to his power requests.

It is not clear which steps the fascists intended to follow once in Rome. Historical research has quite well established that at most the fascist forces comprised 26,000 participants, badly equipped, who would be met by 28,000 soldiers of the Italian army (Repaci 1972: chap. 24). Chances are that if a clash had occurred, the fascists would have fared poorly. The confrontation, however, never took place: the state of siege proclaimed by Prime Minister Luigi Facta was rejected by King Vittorio Emanuele III. Mussolini, who had been negotiating with the government from Milan, was offered a crucial role in a coalition of conservatives and nationalists. At that point, though, he was ready to request more, and he proposed forming his own government. The king unexpectedly accepted. Mussolini was thus officially (and nonviolently) proclaimed prime minister on 30 October 1922. The next day the Blackshirts, who had been waiting around the capital, entered the city in a march that turned out to be a parade, the celebration of a doubtless victory. A picturesque spectacle of variously dressed legionnaires presented itself to the Romans in a rally that involved the monument to the Unknown Soldier and concluded with a salute of homage to the king at the Quirinale Palace.

Was this a revolution, or even a march? Certainly, one can argue, the fascists' planned action was at least potentially destabilizing, an assault on the legitimacy of governmental institutions, and therefore revolutionary. But does potentiality in itself count toward defining an event as revolutionary? Alternatively, the event symbolically marked the beginning of a new era, the fascists will argue, the stepping stone into the 20 years of power that Mussolini started to exercise as a dictator in 1925. Yet, in concrete terms, Mussolini's participation in government in the first two years followed the rules of the traditional political system and was played out within the liberal parliamentary institutions (Aquarone 1965). Well aware of these idiosyncrasies, though, Mussolini never ceased referring to the October events as "revolution." The sacred character he ascribed to such an occurrence induced him to do so. In his Milan speech of 4 October 1924 he affirmed (1934–39: 4:293): "Like it or not, in October 1922 there was an insurrectional act, a revolution, even if one can argue over the word. Anyway, a violent take-over of power. To deny this real fact . . . is truly nonsense." A few months earlier, on 5 July 1924, he told the Senate (1934–39: 4:223): "Fascism did not come to power through normal means. It arrived there by marching on Rome *armata manu*, with a real insurrectional act." A good student of Gustave Le Bon, Mussolini was keen on the importance of using the word *revolution*. "And why do I insist on proclaiming the revolution of October a historical revolution? Because words have their own tremendous magic" (1934–39: 4:66). In this vein, he also explained his fondness for *revolution* to the journalist Emil Ludwig (1932: 106): "That word makes a mystic impression on the masses. . . . It gives the common man the impression of participating in an exceptional movement."

What Mussolini esteemed important was the heroic character of fascism; therefore, the exaltation of revolution went along with dramatic references to blood, despite the fact that the March on Rome had been bloodless. "If in the insurrectional days of October there was no blood—although there had been tens of glorious dead—much blood—very pure—ran in the previous three years." Thus Mussolini (ibid.: 4:223–24) told the Grand Council of fascism on 22 July 1924. In a rhetorical detour, the extraordinary, ethical character of the fascist movement was proved by the bloodshed before the march, as Mussolini (1934–39: 8:120) reiterated on 17 October 1932, during the festivities for the 10th anniversary of the revolution. "Among all the insurrections of modern times, ours has been the bloodiest. . . . The conquest of the Bastille only required a few tens of dead. . . . The Russian revolution did not cost more than a few tens of victims. . . . Our revolution during three years has required large sacrifice of young blood." (The three years Mussolini refers to are those between the foundation of fascism and the March on Rome.)

In Mussolini's vision, not only was the march the culmination of the revolution; it also constituted the apogee of the saintliest, purest, most legitimate revolution. Consecrated by the superior value of blood, fascist violence proved to be morally based, a necessary step toward regeneration and salvation. Not surprisingly, fascist martyrs acquired a prominent role in the mythicization of the movement. The official statutes of the Fascist Party reserved important honors for the fallen; party branches kept shrines in memory of the dead; not only new public works but also pennons of fascist groups were named after the martyrs; the Fascist Association of Families of the Fallen, Disabled, and Wounded was regularly present in official fascist ceremonies; and an updated book of martyrs was religiously kept. With its sacrifice of young blood, fascism proved the spiritual nature of its mission, its unselfish attempt to resuscitate a moribund country. Mussolini's attachment to the word *revolution* and his exaltation of the rhetoric of blood were part and parcel of the fascists' attempt to define their identity in spiritual terms, stress the value of action in a decaying, bureaucratized world, and affirm their role as saviors of a corrupt bourgeois system.

In this sense, fascism's self-proclamation as "revolution" cannot be intended as a merely manipulative tool, a form of propaganda that fascism used to forge people's minds. Rather, fascism's self-identification with revolution allowed Mussolini's movement to construct an image of itself that reinforced and channeled fascism's claims to purity and ideals. The appeal to spirituality was at the core of fascism's historical self-representation. Once contextualized at the source of fascism's revolution, this appeal also gave Mussolini's movement the opportunity to encode memory within a glorified system of signification, a sacred frame. The mythical invocation of blood, together with the mystique of the origins, contributed to the sacralization of fascism's memory. Fascist memory, at the same time, played a performative function: it made sacred what it remembered. The institutionalized staging of myths, such as the 1932 Exhibit of the Fascist Revolution, well exemplifies this process.

THE REVOLUTION BETWEEN HISTORY AND MEMORY

The first major exhibit staged by fascism, the *Mostra della Rivoluzione Fascista*, specifically revolved around the theme of fascism's rise. Originally planned as the history of fascism to date, the exhibit, in the reorganized project sketched by Dino Alfieri and supervised by Mussolini, focused on the years that led to the seizure of power and the revolution.[12] Extending from 1914 (with the beginning of World War I) to 1922, fascism's brief history constituted the thread guiding the *mostra*. The exhibit proposed the themes of war, heroism, and sacrifice, which fascism claimed to represent, and intended to provide an "objective, faithful, chronological reconstruction" (Alfieri and Freddi 1933: 7) of the fascist revolution's origins against the background of Italy's vicissitudes. The sacred memory of the revolution was to be not profaned by history but rather exalted by it. "History," in this case, would be accounted for through documents and memorabilia that definitively and incontrovertibly demonstrated the formidable character of the events leading to the establishment of fascism.[13]

Alfieri strongly appeared to believe in history's objectivity. He insisted on the reconstruction process that the mostra pursued even if he conceded that, in order to re-create the atmosphere of the times, architectonic choices and artistic devices also played a major role in the staging of the exhibit. (As a matter of fact, scholars generally analyze the exhibit from the point of view of fascism's relationship to art. See Schnapp 1992; Stone 1993.) Documentation and evidence were thus a priority for the organizers, as the guides to the exhibit relentlessly emphasized (Alfieri and Freddi 1933). To this end, during the organizational phase of the mostra, notes were sent to the party's federal secretaries asking for assistance in the research and solicitation among private citizens of material connected to fascism's historical origins. The requested items included symbols, photographs, medals, postcards, and other artifacts (Archivio Centrale dello Stato, PNF Direttorio, b 274).[14] By the end of this campaign, an amazing total of 18,040 objects had been received (Alfieri and Freddi 1933: 60).

Notwithstanding the minute search for evidence, the organizers insisted that the mostra was not conceived as a dry presentation of facts, in the mode of a museum. Rather, it aimed at exciting people's fantasy and imagination and renewing their spirit (Alfieri and Freddi 1933: 9). Alfieri claimed that the mostra was not an "exposition" or an "exhibit" in the usual sense, nor "historical reevocation for its own sake," but rather an understandable spiritual representation of all of fascism's accomplishments, both material and spiritual. ("Spirit," indeed, constituted, according to the exhibit plans, one of the four elements that needed to be represented and to dominate the show.) The official art critic of the regime, Margherita Sarfatti (1990: 222), in her turn affirmed that this was not only la mostra (the exhibit) but also *la dimostrazione* (the demonstration) of the fascist revolution, its proof. Sarfatti interpreted the mostra not as a gathering of historical material but as "history in action" (*storia in atto*). In effect, statues, iconic symbols, collages, and other artistic installations at the exhibit offered suggestive scenes and evocative images that, according to several reports, struck the visitors' emotional chords.

The main section of the exhibit consisted of 19 halls laid out on the ground floor of Palazzo delle Esposizioni in Rome. The itinerary for the public was obligatory; there was no possibility of skipping rooms or following an arbitrary order. From Room A on the right side of the building (which recounted the "Beginning of the Great War"), other halls unfolded along the external perimeter of the Palazzo. Then, from the last room on the left side of the building (Room Q: "The March on Rome"), one entered four other rooms in the center, including the special hall dedicated to Mussolini. The exhibit culminated both thematically and structurally with a gigantic and imposing *Sacrario dei martiri* (Sacrarium of the Martyrs). Here it is worth reporting the brief description of the hall that Freddi wrote for the *Guide to the Exhibit* (Alfieri and Freddi 1933: 63):

> To the memory of the Martyrs, whose generous blood flooded the hard roads of the Revolution, is dedicated a hall with the title "Sacrarium of the Martyrs." . . . In the center of the circular hall one finds a pedestal of a red blood color, with a diameter of seven meters in the center of which grows a metal cross, seven meters high, infused with a white light and with the inscription "To the immortal Fatherland." The Martyrs, who are celebrated in six circles along the circular walls of the Sacrarium, answer *Present!* to the mute evocation of the living. The atmosphere of the Sacrarium, all dominated by an azure tonality, is highly mystical and suggestive.

The symbolism of the hall, with its gigantic cross at the center, the names of the dead on the pennons displayed at the bases of the circles, and an allusion to their living legacy through a repetitious display of the word *presente*, was supposed to evoke a sense of respect and awe. Room N ("The Year 1921") had already presented the visitors with the historical documentation of young fascists' tragic martyrdom, including bloody shirts in window cases—an extreme case of the meshing of sacred memory with profane history. Now in the Sacrarium, after the history of fascism's origins and its sacrificial bloody path had been copiously documented, people felt the obligation of remaining silent, according to press reports of the time, and sometimes even of kneeling down, as if in a religious place. The dramatic character of blood was turned into a spiritual presence, in the manner of the Catholic ritual of Corpus Christi. Personal witnesses, as well, stressed the religious quality of the hall.[15]

The Sacrarium was, indeed, staged as a place of cult and solemn observance; its aura emanated from the evocative presence of the dead.[16] Since the dead belonged to fascism, the sacrality of the dead transferred to the movement for which they fought, turning the history of fascism into a hagiography. Fascism, the exhibit proclaimed, was saintly and moral. It had sacrificed itself for the nation; its martyrs were now the whole country's martyrs. This chain of meaning construction that linked blood to martyrs and youth ultimately referred back to fascism as the nation's savior. On the basis of historical records, fascism made a shrine out of its beginning and illuminated it with the auratic, sacred light of memory. Hence, the story that the exhibit chose to tell sacralized fascism's memory. Memory, as displayed throughout the mostra, at the same time showed and proved fascism's sacredness. Room U, the Sacrarium of the Martyrs, demonstrated the final stages of this process in a solemn, somber atmosphere.

The fact that the mostra represented the origins of fascism, not its whole history to the present, eased the operation of endowing the fascist revolution with the halo of sacrality that generally surrounds the past. At the same time, however, the mostra needed to affirm the continuous presence and the consistent quality of the sacred in fascism if it wanted to avoid the risk of representing fascism's past as past, or slipping into a monumentalization that would signify closure rather than continuity. Thus, the exhibit became the occasion to celebrate officially the soul of the regime, the value and purity of its actions, the high scope of its mission. The main narrative line of fascism's origins was not substantially modified from the one circulating in the past. It was, however, reiterated that fascism was not a passing phase in Italian history nor a political movement like many others. The fascist revolution marked the watershed between two institutional eras, two incomparable moments in the life of the country. Fascism came to restore Italy's peace and security, its destiny of glory and grandeur.

Within this narrative context, the challenge that developed for fascism's official symbolic discourse was, rather, that of finding ways to deepen and enforce that self-assessment, to keep it alive at all times as a present reality, to turn that self-representation into a blueprint for the Italians' identification with the regime, and ultimately to make fascism's historical account into a tale shared by a national community. In particular, what was at stake involved the making of such a community, the formation and establishment of a coalesced social body that recognized itself as one under the aegis of Mussolini's regime.

According to Emile Durkheim (1915), the presence of the sacred normally eases the task of achieving social cohesiveness, since the sacred presupposes a community and entails an emotional worshiping of society. Fascism's pursuit of the sacred shows a strong belief in this process. Yet fascism's community was very much a project in the making. Even though the exhibit in part succeeded in solidifying the bond between fascism and the Italians (Schnapp 1992), the regime still needed to supervise and mandate memory, as the case of the Roman myth once again shows.

THE MYTH OF MEMORY

On 3 April 1921, Mussolini delivered a speech in Bologna in which he proclaimed 21 April—anniversary of the mythical founding of Rome—an official fascist holiday. Two years later, at the head of the Italian government, Mussolini instituted the celebration of the Birth of Rome as the new national holiday under his mandate. This was the first of many symbolic interventions that fascism linked to the mythical resonance of Rome's historical past and status; Rome's legendary power, and particularly its imperialistic grandeur, attracted fascism's attention. The fascists' interpretive choice of the Roman past was not inevitable, since historical reconnections to the Romans had traditionally run a whole gamut of possibilities, especially in the years of Italy's unification. During the Risorgimento struggles of the 1800s, the liberal patriot Giuseppe Mazzini evoked Roman civilization as a legacy—a mission that would inspire the Italians and help them establish spiritual unity within Italy and in Europe. Also, the international support for Italy during the Risorgimento was driven by an emphasis on the moral, cultural, and political meanings of Rome, and on Rome's cosmopolitan character (Chabod 1961). For many, Italy's unity was connected to the idea of "mission," a legacy of romantic historiography (Croce 1966 [1928]: 3).

In the late nineteenth century, however, in a climate highly sensitive to imperialistic dreams and expansionist aims, the idea of universal moral missions turned into the pursuit of political grandeur and success, militaristic glories and conquests. By the end of the 1800s Italy began its first, though unsuccessful, colonial war. The circle of those who, in the foot-steps of the Romans, asserted the importance of being militarily strong and powerful widened, headed by the nationalists. Their dreams of power continued to be inspired by the reconfiguration of the Roman past, a transfigured interpretation that, as Antonio Gramsci (1985) lamented, turned the idea of Rome from spur to liability. In the wake of World War I, all these aspirations combined in an exaggerated sense of idealism and heroism that targeted the Italian parliamentary government as the nega-tion of those sentiments, the obstacle to the achievement of extraordinary goals. Not surprisingly, the fascist movement was born out of this cultural context and proposed itself as the carrier of the new political trend. The fascists appropriated the myth of Rome. Through it, they defined them-selves as the repository of a universal mission, the apt interpreters and reenactors of a glorious past. Despite, or maybe in addition to, its claims to absolute novelty, fascism counted on the evocation of shared history as a sign of its link to tradition, a sacred time.

On the second anniversary of the Birth of Rome, the fascist newspaper *Il Popolo d'Italia* reported Mussolini's statement (1934–39: 2:277–78): "The Rome that we honor . . . is not nostalgic contemplation of the past, but hard preparation for the future. Rome is our departure and reference point: it is our symbol or, if you wish, our Myth. We dream of Roman Italy, i.e., wise and strong, disciplined and imperial." Fascism intended to build a powerful Italy on Rome's foundations. Via discipline and military strength, it hoped to lead the country onto a successful path that would ultimately bring back the empire "on the fatal hills of Rome," as Mussolini triumphantly stated 14 years later. In his selective interpretation of Rome, Mussolini exalted the values of work and discipline. He also spelled out his vision of an internally fascistized Italy that needed to be obedient and submissive, trustful and respectful. In 1923 the Birth of Rome became a state holiday and was made to coincide with a new Labor Day that sub-stituted for May First. In the name of Rome, military loyalty and obe-dience, rather than workers' solidarity, was designated as the meaning of Labor Day.

The term *fascism* itself demonstrated this association. Derived from the Latin *fascis*—a bundle of equal rods tied together and to an ax—fasces represented authority in ancient Rome and were carried by minor Roman officials, *lictores*, who preceded the high magistrates in the procession.

Although *fascio* constituted a common political expression at the time and referred to "group" or "association," Mussolini intended to emphasize the original meanings of unity and authority implicit in the term. In its iconographic representation, the fascio actually became fascism's main symbol, its signifier. As Mussolini wrote in *La Dottrina del Fascismo* (1934–39: 8:73): "[Fascism] wants to remake not only the forms of human life, but the content, man, character, faith. To this end, it requires discipline, and an authority that would impress the spirits and dominate them fully. Its sign is thus the *fascio littorio*, symbol of unity, force and justice." Although other countries and political formations had adopted the fascio in the past, or were still using it, the Italian fascists took extreme care in defining the proper design of the symbol and its circulation. Following meticulous historical research, the Roman version with the ax on the side was preferred over the one with the ax in the center, typical of the French Revolution and the Risorgimento (Gentile 1993: 85–87). On 12 December 1926 a decree law made the fascio with that design an emblem of the Italian state. As such, the fascio appeared everywhere, from official documents to toys, from party badges to sewer plaques, monuments, and stamps; it was even used to coin new words.

During the 1920s, the regime did not particularly insist on the image of imperial Rome, although it still emphasized Rome's triumph, strength, and supremacy both in the territorial and, especially, in the spiritual sense. In the 1930s, the theme of Rome's political power became more prominent, even if it continued to coexist with a diversity of spiritual images and thematics. The production of postage stamps testifies to this trend. Several series featuring Rome were printed over 20 years. They portrayed the mythical origins of the eternal city, Rome's role in establishing Christianity as a universal religion, and Rome's imperial and warlike virtues. The regime was not shy about producing a plethora of multivalent images and meanings. Beyond their specificity, these cultural constructs communicated Rome's centrality in Italian history and affirmed a continuity between the latter and fascism. Within an environment already pregnant with Roman rhetoric, the fascist regime, via the myth of Rome, proclaimed itself the natural inheritor of the country's leadership. The reference to the common Roman past, no matter how selectively and ambiguously constructed, historicized fascism's role and presented fascism as the expression of a national tradition.

The ambiguous character of fascism's memory potentially eased the regime's identification with Rome. The fuzziness and interpretive width of the Roman myth also allowed the regime to naturalize its own ideals of superiority and its goals of expansion. In effect, from the multiplicity of the Roman themes it circulated, the regime extracted one common motif: that of Rome's power. Fascism's rhetoric made spiritual and territorial domination into the normal categories of reference in the historical assessment both of Rome and of fascism's own inherited mission. The stamp issued in 1932 for the 10th anniversary of the march, for example, shows the link the regime established between ancient Rome's dominance in North Africa and fascism's vision of its own future. The stamp portrayed a worker shoveling amid Roman ruins and against the background of an African landscape. The caption read: *Ritornando dove già fummo* [Returning where we already were]. The appeal of Africa as a territory of conquest, where Roman "civilization" and art had already left a mark, clearly transpires in this vignette, even if at the time the regime denied any interest in imperial politics.

In September 1937, the regime opened the *Mostra Augustea della Romanità* to celebrate the second millennium of Augustus's birth.[17] The entrance to the exhibit featured in big letters Mussolini's words: "Italians, you must ensure that the glories of the past are surpassed by the glories of the future." Fascism's Roman lineage requested and determined the regime's imperialistic path. In effect, after the 1936 proclamation of the empire in Ethiopia, fascism's ambitions reached such heights that the regime even came to interpret the history of Rome as teleologically announcing the inevitable and successful coming of fascism. A 10-cent stamp, printed in 1937 as part of a series on Italian history, featured the mythical Romulus working the furrow for the foundation of Rome. A phrase by Mussolini captioned the vignette: "The sign of the infallible destiny." In a mythical reversal, fascism was no longer the historical continuation of Rome. Rather, Rome was the antecedent of fascism, its harbinger. A reciprocal relation of influence connected the glorious Roman past to the ever more glorious fascist present-future.

Roland Barthes (1972) claims that mythologies tend to normalize and naturalize meanings and to present them as permanent. Fascism's approach to the myth of Rome operated within this structural space. The regime did not merely invent memory—after all, memory, like history, is always reconstructed, selective, and interpretive. Through its memory/history construct, fascism also invented and interpreted itself as "naturally" powerful, imperialistic, and spiritual, the true carrier of Italy's expansionist and civilizing destiny. Fascism's mythical connection to the immortal Rome ensured the reality of these qualities, while hiding the artificial nature of the "community" fascism claimed to represent.

CONCLUSIONS

In the 1800s the preoccupation with the loss of community and the growing focus on the individualized nature of social relations provoked a sense of anxiety about one's own identity and connectedness to the social world. Lyrically portrayed in Charles Baudelaire's urban poems, and sociologically epitomized by Georg Simmel's city-dwellers, the figure of the isolated individual, whose experience was cut loose from tradition, at the turn of the twentieth century came to represent the outcome of the new industrialized era, with its shattered customs and ties—what Ferdinand Tönnies described as the passage from gemeinschaft to gesellschaft. The anomic character of coexistence envisaged by Durkheim, and the bureaucratization and disenchantment of the world captured by Weber in the image-metaphor of the iron cage, more forcefully stressed the structural changes ushered in by modernity and emphasized their dramatic impact. A pessimistic acceptance of the new reality went along with a sense of nostalgia for the past and an attempt to understand ethnologically and historically the enormous cultural shift that had been occurring.

The relationship between tradition and modernity was central to fascism's historical unfolding and identity construction. Italian fascism, and also German Nazism, as many historians have argued, interpreted and reflected the crisis of representation that affected Europe at the time. The coexistence of apparently irreconcilable differences, the coeval presence of rational and mythological claims in both movements, makes them compelling expressions of the identity crisis striking Western culture at the fin de siècle. Both fascism and Nazism created a cultural-political model, founded on basic contradictions, that allowed them to invoke tradition and at the same time accept and exploit technology; to condemn rationality, while applying rationalistic plans to the government of the social; to applaud the past but also salute themselves as the beginning of a new heroic era. Jeffrey Herf (1984), in his classic work on National Socialism, coined the expression *reactionary modernism* to characterize the specious hybrid that defined National Socialism's identity. The coexistence of incongruent opposites, not the exclusionary and exclusive presence of one or the other, defined, according to Herf, the ideological makeup of Hitler's Third Reich.

The same ambiguity toward modernity applies to Italian fascism, where, even more than in Nazism, the tension between past and future divided those in the movement who were forward-looking from those who believed the past could be the foundation for the future. The position that emerged as victorious insisted that fascism was connected to the fate of Italy; fascism's importance and significance derived from its place in Italian historical development. Yet the tension between past and future was never fully resolved in favor of one or the other, and it continued to constitute a challenge to the regime's self-definition. The presence in fascism of this double-edged nature is, after all, what motivated Benjamin (1969) to warn about the danger of fascist movements. For Benjamin, fascism intended to resacralize the world by bringing back the aura of tradition through the use of modern technological means. Fascism intended to rebuild a sense of community and togetherness, but from above and through imposed rituals and cults. In order to pursue its goals, the fascist regime posited itself as the sacred link uniting the people—the religion that would enable the Italians to fulfill their national myth. And, we might add, it adopted a master narrative that used events, especially founding events, to create a tradition of memory.

In this essay I have argued that fascism, like other critics of the turn of the century, drew a link between memory, community, and tradition. Differently from Benjamin and Halbwachs, however, fascism vowed to reverse the fading of the past by combining, in a truly hybrid operation, the sacred and the profane, the mythical and the secular, subjectivity and objectivity. The regime's original elaboration of the memory/history construct was part and parcel of such a cultural-political project. Fascism invoked the aura of the past to posit the sacredness of its own profane present. It solicited individual passions and emotions while writing and ratifying an "objective" version of history. Ultimately, it relied on the pathos of remembrance to create a historical tale that interpreted and represented fascism as the glorious protagonist of Italy's resurgence, the leading force in the establishment of a "spiritual" community.

Historical exhibits, such as the Mostra della Rivoluzione Fascista, and historical evocations, like that of the Roman past, displayed the sacred foundations of fascism's community and became a source for the regime's own claims to leadership. History allowed fascism to objectify and naturalize its version of memory through a collection of traces that, as in the examples of both the mostra and the myth of Rome, testified to the occurrence of events and posited them as real. The presence of a fascist community was dependent on the accumulation of evidence. The stack of historical "proofs" legitimated fascism's tale while also creating a context for vicarious experience. The aura of the martyrs' displayed blood, and the glory of ancient Romans' deeds, supposedly provided the Italians with the feeling of belonging to a shared past, a common tradition.

Was fascism's community a real community, then, in Benjamin's sense, or even an imagined one? One conclusion this essay draws is that the regime produced an image of community. The master narrator, not Benjamin's storyteller, ensured the vitality of the links among people, the maintenance of sociality. No exchange of counsel or advice occurred between Mussolini and the Italian people. In contrast, vertical relations of power defined the interaction between the Duce and his subjects. The regime undercut the centrality of experience that characterizes the existence of communities. For that centrality of experience it substituted an artificial evocation of tradition, the ambiguous imposition of constructed memory, and a staged sacralization of origins. Embedded between past and future, tradition and modernity, memory and history, fascism created the simulacrum of a national community, a fake organic whole founded on the suppression of traditional social ties and dependent on the absolute submission of its members to the regime. Fascism's aim was to delete differences among its subjects; homogeneity, as symbolized by the fascio, implied discipline, unity, and subordination to the will of the leader.

To be sure, unity is a necessary element in the making of all nations and their symbolic struggles. And master narratives embedded in commemorations are necessary for the creation of a collective identity (see, for example, the case of Israel in Zerubavel 1995). Furthermore, the nation always carries within itself an ambivalence that contains both progression and regression, rationality and irrationality (Nairn 1991); the plurality of voices is normally sacrificed when the fate of the nation is at stake. From this perspective, fascism does not represent the only case in which a dominant, official memory is circulated as the legitimate one and made to work as a sealing agent of national consciousness. Nevertheless, we need to consider that the fascists were not desiring Italy's recognition as a nation so much as its recognition as a fascist and totalitarian state. The political, institutional factor is crucial in the analysis of fascism's use of memory/history, its appeal to the sacred, and generally its ambivalent response to the contradictions of modernity. Situated within a cultural climate concerned with the rapid and inevitable nature of social and economic transformations, fascism imposed an artificial, auratic tradition that, through recourse to aesthetic politics, and by appealing to history as its cultural legitimator, crushed the modern individual and presented Mussolini's regime as the authentic and true expression of the Italian "community."

NOTES

The author wishes to thank Richard Kaplan, Roger Friedland, and the anonymous reviewers solicited by *Social Science History* for their comments on previous versions of this article.
1. On Benjamin's idea of redemption in the context of a messianic age, see Habermas 1979; Honneth 1993; and Wohlfarth 1978.
2. On the question of the novel Benjamin refers to Georg Lukács's *The Theory of the Novel*. See Wohlfarth 1978 for a discussion of the difference between the two conceptions.
3. For a more positive interpretation of Benjamin's theory of the novel, see Brooks 1987.
4. Benjamin's theory of modernity also relied on a secularized notion of aesthetic "aura"—the halo that surrounded past works of art because of their uniqueness and rootedness in the cultic fabric of tradition. See "The Work of Art in the Age of Mechanical Reproduction" in Benjamin 1969. On the relation between social and aesthetic issues in Benjamin, see Paetzoldt 1977.
5. In a 1939 essay on Baudelaire, Benjamin (1969) specified the conditions for these changes and linked the loss of the traditional form of experience to a short-circuited memory via the modern phenomenon of shock. See Honneth 1993: 185 for Benjamin's nonsubjective concept of experience.
6. Benjamin, in fact, believed that storytelling can take place only under specific historical and social circumstances and that it would be a mistake to try to have the kind of

experience today that was typical of the past. He took Marcel Proust's *mémoire involontaire* as a redemptive kind of memory in contemporary society—a positive form of remembrance. See "On Some Motifs in Baudelaire" in Benjamin 1969. See also Goody 1991 and Ong 1982 on the impact of writing on narrative structure.

7. Benjamin (1969) admires Baudelaire's poetry for its ability to reject artificial aura while complaining about its loss.

8. For memory as the art of remembrance in the Middle Ages, see Yates 1966. With the development of print, memory became connected to collecting as means to acquire knowledge through the cataloguing and locating of the material (Bolzoni 1995). See Le Goff 1992 for a general discussion of memory.

9. See Schwartz 1982 for a critique of this point.

10. For a general discussion, see Hutton 1993.

11. Barthes (1972: 153) would define this operation as "neither-norism."

12. Mussolini wanted the title "Exhibit of the Fascist Revolution" rather than Alfieri's suggested title, "Exhibit of Fascism" (Alfieri and Freddi 1933).

13. On the relationship between material artifacts and the idea of preserving culture and history in museums, see Findlen 1994, 1998.

14. See Brandt 1994 on the role of photography in the case of war museums.

15. See Schnapp 1992 on the reception of the exhibit and its religious character. Schnapp (ibid.: 19) affirms, on the basis of archival analysis, that the exhibit "provoked a response quantitatively *well in excess* of the organizers' aims" (italics in the original). Schnapp defines people's response to the exhibit as "participatory enthusiasm."

16. The visitors were also welcomed by the hymn "Giovinezza" (Youth), which emphasized the gravity of the sacrifice. "Giovinezza" was not only the official anthem of fascism; it also stressed the young character of the movement, the young age of the people who had died for the cause. Youth, which was one of fascism's highest values, enlarged and dramatized the dead's actions.

17. On the Mostra Augustea, see Archivio Centrale dello Stato, Segreteria Particolare del Duce, Carteggio Ordinario 1922–43, fasc. 135015.

REFERENCES

Alfieri, D., and L. Freddi. 1933. *Mostra della Rivoluzione Fascista*. Bergamo: Istituto Italiano di Arti Grafiche.

Aquarone, A. 1965. *L'organizzazione dello stato totalitario*. Turin: Einaudi.

Barthes, R. 1972. *Mythologies*. New York: Paladin.

Benjamin, W. 1969. *Illuminations*. New York: Schocken.

Bolzoni, L. 1995. *La stanza della memoria*. Turin: Einaudi.

Brandt, S. 1994. "The Memory Makers: Museums and Exhibitions of the First World War." *History and Memory* 6: 95–122.

Brooks, P. 1987. "The Storyteller." *Yale Journal of Criticism* 1: 21–38.

Chabod, F. 1961. *Storia della politica estera italiana dal 1870 al 1896*. Bari: Laterza.

Croce, B. 1966 [1928]. *Storia d'Italia dal 1871 al 1915*. Bari: Laterza.

Durkheim, E. 1915. *The Elementary Forms of the Religious Life*. London: Allen and Unwin.

Falasca Zamponi, S. 1997. *Fascist Spectacle: The Aesthetics of Power in Mussolini's Italy.* Berkeley: University of California Press.

Findlen, P. 1994. *Possessing Nature: Museums, Collecting, and Scientific Culture in Early Modern Italy.* Berkeley: University of California Press.

——. 1998. "Possessing the Past: The Material World of the Italian Renaissance." *American Historical Review* 1: 83–114.

Galli, G. 1982. "Il fascismo e la violenza come strumento di azione politica," in C. Casucci, ed., *Il fascismo: Antologia di scritti critici*. Bologna: Il Mulino.

Gentile, E. 1993. *Il culto del littorio: La sacralizzazione della politica nell'Italia fascista*. Bari: Laterza.

Goody, J. 1991. "The time of telling and the telling of time in written and oral cultures," in J. Bender and D. Wellbergy, eds., *Chronotypes: The Construction of Time*. Stanford: Stanford University Press.

Gramsci, A. 1985. *Selections from Cultural Writings*, ed. D. Forgacs and G. Nowell Smith. Cambridge: Harvard University Press.

Habermas, J. 1979. "Consciousness-raising and Redemptive Criticism: The Contemporaneity of Walter Benjamin." *New German Critique* 17: 30–59.

Halbwachs, M. 1980 [1925]. *The Collective Memory*, ed. M. Douglas. New York: Harper-Colophon Books.

——. 1992 [1925]. *On Collective Memory*, ed. L. Coser. Chicago: University of Chicago Press.

Herf, J. 1984. *Reactionary Modernism: Technology, Culture and Politics in Weimar and the Third Reich*. Cambridge: Cambridge University Press.

Honneth, A. 1993. "A Communicative Disclosure of the Past: On the Relation between Anthropology and Philosophy of History in Walter Benjamin." *New Formations* 20: 81–92.

Hutton, P. 1993. *History as an Art of Memory*. Hanover, N.H.: University Press of New England.

Le Goff, J. 1992. *History and Memory*. New York: Columbia University Press.

Ludwig, E. 1932. *Colloqui con Mussolini*. Milan: Mondadori.

Mussolini, B. 1934–39. *Scritti e discorsi*. 12 vols. Milan: Hoepli.

——. 1951–63. *Opera Omnia*. 36 vols. Florence: La Fenice.

Nairn, T. 1991. *The Break-up of Britain*. London: Verso.

Nora, P. 1989. "Between memory and history." *Representations* 26: 7–25.

Ong, W. 1982. *Orality and Literacy: The Technologizing of the Word*. London: Methuen.

Paetzoldt, H. 1977. "Walter Benjamin's Theory of the End of Art." *International Journal of Sociology* 7: 25–75.

Repaci, A. 1972. *La Marcia su Roma*. Milan: Rizzoli.

Roth, M. 1989. "Remembering Forgetting: *Maladies de la mémoire* in Nineteenth-century France." *Representations* 26: 49–68.

——. 1991. "Dying of the Past: Medical Studies of Nostalgia in Nineteenth-century France." *History and Memory* 3: 7–29.

Sarfatti, M. 1990. "Architettura, arte e simbolo alla Mostra del Fascismo," in P. Barocchi, ed., *Storia Moderna dell'Arte in Italia*, vol. 3. Turin: Einaudi: 220–27.

Schnapp, J. 1992. "Epic Demonstrations: Fascist Modernity and the 1932 Exhibition of the Fascist Revolution." In J. Golsan, ed., *Fascism, Aesthetics, and Culture*. Hanover, N.H.: University Press of New England: 1–37.

Schwartz, B. 1982. "The Social Context of Commemoration: A Study in Collective Memory." *Social Forces* 61: 374–97.

Stone, M. 1993. "Staging Fascism: The Exhibition of the Fascist Revolution." *Journal of Contemporary History* 28: 225–43.

Terdiman, R. 1993. *Present Past: Modernity and the Memory Crisis*. Ithaca, N.Y.: Cornell University Press.

White, H. 1987. *The Content of the Form: Narrative Discourse and Historical Representation*. Baltimore: Johns Hopkins University Press.

Wohlfarth, I. 1978. "On the Messianic Structure of Walter Benjamin's Last Reflections." *Glyph* 3: 148–212.

Yates, F. 1966. *The Art of Memory*. Chicago: University of Chicago Press.

Zerubavel, Y. 1995. *Recovered Roots: Collective Memory and the Making of Israeli National Tradition*. Chicago: University of Chicago Press.

Idols of the Emperor

◄ ◄ ◄ ◄ ◄ ◄ ◄ ◄ ◄ ◄ ◄ ◄ ◄   MATT K. MATSUDA

A strangled cry breaks the frightening silence that hangs over the crowd. The column shakes. All eyes are fixed on the colossus atop the huge cylinder of bronze and granite as the metal cracks. Oscillating its full length for an instant, the column crashes down. A muffled impact of shattering metal mixes with the breaking of brush, and clouds of dust rise in the air. At that instant an immense clamor breaks out from the crowd, and cries ring out, *Vive la République! Vive la Commune!*[1]

The debris rains down on a site of mathematical elegance, a vast octagon, paved in stone. The architecture of the "Grand Siècle" is borne majestically around the perimeter of the octagon; the Roman arcades of the ground floor are crowned by Mansart's roofs, framed by silent windows and Corinthian columns. The space is an area stunning in the grandeur of its horizontal expanse, lines of sight unbroken—except for one feature: in the exact center of the octagon, a massive pedestal and, for more than half a century, a huge column, 43.5 meters high, bronze and granite; at the summit, a statue of the Emperor.[2]

16 May 1871. A gathering of dignitaries, soldiers, and the curious takes place at the Place Vendôme in Paris; thousands crowd the available space;

the exact numbers are disputed. "The crowd is enormous," reports one paper, remarking on the colorful mix of engineers and laborers, national guard regiments, officials positioned strategically along the balconies, throngs on the floor of the Place. Large barricades and embankments protect the area. A scaffolding rises in three parts around the center of the octagon, and laborers haul in cartloads of sand, brush, and manure to dump at the foot of the pedestal, which is decorated with banners and red flags. Military bands play patriotic airs: the 190th battalion strikes up the Marseilles, and the 172nd the "Chant du départ." Then, an eerie silence falls over the Place.

The column is snared in cables drawn to the summit and back down with pulleys to a capstan. Portals around the square have been shuttered, and windows masked against a concussion. Soldiers turn the capstans. The cables tighten. At the fatal hour, a huge crack suddenly resounds. A shudder runs through the crowd. A capstan has broken, five or six guards have been thrown back by the recoil, miraculously none injured seriously. A half-dozen workers are back on the scaffold, diagonally sawing the stone and bronze at the base of the clumn. The afternoon passes. Another military fanfare. At 4:30 the clarion again sounds. At 5:15 the guard are again at the capstan, slowly winding down the cable. The column resists. "The attention is immense." The cables draw tighter.

The column shudders. The cry—"strangled"—escapes the crowd. With a "slow oscillation" the column trembles and totters. Radical writer Maxime Vuillaume recalls, "A monstrous zigzag suddenly passed before my eyes, like the beating wing of a giant bird. Ah! I shall never forget that colossal shadow" (Villaume 1909: 125). The column tumbles. One gravure shows it toppling in full length; others show it breaking into three sections as it falls. Some renderings show the scaffolding; others do not. The column crashes to the ground, with an explosion of dust but little noise, impact muffled by the cushion of dry brush, sand, and manure. The bronze shatters and collapses into its hollow core. The column is completely demolished. The emperor strikes the ground; a globe and winged Victory fly out of his hand and are never recovered. Fragments are snatched up by the crowd. Dramatic illustrations show dozens of spectators climbing upon the now empty pedestal, waving red flags and cheering. The guard presses forward to the debris, taunting the fallen statue.

The emperor does not actually fall onto the branches and sand, but lies on the stones, head cracked, one hand shattered, face toward the sky.[3]

◄ ◄ ◄

With the surrender of Napoleon III to the Prussians on the battlefield of Sedan on 2 September 1870, a new government under the politician-historian Louis Adolphe Thiers negotiated peace for France. Defiant, the city of Paris rejected the settlement, repudiated Thiers's authority, and constituted itself a revolutionary Commune on the model of 1792. In so doing, Paris set itself against not only the German forces but also Thiers's rival French government, now seated at Versailles.

The Commune would have only 73 days, and the toppling of the Vendôme Column would turn out to be among its last acts, a final spectacle of memory and resistance played out in a ceremony of destruction. What the column celebrated in imperial grandeur, the Communards tried to undo, bringing down an idol to proclaim a euphoric new order, shattering bronze and stone to rupture time and history. The ceremony at the Place Vendôme was an act of anticommemoration, a stopped instant that released the exhilaration and struggle of 73 days' attempts to overthrow the past and initiate a European history of humanity.

Yet as the column fell, not one but many pasts were fractured by the impact, and the act of destruction divided and inflamed its observers, setting left against right, soldier against civilian, aesthetics against honor, liberty against patrimony, history against memory. As one commentator presciently wrote to a colleague on hearing of the fallen monument, "like you I fear that around this column, knocked down by the ones, rebuilt by the others, more and more ardent passions and hatred will be kindled" (Brandat and Passy 1871: 14).

◄ ◄ ◄

The object of all this attention was a triumphal column, consecrated to the memory of the military campaigns of 1805, decreed by Napoleon Bonaparte. To the painter Bergeret were confided the designs for the reliefs that spiraled up the cylindrical face of the column, a "suite of subjects which were like an historical journal of the campaign."[4] Importantly, the bronze for the reliefs was smelted from the cannons captured by Napoleon at Austerlitz from the Russians and Austrians.[5] More than gloriously symbolic, the column was the material commemoration of a historical event. The extravagant romantic reactionary author Jules Amédée Barbey d'Aurevilly proclaimed the bronze of the column a living substance for a living monument, steeped in and penetrated by the blood of soldiers. "The blood of France is there. The blood incorporated with the soul and honor of France!" Thus, "the Column is not a monument like others. The Column is part of the honor of France, and taken down, our honor is likewise degraded."[6]

Inaugurated in August 1810, the column rested on the pedestal of the former statue of Louis XIV at the Place Vendôme, which had itself been overturned in the Revolution. The new Napoleonic monument affirmed imperial greatness, while replacing the memory of one monarch with another. The name itself went through several evolutions: La Colonne d'Austerlitz; de la Grande Armée; finally, la Colonne Vendôme. A single, vertical projection, the column bore at the summit a colossal bronze designed by Chaudet draped in the mantle of a Roman emperor, in one hand resting a globe from which soared a winged victory. Early renderings show the emperor resting on an imposing broadsword, a feature later reduced and attached to his belt, where he grips the knob with a firm hand. Weighing 5,000 pounds and costing 44,000 francs, the statue itself, interestingly, was not cast from the cannons of Austerlitz but from military pieces levied from the arsenal at Mayence. A distinction was always maintained, at least by some, between the different metals and representations. In the debate on the impending destruction of the monument, Jules Simon, Minister of Public Instruction, had favored smelting down the statue—but not the column.[7] Victor Hugo made the same point in verse:

But it's France! Frenchmen
                We are taking down
What remained standing on our darkest horizons
Great France is there! What does
                Bonaparte matter!
Does one see a king when one
                looks upon Sparta?
Lift away Napoleon, the people reappear
Cut down the tree, but respect the
                forest. (Soria 1971: 156)[8]

The emperor and his bronze double were deeply implicated in the political memory of the nineteenth century, for the imperial colossus atop the Vendôme Column followed its own history of triumph, misfortune, resurrection, and reappropriation. Inaugurated and placed originally in 1810, it was taken down at the Restoration and languished in a foundry at Launay for many years. From April 1814 the column was surmounted by the large "drapeau blanc" favored by the monarchy. Contemporary illustrations show the huge white flag flying serenely over the octagon. The statue was nonetheless no more forgotten than Napoleon himself. On 6 April 1814, the prefect of the Seine, the Count of Bondy, requested the reinstallation of the statue "in the name of the inhabitants of Paris." Lazare Carnot, then Minister of the Interior, noted the king's reaction, "His majesty responded that, as the statue had been placed on the column without his order, he did not wish for it to be replaced."[9] In 1831, with Napoleon long since safely defeated and the new Orléans dynasty in search of prestige, Le Moniteur universel reported an audience between Casimer Perier, the président du conseil, and the monarch: "Sire, the column at the Place Vendôme, that monument of immortal victories, lost the statue which crowned it fifteen years ago. This mutilation still continues; it is a sad vestige of foreign invasion."[10]

In 1840 Napoleon did return, in the Orléanist Louis-Philippe's management of the Napoleonic remains and mystique, to bolster the political legitimacy of his own regime. The emperor's body, exhumed from St. Helena, was viewed and claimed to be in perfect condition. Returned to Paris, it made its way down the Seine on a black barge to be interred at the Invalides (esp. Tulard 1986: 81–110). Along with the emperor's exhumed body, his double found its place again atop the column. The new figure, by Seurre, was a popular Napoleon of "the little hat and frock-coat," in a familiar pose, one hand resting in his jacket. The "little corporal" was an extraordinary bit of political artistry—reaffirming Napoleon atop his column—but not Napoleon the emperor. The royal command that ordered the placement of the statue tried to be pragmatic: "the figures in the reliefs of the column being in French military costume, the statue should be equally attired in military costume."[11] The new statue had the intended appeal, at least with some. The publishers of a small guide, a "description" of the column, hoped the new Napoleon would be "part of the solemnités destined to celebrate for the third time the glorious and immortal July revolution," taking Napoleon for a general champion of liberty (Anon. 1833: 20). The great soldier and general, whose other body now rested securely at the Invalides, was the popular hero of French spirit ingeniously divested of the mantle that challenged the authority of the traditional royal lines currently ruling France.

The story does not end there. If troublesome to a few, the imperial Napoleon was a crucial political element to others. With his coup d'état and power consolidated in November 1863, Louis Napoleon, the nephew, regarded Seurre's "little corporal" lacking in grandeur for the background of his own imperial ambitions. As Emperor Napoleon III he ordered the statue replaced with a new version of Chaudet's original. Seurre's piece was thus taken down from the column and reestablished at the roundabout of Courbevoie. The toga of the Roman Caesars returned to the tower at the Place Vendôme, along with the winged victory, the crown of laurels, and the broadsword. So it remained undisturbed, until 16 May 1871.

◄ ◄ ◄

As the column shattered, reactions were instantaneous—particularly from the military. At Versailles, Marshall MacMahon received the news and exhorted his troops to prepare for battle, raising the dignity of the invading Prussian army above the Communards: "Soldiers! The Vendôme Column has just fallen. The foreigner had respected it. The Paris Commune has brought it down. The men who call themselves French have dared destroy, under the gaze of the watching Germans, this witness to the victories of our fathers against the coalition of all Europe" (Claretie 1872: 125). Only five days later the troops would enter Paris by the Point-du-Jour, beginning the final street-to-street warfare, the slaughter, execution, and burning of Paris of the "Semaine Sanglate"—bloody week. Tens of thousands died in the war of France against France. Vengeful mobs, ruthless commanders, and wild female incendiaries crowd accounts of those days as barricades were defended and overrun, prisoners and hostages executed. Public edifices, including the Hotel de Ville, went up in flames. The last resisters were executed at the Mur des Fédérés in the Père Lachaise cemetery.

Military courts shaped the fate of those who survived the carnage. The military and the column in particular dictated the fate of one man who played perhaps the single most important role in the drama of the monumemnt, Gustave Courbet. A renowned and often controversial realist painter, Courbet's major works, *Burial at Ornans, The Stonebreakers,* and *The Artist's Studio,* had excited artistic and social commentary in the Salons and made him "the loudmouth of French painting" (Riat 1906: 292–93).[12] As president of the Fédération des Artistes under the Commune charged, ironically, with protecting art in Paris during the siege, Courbet campaigned vigorously against the column. On 4 September 1870, he issued a communiqué suggesting that the column be knocked down, arguing that it was a monument "lacking in artistic value, tending to perpetuate the ideas of war and conquest of the imperial dynasty."[13] On 12 April 1871, the Commune issued its official statement, agreeing with Courbet that the column was a "monument to barbarism," symbolizing only "brute force and false glory, an affirmation of militarism, a negation of international law, a permanent insult of the victors over the vanquished, a perpetual attack on one of the three great principles of the French Republic, *la fraternité.*"[14] The Napoleonic monument was to be destroyed and replaced by a new figure symbolizing 18 March—the founding date of the Commune itself.

The decision to replace one commemoration with another had perilous personal consequences for Courbet. Anonymous letters signed "a former soldier" or referring to Napoleon, threatened the artist with drowning and daggers if anything should happen to the column. With the return of the Versaillies to control in Paris, Courbet was arrested, jailed, tried for "complicity in the abuse of authority in the destruction of the Column" by a military court, and eventually charged with the full cost of the restoration—a clearly impossible sum. The charge included substantial payments to other artists, including Dumont for restoring the statue, and Mercier for the model of the Victory statuette. Courbet protested that he had acted with good intentions, intending only to take down the column and reestablish its parts at the Invalides or another appropriately museal site—though, in a pointedly ironic "rendering unto Caesar" he had also suggested melting down the commemorative reliefs and stamping them into money (Castagnary 1883; Bonniot 1967: 221–24).[15]

Courbet's correspondence does suggest an apparently sincere respect for monuments and commemoration. In an "Open Letter to the German Army" of 29 October 1870, he had appealed, "let us have your Krupp cannons . . . the last crowned with the phrygien bonnet to be planted on a pedestal which we will raise together at the Place Vendôme. This will be our column, one to the other, the column of Germany and France forever federated" (Reau 1959: 193). Courbet would only inconsistently follow this line, for in his trial arguments he maintained that the verticality of the column disturbed the artfully horizontal lines of the Place Vendôme. "For me, this column obstructed. An individual thing does not have the right to block traffic. This column was badly placed. . . . at the Place Vendôme it was a miserable pretension as a work of art, which made foreigners laugh."[16]

As the internationalist monument he envisioned would also stand at the Place Vendôme, Courbet's argument against the Napoleonic column from a logic of spatial aesthetics was not his honest guiding principle, and it is intriguing that he would regard it as a form of innocence. What Courbet tardily hoped was that art would put him outside and above the real and explosive question: the control of historical memory. If his artist's expertise could prevail in convincing the court of the aesthetic merits of taking down the column, he might be beyond the reach of those—particularly soldiers and veterans—who did not wish to see the Napoleonic memory violated. The letter to the German army demonstrated, at least early on, that Courbet knew the hazards of destroying a military monument; he focused on forging cannons into commemorations—not effacing them. Under wartime circumstances, to destroy a military monument could not be regarded a virtuous act, not even by the Germans, not even in the name of art or brotherhood.

In destroying the column, Courbet's internationalism ran afoul of the traditions and glories of the military which Marshall MacMahon had suggested even the Germans could respect. As an institution charged now with dictating justice in its own name, the military was Courbet's judge and undoing. Harassed and threatened, Courbet fled to Switzerland, where he denied wrongdoing, saying little about the event, commenting on the increased value of his paintings. His friends began to plead his case and try to rehabilitate his memory in issues of a bulletin, *Les Amis de Courbet*. He subsequently died in exile, and his body returned to Ornans only in 1919 with a special "pass for cadavers" from the mayor of Vevey.[17]

◄ ◄ ◄

I have called Courbet's case a struggle over "memory." The event that proved both his political triumph and undoing was well documented by witnesses, yet how much was the event remembered, and how much created in the records? The radical and not-so-radical press, the numerous personal memoirs, the histories and scholarship that center on the column recompose a torrent of words and images—both gravure and photographic—that complement and contradict. Karl Marx seemed to frame the event with the famous last lines of his "Eighteenth Brumaire." His image of the iron statue tumbling from the top of the column, coupled with his later analysis of the "Civil War in France," provided a well-known and defining interpretation of events leading to the Place Vendôme, yet his image of the falling emperor was drawn twenty years before the event, making him more prophet than witness (Marx 1988).

Among the journalists at the site itself, reports ranged fully across the political and rhetorical spectrum. To the left, Jules Vallès headlined his column in *Le Cri du peuple*, "It's fallen! The sentence of the people is executed, justice is done! It's fallen, this column made of cannons bought at the price of so many cadavers." *Le Salut public* of Gustave Maroteau published a biting polemic, "An Emperor on a Dunghill," declaring, "with him the cult of great men crumbles, those famous bandits whose image was hardened with the blood of the unfortunate." As for the monument itself, Maroteau described "the fall of this gigantic urinal."[18] Less enthusiastic was *Le Bulletin du jour*, whose criticisms were somewhat differently directed. In an otherwise prosaic account of the crowd scene, this biting line: "The numerous musicians of the national guard were summoned triumphally to celebrate the only incontestable victory of the Commune." *La Constitution* was not even so gracious in its interpretation of the event: "In the crowd united yesterday around the Place Vendôme there were explosions of hatred and rage. On your guard, members of the Committee and members of the Commune."[19]

The moment of impact was also witnessed differently by different observers—including photographic observers. Prosper Lissagaray, in his *Historie de la commune* (1876), comments, "the head of Bonaparte rolls upon the ground," leaving behind a "purified pedestal." Gravures also show the clean cut between the head and body. The rolling head is a telling image, since photographs taken from many angles, including one close group portrait of Courbet and his associates posing with the fallen statue, indicate that the head of the statue did not in any way separate from the trunk.[20]

Nonetheless the break was a favorite image of the reporting. *Le Réveil du peuple* played with the embedded historical references, "nothing remains but a heap of fragments. The Column is pulverized, the *tricolor* shrouds the decapitated Caesar, resting on a bed of manure." The image of death and the politics of the corpse was attended also by Vallès: "he rests there, somber and sinister, red flags at the four corners of the pile of sticks, as on an immobile catafalque containing the cadavers of imperial glory." Another press account from the Place noted a sailor taking up a paving stone to strike the head of the fallen Napoleon (he was, for some reason, prevented). Maxime Vuillaume also wrote in similar terms. "Caesar rests upon his back, decapitated. His head, crowned with laurels, has rolled like a pumpkin to the edge of the walkway" (Vuillaume 1909: 249–50).[21]

Photography and writing contradict. The head may have been reattached for the pictures, but more likely the journalists were writing less out of observation than political symbolism. The truth of the event was not the seeing, but the meaning of the act: the end of dictators, the head and the trunk, the ruler and the state, now separated, sovereignty returning to the people. Recent history was of course deeply implicated: by shattering Napoleon Bonaparte, the Communards proclaimed their liberty from the nephew, Louis Napoleon. Revolutionary memories would also evoke the statue of Louis XIV which had been overturned in 1792 at the Place Vendôme, or images from the Place de la Concorde, where the guillotine had severed the royal head of Louis XVI. In fact, in addition to the "decapitated Caesar," the "shrouding" of the figure was a determined choice of language. Not mere rage nor effacement of symbols was taking place, but a sacred transition, of both political and spiritual legitimacy.

Lissagaray's, Vallès's, and Vuillaume's imagery and the shadowy memories of the guillotine are arresting in view of a small historical action coincident with the toppling of the column. A *procès-verbal* from the National Archives relates the fate of the third Napoleonic body (after Vendôme and the Invalides), the "little corporal" resting at the roundabout at Courbevoie. On 17 September 1870, the very day the Prussians were to occupy Versailles, the government ordered engineers "to take down the statue called The Little Corporal at Courbevoie and deposit it in the Seine." A few days later, according to the architect in charge, the statue was taken down, during which the head ("in spite of precautions") was separated from the trunk. The whole was bound in 130 meters of tarred cordage, along with the head, which was placed at the feet. Transported upstream from the bridge at Neuilly, "at a distance of 37 meters from the corner (next to the end) of the rue du Bois-de-Boulogne," it was dumped into the river.[22]

The sacrality or desecration of the body ran throughout the tale of the Vendôme Column. Even the choice of 16 May for the ceremony resulted from technical difficulties the engineers experienced with the scaffolding and cutting of the base of the monument. The original date had been 5 May—the day of Napoleon's death. After the fall, speeches were made from atop the debris itself. Citizen Henri Festrine declared to the crowd, "Citizens, we have seen this column fall, as well as the man who now lies on the excrements fated to receive him. This man, who stunned all the courts of all foreign nations, is at your feet, helpless." The broken body was also evoked by Vuillaume, who wrote, "The Column is on the ground, open, its entrails of stone open to the wind."[23] The fall brought low the power and the glory of the Emperor to a corpse. The editors of *Le Père Duchêne* make this point with their customary glee:

> Having thrown down the little man of bronze
> That's not bad
> But that's not all
> And it's far from being enough
> Citizens members of the Commune
> Why only the bronze!
> The justice of the people has quite other relics
> To throw to the winds!

The "other relics" of course, were the remains of "the little man in flesh and bone at the Invalides." *Le Père Duchêne* was unsparing in its attack on the Napoleonic regime, and described an imperial corpse "stuffed with spices in the stomach, for fear that it will spoil!"[24] Jules Vallès also declared war on the injustices of the dead. Vallès, writer, journalist, poison pen par excellence, followed in the tradition of Marat with *Le Cri du peuple:* "The statue of the first Bonaparte as roman emperor is at the refuse dump, and that is very good, but it is not enough. The swaddled carcass of this master rogue is still at the Invalides . . . it must be burned . . . and its ashes scattered to the wind. Enough of these ignoble relics."

Vallès offered little distinction between the two bodies of the emperor; the one shattered at the Place Vendôme and the other whose remains rested at the Invalides, the "swaddled carcass." Here Vallès echoed *Le Père Duchêne*'s suggestions for Napoleon's remains: "Let's go! / Fuck it in a bright bed of lime / Or burn it / Or throw the whole thing into the Seine / Or into the sewers!"[25] The drowning of the body was at least partially accomplished as noted earlier. The burning of the body, the reduction to ashes for *Le Père Duchêne* as well as for Vallès was no consecration, but merely an efficient means to scatter dust so that no more "relics" could remain. It was precisely the antiquarian "sacred" powers of the relic which was the scene of the struggle for them.

◀ ◀ ◀

The battle over memory and monument was not limited to wicked broadsides in the radical papers. The column had equally eloquent defenders who on several occasions turned to verse to make their points. Poetry as a location of political sentiment was common enough in the nineteenth century (think of Lamartine or Hugo), and numerous small booklets proclaimed their own version of the events at the Place Vendôme. In a paean to the column (1874), one Eugene Léveque allowed the monument to speak for itself. At the side of the fallen column, the poet finds the Napoleonic statue declaring "in its vibrant voice resonating everywhere" "the shame with which the crime here was committed" (Léveque 1874: 8). Another defender of the column, Edouard d'Anglemont, in 1872 published *La Resurrection de la colonne*, a telling title to say the least. D'Anglemont lauded the column, and offered his stamp on the Communards, "Bible of our exploits / popular monument / you are no more! / The royal brigands of Paris / possessed of infamy and stupid hatred / have laid down your epic debris in the gutter!" The column becomes proud victim, fallen to the "purveyors of death, kings of the guillotine, hideous profaners of the sainted word: liberty," a pointedly Jacobin imagery. When the column is finally restored, the resurrection image—the rising anew of the body from death—incorporates a new glorious France, "great again among nations" (D'Anglemont 1872: 5–10).

The conjunction of resurrection and nation ran through the conflicts of the Commune. A few weeks after taking control of Paris, on 7 June, Adolphe Thiers's new government had the body of the Archbishop Dar-

boy (executed by the Communards) disinterred, embalmed, and commemorated with a grandiose ceremony at Notre Dame. A few years later
came the grandest, though to its opponents, the most grotesque vision of
expiation and reconciliation of the nation: the building of the basilica of
Sacre Coeur, overlooking all of Paris from the summit of Montmartre
(Loyer 1993: 450–73).

◄ ◄ ◄

The poetic treatments of the column described not only the promise of the
nation as resurrected body, but also the unfolding of history itself in which
words and monument become one. Léveque's 1874 verses (above) open
with an arresting laudation: "Standing with its glorious spiral against the
sky / a bronze monument dominates the city / on its proud flanks it
unrolls the history / of the dawn of the century to posterity" (Léveque
1874: 8). The description here of an unrolling history is noteworthy, for
the Vendôme column, much more than other more pointedly allegorical
statuary, actually *is* an historical mural, 425 plaques, unrolling some 840
feet, over a thousand if fully extended. The bronze spiral of the column
unfolds, in multiple sequential tableaux, Napoleon's campaigns and the
victory of Austerlitz. The story begins 24 August 1805, with the march of
the French armies toward the Rhine, features diplomatic encounters at
Wurtemberg, Louisbourg, and Ulm, and episodes of battle leading up to
Austerlitz on 2 December. The spiral concludes with the cession of Venice
to Italy, and the return of the Napoleonic guard to France.[26] The contemporary (Napoleonic era) costuming of the armies, their formations, and
artillery, wind up and around a monument rendered in imitation of Trajan's victory column at the Forum in Rome, crowned by the Roman drap-
ing of Napoleon himself, after the Royal style made popular in the eighteenth century. By 1871 many layers of empire and memory were already
incarnated at the Place Vendôme.

The story in bronze which the column unrolls is not only a documentary of Napoleonic military campaigns, but itself a treatise on historical
consciousness. As an almost exact copy of Trajan's column, it was at once
triumphal monument and funereal marker. In Trajan's case his ashes
were deposited in a mausoleum in the base of the monument, associating
his person, his memory, and his monument with the geographical center
of Roman authority.

The subsequent embedding of the Roman example in the French was taken very seriously, as Napoleon's self-representation as a Caesar indicates. In 1821, one Alexandre Goujon, a former captain of the artillery, had published a poetic pamphlet dense with the imagery of Napoleon's greatness, placing the general in the line of the "heroes of antiquity." The column was something more than a marker, for "standing upright upon the triumphal column, holding the Victory in his hand, he resembled the commander of Europe!" The personal majesty that linked Trajan to Bonaparte through the column led to Goujon's unsurprising suggestion: "Yes, Napoleon, the column at the Place Vendôme is the only monument worthy of receiving your ashes" (Goujon 1821: 5–7). To consecrate and mix the ashes with the material of the monument itself would unify the two bodies into one sacred relic, the ultimate repetition of Trajan's memorial.

The "memory" of the column was manifest in other ways as well. The iconographies of monuments like Trajan's column were not intended merely to glorify brutal military conquest but to illustrate grand lessons in politics and morality deserving of respect and emulation. A great conquerer hero could not achieve glory merely through military victories, for the source of success was inextricable from worthiness and the exercise of the virtues of "courage, clemency, justice, piety." Like Aeneas leaving Dido to pursue Destiny, the great man was only the incarnation of these virtues, a part of an unfolding, ascending spiral of history. A triumphal column, with its continuous frieze, was an invocation of historical time, a series of images which, in one notable interpretation, "incarnates to our eyes the temporal dimension which draws together the past and the future," and translated to the viewer "the immense effort of the ascension of the Roman world." At a cosmological extreme, the spiral of time was a Dante-like history of the world, unwinding somewhere between the Earth and the moral system of Aristotle, and Paradise—the image of the Ptolemaic heavens.[27]

◀ ◀ ◀

The destruction of the Vendôme Column was much more than an antimilitarist statement or attempt to mock one Napoleonic dictator by bringing down another. To break the column would break and collapse many different histories—those of the Napoleonic regimes of course, but also classical, cosmological, cultural, and national narratives. To efface one without disturbing the others was impossible. As the emperor fell, so also did the patriotic genius of the French revolutionary armies. Tyranny conquered meant a cultural heritage endangered. Virtuous republics tumbled down alongside ambitious dictators.

The politics of memory thus shaped fiercely divided reactions to the Communards' act. One document contemporaneous with the events in Paris neatly outlined the complex terms of the debate. In May 1871, Paul Brandat of a pacifist organization, the *Ligue Internationale et Permanente de Paix*, wrote to his colleague Frédéric Passy, requesting an official position on the tumultuous events taking place in Paris. The entire exchange, which ranged over civil war, world brotherhood, working-class oppression, and the rule of law, was conducted around the singular event of the column's destruction, locating the act between "the art of producing and the art of destroying . . . the politics of life and the politics of death" (Brandat and Passy 1871: 1–2).

Brandat opens the exchange by giving support to the action at the Place Vendôme and the right of "workers, condemned to misery by conquerers," to negate oppressive memory in the name of their own human liberation. He justifies the Communards' action by locating the column in a sinister lineage, drawing not on European history but on Asia and Africa as sites of unspeakable savagery to make his point. "A long time ago, Timour-Beg, an Asian Napoleon, built an edifice of human remains," he begins, matching this horror with an account of a voyage to "the coast of Africa" where he encounters the warrior king of Dahomey, elevating a funereal monument to the memory of his father—"a gigantic tomb of bricks hardened with human blood." Brandat unseats Napoleon from Rome and places him alongside non-European barbarians, neatly serving as signs of a primitive savagery counterposed to antique grandeur. The column, he claims, is nothing but "an immense pile of human debris" (ibid.).

Yet Brandat's support is ambivalent; he finds the destruction of the column an unsettling act, a sign of "serious times." He was right about that: the immediate situation around Paris was explosive for a population trapped "between civil war and foreign war." By 8 May, Thiers had already delivered an ultimatum to the Parisians, and by the 13th his Versailles forces occupied an important fort near Paris, just three days before the column fell. Brandat was careful to lament the destruction of the monument as "the necessary consequence of the cult of force," which he abhorred.

The attack on the column raised a troubling question: was violence justifiable—even against monuments of oppression? For the Commune, what were the legitimate means of its own defense? Frédéric Passy, in his reply to Brandat, judged the events at the Place Vendôme a crime, even if they were directed against tyranny. The blow against the column, he argued, was criminal because it was effected by "a faction, no . . . a band without mandate, without authorization, without title or appearances of any kind of title" (ibid.: 11). The unacceptable fault of the destroyers was not their revolutionary politics, nor particularly their use of force, but that they did not act in the name of what he called "the nation."

But who could claim to speak and act in the name of "the nation"? Clearly, it was not the Napoleonic regime, for whom Passy had no sympathies: "it is not the statue of that great and sterile butcher which should take its place on the summit of this funereal monument, but the statue of his principal victim, *La France*" (ibid.). The Communards had read the column as a monument to tyranny and militarism, thus deserving destruction. In Passy's view, the Communards should only have exchanged empire for *patrie* by replacing ruler's laurels with a symbol of the people's heritage. Breaking the Vendôme Column captured the political shift yet also damaged the incarnated and resurgent nation. His argument has a perplexing circularity: only the nation could destroy monuments, yet the nation would be attacking itself by doing so.

The logic of this conundrum, and the thinking behind its origins, can be illustrated by actions taken at Versailles. On 25 April 1871, less than a month before the events at the Place Vendôme, Adolphe Thiers had presented a *Projet de loi* declaring all public and private property in Paris (especially if seized by the Commune) to be inalienable. The document begins with a declaration of urgency: "The insurrection which dominates Paris and disquiets France has taken on, in its audacious development, characteristics which no legislator could have foreseen."[28] Thiers's bill opens by defending the bourgeois sanctity of property, yet expands this notion to declare the Commune a threat not to anyone's particular wealth, but to the cultural heritage of a nation.

The monuments erected by our fathers, witnesses to our old glories, are threatened, the wealth of our establishments are taken and brazenly presented to the Mint. The hand of the ravagers does not hesitate before the sacred vases which the faithful have given to our churches to contribute to the pomp of their ceremonies. They covet and have begun to pillage all the art objects which the passion of a few amateurs or the enlightened taste of governments from different eras have been able to unite in private and public collections.[29]

The bill establishes as inalienable not only properties belonging to the state, department, and city, but also to churches, workshops, civil and commercial companies, and individuals. Arrest and condemnation await anyone acting in the name of, or under the orders of "one so-called Commune of Paris." The intent of the legislation is quite clear: to punish "plundering and theft" and to place "out of circulation all goods and properties upon which the insurrection would exercise its own accounts."

Behind the proposal however, more was at stake than punishing theft and trafficking. In his bill Thiers wrote, "Before this peril *d'un nouveau genre* which none of our too-numerous revolutions has ever before presented, the legislation appeared insufficient." Thiers, a good historian, was certainly familiar with theft and the willful destruction of icons, images, and art in revolutionary situations—what was "new" about this? His deputy M. Bertrand clarified the position of the Versailles government by denouncing the "pillage and devastation" of everything that "the nation, the department of the Seine, the great city and its individuals hold particularly dear," reviling the Communards as "adventurers without names, and more often without patrie."[30] In attacking the Communards thus, the government at Versailles saw "France" as the injured party, assaulted by outsiders, internationalist fanatics not even French.

Maurice Aghulon has argued that a new language was being shaped at the time of the Commune, a language of visual representations outside of politics. To destroy symbols of despotism was an expected act, "but to demolish one of the celebrated monuments of Paris! That was no longer politics, it was vandalism, barbarism . . . in this new language, Napoleon and the Column were no longer a political symbol; they had become works of art, to be preserved as such. One did not yet speak of 'patrimony,' but the idea was there" (Aghulon 1988: 304–7). Courbet, recall, had tried to defend himself by appealing to aesthetics. Alas for him, the column had itself already acquired a quality of temporal sacrality beyond his or anyone's artistic judgment.

Aghulon is perhaps too modest in emphasizing the historical lateness of transforming political symbols into objects of artistic heritage. Struggles over "patrimony" had begun at least with the French Revolution, and in his exchange with Brandat, Frédéric Passy had defended the column by arguing that "the monuments raised by our predecessors are a sacred patrimony" (Brandat and Passy 1871: 12).[31] On this point he was adamant. In Passy's vision, history and art, or better, history embodied in art, were the markers that resisted time's "incessant destructions." Each shattered monument was a forgetfulness, an oblivion, so to attack the Vendôme Column was to attack not merely Napoleon, but history itself. Such elegant arguments had been employed even earlier by Casimer Perier, who, in remonstrating before Louis Philippe for the return of the Napoleonic statue, had concluded, "Monuments are like history: they are inviolable like it; they must conserve all the nation's memories, and not fall to the blows of time."[32]

◀ ◀ ◀

Yet shaping a patrimony is a process of selection and designation, and the difference between symbols of tyranny and grandeurs of a "nation's memories" is not always obvious. In their committee work, the Communards themselves were often at pains to know exactly what to destroy. One act of obliteration was decreed by consensus on 10 May 1871: "The house of Thiers, located at place Georges, will be torn down." The house of the chief of the Versailles government was completely demolished, but the total project was in no way simple. In a 12 May meeting, Courbet posed a problem to his fellow delegates: "Messr. Thiers has a collection of bronze antiques; I wonder what should be done with them." The delegates decided that a commission would be appointed to conserve and protect them. Demay remarked, "Don't forget that these small bronze artworks are the history of humanity, and we want to conserve the intelligence of the past for the edification of the future. We are not barbarians." Protot differed: "I am a friend of Art, but I am of the opinion that all the pieces representing the image of the Orléans should be sent to the Mint. As for the other artworks, they will obviously not be destroyed." Clemence added another category: "Thiers' collection is also composed of bibliographic riches, for whose conservation I ask that a commission be named." Grousset also: "There are also in Theirs' home pieces belonging to the Archives . . . it would be good if, on the commission we are going to name, there could be historians, men of letters."[33] So the Communards organized their own patrimonies by taste, politics, discipline. One thing was destroyed, another preserved; some useless or offensive articles were to be broken up or burned, consigned to oblivion, others protected, the history of humanity.

◄ ◄ ◄

For the Communards, the breaking of time was the deep logic of their many ritual acts, including the destruction of the column, of Thiers's house, of Orléanist and Napoleonic imagery. The Commune attempted to establish itself in a revolutionary temporality, adopting the Republican calendar for *Le Journel officiel,* and declaring the Commune's founding date the consecration of a "rupture" and "negation" of previous history.[34]

This negation of the past would prove to be one of the most fiercely contested points in the whole debate around the destruction of the Vendôme Column. The poet Léveque, cited earlier, had attacked the Communards for having "soiled forever the French name," raging, "They have pulverized Glory / and attempted to erase History!" (Léveque 1874: 13). The war over the column was a struggle over representing the legacies of the past. Partisans of "patrimony" like Frédéric Passy were vaguely sympathetic to the Communards' anti-imperialism, but found their politics of rupturing time, space, and history anathema to his own. In condemning the radicals, Passy defined what was clearly the true offense of the Place Vendôme: "crime against the present and crime against the past . . . foolish and barbarous pretension to make a tabula rasa of the material works of our fathers as well as of our traditions, ideas, and the laws of human nature itself" (Brandat and Passy 1871: 12).

What Passy shared with the Communards was a certain internationalism, a humane and ideal politics based upon a federalist world order free from political oppression, dedicated to the rightful exercise of work and art. In this, the programs of a hundred Proudhonian, Marxist, Blanquist, Jacobin, socialist, and other workers' movements of the middle and late nineteenth century could find general philosophical agreement. Passy's position against the Communards on the question of the column was something else, however: it was a bulwark against the unsettling possibility that the past had no meaning. He could not fault deposing images of tyrants, yet if monuments could be destroyed, the "material works of our fathers," their embodied traditions, aspirations, and patriarchal lineages would be upset, and with them his attempt to define a "nation."

Invoking the destruction of the column, Passy agrees that the nation has the right to decree such actions, yet only as a "purifying France" answering to a higher principle "like the dens of pagans converted by Christianity given sanctuary by the God of justice and love." At the place of the destroyed column Passy would fashion a new monument. "I would, in the name of France, in the name of humanity, ask that the memory of those whose fathers gathered together the bronze and stone with their blood be sadly inscribed" (Ibid.: 14–16). The moving eloquence of inscribing memories of fathers' blood equates the "name of humanity" with that of France in a patriarchal prescription. The transcendent, encompassing, eternal humanity which Passy invokes, the tears it weeps, the language it speaks is that of a French nation defined as generations of fathers inheriting the classical and Christian worlds. By defending "material works" Passy's reflections also underline another point: this inheritance is a defense of property, in much the way that Thiers's "patrimony" law sought to defend a nation defined through property and ownership. Passy's views on the column outline a bourgeois historical vision, couched as they are in a language of nation as patriarchal, propertied lineage, Christian redemption, and the defense of an abstract humanity in the continuities of a French tradition. Such historical narratives ultimately moved him to disdain the Communards' action in the name of "human nature."

◄ ◄ ◄

Passy's history was extensive, drawing its power from the transmissions of an unrolling legacy of time. Other histories were intensive, fixed on the decisive meaning of moments. The moment of the falling column proposed a special historical scheme to Passy's interlocutor Paul Brandat, for whom the events at the Place Vendôme were less a threat to a redemptive, liberal history than an ecstatic expression of social justice and international politics as a unique instant of lived experience: "Ah! It was a noble festival, a festival blessed by God, as if at that great council of work, the

Universal Exposition, the French people had invited the workers of all the nations to tear down this symbol of war to the sound of a European orchestra, for peace, and peace alone, can emancipate the worker" (Ibid.: 2).

The French, by their action against the Vendôme Column, set the example for the new world order. The character of this world order is breathtakingly characterized in the first lines "Ah! It was a noble festival, a festival blessed by God." The image of the festival (*fête*) in Brandat's vision is striking and was revived forcefully and eloquently by historian Henri Lefebvre (1965) in his bold formulation: "The Commune of Paris? It was first of all an immense and grandiose festival, a festival which the people of Paris, essence and symbol of the French people in general, offered to themselves and to the world" (Lefebvre 1969: 125).[35] For both Lefebvre and Brandat, *festival* is a critical category in understanding the revolutionary actions of the Commune: the celebration of apparent disorder in the face of order, the "destructuring of society" attempted by the Commune's innovative legislation on worker's rights, women's education, and political liberties. Seen in this way, the overturning of the column was simply the most spectacular example of a society playing out festive rites of reversal, making a world upside-down out of politics, class, and culture. This meant inverting hierarchies and rupturing time in the present, creating disorder out of which could be born new orders.

The joyful image of the festival embraces both the excitement of workers' internationals, and the self-congratulation of the Universal Expositions—those late nineteenth-century showcases of bourgeois civilization. Shaped by the French revolutionary tradition of the nineteenth century, the Communards were true indignant believers in this exalted new world order, part Blanquist in taking the Jacobin past as a political and social model, part Fourierist in looking to a worker's society organized on scientific industrial principles. Framing this fervor in terms of the Vendôme Column, the *Journal officiel* of the Commune reported on memories of the future: "Let the world be convinced: the columns put up from now on will never celebrate some historic brigand, but will perpetuate the memory of some glorious conquest in science, work, and liberty."[36]

◄ ◄ ◄

The Communards believed in many things, in justice, work, liberty, science; they also believed that revolution was necessary to achieve those goals, and that revolution was a struggle over memory. Marx had contemptuously denounced the operatic nostalgia of Louis Napoleon's coup d'état and later celebrated the martyrs of the Commune in his writings. The followers of Auguste Blanqui honored the cult of 1793, organizing their political activities around pilgrimages and mythic rituals commemorating the heroes of nineteenth-century insurrection.[37] Yet revolutionary memory triumphant required more than a cult of saints. It required war on the memories of the old order.

From the Place Vendôme, radical writer Félix Pyat delivered his attack: "The Column has fallen, victim of the United States of Europe. Sooner or later its fall will sweep away the Trafalgar Column in London, that of Blucher in Berlin, all the old royal and social forms, all the vestiges of war and hatred, of race and caste."[38] In London and Berlin, just as in Paris, fallen columns inaugurated a new federalist world broken from despotic history. Far from a nurturing and identifying tradition, Pyat recognized the past incarnated in the columns as monopolized memories, the false, intolerable glories of a decrepit order. Humanity would be possible only when such memories were destroyed, the old forms and vestiges crumbling as their props were pulled down.

Pyat's account separated past from future, and the column appears as a marker to conjure a series of rhetorical oppositions, an ethical map of political principles and ironic justice: "This monument of force against law, of empire against republic, of war against peace, of Caesar against the people, has finally been knocked down by the hand of the people themselves."[39] The column defined the moral space of a new history that lay at the base of ethical rule: the resurgent, recaptured justice of "the people." That space was also geographic, the mapping of an entirely new political order of Europe. Writing from the Place Vendôme, Pyat concluded, "It has fallen forever at this place which will henceforth forever be called 'Place Internationale.'"[40] At a reception following the events of 16 May, officials in fact adopted this new name, but time was not on the side of the Commune.

One more report on the column gives an important variation on the spectacular overthrow of history and memory taking place at the Place Vendôme. Venting his rage against the "rigid, brutal, heavy and dumb" monument, Jules Vallès saves a good part of his derision for the ease with which it fell: "to bring it down, the calculations of an engineer and a few rounds of rope were sufficient." Vallès's sarcastic astonishment is tuned not to dramatic moments, but to the altogether commonplace way in which history vanishes: "They thought that this column, that this glory could never fall without a shattering upheaval in the world, without the walls of Paris trembling like those of Jericho to the sound of the trumpets of the soldiers of Israel; the inhabitants waited for a shaking of the ground, at the exits of their homes, for the breaking of their windows. Illusion!"[41]

In wicked overstatement, the invocations of apocalypse become comic-opera, inversions of grandeur and tragedy. The end of history—the crumbling walls, the trumpets of Israel—evokes not disaster, but mockery. The colossus falls, Paris does not tremble, the world of the ancients does not reel. Just like its muffled landing on the brush, sand, and manure in the Place Vendôme, the history encased in the monument crumbles without impression. Illusion! The grand tradition, the glory, the mythical past of the Roman emperors is overthrown by the modernity of a fugitive moment, an unremarkable instant.

Indeed, as history was momentarily broken and memory challenged at the Place Vendôme, the monument itself was desubstantialized, its sacred power of place and material rendered spectral and absent. Barbey d'Aurevilly had declared of the column, "Its bronze is more than simple bronze. The blood of those who perished before the enemy on the battlefield has been drunk in, penetrated, making it a thing human and living" (Murat 1970: 208–11). Such defenders of the sanctity of the metal were no doubt horrified by the reports of 20 April 1871, in the *Journal Officiel de la Commune*. Giving Courbet's original remarks on hauling the column off to the mint a businesslike twist, the *Journal* reports, "The materials which compose the column at the Place Vendôme are for sale. The bronze of the cannons of Austerlitz is supposed to permit the fabrication of a million five-centime coins."[42] *Le Père Duchêne* equally proposed, "It is necessary . . . that this bronze end up by serving the commerce of men, that it be nothing more than a money of exchange representing real work and the force of the People circulating around the world!"[43] Infamy—the wreck of the column, the dignity of its cannons and statues was to be taken up and stamped into money! In the destructive moment of modernity at the Place Vendôme, the sacredness of material, of site were to see their final transformation into the anonymous exchange of the economy.

Regarding this brief moment when history turned at the Place Vendôme, it is hard not to read a disquieting resonance out of this exchange-value vision of the future. In his famous memoires of the Commune, Prosper Lissagaray reports "the people wanted to share in the debris of the Column," by running out after souvenirs as it shattered; "the Mint opposed them on the grounds of the money involved" (Lissagaray 1972 [1876]: 291). Even the champions of the monument use mockingly similar language. Barbey d'Aurevilly reports one enraged suggestion from a patriot of the column to capture and imprison Courbet in an iron cage on the pedestal of the fallen monument, "and the man who suggested this added to the punishment all the filth and degradation of the modern spirit in adding: 'he can be shown for money'" (Murat 1970: 211).

The plans to strike the new money from the shattered reliefs were never carried out: not enough time. Had they been, the coins would undoubtedly have shared the fate of other artifacts, subsequently enshrined in their own institutions of memory. Lissagaray reports: "The pieces struck by the Commune are exceptionally rare. I possess an example of a known type, the same as one can see in the displays at the Musée Carnavelet, where a series of everyday objects recalling the insurrectional period of 1871 are laid out" (Lissagaray 1972 [1876]: 287).

The reliefs were reconstructed and the entire column completely rebuilt by the conservative Republican governments in a few years. Photographs show the engineers and architects replacing the Napoleonic statue just after Christmas Day, 1875. Memories lingered even of this reconstruction project. Lissagaray: "One of the first acts of the victorious bougeoisie was to once again raise that enormous baton, symbol of imperial power. To place the master back on his pedestal cost a scaffolding of thirty thousand cadavers. Like the mothers of the First Empire, how many of our own time can look upon that bronze without weeping?" (ibid.: 291).[44]

◂ ◂ ◂

The Commune is annually commemorated by European leftists and guardians of the 73 days' memory at the Mur des Fédérés, the site where the last resisters were executed by Versailles troops against the walls of the Père Lachaise cemetery. At the Place Vendôme, the column is outfitted with the tricolor on national holidays, and, as a Napoleonic monument, takes wreaths for military commemorations.[45] The Place in the late twentieth century is the locale of luxury boutiques, great banks, insurance companies, and the Ritz hotel. The Commune is nowhere present.

Most of the documents reported above as "testimony" appeared in papers and journals on 17 May 1871, the day following the destruction of the column. Some 80 years later, on the same date, a small news article appeared in one of the Paris newspapers announcing a commemoration at the Place Vendôme. The piece, clipped out and filed away at the Bureau des Batiments, announced the forthcoming 250th anniversary of the inauguration of the Place by the Sun King, Louis XIV, whose own statue there had been overturned by the Revolution. The origin and ordination by monarchs had slipped far enough back in history to claim priority over attempts to break that history. The Place was to be adorned with bowers, and a royal mantle hung in front of the Ministry of Justice. Every night, the façades were to be illuminated so that the whole Place would be covered with a "luminous canopy." In the evening, there were concerts, the release of pigeons, and "an elegant and flowery dinner at the Ritz." "The Big Event," however, at the end of the festivities, would be "a carrousel of elegance in automobiles," around the Place and around the column, which did not even exist in the age of Louis: 25 luxury cars carrying young women presenting the latest dress styles "of our great fashion designers."[46] *Le Père Duchêne* would have to laugh.

NOTES

1. Based on eyewitness accounts, *La Commune*, 17 May 1874.

2. See Alfred Normand, "Architectural Plans" of the Column and the Place Vendôme, collections of the Bibliothèque Historique de la Ville de Paris (BHVP).

3. For reproductions of the essential images of the fallen column, see Auray 1989. Also the many gravure reproductions from Soria 1971. The final whereabouts of the "Victoire" are disputed; some researchers argue it found its way to England or the United States: Albert Mousset, "Les trois Napoleon de la colonne," piece 7, in the archives of the Bureau des Batiments civils et des Palais Nationaux, Paris.

4. Jean Bourguignon (Académie des Beaux-Arts), letter, archives of the Bureau des Batiments Civils, piece no. 9. See also "Monuments et oeuvres d'art à la gloire d'Austerlitz," *La Revue: séance annuelle des cinq académies* (15 November 1951): 338–39. The design and engineering of the column are discussed in Normand and Normand 1897; a journalistic history is recounted in Dementhe 1873: the piece appears as a series, 115–18, 134–35, 150–51, 163–67, 178.

5. French history commemorates the battle as Napoléon's strategic victory over the

Austro-Russian army commanded by the monarchs Alexander I and François II on 2 December 1805. Also called the "Battle of the Three Emperors."

6. Cited by Murat 1970: 211. On the political and sacred qualities of memory and monuments in other contexts, Brossat 1990; Young 1993; *Representations 35: Monumental Histories* 1991.

7. Cited by Reau 1959: 197.

8. See also Victor Hugo, *La Colonne*, piece 8–1431 at the BHVP.

9. On the "drapeau blanc," see the reproduction of the image in Murat 1970: 62–63. Carnot's letter noted in a letter to the Ministre des Affaires Culturelles, piece 622, archives of Bureau des Batiments Civils.

10. *Le Moniteur universel*, 11 April 1831.

11. The Comte d'Argout, *Ordonnance Royale*, Ministre des Travaux Publics, archives Bureau des Batiments Civils, dossier Vendôme Column.

12. Based on notes by Castagnary (Cabinet des Estampes, papiers Courbet), Bibliothèque Nationale, Paris.

13. Communication to the Fédération des artistes, 4 September 1870, cited in Reau 1959: 193.

14. Decree, 13 April 1871, from Bourgin and Henriot 1924.

15. Courbet's remark cited in Reau 1959: 196.

16. Cited in Clement 1980: 74.

17. For the scholarship on Courbet's role in the incident, see: Gagenbin 1963; Borel 1921 (letters and correspondence); Muller 1958–59; Levron 1961: 535–37.

18. Jules Vallès in *Le Cri du peuple*, 17 May 1871; Gustave Maroteau in *Le Salut public*, 18 May 1871.

19. Reported in *Le Bulletin du jour*, 17 May 1871, and "La Chute," from *La Constitution politique et sociale*, 18 May 1871.

20. See the collections of the BHVP, Photographs: Place Vendôme, G.P. IV, 12–14, 29–33, 33–52, 1871.

21. See Claude Lefort's discussion of the guillotine and its role in political symbolism. Prescient analyses in Lefort 1978. Equally indispensable is Ernst Kantorowicz's classic *The King's Two Bodies* (1957) and Bloch 1983.

22. Reported by Albert Mousset, "Les Trois Napoleon de la colonne," archives of the Bureau des Batiments Civils, Paris, dossier: Vendôme Column, piece no. 7. My evocation of multiple Napoleonic bodies should recall the discussion of the *colossos* by J. P. Vernant (1971: 252–53): "It is not the image of the deceased which is incarnated and fixed in stone, it is his life in the beyond, this life which is opposed to that of the living like the night is to day. The colossus is not an image; it is a 'double,' as the deceased himself is the double of the living." See also Dupont 397–419.

23. Festrine's remarks cited by Lefebvre (1969); Vuillaume's words from 1909: 249–50.

24. *Le Père Duchêne*, no. 64, 29 Floreal, An. 79: 3–4.

25. Vallès's editorials in *Le Cri du peuple*, nos. 77 and 78 (17–18 May 1871); remarks from *Le Père Duchêne*, no. 64.

26. For a detailed look at the bas-reliefs and the narrative they relate, see Murat 1970: 186–206.

27. For this interpretation, see Malissart 1976: 116–21. Also, Bressler 1980: 38–39. Discussion of the Vendôme Column and its correspondence with "la triomphale Romaine Trajane à Roma," also in documentation at the Bureau des Batiments civils, Paris dossier Vendôme Column, piece 622.

28. *Projet de loi* (25 April 1871), National Archives, Series F17, carton 2685, dossier 1, piece no. 182.

29. Ibid.

30. M. Bertrand, *Rapport* (1871), National Archives.

31. "Patrimony" has become an essential concept (and practice) in the history of memory. See, especially, Choay 1992; Babelon and Chastel 1980: 5–30; Chastel's article in Nora 1987; Leniaud 1992; Pommier 1991.

32. *Le Moniteur universel*, 11 April 1831.

33. Seance of 12 May 1871 in Bourgin and Henriot 1924.

34. Reported in the daily accounts of the *Journal officiel de la commune*, 17 May 1871. See also the accounts dated 17 September 1870, on the reappropriation of Paris landmarks to their former revolutionary names.

35. Read also the reexamination of Lefebvre's thesis in Edwards 1971: 364–66, and Marcus 1989: 138–47. Consider also Lefebvre's own arguments in *Espace et politique: le droit à la ville* (1973) and *La Pensée Marxiste et la ville* (1972), esp. 109–14, "Engels and Utopia."

36. *Journal officiel*, 17 May 1871.

37. See Hutton 1981, introduction and ch. 1, esp. 8–12.

38. Felix Pyat in *Le Vengeur*, 17 May 1871.

39. Ibid.

40. Ibid.

41. Jules Vallès in *Le Cri du peuple*, no. 78 (18 May 1871).

42. *Journal officiel de la Commune*, 20 April 1871.

43. *Le Père Duchêne*, no. 64, p. 2.

44. On the rebuilding of the monument, see the chronology detailed by architect Paul Domenec in a letter to the Ministry of Cultural Affairs, archives of the Bureau des Batiments Civils, dated 5 May 1966.

45. On the commemorations of the Mur des Fédérés, see Réberioux 1984: 619–49. For images of the column on national holidays and for military commemorations, see Murat 1970.

46. Article, source unknown, dossier Vendôme Column, Bureau des Batiments Civils et des Palais Nationaux, Paris.

REFERENCES

Aghulon, M. 1998. *Histoire vagabonde*. Paris: Ed. Gallimard.
Anonymous. 1833. *Description de la colonne*. Paris: Gauthier.

Auray, M. 1989. "La Commune démolit la colonne Vendôme." *Gavroche*, no. 44 (March/April).

Babelon, J.-P., and A. Chastel. 1980. "La Notion de patrimoine." *Revue de l'art*, no. 49.

Bloch, M. 1983. *Les Rois Thaumaturges*. New ed. Paris: Ed. Gallimard.

Bonniot, R. 1967. "Le Deboulonner: Courbet et la réédification de la colonne Vendôme—interventions de ses amis santais en faveur de Gustave Courbet en exil 1875." *Gazette des beaux-arts*, no. 1185 (October).

Borel, P. 1921. *Gustave Courbet et la colonne Vendôme*. Oeuvres Libres.

Bourgin, G., and G. Henriot, eds. 1924. *Procès-Verbaux de la Commune*.

Brandat, P., and F. Passy. 1871. *La Colonne*. Brest.

Bressler, H. 1980. "La Colonne Vendôme: un monument sans histoire." *Techniques et architecture*, no. 331 (June–July).

Brossat, A., et al. 1990. *A l'est: la mémoire retrouvée*. Paris: Ed. La Découverte.

Castagnary, J. 1883. *Courbet et la Colonne Vendôme*. Paris: Dentu.

Choay, F. 1992. *L'Allégorie du patrimoine*. Paris: Ed. Du Seuil.

Claretie, J. 1872. *Histoire de la révolution*. Paris.

Clement, J. B. 1980. *La Commune et les aristes*. Paris: Nouvelles Editions Latines.

D'Anglemont, E. 1872. *La Résurrection de la colonne*. Paris: E. Dentu.

Dementhe, J. 1873. "Histoire de la colonne Vendôme." *L'Illustration 2.*

Dupont, F. 1989. "The Emperor God's Other Body." In M. Feher, R. Addaff, and N. Tazi, eds., *Fragments for a History of the Human Body, Part Three*. New York: Zone.

Edwards, S. 1971. *The Paris Commune, 1871*. London: Quadrangle.

Gagenbin, B. 1963. *Courbet et la colonne Vendôme*. Geneva: Faculte des Lettres.

Goujon, A. 1821. *Pensée d'un soldat sur la sépulture de Napoleon.*

Hutton, P. H. 1981. *The Cult of the Revolutionary Tradition*. Berkeley and Los Angeles: University of California Press.

Kantorowicz, E. 1957. *The King's Two Bodies*. Princeton: Princeton University Press.

Lefebvre, H. 1969. *La Proclamation de la Commune*. Paris: Ed. Gallimard.

——. 1972. *La Pensée Marxiste et la ville*. Paris: Casterman.

——. 1973 [1968]. *Espace et politique: le droit à la ville*. Paris: Anthropos.

Lefort, C. 1978. *Les Formes de l'histoire: essais d'anthropologie politique*. Paris: Ed. Gallimard.

Leniaud, J.-M. 1992. *L'Utopie française: essai sur la patrimoine*. Paris: Menges.

Léveque, E. 1874. *A propos de la colonne vendôme restaurée moins le couronnement*, part 1, "La Chute."

Levron, J. 1961. "Courbet et la colonne." *Mercure de France*, no. 1175 (July).

Lissagaray, P. O. 1972 [1876]. *L'Histoire de la Commune*. Paris: Maspero.

Loyer, F. 1993. "Le Sacré-Coeur de Montmartre." In P. Nora, ed., *Les Lieux de mémoire*, tome 3: *Les France*, vol. 3: *De l'archive à l'emblème*. Paris: Ed. Gallimard.

Malissart, A. 1976. "La Colonne Vendôme: une colonne Trajane à Paris." *Les Dossiers de l'archeologie*, no. 17 (July–August).

Marcus, G. 1989. *Lipstick Traces: A Secret History of the Twentieth Century*. Cambridge, Mass.: Harvard University Press.

Marx, K. 1988. *The Eighteenth Brumaire of Louis Napoleon, and the Civil War in France*. London: International Publishing.

Muller, G. 1958–59. "De la responsabilité de Courbet dans la destruction de la colonne." *Procès-verbaux et mémoires de l'académie des sciences, Belles-lettres et Arts de Besançon*, vol. 173.

Murat, A. 1970. *La Colonne Vendôme*. Paris: Palais Royale.

Nora, P., ed. 1987. *Les Lieux de mémoire*, tome 2: *La Nation*. Paris: Ed. Gallimard, 1987.

Normand, A., and C. Normand. 1897. "La Colonne Vendôme." *Bulletin de la société des amis des monuments parisiens XI*.

Pommier, E. 1991. *L'Art de la liberté: doctrines et débats de la révolution française*. Paris: Gallimard.

Reau, L. 1959. *Les Monuments détruits de l'art français*. Paris: Hachette.

Réberioux, M. 1984. "Le Mur des Fédérés." In P. Nora, ed., *Les Lieux de mémoire*, tome I: *La République*. Paris: Ed. Gallimard.

Representations 35: Monumental Histories. 1991 (summer).

Riat, G. 1906. *Gustave Courbet, peintre*.

Soria, G. 1971. *Grande histoire de la Commune*. Paris: Robert Laffont.

Tulard, J. 1986. "Le Retour des Cendres." In Pierre Nora, ed., *Les Lieux de Mémoire*, tome 2: *La Nation*. Paris: Gallimard.

Vernant, J. P. 1971. *Mythe et penseé chez les grecs*. Paris: Maspero.

Vuillaume, M. 1909. *Mes cahiers rouge*. Paris.

Young, J. E. 1993. *The Texture of Memory: Holocaust Memorials and Meaning*. New Haven, Conn.: Yale University Press.

Confucius and the

Cultural Revolution: A

Study in Collective Memory

◀ ◀ ◀ ◀ ◀   TONG ZHANG AND BARRY SCHWARTZ

"Confucius declared that he was not an originator, but a transmitter. It was his mission to gather up what had been once known but long neglected or misunderstood. It was his painstaking fidelity in accomplishing his task, as well as the high ability which he brought to it, that gave the Master his extraordinary hold upon the people of his race." Reverend Arthur H. Smith's (1986 [1894]: 115) observation is notable because it defines Confucius as a cultivator as well as an object of traditional reverence. Pastness itself impressed Confucius, just as Confucius symbolizes the pastness his successors embrace. This dual facet of Confucius's image is instructive for the light it throws on our understanding of collective memory.

Two models frame present understandings of collective memory. In the first model, memory is context-dependent and changes as it is invoked across generations. Whether focusing on the politics of memory (Hobsbawm 1983; Alonso 1988; Tuchman and Fortin 1989; Bodnar 1992, Boyarim 1994; Gillis 1994)[1] or memory over the *longue durée* (Halbwachs 1941; Pelikan 1985; Kammen 1991; Peterson 1994; Ben-Yehuda 1996), Western studies endeavor to show how beliefs about the past become hostage to the circumstances and problems of the present and how different elements of the past become more or less relevant as these circumstances and problems change. Memory thus becomes a social fact as it is made and remade to serve new power distributions, institutional structures, values, interests, and needs.

In the second model of collective memory, images of the past are stabilized by the context-transcending requirements of society itself. Every society, even the most fragmented, requires a sense of sameness and continuity with what went before. Society changes constantly, Emile Durkheim observed (1947 [1893]), but the collective consciousness endures unchanged across generations because old phases remain intact as new ones are superimposed upon them (see also Durkheim 1965 [1915]: 414–33). Edward Shils also observed that beliefs about the past outlive changes in the structure of society. "No generation, even in this present time of unprecedented dissolution of tradition, creates its own beliefs." Generations acquire most of what constitutes them from the past (1981: 38). As individuals acquire understandings of the past through forebears (either through oral culture, commemoration, or professional historiography), common memories endow successive generations with a common heritage, strengthen society's "temporal integration," create links between the living and the dead, and promote consensus over time (Shils 1981: 13–14, 31–32, 38, 327. Also see Freud 1939; Bellah et al. 1985; Schwartz 1991; Schudson 1994: 205–21).

Stable images of the past are not always demonstrably true images. Sometimes false ideas are transferred across generations and accepted as if they were true. And sometimes we do not know whether an account of the past is true or not. Truth value and its resistance to revision is plainly not the only source of the past's stability. Nor is the stability of the past necessarily the result of commemorative devices (*lieux de memoire*) that symbolize society's "grand narratives"; on the contrary, the erosion of what these sites and narratives represent, according to Pierre Nora (1996) and Jean-Francois Lyotard (1984 [1979]), is one of the late twentieth-century's distinctive characteristics.

That we should consider the stability of memory as a problem rather than a given is ironic. The pioneers of collective memory research (Cooley 1902; Czarnowski 1919; Halbwachs 1925; Mead 1929; see Coser 1992, Schwartz 1996 for discussion) wondered how a supposedly immutable past could be so readily and so often reinterpreted. So rich has been the evidence of reinterpretation and so convincing the explanations, that the continuity of memory is now problematic. Some reviewers (Zelizer 1995: 227), although focusing on collective memory's malleability, recognize the tension between continuity and change. Their understanding of the means by which continuity is sustained, however, remains unclear; the most pressing problem is still why memories and commemorations are as stable as they are. We propose to address this problem by analyzing the Chinese communist regime's representation of Confucius before (1949–65), during (1966–76), and after (1977–80s) the Cultural Revolution. This case extends the range of collective memory studies from the West, where existing insights have been developed and codified, to the East, where new issues appear.

We are concerned with the concepts of "construction" and "critical inheritance" of the past. Social construction refers to the belief that present understandings of past events are mediated by conceptual and rhetorical apparatuses (Hobart 1989) anchored in group interests.[2] Sociologists and historians have long noted that the tendency to selectively ignore, decontextualize, or otherwise distort past occurrences is especially marked when a regime's legitimacy or a nation's pride is at stake. But what if historical occurrences or figures are too authoritative, important, or authentic to be distorted, let alone forgotten? The Chinese past, to take one example, has been highly resistant to reconstruction, and this resistance is not an isolated trait; it is part of a syndrome of authoritarianism, conventionality, cognitive rigidity, submissiveness to authority, and traditionalism (Yang 1987). In this paper we argue that the construction of the past, although deemed universal, is least pronounced among cultures in which innovation, libertarianism, and cognitive and moral flexibility are least valued.

China's traditionalism, Max Weber's (1964 [1916]) analysis suggests, has deep historical roots. Because the ancient Chinese lacked a transcendental ideal that distanced them from the world, their morality was "completely secularized," devoid of "prophetic zeal and moral dynamism." The result was not an idealistic transforming of the world, but an adjustment to it—a "relentless canonization of tradition."[3] Acceptance of the given meant that authoritative ideas could never be improved and that effective learning consisted of uncritically assimilating classical knowledge. Piety entailed acceptance of the order of the fathers and of duly constituted authorities. Taoism, ancient China's second major religion, rejected Confucianism's concern for ritual and form but shared its aversion to individualism, nonconformity, innovation, and this-worldly activism (for detail, see Liao 1989, 1993).

Confucianism's cultural power would not be what it was and is if tradition and memory were constantly revised. The Chinese people's reverence for Confucius has varied from generation to generation, but they have never felt free to reconstitute his life and teachings. This does not imply that they agree on what his life and teachings mean. How much emphasis to put on Confucius's defense of slavery or on certain statements that acknowledge materialism, what he had in mind in advocating universal education, whether his conception of ethics is consistent with contemporary conditions—these questions have always been subject to debate. That Confucius stands for order, hierarchy, and tradition, however, has been beyond debate. To recognize that each generation has succeeded in finding itself in Confucius and has assigned him more or less prestige is not to say that it has transformed or "reconstructed" him. Our paper seeks to document the stability of Confucius's image and to explain how it is maintained by "critical inheritance."

METHOD AND DATA

Much has been said about the Cultural Revolution's anti-Confucius crusade (see, for example, Fran 1975; Whitehead 1976; Louie 1980); little has been said about its failure. Drawing our analysis through the changing "discursive surround" of Confucius, we attend to the social talk that constitutes and interprets him across time. We assume that recent ideas about what Confucius means to China, how to assess them, and how, once constituted, they ought to be represented, are strongly affected by the specialized discourses of the Chinese Communist Party. Our analysis of Confucius discourse moves back and forth between party officials and their environment by attending to what they say during eras of institution building and crisis.

To grasp the Chinese Communist Party's assessment of Confucius before, during, and after the Cultural Revolution, we rely on firsthand data from three sources:

(1) Two leading newspapers, *Ren Min Ri Bao* and *Guang Ming Ri Bao*,

express official attitudes toward important events of the day. *Ren Min Ri Bao* is the organ of the Chinese Communist Party; *Guang Ming Ri Bao*, the major newspaper in the field of culture. Within a given era, Confucius's portrayal in these newspapers is consistent and, although we have undertaken no formal content analysis, the materials we select for illustration capture the newspapers' essential interpretations.

(2) China's officials commonly introduce political directives and explain their rationale through closely integrated public speeches, a selection of which (again for the purpose of illustration) comprises a second source of data.

(3) For supplementary data one of the authors interviewed a nonrandom sample of ten mainland Chinese living near a large state university in the United States. Since all respondents left mainland China for the United States in the 1980s, all lived through the Cultural Revolution. The purpose of these interviews is to provide a basis for speculating on the influence of official evaluations of Confucius. The respondents were asked to identify the source of their earliest and later conceptions of Confucius, the time these conceptions were formed, and to explain their meaning. In order to generate as much information from respondents as possible, the author chose interviewees aged 27 to 56. She focused on the seven respondents over 40 because they lived through the Cultural Revolution as adults. To gauge generational differences, she also interviewed three respondents under 40 years of age who lived through the Revolution as children.

Eight of the respondents are graduate students in philosophy, comparative literature, education, entomology, economics, statistics, and ecology. The author also interviewed a visiting scholar and an immigrant from China. She took notes during the private interviews and transcribed them immediately afterwards.

CONFUCIUS

Confucian doctrine is distinguishable from Confucius the man, but in most cases affection or hostility for one goes together with the other. Confucius, the Latinized form of *K'ung Fu-Tzu* (c. 550–476 B.C.), was a statesman, philosopher, and educator who lived at the end of "the Spring and Autumn Period" (770–475 B.C.) of Chinese history. This was a transitional period during which China developed from an ancient slave society into a feudal society. During the next 250 years, the period of "A Hundred Schools of Thought Contending," Confucianism was but one philosophy among many, including Mohism, Taoism, and Legalism. To strengthen his power, Han Wudi (140–87 B.C.), emperor of the West Han Dynasty, followed the advice of the renowned scholar, Dong Zhongshu (179–104 B.C.), by rejecting all philosophies except Confucianism. Since then all feudal rulers have followed Confucianism and enforced it as a secular religion.

Even at the end of the twentieth century, Confucius's influence on Chinese culture and social life remains powerful. The Confucian tradition, Tu Wei-Ming (1990) observes, "remains the defining characteristic of Chinese mentality" (136). The power of this tradition is evident in our interviews. Six of the seven respondents who agreed to rank Confucius placed him first among ten renowned Chinese historical figures, one ranked him second. The reason given for Confucius's high ranking is his influence on Chinese culture.

The core of Confucian doctrine consists of the concepts *Ren* and *Li*. Confucius defined *Ren* as "love all men." To put this definition into practice he taught his students: "Do nothing to others that you would not wish done to yourself," and "the man of virtue, wishing to be established himself, seeks also to establish others." Since "Ren makes man a man," the meaning of a person's life is defined exclusively by his fellowmen and by his community (*Analects*).

Ren also found expression through the performance of Li, which encompasses rituals, social and political structures, and status-specific behavioral norms. According to Confucius, the prince, minister, father, and son had to conform to strict codes of conduct, and in this conformity much was at stake. Only if the nation's men—from prince and minister to fathers and sons—conform to proper rules of conduct can social order be maintained. This is because the correct observance of rites signifies commitment and deference to authority. Confucius declared: "Ren means to restrain oneself and observe Li." Since Li required people to behave according to their status and rank, Confucius's influence on the formation of Chinese culture and social life cannot be separated from his "use value" (Maines et al. 1983) in legitimating political structures.

How Confucius is remembered: the uses of "critical inheritance." Radical intellectuals have always criticized Confucius because his doctrines of self-restraint and conformity stand in opposition to ideologies of change (Louie 1980: 1–16). On the other hand, Confucius has been useful to all establishments. The communist establishment, assuming power in 1949, was simultaneously drawn to Confucius because his memory legitimated its hegemony and repelled by Confucius because his ideals opposed its revolution. This dilemma was resolved by "critical inheritance"—a form of collective memory that has no close Western counterpart. The term "critical inheritance" appears mainly in political and academic discourse, but it is universally understood to mean a deliberative process wherein both positive and negative aspects of historic figures are recognized. Critical inheritance upholds traditional authority because it sustains the dignity of the past while recognizing the need of successive generations to reevaluate it. Thus, Confucius can be revered—must be revered—by the institutions and individuals that reject his political convictions.

BEFORE THE REVOLUTION

The Communist Party, after eight years of Anti-Japanese War and three years of civil war, assumed control of China and established comprehensive reforms. From 1949 to 1966 the regime undertook two agricultural programs. The first program (1949–52) was based on a land policy permitting retention of private farm ownership. The regime turned to Confucius, symbol of the authority of the family, to legitimize this effort because the party's plan for economic decentralization was based on the family unit as the pivot of agricultural production. The second phase of reform, in contrast, included the socialization of private lands and the Great Leap Forward (1953–66)—a disaster that led to 20 to 30 million deaths between 1958 and 1962. Never was the Confucian legacy of asceticism more serviceable in sustaining loyalty to a regime than during this period of indescribable suffering.

In theory, the transition from civil war to peace requires a shift from the pursuit of revolutionary projects to economic and social development. Institution building, however, does not always progress as planned, and Mao knew that his party's survival required the establishment of a strong central power (Fairbank 1992: 361). Given the masses' commitment to the Confucian tradition of deference and hierarchy, political leaders seeking to legitimate their policies complimented Confucius in official publications. Our task, said Mao Zedong, "is to study our historical legacy and evaluate it critically with the Marxist method. Our nation has a history of several thousand years, a history which has its own characters and is full of treasures. . . . We must make a summing-up from Confucius down to Sun Yat-sen and inherit this precious legacy" (Mao 1940). Mao extolled Confucius's school in Qu Fu (1955) and deemed "the doctrine of the mean," Confucius's philosophy of moderation, a great achievement meriting close study (Hou 1987). Liu Shaoqi, late president of the People's Republic, called on "every communist who wants to become a good, politically mature revolutionary" to "make great efforts in self-cultivation" by following Confucius's example. Confucius was a feudal philosopher, Liu conceded in his famous lectures, *How to be a Good Communist,* but "he did not consider himself to have been born a sage." Confucius realized that his achievements were facilitated by his environment (Liu 1964).

Communist ideologues, however, could not ignore the way Confucianism contradicted socialism. This is why Mao stressed the "critical" aspect of "critical inheritance." Mao's dilemma involved the antinomy of tradition and modernity: on the one hand, his regime was inclined to negate traditional symbols that could not be assimilated into communist ideology; on the other hand, his regime found in these symbols great sources of energy and attempted to exploit them by detaching them from their former contexts. In his "On New Democratism," Mao wrote: "Those who worship Confucius and advocate reading the classics of Confucianism stand for the old ethics, old rites and old thoughts against the new culture and new thought. . . . As imperialist culture and semi-feudal culture serve imperialism and the feudal class, they should be eliminated" (Mao 1940). "Compared to Confucius's classics," therefore, "socialism is much better." If Mao and his associates rejected Confucius's ideas, however, they identified themselves with his eminence. The problem, in Mao's words, is to "keep the good things from the past while rejecting harmful feudal ideas" (1955).

Since Mao's notion of feudal ideas included capitalist ideas prevailing before the 1949 Communist Revolution, his rhetoric about Confucius was inherently ambivalent. Mao could construe Confucius his countryman but not his political ancestor. The problem appeared with great clarity in our interviews. Nine out of the ten respondents said they regarded

Confucius as a great thinker and educator, but some respondents never-theless repudiated him. Two respondents, both over 50, mentioned a 1951 film, *The Life of Wu Xun*, which was criticized on its release for eulogizing the central character's readiness to submit to the landlord class. Both respondents saw Wu Xun as the embodiment of Confucius's philosophy. Another respondent, age 44, who lived through the pre–Cultural Revolu-tion reforms said that the simultaneous embracing and rejecting of Con-fucian values paralleled the political and economic situation. During the 1958 education revolution, he recalled, Confucius was rejected; but in the aftermath of the post-1961 famine, Confucius was embraced. At this time (five years before the onset of the Cultural Revolution) the memory of the ancients consoled and there was a nationwide upsurge of Confucius-worship.

Reconstruction vs. Critical Inheritance

The concept of critical inheritance is not subsumeable under the concept of reconstruction. *Reconstruction* is a metaphor (used synonymously with *fabrication, invention, representation, framing*) for the process of reinterpre-tation. Designed to convey the assumption that knowledge of the past is affected by the context in which the past is considered, this metaphor has been applied so indiscriminantly that it has confused more than it has clarified. Efforts to reconstruct the past include, in fact, (1) the exaggera-tion of certain aspects of an authenticated event, (2) the focus on one phase and ignoring of other phases of an event, and (3) the dissociation of an otherwise accurate account of an event from related events.

The above interpretations are "constructions" in the weak sense, for their function is to distort rather than to invent or negate the past. Con-structions, however, can also involve the (4) making of imaginary events or (5) the denial of real events. Constructions of the past might also (6) falsely define an individual into or out of existence, or, less dramatically, (7) falsely ascribe characteristics to an individual or event. These last four transformations, whether resulting from unintended or deliberate misin-terpretation, may be described as *reconstructions* in the strong sense.

Changing images of Western deities, heroes, and villains are, for the most part, reconstructions in the weak sense. To refer to such construc-tions as weak, however, is not to suggest they are inconsequential. It is precisely differential selection, emphasis, and contextualization that transformed Emma Goldman, a bloodthirsty anarchist through the 1920s, into a kindly Jewish grandmother by the 1980s (Frankel 1996). Benjamin Franklin and Thomas Jefferson, like many if not most enlightened men of the late eighteenth century, considered Jesus a nondivine epitome of reason and author of revolutionary ethical codes. By mid-nineteenth century, however, Jesus had become the Great Liberator—divine champion of the oppressed and enslaved (Pelikan 1985: 189–93; 206–19). George Washington, America's first hero, was the consummation of gentility in the early nineteenth century, a counterpoint to plutocracy during the progressive era, and a model for captains of industry during the 1920s. The most popular of American heroes, Abraham Lincoln, has been the most malleable. During the Industrial Revolution Lincoln was the champion of the free market; by the Progressive Era he had become the first labor reformer. Among whites, Lincoln was an ardent segregationist; among blacks, a compassionate friend. During the New Deal he personified the rights of racial justice as well as labor; in the late twentieth century he stood for racial integration. For every generation of conservatives, Lincoln has been the great individualist who pulled himself up by his own bootstraps; for every generation of liberals, the model of compassion for the underdog (Schwartz 1991, 1997).

The image of Confucius has never lent itself to such diverse interpretation. This is because the malleability of heroes is not in the quality of their lives but in the nature of their culture. Since critical inheritance is a collective representation, our concern is to understand it in cultural contexts. We have examined one of these contexts—the early years of the communist regime. We now move into the next phase.

CULTURAL REVOLUTION

The sociology of memory, to turn a phrase from Clifford Geertz (1973: 212), "ought to be called the sociology of meaning, for what is socially determined in not the nature of conception but the vehicles of conception." What is problematic about Confucius, then, is not his fate during the Cultural Revolution but why the customary vehicle of conception, critical inheritance, could no longer be applied to him.

Confucius, when vested with political authority, executed reformers and razed rebellious cities. His most powerful concepts, including "The

Way," "Rectification," "Benevolence," "Filial Piety," "Fraternal Duty," "The Will of Heaven," "Fate," and "Innate Knowledge" were designed to maintain slavery. Yet, his influence endured long after slavery had disappeared, legitimating feudalism and, in modern times, fascism and capitalism (see, for example, Yang 1974). Communism, too, accommodated Confucius, but only as long as it accommodated tradition. When its cultural revolution broke with the past, Confucius had to be totally rejected.

"At the beginning of the Cultural Revolution," one of our respondents recalled during his interview, "Mao Zedong attacked the old Confucian culture rather than Confucius himself. There was a campaign against the Four Olds: old thought, old culture, old tradition, and old custom." This campaign intensified because. the contrast "Old vs. New" resonated so intensely with "Bourgeois vs. Proletarian" and "Xenophilia vs. Nationalism." As Confucius embodied the old, he inevitably became the personification of capital and foreign influence. He could no longer be reverently ignored, for he was no longer inheritable.

As the party's campaign against the Four Olds became more energetic, the measures it took against Confucius became more radical. The revolutionaries had to destroy every reminder of Confucius—temples and relics, statues, shrines, monuments, and sacred texts (especially those located in Qu Fu, Confucius's birthplace)—to articulate fully their contempt for the old system's corruptness. Another respondent, in high school at the time, recalled: "Around March of 1974 we stopped classes for an entire month to study the history of the struggle between the Legalist School and Confucianism. Our political textbook contained criticisms of Confucius, and we were all required to criticize him in our composition." It was not that tenets of antique Legalism, which existed more than 2,000 years ago, were congruent with the Cultural Revolution; it was a matter of the regime appropriating Legalism as a precedent, a second language, with which to condemn Confucius. A third respondent recalled an instance of guilt by association: "The regime's resentment of the intelligentsia extended to Confucius, a worshiper of scholarship and leader of the intelligensia of his own day." A fourth respondent reported: "In the campaign against the Four Olds, I saw pictures and statues of Confucius among the antiques confiscated." All the media our respondents remembered— newspapers, magazines, radio broadcasts, Party Central Committee documents, journals, textbooks, political study materials—condemned Confucius in the harshest terms. (For commentary on the anti-Confucius theme in the era's children's books, see Liao 1985.)

The rhetoric of condemnation was overdetermined. It not only disparaged the past but also legitimated the Cultural Revolution, whose official targets included the local elites that Mao had himself created. His reform was an effort to make "democratic centralism" more centralized by wiping out what Alexis de Tocqueville (1945) called the *corps intermédiare*—local institutions protecting the individual from the tyranny of the state. This intermediate body consisted of not only the school, family, and religious organizations but also the entire stratum of carefully trained ministers, subordinate officials, army officers, and specially privileged party officials.[4] The party ideologists targeted Confucius's concepts of *Ren, Li,* and *Rectification* because they sanctified the decentralizing power of these local elites. In Confucius's own words: "Ren is self-restraint, strict observance of the rituals, and adaptation to the [decentralized feudal] political and social system (Li)."

Mao's attack on Confucius was designed mainly to deal with critics of his own policies and record. The great 1958–62 famine, resulting from Mao's reorganization of agricultural production, led party officials, including Liu Shaoqui and Deng Xiaoping, to attack him directly. Liu (an urban organizer formerly prominent in the party hierarchy who deeply admired Confucius) defined the famine a "man-made calamity" and identified Mao as its cause. So intense was the criticism of Mao for his inept management of this and other matters that he had literally to institute a counterrevolution in order to maintain his power. The country approached civil war as Red Guard factions fought one another as well as the People's Liberation Army. Between 1966 and 1976, 60 percent of party officials were purged, a million people were persecuted, and the economy collapsed (Fairbank 1992: 383–405).

Concurrently, Confucius became antiquity's greatest villain. *Guang Ming Ri Bao,* to take one example, attacked Confucius's authorship of ruling-class hegemony. His extolling of filial and fraternal devotion was not an end in itself but a means of preserving the order of the slaveholder (22 September 1973). *Ren Min Ri Bao* attacked Confucius's educational philosophy on the same grounds. His belief in the meanness of manual labor, the revolutionary ideologues explained, was developed by Mencius (372–289 B.C.), China's "Second Sage" and the most influential follower of Confucius, into a reactionary precept: "Those laboring with their brains govern others; those laboring with their brawn are governed by others." Confucius's class prejudice ramified widely and contributed to centuries of working-class misery. (Feng Youlan presented similar criticisms of Ren, Li, Rectification, and "The Restraint of Self and Response to Li" in his book *On Confucius* [1975].)

The regime's reinterpretation of Confucius was required by the logic of its new political cause, but the significance of that new interpretation cannot be reduced to the political interests it served. Karl Mannheim (1936: 109–91) observed that all knowledge is partial because the interests in which it is rooted are partisan, but he believed this connection to be a source of enlightenment, not ignorance. Particular social standpoints yield visions of the past that are unavailable from any other standpoint. Thus, as the Communist state imposed its revolution, it created conditions that not only brought Confucius's vices into sharper view but also revealed them to be more definitive of his character than previously believed.

Since moderation and self-possession were, in Confucius' philosophy, the virtues of the "superior man" of the ruling aristocracy, his "doctrine of the mean," formerly applauded by Mao himself, was now condemned as a rationalization of the status quo. A *Ren Min Ri Bao* commentator explained: "[Confucius's] 'doctrine of the mean,' from the first day it was created, has stood in opposition to rebellion, progress, reform and dialectics." This doctrine is expressed in Chinese as *Zhong Yong*, where *Zhong* is embodied in Li, whose ultimate referent is slave society, while *Yong* translates into "constancy" or "changelessness." Thus, *Zhong Yong* denotes the eternal universality of the principles of slavery, which can be neither destroyed nor mitigated. The article concludes: "It has been proved by history that 'the doctrine of the mean' is an insidious and deadly ideological weapon. It is a reactionary philosophy employed by capitalist cliques to launch a vindictive comeback and to suppress the revolutionary people. It has the reactionary essence of stubbornly defending the old things in the disguise of eclecticism. It stands in opposition to revolutionary dialectics and the philosophy of struggle" (*Ren Min Ri Bao:* 3 June 1974).

The "Anti-Confucianism Campaign" attacked every aspect of Confucius's thought: his preoccupation with the golden age of the past rather than the future, his male chauvinism (Liao 1990), his fetishizing of self-conquest and intellect (which lead inevitably to capitalist careerism and elitism), his inability to recognize that ethics are class-based rather than universal, the affinity of his ideas with the interests of China's seemingly indestructible clique of capitalist sympathizers and counterrevolutionaries (Whitehead 1976). And no one had forgotten that Mao's archenemy, Chiang Kai-shek, had invoked Confucian teachings against the communists throughout the 1930s (Fran 1975: 95; de Bary et al. 1960: 796–812).

Anti-Confucius sentiment was overdetermined in yet another sense. Cultural revolutionaries' perception of wayward political leaders (including General Lin Biao, once Mao's heir apparent who allegedly turned against the Revolution[5]) made more sense in light of the traitors' devotion to Confucius. As one of our respondents observed, "To criticize Lin Biao effectively it was necessary to connect him to Confucius." Just as "Confucius was criticized for restoring the Zhou [slaveholder] dynasty," another respondent explained, "so Lin Biao was criticized for counterrevolutionary efforts to reinstate capitalism." In short, Lin was a twentieth-century Confucius; Confucius, a fifth-century (B.C.) Lin. As Lin, like Liu, venerated Confucius, he made the perfect target. *Guang Ming Ri Bao*'s (6 December 1973) claim is typical: "In order to restore capitalism, Liu Shaoqi and Lin Biao dug Confucius out of his grave and extolled him to the skies." Eight out of our ten respondents referred to the attacks on Lin and Liu and said they recognized the ulterior motive behind them.

Ironically, the regime's attack on Confucius was inspired by Confucius's own legacy. "Conspiracy," according to John Fairbank, "was a continual part of Imperial Confucianism because the ruler's legitimacy was assured only when his proper conduct produced harmony between ruler and ruled." Criticism by invocation of historical exemplars makes sense in a society in which political consensus is so idealized. As dissent is disharmonious it must be expressed secretly (1992: 403), which justifies the ruler's assumption of a world filled with hidden enemies and traitors and his need for symbols to represent them.

The Confucius of the Cultural Revolution is but one part of a broader "cultural profile" consisting of "images of the past, rhetorical styles, attributions of responsibility" (Olick 1994: 12). All the concerns, events, and aspirations associated with the Cultural Revolution—the bridging of the gap between elite and masses, centralization of power, fear of counterrevolution, economic failure, the empowerment of the young, the excesses of the Red Guards—form this profile, this articulated whole in which it became necessary to "use Marxism-Leninism–Mao Zedong thought as a weapon [to confront] Confucius's reactionary ideas and eliminate their pernicious influence so that people will not be poisoned by the ghost of Confucius again" (Yant 1974: 66).

Since the Cultural Revolution's characterization of Confucius conveys no information about him that was unknown in previous years, it cannot be a "reconstruction." It was a matter of previous interpretations of Confucius—explicitly selective recognitions of his virtues and vices—losing resonance and of the regime rejecting him totally rather than inheriting him critically. That this regime did not reconstruct Confucius is, indeed, the problematic element in its reaction to him. Why could the party not construe itself as the ultimate realization of Confucius's ideals? As certain scholars (Fan Wenlan and Lu Zhenyu) had actually defined Confucius as a progressive for his time, could it not be argued that he was a protocommunist? The French left, after all, had convinced itself that Joan of Arc was the first socialist. Why could not Confucius be thus transformed? This question assumes special relevance because the original Chinese revolution had extended rather than broken with Confucian despotism.

Liu Xiaobo, a contemporary philosopher (cited in Chong 1993), has observed that the "totalitarian Confucian value system still persists in a Marxist-Leninist guise" (125). Liu's observation on the 1949 communist revolution is paralleled by Fairbank's (1992: 252) observation on the 1912 republican revolution. The new military governors and provincial assemblies, far from adopting an active attitude toward the world, had inherited the gentry's Confucian aversion to disorder and never developed alternatives to the patriarchal tyranny of the Confucian family system (264). Even in Chinese cities, critical social movements "combined popular righteousness with a continued subservience to authority" (274). The rigid cultural climate at once reflected and helped to sustain Confucian values.

To affirm the stability of Confucius's image in the face of radical change is not to exaggerate its uniqueness. The case of Confucius actually conforms to many of the contours of recent collective memory studies, as Zelizer (1995) has described them. Confucius's memory is *processual*—constantly unfolding, changing, and transforming; it is *unpredictable*—embraced by the new communist regime and rejected unexpectedly during its Cultural Revolution; it is *partial* in that Confucius's positive and negative qualities are more or less visible according to the conditions under which they are contemplated; *usable* because invoked as a tool to defend party aims and agendas; at once *particularistic* among communists aware of its class-linked source and *universalistic* among Confucianists seeing its transcending of class and national boundaries; and, finally, Confucius's image is *material*—embodied in physical objects and places. Thus, the unreconstructability of Confucius hardly revolutionizes our conception of collective memory, but it does modify our conception in a way that becomes clearer as we move into the postrevolutionary period.

AFTER THE REVOLUTION

The campaign against Confucius grew in intensity as the Cultural Revolution gained momentum, but as the Revolution played itself out Confucius's prestige rose to a level higher than it was when the Revolution began. The new Confucius was affected by the new policies, conditions, actors, goals, and anxieties of China's present; but it was the perceived reality of the old Confucius that defined the present's moral relevance.

In 1976 Mao Zedong died, the Cultural Revolution ended, Deng Xiaoping soon assumed power, and China entered a new phase of political development. The aftermath of the Cultural Revolution included the same erosion of social values and tradition that attended the West's industrial revolutions. The first step towards stabilizing this political environment was to rehabilitate the hundreds of thousands convicted of political crimes; the second, to condemn the Cultural Revolution itself and punish its principal leaders, the Gang of Four. Mao, on the other hand, could not be summarily denounced without undermining the regime's own legitimacy. Party spokesmen resolved the dilemma by dividing his life into a good early phase, accounting for about 70 percent of his influence, and a bad late phase accounting for about 30 percent. Mao was critically inherited, and so again, after a decade of Cultural Revolution, was Confucius.

The ultimate goal of Deng Xioping's regime was to move China not to its pre–Cultural Revolution state but to a new place in the world. To achieve this goal, China's moral order had to be reinforced. Before the Cultural Revolution, Confucius helped to legitimate a new and inexperienced Communist regime. After the Cultural Revolution, he was pressed to the service of broader and more ambitious ends—to dignify and stabilize a backward society seeking a place in the modern world. To this end, an old vehicle of meaning, critical inheritance, had to be restarted.

After the new authority assumed power, it restored the Confucian shrines that the Red Guard had pillaged and punished vandals severely; some, with death. Simultaneously, it denounced the Gang of Four for its criticism of Confucius. The discursive logic centered on the relationship between present and past. One commentator, after making a positive assessment of Confucius's pedagogy, exclaimed: "let us thoroughly criticize the Gang of Four for its anti-history fallacy of breaking completely with all the cultural heritage and totally repudiating Confucius. Let us take over all the good cultural heritage of our nation and work hard to establish a new system of proletarian education" (*Ren Min Ri Bao:* 18 July 1978). An academic writer recalled that during the Cultural Revolution "restraining oneself and observing Li" were interpreted as Confucius's principles for restoring slavery. In fact, observing Li should be explained not as restoring Li but as "practicing its virtues." Confucius, after all, sought order without oppression (*Journal of Northeast Normal University* 1986: 2). On a more concrete level, *Guang Ming Ri Bao* reaffirmed Confucius's relevance to China's present situation by refuting the Gang of Four's claim that he was too genteel to be bothered with farming and military matters (*Guang Ming Ri Bao:* 12 September 1978). Both levels, the philosophical and the mundane, were infused by the same egalitarian logic.

Pro-Confucian discourse became more animated as China's economy opened to trade and state-regulated market enterprise in the late 1980s; yet many young scholars saw traditional Confucian culture as an insular hindrance to modern China's development. The only way for China to survive, they said, is to replace Confucianism with Western individualism. Part of the regime's conscious effort to merge the traditional with the modern (a practice more widespread in Asia than in the West [Lipset 1996]) was its establishing the Chinese Association of Confucius Study in Qu Fu. Confucius's every vice must be rejected, but his virtues must be recognized and assimilated into the Four Modernizations—industry, agriculture, national defense, and science and technology. Such was the association's mandate.

As the Four Modernizations exposed China to the outside world and made it vulnerable to the social maladies of Western commodity societies, the new Confucianists insisted that reformed governmental, business, and family ethics would preserve tradition as China modernized. Thus, in 1989, when the state decided to make explicit its acceptance of the Confucian tradition by commemorating the 2540th anniversary of Confucius's birth, Gu Mu, member of the State Council of the Peoples Republic and nominal head of the Confucius Foundation, delivered the defining address. The attendance of the General Secretary of the Chinese Communist Party, Jiang Zemin, Vice-Premier Wu Xueqian, as well as the timing of the ceremony (soon after the Tiananmen Square Massacre), underscored the significance of Gu's speech. Gu Mu extolled Confucius in the name of the party and the nation:

> China has a long history and splendid ancient culture. The Chinese culture represented by Confucianism once shined brilliantly in our history but has become dimmer during the last two hundred years [the decline of empire and ascent of republicanism]. Since the foundation of the People's Republic of China, however, we have made rapid progress in economic and cultural construction. We are beginning to see a bright future. Vicissitudes of a country may be due to complex objective causes as well as subjective causes. We should have an introspective analysis of this problem. (Gu 1989)

The objects of such "introspective analysis" included Mao; the instruments, Confucianism. Gu had avowed the historical role of Confucianism and the achievements of the Chinese Communist Party while calling for detailed study of the Cultural Revolution's disastrous effects (part of communism's "vicissitudes"). Doing so, he refuted radicals who would negate both the recent (communist) and remote (Confucian) past. Neither communism nor Confucianism, he said, are responsible for China's underdevelopment.

Towards the end of his speech Gu Mu stressed the Confucian concept of "the preciousness of harmony." The Tiananmen Square Massacre (4 June 1989) made Gu's statement resonant. Chinese officials construed the Tiananmen demonstration as an example of the threat posed by antitraditional (democratic) trends and condemned it by broadcasting quotations from Confucius (*Christian Science Monitor*, 12 October 1989: 6).

As Gu Mu emphasized tradition, he condemned the rejecters of Chinese culture and uncritical worshipers of Western culture. Understanding Confucius is essential to the task of balancing tradition and modernity, but Gu made no effort to reconstruct Confucius, mold him into a founder of modern China, deny the feudal framework of his philosophy, or conceal what is objectionable in his teaching. The problem, after the Cultural Revolution as before, is to know Confucius as he was, to cherish what is useful and good in his thought, and to reject everything else. In Gu's words, "We can neither eulogize Confucianism blindly nor repudiate it simply. The correct attitude is to inherit it critically" (cited in Mu 1989: 19).

The ideological importance of critical inheritance was evident in methodological reform. In academic circles, the "method of class analysis," the major method of studying Confucius before the Cultural Revolution, was replaced by the "method of equivalence" and the "method of three divisions." The "method of three divisions," based on the view that Confucius's thought can be divided into categories that are totally acceptable, totally rejectable, or acceptable and rejectable in part, is the methodological component of critical inheritance. Scholars adopting the "method of equivalence" hold that the class interests with which Confucius was identified are irrelevant to the evaluation of his historical role. The issue is whether Confucius's thought reflected the progressive or regressive trends of his own society.

The slippage between political structures and images of the past are particularly evident in the present case, which shows two very different regimes—Mao's prerevolutionary regime seeking to establish itself and become self-sufficient and Deng's postrevolutionary regime seeking to transcend self-sufficiency and become part of a modern world—conceiving Confucius almost identically. We say "almost identically" because the need for Confucius was based on different grounds—political legitimation in the first phase; the need for meaning, national identity, and roots in the second phase. It would be fair to say that in this second phase the public was receptive to Confucianism because it sustained the tradition and proud heritage that the Cultural Revolution had deliberately attacked.

CONCLUSION

The less traditional the culture, the more that can be done with the past interpretively. This is why American heroes, emerging in a tradition-weak society, meet the minimum definition of reconstruction while Confucius, emerging in a tradition-steeped society, does not. For reconstruction of the past to occur, moral sentiments, in Emile Durkheim's words, "must not be hostile to change, and consequently must have but moderate energy. If they were too strong, they would no longer be plastic. Every pattern is an obstacle to new patterns, to the extent that the first pattern is inflexible" (1950 [1895]: 69). Chinese consciousness is not inflexible, but it is highly stable, and this is why, by studying it, we gain knowledge of how collective memory resists social changes that would elsewhere induce its reconstruction. We have emphasized, in this connection, that the communist regime's quest for unity took form in continuity with the very tradition it disparaged. As Fairbank put it, "The totalitarian claims of Leninism perpetuated the claims of the imperial autocracy. The Neo-Confucian doctrines as absolute truth were substituted by Marxism-Leninism, which was equally all-embracing and absolute" (1992: 430). These ironic continuities have affected deeply the workings of Chinese memory. Unlike Joan of Arc and Abraham Lincoln, who are ambiguous enough to be loved by anyone for any reason (Kertzer 1988: 71), Confucius can be unconditionally loved (uncritically inherited) only by the status quo's defenders. The core of Confucius's doctrine, which includes the concepts of "the preciousness of harmony," "the doctrine of the mean," *Ren*, and *Li* endorses the status quo and opposes revolution—cultural as well as political.

Reverence is no less profound for being conditional. If reverence for Confucius can be officially suspended, his place in the collective imagination is too deeply installed to be altered fundamentally. Confucianism's unchanging core does not mean that different generations and different people evaluate Confucius in unchanging ways. Each generation passes on to the next an image of him that differs from the image it inherited. This new image includes new evaluations of the different parts of Confucius's life and doctrine and changing levels of prestige, but its content remains stable. This is the essence of critical inheritance: the past serves present interests not by unwitting reconstruction but deliberately selective appreciation and condemnation.

That critical inheritance is useful for a society pulled in the direction of both modernity and tradition is evident, for when this tension dissipates— when society pulls in one direction only: away from the past, as it did during the Cultural Revolution—critical inheritance is abandoned and the orienting past tense of tradition is lost. The two dimensions of critical inheritance, when in use, embody Michael Schudson's observation that "the past is constantly being retold in order to legitimate present interests." Had Confucius's assumed character and teachings not been applicable to China's changing conditions and needs, he could have never been idolized for so long. Yet, Confucius's ancient and modern images possess similar elements, which reflects Schudson's (1987) complementary belief that "the past is in some respects, and under some conditions, highly resistant to efforts to make it over" (105). Tradition, Schudson added, offers the most potent resistance. The ways people reconstruct the past are "confined to the experiences of their own traditions" (108–9). Contemporary Chinese, given their valorization of piety, self-restraint, hierarchy, and tradition, have come to know and revere the same Confucius that was known and revered in earlier times.

Now, as before, "the centre stage in almost all approaches to Chinese social behavior is commanded by Confucius" (Bond and Hwang 1987: 214). Might this statement be exaggerated? As China develops technologically and becomes more open to Western influence, reverence for the past, and for Confucius in particular, must become mitigated. Indeed, the process of attrition, first articulated by the republican ideologues of the May Fourth Movement of 1919, has been evident since the beginning of the century. Confucius, although remaining at the core of the still vibrant "habits of the heart" of the Chinese people (Wei-ming 1991: 5), cannot be revered in an urban-industrial society to the same extent as he was in traditional China's agricultural society. Such is the position of China's progressives.

As China's economy moves away from orthodox socialism, however, its government finds nationalism a necessary source of ideological support. The "return to the ancients" and new interest in their great monuments and shrines are presently invoked to articulate nationalist sentiment, and no theme in the literature on the changing China is more visible than the "remarkable comeback" and increasing relevance of Confucius as a moral model (Bordewich 1991; Spence 1993; *Christian Science Monitor*, 24 May 1993: 10; Engardio 1995). Indeed, Gu Mu, in his speech to the first meeting of the International Confucian Association on the 2,545th anniversary of Confucius's birth gave expression to the present "Confucianism Craze" (for detail, see Hongyan 1997) by announcing that

Confucius remains not only the Great Presence of China but will be China's greatest gift to the world (Ching 1994: 37).

To appreciate the gift of Confucius in China, however, the role of "fabrication"—the intentional effort of one or more individuals to manipulate or even falsify history—must be discounted (see Goffman 1974: 83–123). What motives, then, should we attribute to party officials resorting to Confucius? What should we make of the work of editors, political information bureaus, and other publicists? Is Confucius's image invoked by the state and the media as Christ's image is invoked in the West by the church? Or is his image used to manipulate the masses into supporting a cause toward which they might be otherwise indifferent?

Chinese officials do not always consciously manipulate; they often believe that their efforts to affect others' opinions are in the general interest. The fabrication concept is useful, however, because it helps distinguish influencing agents who share their audience's values from agents who induce their audience to adopt values to which it is not committed or of which the agents alone approve. Conflict theories of memory are referring to this kind of fabrication when they assert that any image of the past is "a product of elite manipulation" (Bodnar 1992: 20). Since the dominant class's images celebrate the dominant ideology, Baigell (1993: 201, 204) observes, they "can be seen as a form of oppression" or, at best, baneful influence. The conflict theories, however, assume dissensus to be the natural state of society, dismissing the possibility that image-makers, even in an authoritarian society, might embrace the same values and goals as their audience and invoke shared symbols to articulate, rather than to manipulate, its sentiment. This second point is the most fundamental. To focus exclusively on the use of Confucius's image by the Chinese Communist Party leads to a supply-side theory that attends to the production of images but ignores how the images are received. Reception, however, is always problematic. The state's success or failure in generating support for itself by appealing to Confucius is determined by the public's endorsement of the values Confucius symbolized, the public's belief that those values are worth preserving, and its perception that the state is their custodian rather than their exploiter. Between the remembrance of Confucius and the immediate problems of maintaining authoritarian control in a rapidly democratizing world exists a relation that neither the concepts of manipulation and propaganda, nor the related concepts of dominant ideology and false consciousness, can formulate.

Thus, it will not do to universalize Maurice Halbwachs's observation that "collective memory is essentially a reconstruction of the past" (1941: 353). Since critical inheritance warrants the embracing of Confucius without the total acceptance of his doctrine, it enables collective memory and tradition to subserve, yet subsist independently of, present powers and policies. Allowing expression of positive attitudes toward Confucius without enshrining his negative legacy, critical inheritance seeks to preserve tradition while legitimating uninhibited modernization. Thus, Confucius, unreconstructed, remains relevant in contemporary China.

NOTES

The authors are grateful for comments on earlier drafts by Grace Chen, Tim Futing Liao, Shun Lu, Mik-Young Park, and Howard Schuman.
1. In a second strand of the politics of memory literature, power is diffused rather than concentrated, and collective memories emerge out of a context of cross-cutting coalitions, networks, and enterprises. Writings on the fate of artistic (Lang and Lang 1990) and presidential (Fine 1996) reputations, Holocaust memories (Irwin-Zarecka 1994), place-naming and monument-making (Gregory and Lewis 1988; Zelinsky 1988; Wagner-Pacifici and Schwartz 1991), and the organization of museums (Barthel 1996) all link memory to pluralistic networks of interest and power.
2. The "symbolically reconstructed past," for Mead, refers to a fictive past that is created to manipulate social relationships in the present (Maines, Sugrue, and Katovich 1983). Howard Schuman and Jacqueline Scott (1989), on the other hand, demonstrate how the collective memory of generations is affected by a psychological imprinting phenomenon.
3. So intense was the Chinese determination to adjust to rather than master the world that it seemed to many to be a biological inheritance. Weber took this claim seriously at first, but concluded that the "traits which are considered innate may be the products of purely historical and cultural influences" (Gerth: 229).
4. It is probably no coincidence that the first systematic anti-Confucius campaigns took place during the Qin dynasty. Shi Huangdi became emperor in the third century B.C. under the influence of Legalist reforms that rivaled Confucianism by emphasizing government by formal rules and centralized administration. At this time came to pass *Fenshu Kengru*, meaning literally the burning of books and the burying of Confucianists.
5. Lin Biao was the appointed successor of Mao Zedong during the Cultural Revolution. According to the mass media, Lin Biao and his clique tried but failed to start a

military coup d'etat in September of 1971. The campaign against Lin Biao and Confucius began after this event.

REFERENCES

Alonso, A. 1988. "The Effects of Truth: Re-Presentations of the Past and the Imagining of Community." *Journal of Historical Sociology* 1: 33–57.

Baigell, M. 1993. "On the Margins of American History." In W. Ayres, ed., *Picturing History: American Painting, 1770–1930*. New York: Rizzoli.

Barthel, D. 1996. *Historic Preservation: Collective Memory and Historical Identity*. New Brunswick, N.J.: Rutgers University Press.

Bellah, R. N. 1970. "Civil Religion in America." In *Beyond Belief*. New York: Harper and Row.

Bellah, R. N., et al. 1985. *Habits of the Heart*. New York: Harper and Row.

Ben-Yehuda, N. 1996. *The Masada Myth: Collective Memory and Myth Making in Israel*. Madison: University of Wisconsin Press.

Bodnar, J. 1992. *Remaking America: Public Memory, Commemoration, and Patriotism in the Twentieth Century*. Princeton, N.J.: Princeton University Press.

Bond, M. H., and K. Hwang. 1987. "The Social Psychology of Chinese People." In Michael H. Bond, ed., *The Psychology of the Chinese People*. New York: Oxford University Press.

Bordewich, F. M. 1991. "Kong." *Conde Nast Traveler* 26: 122–125.

Boyarin, J., ed. 1994. *Remapping Memory: The Politics of Time Space*. Minneapolis: University of Minnesota Press.

Ching, F. 1994. "Confucius, The New Saviour." *Far Eastern Economic Review* 157 (November 10): 37.

Chong, W. L. 1993. "The Tragic Duality of Man: Lin Xiaobo on Western Philosophy." In K. W. Radtke and T. Saich, ed., *China's Modernization: Westernization and Acculturation*. Stuttgart: Franz Steiner Verlag.

Cooley, C. H. 1918. *Social Process*. New York: Charles Scribner's Sons.

Coser, L. A., ed. 1992. *Maurice Halbwachs on Collective Memory*. Chicago: University of Chicago Press.

Czarnowski, S. 1975 [1919]. *Le Culte des Héros et ses Conditions Sociales*. New York: Arno Press.

de Bary, W. T., W. Chan, and B. Watson. 1960. *Sources of Chinese Tradition*. New York: Columbia University Press.

de Tocqueville, A. 1945. *Democracy in America*. Part 1. New York: Knopf.

Durkheim, E. 1964 [1893]. *The Division of Labor in Society*. New York: Free Press.

——. 1950 [1895]. *Rules of the Sociological Method*. Glencoe, Ill.: Free Press.

——. 1965 [1915]. *The Elementary Forms of the Religious Life*. New York: Free Press.

Engardio, P. 1995. "China: Move Over, Karl Marx—Here Comes Confucius." *Business Week* (May 29): 53.

Fran, K. T. 1975. "Why China Criticizes Confucius." *Critica Sociologica* 35: 89–96.

Fairbank, J. K. 1992. *China: A New History.* Cambridge, Mass.: Harvard University Press (Belknap).

Feng, Y. 1975. *On Confucius.* Jiangsu Province: People's Publishing House.

——. 1985. "Confucius, Confucius, How to Study Confucius." *Tuan Je Bao* (Solidarity) January 1.

Fine, G. A. 1996. "Reputational Entrepreneurs and the Image of Harding." *American Journal of Sociology* 101: 159–93.

Frankel, O. 1996. "Whatever Happened to 'Red Emma'? Emma Goldman, from Alien Rebel to American Icon." *Journal of American History* (December): 903–42.

Freud, S. 1939. *Moses and Monotheism.* New York: Viking.

Geertz, C. 1973. *The Interpretations of Culture.* New York: Basic Books.

Goffman, E. 1974. *Frame Analysis: An Essay on the Organization of Experience.* New York: Harper and Row.

Gillis, J. R., ed. 1994. *Commemorations: The Politics of National Identity.* Princeton, N.J.: Princeton University Press.

Gregory, S. W., and J. M. Lewis. 1988. "Symbols of Collective Memory: The Social Process of Memorializing May 4, 1970 at Kent State University." *Symbolic Interaction* 11: 213–33.

Gu, M. 1989. "Speech at the Opening Ceremony Commemorating the 2540th Anniversary of Confucius' Birth and a Symposium on Confucianism." *Study of Confucius,* vol. 4.

Guo, M. 1954. *The Book of Ten Criticisms.*

Halbwachs, M. 1926. *Les Cadres Sociaux de la Mémoire.* Paris: Presses Universitaires de France.

——. 1941. *La Topographie Légendaire Des Evangiles en Sainte Terre.* Paris: Presses Universitaires de France.

Hobart, M. E. 1989. "The Paradox of Historical Constructionism." *History and Theory* 28: 43–58.

Hobsbawm, E. 1983. "Mass-Producing Traditions, 1870–1914." In E. Hobsbawm and T. Ranger, ed., *The Invention of Tradition.* Cambridge, England: Cambridge University Press.

Hongyan, L. 1997. "Developments in the Study of Confucianism on the Mainland of China in Recent Years." *Social Sciences in China* (spring): 17–30.

Hou, X. 1987. "Mao Zedong's Criticism and Inheritance of 'the Doctrine of the Mean.' " *Qi Lu Journal,* vol. 4.

Irwin-Zarecka, I. 1994. *Frames of Remembrance.* New Brunswick, N.J.: Transaction.

Kammen, M. 1991. *Mystic Chords of Memory.* New York: Knopf.

Kertzer, D. 1988. *Ritual, Politics and Power.* New Haven, Conn.: Yale University Press.

Lang, G. and K. Lang. 1990. *Etched in Memory: The Building and Survival of Artistic Reputation.* Chapel Hill: University of North Carolina Press.

Liao, F. 1985. "Virtues Reflected in Children's Picture Story Books During the Chinese Cultural Revolution." M.A. thesis. Department of Sociology, University of Georgia.

——. 1989. "Positive Alienation and Its Reflection in Taoist Thought." *International Sociology* 4: 5–17.

——. 1990. "Women in the Taiping Movement in Nineteenth-Century China." In Guida West and Rhoda Lois Blumberg, eds., *Women and Social Protest*. New York: Oxford University Press.

——. 1993. "Sitting in Oblivion as a Taoist Practice of Positive Alienation: A Response to Negative Alienation in the Tang Dynasty." *International Sociology* 8: 479–92.

Lipset, S. M. 1996. *American Exceptionalism*. New York: W. W. Norton.

Liu, S. [1939] 1964. *How to Be a Good Communist*. Yenan, China: Institute of Marxism-Leninism.

Louie, K. 1980. *Critiques of Confucius in Contemporary China*. New York: St. Martin's Press.

Lyotard, J.-F. [1979] 1984. *The Postmodern Condition*. Minneapolis: University of Minneapolis Press.

Maines, D. R., N. M. Sugrue, and M. A. Katovich. 1983. "The Sociological Import of G. H. Mead's Theory of the Past." *American Sociological Review* 48: 163, 164, 169.

Mannheim, K. 1936. *Ideology and Utopia*. New York: Harcourt, Brace and World.

Mao, Z. 1938. "Role of the Chinese Communist Party."

——. 1940. "On the New Democratism."

——. 1955. "A Comment on the Article 'An Agricultural Producers' Cooperation Which Increased Production by 67% Within Three Years.'"

Mead, G. H. 1929. "The Nature of the Past." In J. Coss, ed., *Essays in Honor of John Dewey*. New York: Henry Holt.

Mu, Z. 1989. "The Destiny and Prospect of Confucianism in Modern China." *Study of Confucius*, vol. 2: 16–23.

Nora, P. 1996. *Realms of Memory*. New York: Columbia University Press.

Olick, J. K. 1994. "Collective Memory and Discursive Process: The Nazi Past in West German Politics, 1949–1989." Presented at the Annual Meeting of the American Sociological Association, August 12, Los Angeles, Calif.

Olick, J. K., and D. Levy. 1997. "Collective Memory and Cultural Constraint: Holocaust Myth and Rationality in German Politics." *American Sociological Review*. In press.

Pelikan, J. 1985. *Jesus Through the Centuries*. New York: Harper and Row.

Peterson, M. D. 1962. *The Jefferson Image in the American Mind*. New York: Oxford University Press.

Schudson, M. 1989. "The Present in the Past Versus the Past in the Present." *Communication 1989*, vol. 11: 105–13.

——. 1994. *Watergate in American Memory*. New York: Basic Books.

Schuman, H., and J. Scott. 1989. "Generations and Collective Memories." *American Sociological Review* 54: 359–81.

Schwartz, B. 1991. "Social Change and Collective Memory: The Democratization of George Washington." *American Sociological Review* 56: 221–36.

——. 1996. "Introduction: The Expanding Past." *Qualitative Sociology* 19: 275–82.

———. 1997. "Collective Memory and History: How Abraham Lincoln Became a Symbol of Racial Equality." *Sociological Quarterly* 38: 469–96.

Shils, E. A. 1981. *Tradition*. Chicago: University of Chicago Press.

Smith, A. H. 1986 [1894]. *Chinese Characteristics*. Singapore: Graham Brash Ltd.

Spence, J. D. 1993. "Confucius." *The Wilson Quarterly* 17: 30–38.

Tuchman, G., and N. Fortin. 1989. *Edging Women Out: Victorian Novelists, Publishers, and Social Change*. New Haven, Conn.: Yale University Press.

Wagner-Pacifici, R., and B. Schwartz. 1996. "The Vietnam Veterans Memorial: Commemorating a Difficult Past." *American Journal of Sociology* 97: 376–420.

Weber, M. 1964 [1916]. *Religion in China*. Glencoe, Ill.: Free Press.

Wei-ming, T. 1990. "The Confucian Tradition in Chinese History." In P. S. Ropp, ed., *Heritage of China: Contemporary Perspectives on Chinese Civilization*. Berkeley: University of California Press.

———. 1991. "Cultural China: The Periphery as the Center." *Daedalus:* 1–32.

Whitehead, R. L. 1976. "The New Ethic in China and the Anti-Confucius Campaign." *Australian and New Zealand Journal of Sociology* 12: 16–21.

Yang, K. 1987. "Chinese Personality and Its Change." In M. H. Bond, ed. *The Psychology of the Chinese People*. New York: Oxford University Press.

Yang, Y. 1954. *The History of Chinese Ancient Thought*.

———. 1974. *Confucius: "Sage" of the Reactionary Classes*. Peking: Foreign Languages Press.

Zelinsky, W. 1988. *Nation into State: The Shifting Symbolic Foundations of American Nationalism*. Chapel Hill: University of North Carolina Press.

Zelizer, B. 1995. "Reading the Past Against the Grain: The Shape of Memory Studies." *Critical Studies in Mass Communication* 12: 214–39.

Zhang, D. 1989. "Explore the True Meaning of Confucius' Thinking." *Study of Confucius*, vol. 3: 32–34.

Newspapers and Journals
Guang Ming Ri Bao
    30 October 1961
    3 December 1973
    22 September 1973
    6 December 1973
    12 September 1978
Ren Min Ri Bao
    3 June 1974
    30 December 1976
    18 July 1978
Journal of Northeast Normal University
    February 1986

Institutional Legacies and

Collective Memories: The Case of

the Spanish Transition to Democracy

◄ ◄ ◄ ◄ ◄ ◄ ◄ ◄ ◄ ◄ ◄ ◄ ◄   PALOMA AGUILAR

In both Europe and the United States, the impact of the past on the present has become a central research focus for sociologists, political scientists, and historians alike. After decades of concentrating on more tangible, or structural, aspects of the links between historical evolution and political developments, many analysts now stress the importance of the collective memory of societies, and of the different groups that comprise them, as well as of the formal and informal legacies inherited from authoritarian experiences. This interest in the use and abuse of the past has been prompted in part by the general resurgence of nationalist movements, which tend to legitimize current grievances with reference to historical events. Such events are all the more debatable, the more remote they are.

The role played by the memory of the civil war (1936–39) in shaping the transition to democracy in Spain (1975–78) differed according to each region. Thus, in addition to underlining the importance of memory in explaining the change in regime in Spain, and its institutional design,[1] this article also offers a first approximation of the particular role played by the collective memory of the war in the transition in the Basque country. I shall refer not only to the civil war itself but also to the Franco regime, and chart the evolution of accounts of the war as well as the different uses made of them by leading political forces. Only in this way can the role played by the war in the years following Franco's death be properly understood. This approach also allows us to trace the specific legacies of the authoritarian regime in various areas of the country and to assess the differing impact that the Francoist period had on the capacity of distinct regional elites to act.

In Spain, the traumatic memory of the civil war helped ensure that both the political elites and Spanish society in general did everything possible to avoid repeating the past errors that had undermined Spain's only previous democratic experience, the period of the Second Republic (1931–36). Political adversaries tried not to transform the past into a destabilizing tool, which many feared could render impossible any peaceful dialogue among the heirs to the ideological positions that had been contested in the civil war. This caution helps to explain the policy of national reconciliation that came about based on the implicit recognition of collective culpability for crimes committed during the war and the unanimous desire that a similar drama should never be repeated. Consensus, rather than confrontation, was thereby confirmed as the most legitimate form of negotiation between different political and social players (Aguilar 1996).

In the Basque country, the traumatic character of the memory of struggle helps explain many of the attitudes adopted by the different protagonists in the transition. However, it is clear that this region represented the most atypical example within the Spanish context since, during this period of political change, maximalist and violent stances were not so clearly in the minority as they were in the rest of the country. Indeed, levels of political and social mobilization were far higher, especially when these began to decline in other areas.[2] Moreover, the transition's two referenda— on the Political Reform Law (1976)[3] and on the Constitution (1978)[4]— produced the highest levels of abstention in the Basque country, demonstrating both the specificity of this case and the need for a detailed study of collective memory in the region.

If Basques, especially nationalists, did not feel obliged by the "consensual" spirit that characterized Spanish transition, and we have defended the idea that this was based on the recognition of collective guilt for the war, what were the consequences? Might it be that the Basques did not have the same political priorities as other Spaniards? If so, how did this memory of the civil war permit them to adopt a different attitude during the transition? Did they not perceive that they were equally guilty for the unrest of the Second Republic and the brutality of the war? I try to answer these questions by dealing with the issue of how the nationalist interpretation of the civil war altered its meaning and allowed the emergence of different lessons to be applied in the transition.

This essay also analyzes why such attitudes emerged by demonstrating the existence of a unique memory of the war—duly fashioned by Basque nationalist elites—that was sufficiently distinct from that of the rest of Spain as to have a different political impact. This is not to claim that collective memory is the variable that best explains the delay in the transition to democracy in the Basque country but rather to underline the importance of attempts by political elites (in this case nationalists) to manipulate the past, and to explore the repercussions of such attempts on the values and beliefs of a society trying to recover from a deeply complex memory.

Although political elites have often tried to use the past for their own purposes, I defend the idea that most of the time they have not been able to do so. The context in which the transition to democracy took place and, more specifically, the formal and informal legacies inherited from the past, help to explain the restrictions with which the elites had to deal in this period. Therefore, I also try to show that the Basque nationalist elites had the capacity to impose their demands in the aforementioned way precisely due to the nature of the Francoist dictatorship. This regime was so obsessed with the preservation of national unity (one of the declared aims of the Francoist side in the civil war was to annihilate the so-called separatist desires of Basques and Catalans) that it acted with extensive violence in those regions possessing greater linguistic and cultural peculiarities. All of this contributed to the extreme deterioration of the statehood issue facing the Spanish Second Republic (1931–36). It was not by chance that the Basque terrorist organization ETA was founded during the Francoist period.[5] The so-called Basque problem, in the violent and radical sense we know it today, would have been very unlikely had it not been for the existence of the Francoist regime. The fact that ETA's actions had the highest visibility of all the political groups opposed to the dictatorship, and very specifically, the fact that ETA killed Almirante Carrero Blanco (Franco's designated successor), helps to explain the initial popularity of the terrorist organization and the more or less explicit support it received from different leftist groups.

With the death of Franco, there was no widespread popular demand for the prosecution of those responsible for the human rights violations committed under the dictatorship. Most of the opposition parties that had talked about the possibility of purging both the civil and military organizations of the dictatorship finally decided to omit this demand from their political programs for two principal reasons. First, the existing social climate was not conducive to such a delicate political measure in a period characterized by uncertainty and unpredictability. Second, the civil and military elites of the Francoist regime still retained enough political resources to oppose such initiatives. The possibility of a coup d'etat was not unlikely, especially because the military and police forces were the main victims of the terrorist attacks.

This situation was perceived very differently in the Basque country, where the more radicalized sectors of the nationalist organizations openly demanded the purge of Francoist elites and the immediate replacement of the existing military and police forces. That the armed forces were so visible in the Basque country during the last decade of the dictatorship contributed to the diffusion of the image, created by the radical nationalists, that an "occupation foreign army" was "invading" their territory.[6] This helps to explain why, when it became evident that no purges were going to take place, both the radical nationalists and the extreme left began to refer to the transition as *post-Francoism*, at once emphasizing the continuities with the previous dictatorship and calling into question the genuineness of the political change.[7]

THE MEMORY OF THE CIVIL WAR IN SPAIN

When the civil war ended, the Franco regime tried to consolidate its rule on the basis of its victory. During the regime's early years, political authorities refused to accept there had even been a civil war, claiming instead that battle had been waged against the "foreign invader" and international communism. However, when a regime's foundational myth is a fratricidal conflict, its legitimacy is unlikely to be sufficiently solid if not reinforced by other elements. In practice, the notorious initial illegitimacy of the Francoist regime was such that, in those early years, it had to maintain its political authority through a strategy of repression and exhaustive political control. The regime's progressive withdrawal from that initial stance coincided with a period of economic liberalization that allowed the country to benefit from the wave of prosperity that swept through the Western world during the 1960s. It was during this period that the regime's rhetoric stopped focusing directly on the war, instead placing greater emphasis on the economic achievements and social transformation that took place during this decade.

In this second stage of the regime, economic growth and prosperity, together with growing international recognition for Francoism, lent the regime a significant degree of legitimacy. This enabled the heroic version of the war that the regime had disseminated until then to be gradually replaced by a tragic vision in which the war was no longer presented as something necessary but rather as an unavoidable accident. In the final stage of the regime, many considered this past a shameful episode, and some even suggested that the best way to overcome it was simply to forget, since they were convinced that any open debate on the subject would reopen old wounds and threaten coexistence in Spain.

By the time of Franco's death, Spanish society had managed to reach, if not an uncontested account of what had happened during the civil war, at least an agreement as to the lessons to be derived from this traumatic experience. During the transition it was accepted that the two warring sides were equally responsible for barbaric acts. In this way, no one party bore more guilt than the other, since both sides had committed unjustifiable atrocities. The exorcism of past brutalities was possible thanks to an interpretation of the struggle as a kind of "collective madness." Finally, the principal lesson derived from the transition was "never again." All forces—political, social, economic—had to ensure that Spain would never again witness a similar drama. Recognizing this solution is essential to understanding the full complexity that underlay both the generalized consensus that governed the transition up until the adoption of the constitution in December 1978 and the policy of national reconciliation that was attempted from the outset.

For an event that had occurred 40 years earlier, the dramatic memory of the war had a vivid presence during the transition. Although over 70 percent of the Spanish population had not experienced the civil war directly, the memory of the event was transmitted from generation to generation, kept alive and resonant as part of a bitter collective memory. The endurance of the trauma derived from the war and the survival of certain Francoist legacies in Spanish political culture can be traced in opinion polls of the period.[8] It was when society perceived—consciously or unconsciously, and in a more or less justified manner—certain similarities between the situation in the 1970s and that of the 1930s, that the memory of the struggle reemerged.

By the mid-1970s Spanish society had gone nearly 40 years without democratic institutions. Thus, at the time when parties, unions, elections, and parliamentary life were all gradually starting to appear, many Spaniards had no direct experience of them. These institutions were not, however, new to Spanish history. A minority of Spaniards had known them during the Second Republic, which had been destroyed, together with its institutions, during the civil war. Throughout its existence the Franco regime reviled the republican experience. The regime's arguments were not shared by a considerable portion of the Spanish people, but in the 1970s there were many who remained critical of the republican period for other reasons.

Widely criticized were the republic's weaknesses and excesses, along with its reluctance to accommodate minorities, its military and religious policy, the imposition of a nonconsensual constitution, and other issues. For many, the failure of the Second Republic, which culminated in the civil war, was partially due to its own mistakes and, furthermore, to an institutional design that exacerbated these errors, along with an international context that effectively offered little help to a weak and incipient democracy.[9] The exclusionary attitude of the political majorities promoted, in many occasions, the anticonstitutional maneuvers of the minorities, regardless that some of them were, from the very beginning, totally hostile to the republican regime. In addition, sectors from certain nationalist parties, such as some within the Partido Nacionalista Vasco (PNV, Basque Nationalist Party), had begun to call into question something even more delicate than the political regime, that is, the legitimacy of national borders, with the subsequent denial that they belonged to the Spanish *demos*. During the republican period very few political actors had the will to put aside their own ideological interests in order to contribute to the stabilization of the newborn democracy. In this sense, the consensus and negotiations among the main political adversaries that during the seventies became the rule, were in the thirties, without any doubt, the exception.

The great contrast between these two democratic experiences helps to explain why, according to a number of surveys, today's democracy receives higher marks than the republican one. However, what really stands out is that Francoism is held in higher regard than the Second Republic.

The fact that the memory of the collapse of the republic remained associated with the tragic experience of the civil war may help to explain the period's poor rating. During the transition, when institutions that had been in place during the republican period were revived, it was logical that Spaniards should recall both this failed experiment and its ill-fated end.

This is why Spanish society tried so hard not to reproduce the errors attributed to the Second Republic and thus avoided repeating its institutional design. The past demarcated what was and was not possible in the political transition: given the uncertainties and caution that surrounded this period, Spain seized upon any clue as to what might happen if certain institutions were established. For history, logically, is a fundamental source of stability and legitimacy for democratic regimes. Every effort was also made to ensure that political adversaries did not turn the past into a political weapon, which many feared would render impossible any peaceful dialogue between wartime opponents. It was a question of forgetting the rancor of the past, of retaining the lessons of history without stirring them up so that, above all, a future of peaceful and democratic coexistence could be constructed.

For many people, however, this recourse to silence amounted to a form of resignation and finally spilled over into frustration. Yet, the principal objective—the peaceful consolidation of democracy in Spain, something that had not previously been possible—was achieved. This allowed the transition to become the basic foundational myth of democracy and its memory to become a political resource of great importance. The events that cast the largest shadow over the process were directly related to the course of the transition in the Basque country—the notable increase in ETA's terrorist activities and the high level of abstention, in two of the three Basque provinces, in the constitutional referendum. The 1978 constitution, a milestone in the transition from the dictatorship and proclaimed as the constitution of Spanish reconciliation, was approved throughout the country, yet the campaign by Basque nationalists in favor of abstention

Table 1. Question: "In general terms, when do you consider that Spain has been better off in political terms in the last 60 years?"

	1984	1985	1986	1987	1988	1989	1990
The Primo de Rivera dictatorship	3%	2%	2%	1%	1%	1%	1%
The republican years	5%	3%	3%	4%	2%	2%	3%
The Francoist period	21%	16%	15%	15%	12%	7%	8%
Today's democracy	58%	58%	62%	62%	67%	77%	76%
Doesn't know	9%	18%	13%	13%	13%	10%	10%
No answer	4%	3%	5%	5%	5%	3%	2%
Study number from CIS (Centro de Investigaciones Sociológicas)	1441	1495	1558	1715	1764	1851	1908

enjoyed unexpected success in their own territory. Over and above the reasons given by the nationalists at the time to justify abstention, we need to ask why they, unlike other Spaniards, felt no obligation to support the policy of consensus and reconciliation. What role did the memory of civil war play in the adoption of such a stance?

THE CIVIL WAR IN THE BASQUE COUNTRY:
A WAR AMONG BASQUES

Throughout the Second Republic, the attitude of the PNV had not exactly been characterized by ideological coherence.[10] Although its leaders formed an electoral coalition with the reactionary Carlists in 1931, in both 1933 and 1936 they decided to go it alone. By 1936, however, the party had moved much closer to the republican and leftist parties with whom the PNV collaborated during the war. This volte-face resulted in a number of desertions from its ranks and something of an electoral slump.[11] When the military uprising against the republic came on 18 July 1936, the PNV— hegemonic in much of the Basque country—found itself obliged, unhappily, to side with one or other of the warring factions. Initial doubts were dissipated when the Francoist forces that had triumphed in Navarre[12] and Álava began to victimize individual members of the PNV. Moreover, it seemed far more likely that they could achieve their statute of autonomy— then awaiting approval in the *Cortes*—from the republicans.

The first thing that needs to be emphasized in regard to the Basque country as a whole, given the apparent oversight that tends to characterize the nationalist account, is the division produced in the very heart of the Basque community by the military uprising. Although Vizcaya and much of Guipúzcoa ended up supporting the republic (although with some reservations on the part of the PNV), in Álava and Navarre not only did many side with the rebels, but in fact the Álavese, and particularly the Navarrese Carlist militia, formed Franco's biggest contingent of volunteers. More significant still is that even in the provinces where the coup d'état triumphed (and unlike all other parties that sided with the republicans) the PNV's headquarters were not immediately closed down. At least until shortly before the approval of the Basque Statute and the establishment of the first Basque government in October 1936, the Francoist forces believed that the PNV would eventually come over to them.[13]

The overtly confessional nature of the PNV gave it a distinctive status on a side where agnosticism and, in many cases, a violent and intransigent anticlericalism dominated. This meant that many Basque nationalists feared their own allies (especially the anarchists, communists, and radical socialists) as much as they did the Francoists. Certainly, the militant wing of the PNV tried to maintain more cordial relations with the enemy during the war, whether because the enemy was also Basque or because of certain ideological, religious, and cultural affinities. This is only logical, given that fighting on one of the two sides was a more forced, accidental affair rather than the result of a clear and enthusiastic decision, as was the case with other parties.

The development of the civil war in the Basque country was marked by some specific features that have been extensively researched: the nationalists' reluctance to fight until they had secured their statute of autonomy, the lack of understanding between the republican and Basque nationalist military hierarchies, the mutual mistrust between nationalists and leftists, the many desertions to the enemy camp, the rapid surrender of Basque battalions in Guipúzcoa, and, finally, when the fall of Bilbao was imminent, the nationalists' refusal to destroy their heavy industry so that this arsenal would not fall intact into Francoist hands.

Probably the most significant issue was the reluctance of the *gudaris* (Basque soldiers) to fight outside the Basque country once they had finally been mobilized by the nationalists. Many witnesses have affirmed that, for them, the war finished when their territory fell into Francoist hands; hence the thorny matter of the Pact of Santoña. The negotiations that some within the PNV began with the Italian fascists linked to Franco are well known. An offer of surrender was made to the Italians in exchange for the nationalists being allowed to evacuate their battalions and part of the civilian population. Effectively, the surrender *did* take place but not the evacuation nor the respect for the civilian and military populations; although the Italian army was prepared to implement the treaty, the Francoist authorities were more than ready to break it. Much as in any other area taken from the republicans, the entry of the victorious troops led to numerous arrests and executions, although the Basque church—which repeatedly intervened in favor of the Basque nationalists on account of their conservatism and exemplary Catholicism—helped to moderate the reprisals.

The repression exacted during the conflict and early postwar years has been one of the most controversial issues in the recent historiography of the period. However, beyond disputes over the number of deaths attributable to each side and the organization of reprisals by both rearguards, it is widely accepted that the Francoist repression in republican areas was most severe in those provinces where nationalist consciousness was strongest. Certainly in Vizcaya and Guipúzcoa jurisdictional privileges were lost (such as the *conciertos económicos*, a special taxation system). However, as a reward for their stance during the war, both Navarre and Álava were allowed to retain these privileges.

Throughout the Franco regime the cultural repression exercised over the whole nation was particularly severe in those regions where a language other than Spanish was spoken, as people were prevented from communicating in their own tongue (a situation much more marked in Catalonia than in the Basque country since, in the former, the proportion of people who used the vernacular was much greater). Nevertheless, evidence exists to suggest that, despite the claim of victimization sustained by Basque nationalism throughout the transition, reprisals in the three Basque provinces at the end of the war were no greater than elsewhere in Spain. Nor was the Basque country the area that suffered the most shortages during the postwar period.

In fact, many authors have asserted that "the repression during and immediately after the war was, in the Basque country, much 'softer' than in other parts of Spain. . . . Moreover, with regard to those most directly involved, practically all those subject to reprisals as a result of the war had returned by 1945" (Garmendia and González Portilla 1993: 191). The myth that repression was greater in the Basque country, carefully nurtured in Basque nationalist discourse, has been called into question by Andrés de Blas, based on works by Salas Larrazábal and Ibarrábal (Ibarrábal 1978). This last author has claimed that, after 1943, there were no nationalist prisoners in Franco's gaols (cited in de Blas 1988: 84).

A PECULIAR TRANSITION TO DEMOCRACY

The batallion that handed over Bilbao's factories intact to Franco's forces in 1937, thereby contravening the republican hierarchy's demand that they be destroyed, was under the command of the PNV. At the beginning of the transition, "the PNV vindicated this act through one of its well-known leaders, Xavier Arzallus, at the first authorized public rally held by the party" (Jiménez de Aberasturi 1979: 260). The PNV's nationalist reading of the past, according to which all Basques lost the war, justified placing the interests of their own region before those of their political allies. This order of priorities, which was widely criticized, was proudly defended by the PNV in an attempt to distance itself from the "Spanish" parties before a new electorate with more radical nationalist demands. In this way, events that at the time were seen as a betrayal of the republican cause (such as the Pact of Santoña or the handing over of the Bilbao factories) came to be seen as a virtue for those whose principal aspiration was to defend "all things Basque." Not for nothing would the two main architects of the Santoña surrender become the most emblematic figures of Basque nationalism during the transition: Jesús María de Leizaola, the president of the Basque government in exile, and Juan Ajuriaguerra, the historic leader of the underground party. Curiously, their honor was never called into question during the transition, and in the mid-1970s Ajuriaguerra was even considered the person with the greatest moral authority in the Basque country.

It is certainly the case that no other political force had its past scrutinized, the result of a sort of tacit agreement not to stir up old issues, especially those related to the conflict, in order to avoid them being used as political weapons. If the PNV and the socialists, who experienced very difficult relations during the 1930s, had engaged in mutual recrimination over their activities during the war, it would have been difficult to achieve the climate of reconciliation and consensus that characterized most of the negotiations during the transition. This allowed the PNV, like the rest of the opposition, to ameliorate its former image and to claim, in defense of its proabstention campaign over the constitutional referendum, "[o]ur deputies did not endorse the republican Constitution, and yet there is the historic evidence of the loyalty of the Basque Government, of the loyalty of a part that, although it did not vote for the Republican Constitution, none the less defended its autonomy, as well as the regime and the Constitution that made it possible, both during the war and for so many years afterwards" (PNV 1978: 146). According to circumstances, the PNV stressed either its unconditional loyalty to the republic or else its major reservations over having had to take part in a war that was alien to them, referring, for example, to the Pact of Santoña, and the resulting moral justification of prioritizing Basque interests over any others, such as defense of the republic.

Another important aspect of Basque nationalist moral authority during the transition derived from the democratic opposition's recognition of the Franco regime's particular barbarity towards the Basque country from the end of the 1960s. Also significant was the "halo of heroism" accorded ETA for having been the most visible source of resistance to the regime and the group whose actions had done most to undermine the chances of the dictatorship continuing after Franco's death.[14] That the opposition was blind to the fact that ETA's struggle, from the outset, had a different objective, is remarkable.

In fact, ETA saw the fight against the dictatorship as accidental: their real goal was freedom for the Basque homeland and the expulsion of "the invader." Despite its differences with radical nationalism, the PNV derived considerable benefit from ETA's armed resistance, both through its unquestioned contribution to the resurgence of Basque consciousness (Fusi 1984: 225), and also through the possibility of indirectly using the threat of terrorism in its negotiations with the central government. Thus, while the party in power during the transition, the *Unión de Centro Democrático* (UCD, Union of the Democratic Center), justified the delays and limitations in certain political measures of great significance for the Basques (for instance, the legalization of the Basque flag, the granting of amnesty,[15] and the constitution of the Basque General Council) on the basis of pressure from the intransigent sector of the army, the PNV also sheltered behind terrorist acts in its attempts to convince the government to act more speedily.

The two most pressing problems of the transition were terrorist blackmail and the threat of military intervention. The armed forces represented a direct legacy of the Franco regime and, although a generational shift had brought about a marked change in mentality among many of its members, it is clear that the most entrenched sections were able to exert considerable pressure on the process of democratization. The fear of a coup d'état led those pressing for democracy to moderate some of their demands, since it was hardly appropriate to force the hand of those already suspicious of the whole process of democratization (especially in regard to territorial decentralization) who, furthermore, were already the favored target of terrorist attacks.

It is odd that the threat of a coup was seen as far less dramatic in the Basque country itself, where the most serious threats to public order had taken place, where the level of social and political mobilization was highest, and where the most radical political forces—on both nationalist and ideological axes—had been driven underground.[16] Fear of a coup d'état (like the one that eventually ended the Second Republic), so clear to many national Spanish parties, hardly figured in the discourse of most Basque nationalist parties, nor has it been a feature of studies of the transition in the region. Some PNV leaders were not so clearly moved by the feeling of collective responsibility that obliged other political forces to temper their demands, even to the extent of seeking to demobilize their followers. For example, one leader stated that if the risk of military intervention existed, it had nothing to do with his demands and was due to an "atmosphere contrary to democratic legality" rather than "flag wars" or "terrorist violence."[17] In this way, the PNV sought to absolve itself in advance of any responsibility for what might happen in order to avoid, at least explicitly, having to moderate its stance.

However, one key leader of *Euskadiko Ezquerra* (EE, Basque Left) recognized that the actions of ETA played into the hands of military plotters, since they deliberately sought to foster a climate of conflict.[18] He underlined that "the war is over" and that it was now a matter of searching for a "solution and a means of conciliation so that, with peace achieved, the consequences of war should disappear."[19] Another key leader of the EE criticized those who said "Euskadi is at war," and claimed that this argument was used not only by ETA sympathizers and militants but also by Arzullus when he was unable to achieve his objectives, thereby encouraging ETA violence as well as confirming his own claims.[20]

The fear of a coup d'état felt throughout Spain was intimately linked to the traumatic memory of the civil war, given that the 1936 conflict had begun in such a manner. However, since in the Basque country there was a different memory of the war's significance and causes, there was also a different view as to the danger of military plotting. Conversely, Basque nationalism seemed on occasion to use the widespread fear of a recurrence of fratricidal conflict, possibly unleashed by a military coup, to achieve its objectives, claiming that only by acceding to its demands could radical elements be contained.

Since then, many of Basque nationalism's growing demands have been based on the urgent need to secure peace in the Basque country and on the impossibility of doing so without certain conditions being met. A PNV leader from Pamplona claimed in June 1978 that, although ETA's violence could not be justified, the state had tried to wipe out Basque culture, and "until the Spanish State takes clear and effective measures to alleviate discrimination against Basque culture, it will be very difficult for us to explain to ETA why they ought to lay down their arms . . . ETA will not renounce violence until our demands are met."[21] Similarly, one of the PNV's foremost leaders, a deputy for Guipúzcoa, recognized in an interview in June 1983 that ETA's actions had advanced the cause of Basque autonomy, especially under the UCD government, since this government "was very concerned about containing violence and therefore supported approval of the Statute of Autonomy." In a well-worn argument, he also insisted that to get rid of ETA more autonomy would have to be given to the Basque country.[22] Another PNV politician saw the vote for *Herri Batasuna* (HB, United People), the political wing of ETA, as the result of Basque "frustrations," as well as a clear warning to his own party's "moderate" tendencies and to the "anti-Basque" stance in Madrid.[23] Whatever the case, it is clear that the PNV knew how best to exploit the UCD's obsession, and that of a large part of the Spanish population, with keeping the peace.

Another possible reason that the democratic opposition did not question the PNV's political credibility was its desire to persuade the moderate nationalists to enter negotiations with nonnationalist parliamentary groups rather than create a "Basque national front," the high point of radical ambition. The major trauma of the war for Basque nationalists had been its fratricidal element among Basques, which explains why they were so concerned about fragmentation and polarization.[24] In this way, as a result of its determination to avoid a new rupture in the heart of the Basque community, the PNV oscillated between support for the government (supporting, on many occasions, the politics of consensus) and collusion with the radicals (refusing, for example, to approve the constitution or to condemn terrorist activities outright). To the radicals, whose electorate they were also trying to attract, the PNV had to demonstrate that its priority was the defense of Basque interests and not striking agreements with other parties. In Parliament, meanwhile, the PNV tried to compromise and support any consensual measures that did not affect its own interests, aware that, if Spanish democracy were not consolidated, it would be very difficult for the Basque country to achieve its goal of self-rule. Thus, the principal lesson the PNV derived from the struggle, although rarely acknowledged explicitly, was that a civil war between Basques must never happen again.

Both the first ETA militants and the most radical sector of the moderate nationalists had a deep respect for some historic leaders of the PNV, but they felt their strategy based on compromise and pacts had borne little fruit. What now had to be achieved at all costs was the reconstruction of the Basque identity, even at the price of destroying consensus with other parties. Thus, in the constitutional debates, the PNV sought to defend, more than Spanish constitutional legality, an earlier, jurisdictional legality, so as not to hinder the possibility of claiming the right to self-determination, and also to avoid breaking definitively with the radical nationalists. The PNV did all it could to reconcile these elements, even at the cost of slightly slipping outside the political game. Keeping in line with nationalist logic, the main objective was to safeguard the national community.

THE SPANISH CIVIL WAR ACCORDING TO BASQUE NATIONALISM

ETA's first terrorist act took place on 18 July 1961. The target was a train carrying veterans of the Franco regime. The attack was followed by a massive police persecution that forced many ETA militants to flee to France. The symbolic significance of both the target and the date chosen for the attack—the 25th anniversary of the coup d'état that led to the civil war—demonstrates the endurance of the memory of the civil war and the desire to attack the legitimating myth of the victors.[25]

Debate over using violence did not become an issue within ETA's leading echelons until 1962, and it was not until the third assembly, held two years later, that the organization, heavily influenced by Federico Krutwick's *Vasconia*, opted definitively for "revolutionary warfare." The fact that radical Basque nationalism did not acknowledge the civil dimension of the war is fundamental to understanding the adoption of this strategy and the very different lessons they derived from the experience of the war.[26] According to them, the 1936 conflict was a war waged against a foreign Spanish enemy. Although obviously serious, it was far less important that the Basque country was subject from that point to a dictatorship than that it was "occupied" by a foreign power. The struggle against Francoism was therefore purely accidental, since the central battle of that war—which for ETA had still not ended—was the one that would subsequently be waged against the Spanish state.

Mikel Azurmendi argues that tens of thousands of voters in the Basque country "believe they are at war today." According to him, "ETA was born in order to give new meaning to the Spanish Civil War; what it demands is the pursuit of what was left unresolved in that conflict, and which the PNV, in exile, did not want to follow up, preferring instead to wait for a peaceful resolution to be brought about by the US and European democracies. ETA was born to fight, and to continue the war" (Azurmendi 39).

Crucially, however, it is not only radical nationalism that appeared to question the "civil" nature of the war waged between 1936 and 1939.[27] Throughout the transition, the PNV was also reluctant to join the implicit pact of silence over the wartime past that other parliamentary groups had put into practice. In fact, according to the radical nationalist, Francisco Letamendía, the PNV,

> in contrast to Spanish parliamentary forces—for whom "national reconciliation" meant, as Carrillo had confirmed, "not digging up the past"—began after June 1977 to commemorate the anniversaries of numerous Civil War incidents in Euskadi. In the same way that, during

the 1970s, the State saw this as a war between brothers, in Euskadi, where a government of National Concentration presided over by José Antonio Aguirre had brought about Basque unity, the Civil War continues to be seen as a fight of national resistance against a foreign occupier. Hence the cult of the "gudari"; hence also the symbolic force of comparing "yesterday's" gudari with "today's" gudari. (Letamendia 1994: 2: 89)

Political documents by moderate Basque nationalists during the transition avoid reference to the 1936–39 conflict as a civil war. The first postwar PNV assembly, held in Pamplona in 1977, supported the same myth as the radical nationalists, claiming the existence of a constant "struggle" from Sabino Arana to the present, without ever referring to the civil war as such. Delegates spoke of a "struggle against the successive foreign dictatorships this country has suffered; struggle in the trenches, arms in hand, against those who forced us into a war we did not want; struggle in prisons and in exile; an underground struggle by all possible means" (PNV 1977: 1). As its natural electorate was nationalist, such occasions were used by the PNV to pay homage to the gudari who perished during the war, especially since it was believed that the gudari gave their lives "for Euskadi" and not for the defense of the republic, which, ultimately, was a "Spanish" regime they had not helped bring about, and whose constitution they had not approved. Furthermore, by paying homage to those who fought "throughout Euskadi" defending what they thought best for their land, they appeared also to be addressing those Basques who, as Carlists, had lined up on Franco's side.

The existence of a new generation of Basque youth, more radically nationalist than the youth of the republican period, ensured that the PNV's attempts to win the new generation overemphasized the Basque dimension of the 1936 war, stressing that their topmost priority was always the defense of Basque interests rather than defense of the republic. During the Pamplona assembly, one speaker referred to the "torrents of blood spilt . . . for the Basque cause," and, again without using the expression *civil war*, to "this tremendous drama, of so much blood, so much pain, so much overwhelming sentiment" (PNV 1977: 5).

Because the memory of what happened between 1936 and 1939 as passed down by Basque nationalism was not that of a civil war (not least because this side-stepped the Pact of Santoña betrayal), the lessons derived from it were different from those learned in the rest of Spain, where the fact that a civil war took place was not questioned.[28] By telling Basque society that it was a war "between Spaniards" in which Basques were obliged to fight against their own volition, and then only to safeguard, as far as was humanly possible, the interests of their homeland, both the PNV and ETA demonstrated the following lesson: Through having in the past made a pact with Spanish forces, we suffered a bloody war that did not concern us and an oppressive dictatorship that "occupied" our land for 40 years. Therefore, we must think long and hard if we are once again to make a pact with Spanish forces since our central concern is, and must be, the Basque community.

A DIFFERENT POLITICAL CULTURE

A summary analysis of the main opinion polls carried out during the transition indicates some striking contrasts between Basque political culture and that of Spain as a whole. According to the 1975 FOESSA Report, while 51 percent of people in Spain as a whole were authoritarian and 49 percent liberal (according to the researchers' own indices), the figures for the Basque country were 31 percent and 69 percent, respectively (Fundación FOESSA 1975: 1159). Although nationally 80 percent agreed with the comment, "In Spain, the most important thing is to maintain order and peace," in the Basque country the figure was only 67 percent (ibid.: 1186).

A later FOESSA report found, first, that while 40 percent of Spaniards in general considered the maintenance of order preferable to the maintenance of liberty, only 26 percent of Basque and Navarrese people agreed (the lowest percentage in any of Spain's regions); furthermore, only 17 percent of Spaniards prioritized liberty over order compared with some 25 percent of Basques and Navarrese (again, the highest figure of any Spanish region). Secondly, while 29 percent of Spaniards as a whole defined themselves as Francoist and 36 percent anti-Francoist, the equivalent figures for the Basque and Navarrese population were 10 percent and 56 percent, respectively, the first being the lowest regional figure, the second the highest. Finally, while 60 percent of Spaniards defined themselves as monarchists and only 20 percent republicans, the figures in Navarre and the Basque Country were 35 percent and 33 percent, respectively, again the lowest and highest regional figures (Fundación FOESSA 1981: 154).

In 1979, a questionnaire was designed that combined a general survey of Spain with specific surveys of historic regions such as the Basque country.[29] Further analysis of the results demonstrates some statistically significant differences between the Spanish and Basque cases. When interviewees were asked whether they favored a monarchy or a republic, 33 percent of Basques and 62 percent of Spaniards chose the former, while 67 percent of Basques and 37 percent of Spaniards opted for the latter. When asked whether they identified with Francoism or anti-Francoism, although 25 percent of Spaniards chose the former, only 7 percent of Basques did so, compared with 93 percent of Basques who chose the latter option and 73 percent of Spaniards. The ideological distance between the two groups is also noteworthy: on a scale of 1 to 10 (where 1 represents the extreme left and 10 the extreme right), Spaniards as a whole located themselves at 5.9, and Basques at 4.4.[30]

Evaluations of the political situation at the time also differed significantly, since only 33 percent of Basques agreed with the phrase, "There are still many problems to resolve, but on the whole we cannot complain," compared with 56 percent of Spaniards. Similarly, the phrase, "The situation is growing steadily more serious, it cannot continue this way," found agreement among 67 percent of Basques but only 44 percent of Spaniards.

Particularly significant for this study of the memory of the civil war was the response to the question, "As far as you are aware, whether or not you lived through those years, which side did you or your family support in the 1936–39 war: republican or nationalist?" Among Basques the answers were 22 percent nationalist and 42 percent republican, whereas the equivalent figures for Spaniards in general were 36 percent Francoist and only 25 percent republican. Paradoxically, just over 30 percent of both groups stated they had fought for neither side, and just over 5 percent said they had fought for both.[31]

In 1991 CIRES conducted another opinion poll on political culture, using a general survey for Spain as a whole and three specific ones for the Basque country, Catalonia, and Galicia.[32] The differences in the memory the two groups had of the war had been slightly attenuated with the passing of time: in 1991, 27 percent of Basques and 34 percent of Spaniards acknowledged that a family member had fought on Franco's side, whereas 40 percent of Basques and 31 percent of Spaniards said a family member had fought for the republic. Some 22 percent of Basques stated that all members of their family of fighting age had defended the republic, while in Catalonia the equivalent figure was 20 percent and the national average was just 12 percent. Nevertheless, if we focus on the family members, friends, and acquaintances of the interviewees who lost their lives during the war, the figure for the Basque country is 8 percent lower than the national average. However, in the Basque country, the figure for those who were "held in prison" is 6 percent above the national average (CIRES 1992: 623).

Clearly, all these questions are based on the memory held by members of society at the beginning of the 1990s, through either lived or inherited experience of an event that had taken place in the 1930s. As memory evolves, so events that take place after these remembered events can modify their recollection. It is curious to see how the traumatic experience of the Franco regime in the Basque country during the 1960s was able to distort memories of experiences during the war and in the postwar period. Thus, it is possible that the recollection in the survey of the number of prisoners held in the Basque country during the war was distorted by a much more recent memory concerning the number of Basque activists imprisoned throughout the 1960s and 1970s. Although it is difficult to determine exactly how many Basques were among the high number of postwar prisoners, some provisional conclusions can be derived from official figures of court cases, broken down by province.[33] By cross tabulating these figures with the number of inhabitants in each province, we can obtain a national average of "trials initiated" in 1939: a figure of 0.149 percent. Both Guipúzcoa (0.025 percent) and Álava (0.143 percent) fall below this figure; Navarre matches it exactly (0.149 percent), while only Vizcaya, at 0.194 percent, is clearly above the national average. Furthermore, the combined average of these four provinces, at 0.127 percent, is again below the national average.

Worth highlighting in these opinion polls is the notably more negative perception of the Franco regime in the Basque country, even when compared to Catalonia.[34] It is highly probable that the scale of this perception is influenced by events that took place during the final decades of the Francoist regime, especially following the Burgos trials.[35] In fact, throughout the 1940s and 1950s, the Basque country was, at least in some ways, much better off than average in terms of Spanish society as a whole. In 1942, for example, mortality rates by province averaged 14.60 percent; for Álava, Guipúzcoa, Navarre, and Vizcaya, the figures were 13.54 percent, 13.76 percent, 13.19 percent, and 12.84 percent respectively.[36] Figures for infant mortality in these four provinces are even more striking, being below the national average for children up to the age of four. Mortality rates are usually highly significant because they reflect, albeit indirectly, nutritional, sanitary, hygienic, and, therefore, economic conditions. It is obvious that the trauma of the memory of a postwar period cannot be measured solely in light of these figures, but it is also true that the less precarious the situation in regard to food, hygiene, and sanitation the more bearable it seems.

What we are dealing with here is absolutely *not* a case of measuring "who suffered most" during the war, the postwar period, or the dictatorship (even if an adequate method of measuring and comparing different types of suffering existed). What we are seeking to demonstrate is that, contrary to what Basque nationalism has maintained, first clandestinely and then openly, the overall situation in the Basque country (at least during the war years and immediately after) was not clearly worse than in the rest of Spain but, in terms of certain indicators, substantially better. Certainly, these figures relating to "material" conditions should be tempered by others related to "cultural" repression, which although widespread most affected those areas with deep-rooted linguistic and cultural differences. However, the situation in certain areas of Andalusia, Extremadura, and La Mancha (to give just three examples) must also have been critical, since their mortality rates and, on occasions, their indices of political repression were much higher than the national average during the years analyzed.

What really seems to have occurred is that, based on a period of repression that was indeed notably more intense in the Basque country than in the rest of Spain from the end of the 1960s, nationalist rhetoric has engaged in a reconstruction of history "in reverse" which maintains that the Franco regime always operated with particular severity toward the Basque country. As Juan Linz states, the memory of the repression exacted by the dictatorship "is without doubt one of the determinants of present attitudes, even when circumstances have changed. A wide section of Euskadi's populace was not prepared to forget this past and look to the future."[37] According to the CIRES poll cited above, the percentage of Basques in agreement with the phrase, "What happened in the civil war was so terrible that it is better to forget about it than talk about it," is lower than in the rest of Spain. The Basques are also the people least in agreement with the following phrase: "The horrors and negative consequences of the civil war were suffered only by those that lived through it, or in its immediate aftermath" (CIRES 1992: 634).

According to this logic, it is usually maintained within nationalist circles, underpinned by the vast symbolic power of the bombing of Guernica,[38] that it was also the Basques who suffered most throughout the war, a conflict which still continues for those who today call themselves *gudari* (ETA activists). In fact some radical nationalists believe that the postwar period lasted right up to the end of the dictatorship, even up to the present day. Such a belief allowed the radical nationalist, Francisco Letamendía, in a speech delivered to the Cortes in 1978, to portray himself as a spokesman for a part of Basque society "that had not been able to forget the horrors of the postwar period because it has seen them reproduced in a succession of deaths, arrests, exiles and imprisonments . . . in some cases, just a few months, or even weeks, ago" (Letamendía 1994: 2: 132).

TRANSITIONS TO DEMOCRACY IN PLURINATIONAL STATES

This crucial issue has been treated, in the last few years, by some of the most well-known experts in transitions to and consolidations of democracies, such as Juan J. Linz and Alfred Stepan. In addition to the political and economic dimensions of most of the transitional periods (the latter being especially relevant in the former communist countries), when dealing with plurinational states we also have to take into account a third element related to the territorial organization of the state. One of the pioneers in emphasizing the importance of this issue was Dankwart Rustow, who pointed out that the only necessary, though not sufficient, "background condition" for a transition to take place was that the national borders of a given country should not be questioned by a majority of the population.[39] In his article, he criticized the determinist view of political change and democratic survival and rejected theses based on the existence of "necessary conditions" for a democracy to emerge. No level of economic, social, or cultural development was required to initiate a transition from dictatorship to democracy, given that most of the society agreed on the territorial definition of the country. As he wrote: "the vast majority of citizens in a democracy-to-be must have no doubt or mental reservations as to which political community they belong to." He added: "Democracy is a system of rule by temporary majorities. In order that rulers and policies may freely change, the boundaries must endure, the composition of the citizenry be countinuous" (Rustow 1970: 350–51).

This factor has not been much dealt with in most of the "transitional" literature, perhaps because it did not become a salient issue until the political transformations in former communist regimes took place. However, this was also an issue in the Spanish transition to democracy, where a major transformation of the territorial organization of the country had to be designed. The difference between the Spanish case and some of the excommunist countries is that, although it is true that statehood was also an issue in the Spain of the seventies, most of Spanish society did not consider their belonging to the Spanish state problematic. Again, this was a special conflict mainly in some sectors of the Basque country,[40] but not in most of Spain, in contrast to what happened in the former Yugoslavia.[41] What was a very controversial issue was the final shape that the administrative and territorial organization of the state should adopt.

In a plurinationalist country such as Spain, this was an additional impediment to the general political process. As we have seen, the statehood problems were rather obvious among the Basque nationalists, given their reluctance to consider themselves as part of the Spanish demos, especially after experiencing a brutal dictatorship absolutely obsessed with the preservation of national unity through the oppression of subnational diversity. If the definition of the demos is not clear enough (a significant part of the Basque population consider themselves as being "only Basques" or "more Basques than Spanish") this might generate serious problems of legitimacy and political stability.

The nationalist ideology of the PNV allows the party to order its political preferences in a very peculiar way. Apart from its attempts to monopolize the representation of the "national interest" of the Basque "community," the PNV ignored the consensus spirit that governed the Spanish transition by arguing that this spirit was contrary to its primary priorities. The loyalty dilemmas that tend to arise in plurinationalist states can be dealt with, according to David Laitin, through the articulation of "credible commitments" between the two main actors in conflict.[42]

Laitin does not agree with the primordialism of certain authors, according to which cultural identities are fixed and, as a consequence, tend to be responsible for the lack of understanding among actors. On the contrary, Laitin maintains that, in most cases, this problem (that, under certain circumstances, can lead to armed conflict) is due to a defective institutional design as well as to the existence of inadequate strategies by both actors. In order to deal with these issues it is necessary that each side fulfills certain conditions. Both have to be able to display a "credible commitment" containing both a "threat" and a "promise." On the one hand, the state has to be able to demonstrate that it is the one determining the final distribution of political resources in society. So it should not allow regionalist forces to think that it will accept all sort of demands if it does not want to have to face, at least in the short run, secessionist demands. On the other hand, the state has to be able to promise "that if regional leaders accept early concessions for devolution of power, the center will not take advantage of the ensuing political quiescence of the region to build up sufficient strength to recentralize the polity." Regional leaders have to be able to transmit the threat "that if there is no devolution of power to the region, a civil war might follow" (Laitin 1995: 25). But also they have "to make a credible promise that if they receive autonomy, they will not use their new power to escalate demands (for complete sovereignty) or to maltreat minorities within their region" (Ibid.: 25–26).

These are very suggestive theses for our case. It seems evident that neither the republicans nor the Basque nationalists were able to make credible commitments to each other, especially "promises," during the republican period and the civil war. The deep mistrust that governed the relationship between them is evident throughout the testimonies of the period. Actually, the republicans did not believe in the Basque nationalist loyalty because they always thought the latter had too many similarities with the Francoist forces (because of their political conservatism and their clericalism). In fact, as we have seen, the Basque nationalist authorities signed a secret agreement with the Italian fascists during the war in a bid to get special treatment after the conflict. On the other hand, Basque nationalists did not trust the republicans either, as they could not agree with atheists, leftists, and people supporting collectivizations during the war.

This problematic relationship was somewhat improved after the war, as both the Basque nationalists and the republicans had to go into exile, and then it was clear that the common enemy to beat was Franco. However, as their mutual mistrust had such deep historical roots, it was not easy to follow Laitin's advice during the transition to democracy. I believe, along with Laitin, that cultural identities are not fixed, but it is also evident that memories of previous treasons and a history of deep misunderstanding may make the process of creating mutual trust and credible commitments more arduous—especially in a transitional period in which there are no fixed rules and the very institutions for dealing with conflicts are being created under circumstances of high uncertainty.

The difficult equilibrium that was reached during the transition was partially broken in the constitutional debates, where the Basque nationalists were partly marginalized in the commission in charge of writing the first draft, as their interests were only represented by a nationalist Catalan. This small commission was elected according to the parliamentary seats of the main political forces, but given that the "Basque issue" was one of the most problematic during the transition, politicians should have foreseen that it was necessary to include moderate Basque forces in the institutional design of the new regime. That this was not taken into account certainly was, according to Laitin's logic, a wrong strategy. Basque nationalists, on the other hand, used their absence from the commission to exaggerate their disagreements with the final text, when actually the real differences were mainly about one article that was finally written in such abstract terms that it could have been interpreted in many different ways.

In the end, none of the Basque nationalist forces voted in favor of the constitution, which nonetheless passed with the vast majority of the votes in Parliament. The PNV even recommended its constituency abstain in the constitutional referendum of December 1978, taking advantage of the higher level of abstentions that were usually seen in the Basque country. The result of the referendum was that the constitution was clearly approved by the Spanish people, but the affirmative turnout did not reach 50 percent of the votes in either Guipúzcoa or Vizcaya. In spite of this, the affirmative vote of these two provinces was clearly higher than the negative one, but the fact that the abstention was even higher has been used ever since by the Basque nationalist forces to "show" the Basque disaffection toward a constitution that does not recognize any previous source of legitimacy.

The refusal of Basque nationalist parties to vote for the 1978 constitution (the so-called constitution of the "consensus" and "national reconciliation") can be interpreted in this way: whenever genuine nationalist political forces perceive a conflict between the interests of the state and the ones of their own community, they will pursue the latter. In the Basque case, the political learning component that underlies this argument is that nothing can be worse, under the nationalist logic, than to see their "nation" divided again, as it was in the civil war, and even under Francoism (although this is rarely made explicit). Whenever we find the coexistence of two national loyalties it is very likely that they will compete and, sooner or later, enter into conflict. This explains why nationalist forces tend to order their political preferences in peculiar ways, as the first priority is to satisfy what they consider to be their "natural" constituency, regardless of whether this causes a worse relationship with the rest of the democratic forces with respect to crucial aspects, such as the drafting of a constitution.

CONCLUSION

It is possible that the memory of the civil war had a more dramatic hue in the Basque case, but this is not, as the nationalists have so often suggested, because the war was more destructive there, or because the postwar period was harsher, or even because the political reprisals of the time were more extensive. Rather, if we leave aside the celebrated bombing of Guernica and a few other disastrous episodes, the destruction in the Basque country was less than that suffered in other areas, while survival after the war was not as difficult as elsewhere. I have also alluded to the mediating role played by the Basque church throughout the regime, which made considerable efforts to avert executions and reduce the number of convictions.

Rather, the memory of the civil war in the Basque country has such dramatic meaning because of the doubly fratricidal nature of the struggle there, especially for the nationalists. The fact that Basque and Navarrese territory was divided between those who fought to the death for the Francoist forces, supporters of the republic, and nationalist partisans, gives this conflict an even greater resonance, since it suggests the symbolic rupture of a supposedly natural collective identity, the Basque nation. Furthermore, even though both Vizcaya and Guipúzcoa lost their *conciertos económicos*, it is also the case that Álava and Navarre kept their jurisdictional privileges as a reward for their loyalty to Francoism.

A related issue is the greater level of repression unleashed by the dictatorship in the Basque country at the end of the 1960s. This became especially brutal following the emergence of ETA and its recourse to terrorism. From that point onward, the Basque country was subject to many states of exception and, at the time of Franco's death, had the largest prison population in Spain. This atmosphere of tension and confrontation allowed ETA to perpetuate the myth that they were continuing the war that began in 1936 between, according to their version, Basques and Spaniards. For them, this struggle will not cease until Euskadi is independent from the Spanish state.

For their part, moderate nationalists claim they felt obliged to take part in a war that did not concern them, since their priorities had nothing to do with those of either of the warring sides. Despite feeling compelled to fight, they always tried to prevent atrocities and reprisals and, above all, to preserve the integrity of the national community. This interpretation allowed them to justify the Pact of Santoña, particularly to a new electorate that was much more clearly nationalistic than that of the 1930s, and for whose loyalty they had to compete with another nationalist force which, for the first time in history, threatened their hegemony. The PNV now has to be much more cautious in its relations with "Spanish" parties, as there are many who attribute all the ills that have afflicted the Basque Country since 1936 to the policy of cooperation.

Thus, the principal task of moderate nationalism during the transition, while not publicly declared, was to avert the fratricidal conflict of the civil war. The issue at hand was to unite the Basques, even if this meant a worse relationship with the rest of Spain's democratic forces. In contrast to these, the PNV claimed to feel no remorse over the 1936 war. Nor did the party share the maxim implicitly adopted by the greater part of Spanish society: *todos fuimos culpables* (we were all guilty). It is this lack of a sense of guilt that led them not to make the same concessions as others felt obliged to, as they felt they had nothing to purge. According to this logic, consensus is based on feelings of guilt that are not shared by moderate nationalism. Moreover, in line with this same logic, if the nationalists suffered the most under the Franco regime and were the ones who most heroically fought the dictatorship, then it is the rest of Spanish society that is indebted to *them*, and not the reverse. This is the party rhetoric, even though its political practice, as is well known, has been much more inclined towards pacts and negotiation than might be expected from the arguments they present. However, it is obvious that statehood problems are still important in Spanish politics and that these were worsened, and nationalist demands much radicalized, by the very nature of the Francoist regimen, obsessed with the unity of the country and with the absolute centralization of political decisions.

NOTES

Previous versions of this text have been published as a working paper in the Institute of Latin American and Iberian Studies of Columbia University, New York, in 1999, and in a special issue of the *West European Politics Journal*, 21.4 (1998).

1. Part of the new institutionalist literature (particularly in its sociological and historical versions) could be very helpful in this respect, as it emphasizes the importance of historical legacies in the design of new institutions. See Steinmo, Thelen, and Long-streth 1992, and also Hall and Taylor 1996.

2. First, we should begin to call into question the "peaceful" nature of the Spanish transition, especially if we take into account that between 1975 and 1980 more than 460 people died in a violent way, whether in terrorist attacks from both extremes of the political spectrum, or in the frequent confrontations between police forces and demonstrators. Of the sixty-three deaths that have been recorded by Ramón Adell in the collective actions of this period, more than half of them took place in the Basque country. See Adell 1997. Second, the most popular demonstrations of the Spanish transition, those in which the main demand was total amnesty for political prisoners (irrespective of the result of their actions), were especially abundant and violent in the Basque country, given that most of the political prisoners of that time belonged to ETA.

3. The highest rates of abstention occurred in Guipúzcoa (55 percent) and in Vizcaya (46 percent), compared with the national average of 22 percent. See Llera 1984: 95 and Coverdale 1985: 233.

4. The percentage of votes against was greater in the Basque and Navarrese provinces (around 20 percent) than in the rest of Spain (almost 8 percent). See Coverdale 1985: 241–43. For a synthesis of electoral participation in the Basque country and the rest of Spain between 1977 and 1979, see Linz 1986: 179.

5. *Euzkadi Ta Askatasuna* (Basque Country and Freedom), the terrorist organization of radical nationalism founded in 1959. It has its origins in the EKIN group (Action), founded in 1952 by members of the youth organization of the PNV (Partido Nacional Vasco, or Basque Nationalist Party), the EGI (*Eusko Gaztedi*, or Basque Youth), and another Basque student group, EIA (*Eusko Ikasle Alkartasuna*, or Union of Basque Students). The split between the PNV and EKIN did not occur until 1958, a year before the foundation of ETA. Despite this, there were still significant transfers from EGI to ETA, even though ETA's strategies were clearly different. With the rise of ETA, the PNV had to face for the first time a serious nationalist rival. This led them, especially in the first electoral campaigns of the transition, to incline on occasion towards radical nationalism in order to ensure that the youth vote was not attracted, en masse, to this new force which soon had its own political wing, HB (*Herri Batasuna*, or United People).

6. According to Ander Gurruchaga, "of a total of eleven states of exception decreed by the regime between 1956 and 1975, ten affected either Guipúzcoa or Vizcaya, or both at the same time" (1985: 289). The same author also stresses the importance of the "stigma of defeat" that prevailed in the Basque country throughout the Franco period.

7. All these questions are related to a recent theoretical debate that is taking place in political science. Many of the authors dealing with the process of transition and consolidation have already referred to the issue of prosecuting the political elites of authoritarian regimes, to the appropriateness of purging the civil and military organizations in order to facilitate political change, and to the possibility of compensating in economic terms or, at least, of symbolically rehabilitating the victims of the dictatorships. Recently, precisely because of what has been called the "third wave" of democratizations, this debate has acquired an enormous relevance and has been called "transitional or political justice." Some of the most important contributions in this respect are Kirtz 1995 and McAdams 1997. The most recent article on this topic is Elster 1988.

8. On the endurance of certain authoritarian values, see Torcal 1995.

9. For such an account of the Second Republic, see Payne 1990.

10. Founded by Sabino Arana in 1895, the PNV was, and remains, the most important Basque nationalist party.

11. On the attitude of the PNV in the 1930s, see Fusi 1979 and de la Gramja 1986.

12. Navarre is not part of the Basque country but constitutes an independent autonomous community. Nor were these communities integrated into the same region in the 1930s. However, according to the Basque nationalists, Navarre forms part of the *Euskalerria* (Basque homeland) along with other regions in the south of France.

13. On contacts between the rebels and the PNV, see Payne 1974: 220–22, and Jiménez de Aberasturi 1979: 179.

14. As suggested by a PNV politician, a "moral identification" with ETA developed among all the democratic parties since it was the only "armed opposition" to Francoism (interview carried out by Hans-Jürgen Puhle, 20 September 1983, Code B4/C64: 17–18). These interviews are cited anonymously at the behest of those involved. I have been allowed access to them, with the permission of Professor Richard Gunther (who carried out most of them), in the library of the Juan March Institute.

15. On the amnesty demonstrations, their intimate connection with the memory of the civil war, and the specificities they acquired in the Basque country, see Aguilar 1997.

16. It also seems that the Basques were less afraid than other Spaniards of the possible outbreak of a new civil war. See the results of the CIRES poll (1992: 636) on fears that this might happen on Franco's death, with the legalization of the PCE (Spanish Communist Party), after the coup d'état of 23 February 1981, or after the PSOE (Socialist Party) took power in 1982.

17. Interview with a representative of the Basque government carried out by Richard Gunther, 20 September 1983, Code B4/C64: 18.

18. Interview with EE leader carried out by Gunther, June 1983, Code B4/C56: 5–6. EE was the nationalist political force that most explicitly articulated in the Basque Parliament fears of a repetition of fratricidal conflict. See *Diario de Sesiones del Parlamento Vasco*, 18 December 1980 and 12 February 1981.

19. Interview with EE leader, cited in former note, 6.

20. Interview by Gunther, 20 September 1983, Code B4/C63: 11.

21. Interview by Gunther, 27 June 1978, Code B1/53: 263–64.

22. Interview by Gunther, June 1983, Code B4/C58: 4.

23. Interview by Gunther, 21 June 1979, Code B1/A20: 221.

24. This fragmentation indeed exists and is reflected in the party system. See Montero and Torcal 1991: 154. Other authors highlight the existence of a divided nationalist political élite, in contrast to the Catalan case; see Laitin 1993: 22.

25. Both the PNV and ETA dedicated no little effort "to the 'mutilation' of monuments commemorating Franco's victory in the Civil War" (Sullivan 1988: 46). According to Jaúregi 1985, after 1967 ETA planned "to eliminate, with explosives, all memories of the Revolt" (456).

26. The youth of EKIN, and later of ETA, blamed postwar repression in the Basque country on the failure of the "pactist" strategy of the PNV, who should never have negotiated with the "Spanish" republican authorities.

27. For example, Telesforo Monzón (an historic PNV militant who left the party to form the first Mesa Nacional of the HB), established explicit parallels between the present dispute and that of the 1930s. "For me," says Monzón, "the war has not yet finished. The *gudaris* of today are the continuation of the *gudaris* of yesteryear" (Letamendía 1994: 2: 204).

28. The reading of the civil war as a "war against Spain," to which both nationalists and sometimes moderates subscribe, helped create the foundational myth of a future "Basque state." While the Basque government was in existence, at the height of the war, the nationalists forged the illusion that it was they who had constructed the state, to the extent that they even came to mint their own coins. The implications of this mythical construct are difficult to exaggerate since it led to the idea that only when open warfare "against Spain" was launched would it be possible to build an "independent Basque state." One author has recently commented, "Why did the memory of the Civil War have such an unparalleled impact on Basque nationalists? Was not the Civil War equally associated with national oppression in Catalonia? Unlike in Catalonia, the Civil War in the Basque Country was experienced as a nationalist war. The nationalists had their own army, the *gudariak* (Basque soldiers) . . . who created a myth of armed resistance" (Conversi 1997: 224).

29. This poll was designed by Richard Gunther, Giacomo Sani, and Goldie Shabad, who dissected these facts in the elaboration of their book, *El sistema de partidos políticos en España: Génesis y evolución* (1986). Linz 1986 also makes use of this data.

30. Ten years later the Basque electorate was still the most left-wing of all the autonomous communities with a figure of 3.9 percent compared to a Spanish national average of 4.7 percent. See Montero and Torcal 1991: 162.

31. These findings are based on the raw data in the 1979 poll.

32. Juan Díez Nicolás and Juan Díez Medrano generously allowed me to insert questions relating to the memory of the civil war in their questionnaire.

33. "Causas incoadas en los Juzgados de Instrucción, por provincias, clasificadas por los títulos del Código Penal," *Anuario Estadístico de España* (ANE) (Madrid, 1943), 1073.

34. Some 33 percent of Basques had a "very negative" opinion of the Franco regime's achievements, against only 18 percent of Catalans and 15 percent of Spaniards. See CIRES 1992: 639.

35. Many authors have stated that this event is crucial to understanding the evolution of radical nationalism and the popularity it gained in the upper echelons of Basque society.

36. Figures represent the coefficient of provincial mortality per 1000 inhabitants (ANE 1943: 147).

37. Linz, 1994, 2: 663. After the 1979 referendum on the Statute of Autonomy, 69 percent of Basques thought it better to "forget the past and think of the future," compared to 30 percent who thought that "the past cannot be ignored." See ibid., 664.

38. The bombing of Guernica was a military defeat transformed into a propaganda victory by being presented as an attempt by international fascism to annihilate the Basque country. Basque leaders also accused the republican government of not having offered them sufficient help. An important part of the victimization claim in nationalist discourse depends on the mythologizing of Guernica.

39. See the classic though still very pertinent article by Dankwart Rustow (1970).

40. In 1995 a survey on "patriotism" was undertaken by the National Opinion Research Center at the University of Chicago. More than 28,000 people were interviewed in twenty-three countries, and Spain was, along with other nations, in the top of the list measuring "National Pride in Specific Achievements," with a score of 33.1 out of a possible 50 (Ireland got the highest score with 39.3). At the bottom of the list were the countries of the former Soviet bloc, such as Hungary, Slovakia, Poland, Russia, and Latvia. See http://www.norc.uchicago.edu/new/pats.htm.

41. The former Yugoslavian case is very different but also useful to illustrate our thesis. In this case we also find the memory of a cruel civil war that took place during the Second World War. However, just to mention one important difference, in Yugoslavia this memory was used by the elites as a political weapon—just the contrary to what happened in Spain. To understand these differences, we have to take into account that the Yugoslavian civil war that took place in the forties was fought through ethnic alignments, whereas the Spanish civil war of the thirties was fought through ideological ones. According to one of the main experts in civil war studies, Roy Licklider, the likelihood of a civil war to be repeated in the future increases if that war has been fought through ethnic alignments (Licklider 1993). Also, the survey studies that we find analyzed by Dicker show, even in the seventies, the lack of willingness of an important part of the Yugoslavian society to share a common future. See his chapter in Brown and Gray 1977.

42. See Laitin 1995. I thank Ignacio Sánchez-Cuenca for having suggested this reading to me. He himself has written an excellent article on a related topic (Sánchez-Cuenca 1998).

REFERENCES

Adell, R. 1997. "Manifestations et Transition Démocratique en Espagne." *Les Cahiers de la Sécurité Intérieure*, no. 27: 203–22.

Aguilar, P. 1996. *Memoria Olvido de la Guerra Civil Española*. Madrid: Alianza Editorial.

——. 1997. "Collective Memory of the Spanish Civil War: The Case of the Political Amnesty in the Spanish Transition to Democracy." *Democratization* 4, no. 4 (winter).

Azurmendi, M. "Vascos que, para serlo, necesitan enemigo." *Claves* 70.

Brown, A., and J. Gray, eds. 1977. *Political Culture and Political Change in Communist States*. London: MacMillan Press.

CIRES. 1992. *La realidad social en España 1990–1991*. Bilbao: Fundación BBV/Caja de Madrid.

Conversi, D. 1997. *The Basques, the Catalans, and Spain. Alternative Routes to Nationalist Mobilization*. Reno: University of Nevada Press.

Coverdale, J. F. 1985. "Regional Nationalism and the Elections in the Basque Country." In H. R. Penniman and E. M. Mujal-Léon, eds., *Spain at the Polls, 1977, 1979, and 1982*. Durham, N.C.: Duke University Press.

De Blas, A. 1988. "La izquierda española y el nacionalismo. El caso de la transición." *Leviatán* 32.

De la Gramja, J. L. 1986. *Nacionalismo y Il República en el Pais Vasco*. Madrid: CIS/Siglo XXI.

Elster, J. 1988. "Coming to Terms with the Past. A Framework for the Study of Justice in the Transition to Democracy." *Archives Européennes de Sciologie* I, 39: 7–48.

Fundación FOESSA. 1975. *Informe sociológico sobre la situación social de España*. Madrid: Euroamérica.

——. 1981. *Informe sociológico sobre el cambio politico en España (1975–1981)*. Madrid: Euroamérica.

Fusi, J. P. 1979. *El problema vasco en la Il Republica*. Madrid: Turner.

——. 1984. *El Pais Vasco. Pluralismo y nacionalidad*. Madrid: Alianza Editorial.

Garmendia, J. M., and M. González Portilla. 1993. "Crecimiento económico y actitudes politicas de la burguesia vasca en la postguerra." In Isidro Sánchez et al., eds., *España franquista. Causa general y actitudes sociales ante la dictadura*. Albacete: Universidad de Castilla La Mancha.

Gunther, R., G. Sani, and G. Shabad. 1986. *El sistema de partidos politicos en España: Génesis y evolución*. Madrid: CIS / Siglo XXI.

Gurruchaga, A. 1985. *El código nacionalista vasco durante el franquismo*. Barcelona: Anthropos.

Hall, P. A., and R. Taylor. 1996. "Political Science and the Three New Institutionalisms." *Political Studies*, vol. 44: 939–57.

Ibarrábal, E., ed. 1978. *Cincuenta años de nacionalismo vasco*. Bilbao: Ediciones Vascas.

Jaúregi, G. 1985. *Ideologia y estrategia politica de ETA. Análisis de su evolución entre 1959 y 1968*. Madrid: Siglo XXI.

Jiménez de Aberasturi, J. C., and L. M. Jiménez de Aberasturi. 1979. *La guerra en Euskadi*. Plaza y Janés.

Kirtz, N. J. 1995. *Transitional Justice*. 3 vols. Washington, D.C.: United States Institute of Peace Press.

Laitin, D. 1993. "National Revivals and Violence." *Estudios/Working Paper* 49 (June).

Linz, J. J. 1986. *Conflicto en Euskadi*. Madrid: Espasa-Calpe.

———. 1995. "Transitions to Democracy and Territorial Integrity." In A. Przeworski, ed., *Sustainable Democracy*. Cambridge: Cambridge University Press.

Letamendía, F. 1994. *Historia del nacionalismo y del ETA*. 3 vols. San Sebastián: R&B Ediciones.

Licklider, R. 1993. *Stopping the Killing: How Civil Wars End*. New York: New York University Press.

Llera, F. J. 1984. *Postfranquismo y Fuerzas Politicas en Euskadi: Sociologia Electoral del Pais Vasco*. Bilbao: Universidad del Pais Vasco.

McAdams, J. 1997. *Transitional Justice and the Rule of Law in New Democracies*. Notre Dame: University of Notre Dame Press.

Montero, J. R., and M. Torcal. 1991. "Autonomias y comunidades autónomas en España: preferencia, dimensiones y orientaciones politicas." In A. Figueroa and E. Mancisidor, eds., *Poder politico y Comunidades Autónomas*. Vitorio: Parlamento Vasco.

Payne, S. 1974. *El nacionalismo vasco*. Barcelona: DOPESA.

———. 1990. *Spain's First Democracy. The Second Republic, 1931–1936*. University of Wisconsin Press.

PNV. 1977. *Iruña 77*. Pamplona: La Asamblea.

———. 1978. *El PNV ante la Constitución. Historia y alcance de unas negociaciones*. Zarauz: Itxaropena.

Rustow, D. 1970. "Transitions to Democracy: Toward a Dynamic Model." *Comparative Politics* 2, no. 3: 337–63.

Sánchez-Cuenca, I. 1998. "Institutional Commitments and Democracy." *European Journal of Sociology*, vol. 39: 78–109.

Stenmo, S., K. Thelen, and F. Longstreth. 1992. *Structuring Politics. Historical Institutionalism in Comparative Analysis*. Cambridge: Cambridge University Press.

Sullivan, J. 1988. *El nacionalismo vasco radical 1959–1986*. Madrid: Alianza Editorial.

Torcal, M. 1995. "Actitudes politicas y participación política en España: pautas de cambio y continuidad." Ph.D. diss., Universidad Autónoma, Madrid.

When Do Collective Memories Last?: Founding Moments in the United States and Australia

◀ ◀ ◀ ◀ ◀ ◀ ◀ ◀ ◀ ◀ ◀ ◀ ◀ ◀   LYN SPILLMAN

In 1876, there was a huge commemoration of the centennial of American independence. The year was marked in many ways, by many groups, in many parts of the country. The central event, though, was a grand International Exhibition in Philadelphia, four years in the making. Planners first met in 1872 in Independence Hall and spoke at length about the sacredness of the venue: "It is altogether fit and wise that we should take our first step and utter our first words in this hall. There sat John Hancock, presiding over that immortal body. There came Jefferson, Franklin, Adams, Sherman, and Livingston presenting the sacred declaration. There lies the broken and silent bell, which at the word proclaimed liberty throughout the land to all the inhabitants thereof" (USCC 1873: 24–25). The theme was taken up by many others in many different ways. Images of the Liberty Bell, Independence Hall, Washington, and Franklin were scattered throughout centennial ceremonies, buildings, poems, histories, and other documents. The revolution was used as a touchstone in talk about the exhibition and as a rich source of national symbolism.

The language of the nineteenth-century commemoration can seem somewhat inflated for twentieth-century tastes, but the grounding of such claims and sentiments remains familiar. In many circumstances, the events and personalities of the American Revolution seem to exist as significant, influential, and constraining dimensions of the national past. A sense of shared experience through time seems crucial to national identity. And for "new nations" such as the United States, founding moments like the Revolution seem integral to the shared national past (Anderson 1991; Lipset 1979: 74–98).

Although founding moments of new nations can seem intrinsically significant, scholars of collective memory will be quick to note the many ways in which the meanings of events like the Revolution are constructed on the basis of contemporary cultural politics. Indeed, this is suggested in the very occasion of the address above, a meeting of predominantly East Coast economic and political elites planning a national centennial celebration only a few years after the Civil War. The place of the American Revolution in national collective memory provides good ground for claiming both that the past is malleable and that it is fixed.

For this reason, American memory of the revolutionary period makes an especially charged case for investigating a key debate about the nature of collective memory. In the following section I outline both competing claims about the constraining power of past events and competing explanations for why some collective memories are robust (see Schwartz 1991: 221–22). While I locate cultural action formulating collective memory in the present, I suggest that it is necessary to go beyond constructionist assumptions that would attribute all apparent persistence in collective memory to contemporary cultural production. I identify ways in which the intrinsic meaning of the past may, indeed, constrain or enable those actions. I argue for a new way of mediating the sense that the past is fixed and knowledge of the past is malleable, an approach that explains why some collective memories are persistent and some are not.

Grounding this argument is a close comparison of collective memory in American and Australian centennial and bicentennial commemorations. The two countries share many historical experiences that could provide cultural resources for claims about collective memory, and the commemorations were produced in very similar ways. Perhaps unexpectedly, and as the following analysis will demonstrate, these similarities were more important for formulations of collective memory than differences in the timing of formal unification were. These events in these countries allow an argument about the persistence of collective memory based on the logic of similar-case comparison: competing explanations for different outcomes can be eliminated due to the similarity in background factors (Smelser 1976). In the second section of this essay, I discuss the context in which collective memories were mobilized. I pay particular attention to producers, audiences, and critics of claims about each national identity.

The third part of this paper assesses the importance of founding moments in collective memories during American and Australian centennial and bicentennial discourse. I show first how the American emphasis on the "founding" events of the 1770s persisted as a key element of collective memory in both 1876 and 1976. I then outline the somewhat counterintuitive counterpoints provided by the Australian case. The Australian emphasis on the founding moment of British invasion and settlement was surprisingly important in 1888 but had evaporated in central constructions of national history by 1988.

What could account for these different outcomes? In the fourth section, I argue that the period of the founding moment has remained symbolically compelling to Americans because, in contrast to the Australian founding, it offers multivalent symbols to bridge gulfs between mainstream cultural producers and their critics. As a result, it has been a persistent and robust element of national collective memory.

MALLEABILITY AND CONSTRAINT
IN COLLECTIVE MEMORY

"Selective traditions," as Raymond Williams (1973: 9) put a well-canvassed point, are characterized by the "way in which from a whole possible area of past and present, certain meanings and practices are chosen for emphasis, certain other meanings and practices are neglected and excluded . . . [and] some of these meanings and practices are reinterpreted, diluted, or put into forms which support or at least do not contradict other elements within the effective dominant culture." Collective memories are malleable, and on this view, the ways we know history are determined more by contemporary concerns than by history itself (if the notion of a history independent of the present can be meaningful at all).

Contemporary concerns may be understood as the interests of dominant groups (Hobsbawm and Ranger 1984; Benson et al. 1986; cf. Schudson 1992: 52–54): in this sense a "social" history recapturing marginalized voices challenges orthodox collective memory. But the influence of contemporary concerns may also be understood more broadly. For instance, as Barry Schwartz (1982: 396) argues in his study of Capitol iconography, "America's originating events and early leaders are not symbols of national unity because of their priority and factual importance but because . . . [they are] convenient objects of consensus among later generations." The general arguments of Maurice Halbwachs and George Herbert Mead for the malleability of history support studies that demonstrate interested manipulation, but they also make a broader case for present-dependent pasts. In Halbwachs's terms, contemporary ideas prevail because "such ideas correspond to a collective experience, if not as ancient, at least much larger" (Halbwachs 1992 [1952]: 184; Maines et al. 1983).

Evidence of the influence of contemporary concerns on collective memory abounds for the United States as elsewhere. Studies of changing and different interpretations of the same cultural object, such as the Revolution or Columbus (e.g., Kammen 1978; Trouillot 1990); studies of different memories and interpretations of history among different groups (e.g., Fabre and O'Meally 1994; Schultz 1991; Bodnar 1992); and studies of historiographical and commemorative politics (e.g., Gillis 1994; Glassberg 1990; Kammen 1991; Warner 1959: 107–225) all illustrate in different ways the malleability of the past. In this line of research and argument, changes in collective memories are attributed to active processes of memory construction by groups and individuals responding to contemporary sensibilities and interests (Thelen 1990: xvii). That is, broadly considered conditions of cultural production—political alignments and fissures as expressed in memory-producing organizations and practices— carry the full theoretical weight of explaining persistence and change in collective memory. The connection between processes of social construction and emergent or fading meanings themselves is often established in close empirical analysis, but among those who argue for the malleability of collective memory, generalization about the specifically cultural processes involved is rare (cf. Olick and Levy 1997).[1]

Karen Cerulo (1995: 145–65) remedies this weakness by developing an analytic framework for understanding cultural processes involved in symbolic change. She argues that charged symbolic associations fail when they are blocked or suspended—when old symbols are too concrete for referents that have changed, or when old become irrelevant. Her study of patterns of change in anthems and flags shows that the most concrete national symbols are most susceptible to change because a charged bond between concrete symbol and referent is more easily blocked or suspended than that between a more abstract or multivalent symbol and referent. Of particular relevance here is her finding that where referents are dynamic, as the "nation" is, more abstract, multivalent symbols are more robust. Cerulo's theory of symbol change suggests a cultural framework for integrating accumulated evidence of the constant reinterpretations and frequent elisions of collective memory. A number of scholars have assumed or argued the point that, as David Kertzer puts it, "it is the very ambiguity of the symbols employed in ritual action that makes ritual useful in fostering solidarity without consensus" (1989: 69). But Cerulo's work specifies and develops this general point by analyzing conditions under which ambiguity might vary.

Such a theoretical development may not be considered necessary by those who place the entire weight of accounts of collective memory on the varying politics of cultural production. But to take this view is to ignore arguments that some transgenerational character is intrinsic to collective memory. Some scholars, though they do not deny the busy process of construction and reconstruction, resist any implication that memory entrepreneurs have a blank slate. Past events often seem to exercise some nontrivial constraint on collective memory: "Traditional patterns of belief and conduct . . . are very insistent; they will not wholly release their grip on those who would suspend or abolish them" (Shils 1981: 200). While they recognize dissent, innovation, and apathy regarding memory and tradition, some argue that there must still be something more—at least some continuous cultural object of dissent, innovation, and apathy.

On this view, there are both functional and charismatic reasons for the persistence of the past, although these two different sorts of reasons are not always clearly distinguished. Functionally, groups and societies rely on a "pattern which guides the reenactment" of particular states of mind, actions, ideas, and social relationships (ibid.: 31): every society requires some fixed continuity with past concerns. In particular, shared collective memories provide "a temporal order . . . [that] contributes to the establishment of intergroup boundaries" and thus solidarity (Zerubavel 1981:

6; see also Schwartz 1991: 222). Further, socially diffused propensities for and attributions of charisma are generated by "whatever embodies, expresses or symbolizes the essence of an ordered cosmos or any significant sector thereof" (Shils 1965: 203).

Persistence in national collective memory receives most nuanced empirical attention in Schwartz's studies of national heroes (Schwartz 1982, 1987, 1990, 1991). While he recognizes ongoing innovation in the images of Washington and Lincoln, he argues that there is also significant continuity. Change comes about more through superimposition than through displacement; societies sustain variant memories at the same time, including more traditional formulations (1982: 396; 1991: 234). Fundamentally, older images persist because of "the endurance of the social relations they symbolize" through large-scale change (1991: 233; see also 1990: 104), and the continuity sets limits to changes in collective memories of the heroes. The past is somewhat malleable, but important constraints on changes to contemporary interpretations do exist.[2]

Arguments for the general necessity of tradition do not imply that any particular event, person, or interpretation is necessary to collective memory. But taken together, such arguments are mobilized to limit the theoretical scope of generalization from constructionist observations. They are especially important here because national founding moments are compelling candidates for continuity and constraint in collective memory. Selected " 'beginnings' of chronological eras" are particularly important for the group solidarity temporal orders can generate (Zerubavel 1981: 86). If any past events "demand narration," constitutive moments of nation-states would seem to do so (Shils 1981: 211).[3]

Both perspectives on collective memory provide leads for a "systematic analysis of factors that lead events or objects to be retained or lost" (Swidler and Arditi 1994: 309). What sorts of things account for persistence or change of elements of collective memory? Some factors are considered important on both sides of the issue. One line of argument and research identifies individual-level determinants and processes such as generational experience and identity investment (Schuman and Scott 1989; Schudson 1989: 109–12; Middleton and Edwards 1990). More relevant to longer-term collective memories such as national founding moments, an important set of factors accounting for either persistence or change concerns institutions and processes of cultural production

(Schudson 1989; Spillman 1997: 33–37; see also Peterson 1994). Records, memorials, the "memory industry," professions, historiographical conventions and attitudes, teaching conventions, holidays, commercially produced cultural objects, and so on may all influence what may be remembered and forgotten. Institutional interests and identities may be structured in ways that encourage or allow continuous collective memories. But they may also be the sites of cultural politics that generate important new additions, omissions, and variant interpretations of the ways in which the past is perceived.

Where malleability and constraint perspectives differ most is in the analytic resources they offer for accounts of why and how some events and cultural objects can be *meaningful* across generations and across patterns of institutional change. How can we account for long-lasting and persistent collective memories? Empirical studies that presuppose malleability attribute persistence to dominant institutional investments. Such an account becomes less plausible, though, the older a collective memory is: in the course of a period of more than a couple of generations, institutional determinants like professional organizations, historiographical conventions, memorials, and holidays change in important ways. Indeed, evidence of such change—and many cases of resulting historical amnesia—is often suggested by malleability studies themselves. There seems to be something more than institutionalized cultural production that gives collective memories long-term meaning.

Those who would argue for the strength of traditional constraints on changes in collective memory on the grounds of institutional interests and inertia also face this problem in accounting for persistent collective memories. However, many "constraint" arguments are based as much on the power of meaning as on the power of culture-producing institutions. Memories are at least partly sustained by the charisma of shared cross-generational narratives, a charisma based on a functional imperative for some shared temporal order. Proponents of the power of tradition, then, would account for persistent collective memories in terms of their meaning as much as their institutional base. Regardless of institutional forces, something *intrinsic to the meaning* of some past events generates their sustained collective memory.

An account of collective memory based entirely on a postulate of malleability provides only a weak explanation of sustained, powerful, and persistent collective memories. An account based entirely on a postulate of constraint provides a stronger explanation of persistent collective memories, by locating part of their power in the meaning of the past event itself. But if constraint theories account better for charismatic memories, they cannot then account well for changes in memories that *have been* charismatic. If some memories persist because of something intrinsically compelling about them, later historical amnesia about those events becomes inexplicable.

This impasse is best resolved by combining virtues of both postulates. Drawing from constraint perspectives, I suggest here that intrinsic properties of the meaning of some past objects and events do sometimes influence their power and persistence in subsequent collective memory. But these properties are aspects not of their inherent, necessary, constitutive charisma but rather of their potential semiotic multivalence, which generates links between symbol and referent less likely to be blocked or suspended. Ongoing construction and reconstruction of collective memory, emphasized in malleability perspectives, characterize processes generating persistence, as well as change. But some past events and objects intrinsically offer more meaningful ground for construction and contention, and these are more likely to persist in collective memory.

The events of the past may offer either thin or rich possibilities for grounding contemporary critical claims. If they offer rich symbols for grounding later critique, they may be more persistently remembered. If, on the other hand, they are better objects of criticism than grounds of critique, they will be less robust in the face of later social changes. That is, the cultural richness and multivalency of past events does influence subsequent possibilities in collective memory. At the same time, if the cultural possibilities are decided in the past, the action that makes collective memory is firmly located in the present.

CENTENNIALS, BICENTENNIALS, AND THE PRODUCTION OF NATIONAL IDENTITY

Centennials in 1876 and 1888 and bicentennials a century later were transient but very intense occasions organized by coalitions of groups constituting a cultural center, aiming to evoke widespread participation and to avoid extensive dissent.[4] Organizers addressed their peripheries in ways that would encourage national participation; those who ignored attempts to make a celebration threatened their project of enacting national community. In each event, organizers also took particular pains to defuse the claims of their most vocal critics. Within this framework, the constitution of cultural centers and their peripheries varies across time and place, in ways that can be specified against the background of the shared form of cultural production (Shils 1988; Schudson 1994).

The forms and organizational structure of the centennials, and later the bicentennials, were remarkably similar. This makes the comparison of claims about national identity possible, despite the fact that Americans were commemorating their revolution and Australians were commemorating what was, on the face of it, the much less inspiring occasion of invasion and first convict settlement on the continent. Even the fact that Americans were celebrating a century of formal sovereignty, and Australians in 1888 were not yet formally unified, had little influence on the production of claims about national identity in these events. For Australians, a language of national identity was well developed and available for mobilization by 1888: in some ways, Australians found it even easier to talk about national identity than did Americans, who faced problems due to the consequences of the Civil War.

Because of the need for the appearance of national inclusion (at least by contemporary lights), and because of the wide vernacular appeal of patriotic claims, discourse about national identity was not confined to organizers: in each of these events, a large number and wide variety of mainstream and oppositional groups had something to say about what their nations meant. What they said was recorded in rich stores of documents ranging from commemorative volumes through poems, sermons, newsletters, and magazines, to minutes and videos and ephemera such as banquet programs and promotional flyers. While organizers' records of centennial and bicentennial reflections on national identity are richest, numerous records of "civil society" groups that mobilized for the celebration, businesses taking advantage of the commemorations, critical groups antagonized by organizers, and local events, speeches, and poems also form the basis of the following analysis.

Central organizers of the American centennial in 1876 were East Coast business and professional elites (Rydell 1984).[5] Adopting a genre that was spreading worldwide, they held an international exhibition in Philadelphia, which provided the focus for activities of many states, businesses, and foreign countries, and many special-interest groups in civil society, including, among many other types, professionals, businessmen, and women's groups. Organizers worked hard to mobilize many of these groups and organizations with early promotional letters; others attached their interests and causes to the event independently. In the process, a wide variety of identities and interests within contemporary society were associated with national identity. But though the Philadelphia exhibition was the central event of the year, events and reflections on the centennial were also made throughout much of the country, especially in Fourth of July speeches and parades but also in poems, articles, sermons, commercially or locally produced histories, and ephemera such as almanacs or books that published the work of schoolchildren (cf. Campbell c. 1980; Randel 1969; Brown 1966).[6]

Mobilization efforts and widespread vernacular interest were not enough, of course, to create universal inclusion, and critique, indifference, and both active and unconscious exclusion also characterized the centennial construction of national identity. Organizers had only limited success in mobilizing federal government support: unlike most other such events, the American centennial was not created under the umbrella of the state.[7] A related problem for organizers, and one central to the way they directed their efforts, was regional inclusion. Only a decade after the Civil War, southern disaffection remained strong, and southern states refused to participate in the exhibition, although numerous individuals and some southern groups did take part privately. Participation in the West was also somewhat weak, although far less contentious than that in the South. Organizers saw regional integration as one of their central cultural goals, and they met with some of their most difficult critiques from regions still culturally, economically, and politically distant from the settled East.

American organizers also met with critique and more subtle resistance from a number of women's groups. Some mobilized independent networks that supported the centennial along with women's issues and ultimately produced a widely noticed Women's Pavilion for the exhibition, as well as numerous other centennial markers. More radical feminists demonstrated at Fourth of July ceremonies in Philadelphia to draw attention to women's issues (Greenhalgh 1988: 174–78; Andres 1976–77).

Other problems in the national public sphere were less central to public discourse about national identity at the time, although they are clear in hindsight. Surprisingly, immigrants were little noticed in discourse about national identity, although some immigrant groups did meet to mark the occasion in Philadelphia. Labor and labor groups were little recognized as part of the "nation" and took little part in the occasion.[8] Perhaps less unexpectedly, African Americans did attempt centennial participation but were met with active exclusion and were barely noticed in patriotic discourse (Foner 1976; Rydell 1984: 27–29; cf. Litwak 1989). Native Americans were more central to mainstream public discourse than either immigrants, labor, or African Americans in the centennial year, but they constituted an interior "other" for the construction of national identity (Rydell 1984: 23–27; Trennert 1974). The surviving documentary evidence of centennial discourse is so rich that some reflections on and by each of these groups can be found; but on the whole, none of these groups were considered relevant in the central construction of national identity, and little critique or national vision originating with these groups entered the public sphere.

As in the United States in 1876, the Australian centennial of 1888 was organized by elites to invite the participation of all members of the nation as they imagined it, and these elites successfully mobilized a wide variety of commercial, professional, state, religious, and other mainstream groups. Unlike in the United States, the elite umbrella was created by the state: colonial governments in New South Wales and Victoria, the two most important and populous colonies on the continent, held big "national" events. Around Australia Day in January, New South Wales held a week of celebrations in Sydney that evoked widespread participation and brought many official and unofficial visitors from provincial areas and from all other colonies (Moore 1888; Davison 1988a). These official and unofficial notables traveled to mark the centennial again in August, when Victoria held an exceptionally well-attended Centennial International Exhibition (Davison 1988a). More modest events and commentary marked the centennial in more remote colonies and country towns. Although the stronger, though colonial, states took a greater role in Australian centennial organization than Washington did in 1876, the Australian colonial governments also played a more active role in economic development than Washington did, and the Australian events were equally influenced by economic elites.

Critique was, on the whole, less explicit and challenging to organizers of the Australian centennial than it had been to American organizers, but organizers of the Sydney and Melbourne events were immersed in somewhat similar issues. Again, regional integration was high on the agenda. Future federation of the colonies was widely expected, and talk of federation was a commonplace of public discourse, but each colony still had a separate government, and colonies competed and quarreled over many mundane issues. Competition between New South Wales and Victoria over the celebration of the centennial (a centennial of the founding of New South Wales as a penal colony) was resolved, with some chagrin, by holding both the Sydney celebrations and the Melbourne exhibition. While many in each of the four other, less developed colonies spoke of Australian identity along with colonial identities and participated in some way in marking the centennial, these colonies were culturally and economically more distant. Regional integration was not as contentious as it had been in the United States, but it was certainly a public issue.

The challenges and silences of other groups in response to Australian centennial mobilization make an intriguing comparison to the American case. There was an active labor movement in Australia by 1888: the voice of labor was recognized and, to some extent, included in centennial discourse, in somewhat the way that American women challenged mainstream constructions within the national public sphere. By contrast, Australian women's organizations seem to have taken little independent part in the centennial, and the imagined nation of centennial discourse was mostly masculine. Immigrants were little noticed in Australian centennial discourse: the mostly British newcomers were part of the cultural center organizing the nation. Australian aborigines were not included and received little attention in centennial events. When noticed, they constituted an interior "other" and, like Native Americans, provided a contrast by which national identity was defined. However, aborigines were not characterized as threatening to "Australians" in the way Native Americans often were to "Americans."

The production of national identities in bicentennials in 1976 and 1988 also took place in a process of organization by coalitions of central groups encouraging the marking of the occasion by innumerable more peripheral "civil society" groups. In both bicentennials, as in both centennials, organizers aimed to encourage widespread participation, and in the process they attempted to preempt opposition, critique, and apathy.[9]

Exhibitions were no longer viable centerpieces of national celebration by the time of the bicentennials.[10] Rather, thousands of particular events and activities were organized, some directly by the Australian Bicentennial Authority (ABA) and the American Revolution Bicentennial Administration (ARBA), and many more by the numerous groups they mobilized. For instance, a central program in each year focused on "bicentennial communities." These programs linked central organizations with local events through promotional activities, registration, and recognition. More than 12,000 communities received recognition under ARBA's Bicentennial Communities Program, and over 66,000 community activities were registered in their Binet database. In Australia, most of the 845 local government areas formed Bicentennial Community Committees, and over 24,000 activities were registered.

Two key differences in center-periphery relations marked both bicentennials by contrast to events a century earlier. First, federal governments were more important for generating bicentennial activity than had been possible in either country (for different reasons) 100 years earlier. The ABA and ARBA were formed by the respective national governments: they were umbrellas to the many other groups involved (e.g., communities, interest groups of all sorts, corporations and other commercial interests, the media, educational institutions, states, etc.). Second, central organizers in the late twentieth century faced the need to address, mobilize, and preempt criticism from a wider public sphere if they were to create a plausible expression of imagined community. Whereas issues of regional integration had been most important to centennial organizers, their successors found the attempted symbolic inclusion of marginalized groups highest on their agenda. American organizers were especially influenced by critique from New Left youth groups, women's groups, and ethnic and racial groups. Australian organizers attempted to address women's and immigrants' issues, and their greatest challenge came from aboriginal groups and their supporters, as I show later.

In each of these four events, expressions of national identity were created in a process of cultural production best characterized by examining the dynamic interrelations of cultural centers and peripheries. The constitution of these centers and peripheries differed according to national and temporal context. But in each case, coalitions of elite groups formed a cultural center that went to enormous if long-forgotten trouble to mobilize "the nation" as planners imagined it. Many groups active in civil society responded to this mobilization, and the events also generated uncountable local and vernacular patriotic expressions. Organizers oriented their actions to countering disaffection and salient dissent, too, and in this way critical groups also sometimes influenced expressions of national identity. Political pressures always mattered in the making of these national celebrations, but the nature of the relevant political pressures changed markedly between the nineteenth and twentieth centuries and differed somewhat between the United States and Australia. Beyond the influence of active critique, some groups remained victims of deeper, unrecognized national exclusion, beyond the boundaries of the relevant public sphere. In this production context themes of national identity were developed and contested. Among those themes, collective memory of founding moments played an important part.

FOUNDING MOMENTS IN NATIONAL COMMEMORATION

The American Revolution resonates as the classically charismatic constitutive moment in national collective memory over two centuries. In both centennial and bicentennial years, history was told mostly as a history of the 1770s, largely distanced from the myriad other significant events and processes of the intervening centuries. The commemorations of 1876 and 1976 were never simply occasions for broader national reflection: they demanded elaborate and rich discourses on the revolutionary period itself.

Revolutionary history was often seen as sacred and always as worthy of reference. As the author of one elaborate volume produced for the commemorative market put it: "Who is there amongst us that, at least, does not revere all matters connected with the birth of his country?" (Brotherhead c. 1872: iii). The Declaration of Independence was central in every speech and ceremony because "it has kept its place in history; . . . it will maintain itself while human interest in human institutions shall endure" (Evarts 1876: 76). References to Washington and the revolutionary period also appeared in most of the unofficial literature of the centennial, in guides, almanacs, poems, and speeches produced by many different groups. Fireworks, interpreted elaborately, included displays like the one that supposedly represented an "Allegory of Independence . . . at the termination of which will appear America, with her right hand pointing to the old Independence Bell" (Centennial Board of Finance 1875: 14).

The revolutionary era also provided a widely used basis for claims to inclusion in the nation. Writers and speakers in a wide range of groups used a link with the founding moment to establish the legitimacy of their participation in the celebration. Catholics pointed to John Carroll's part in the Revolution (e.g., Clarke 1876: 16); women's groups drew attention to heroines like Washington's mother, "who nobly reared Virginia's godlike chief" (Ladies' Centennial Committee of Rhode Island 1875: 1). As did all who could, New Jersey participants in the celebration likened their support to their state's earlier revolutionary role: "As in the Revolution, when the dark days came, New Jersey made her small subscription at the moment when it was most needed and gave most encouragement" (New Jersey State Centennial Board 1877: 87).

A hundred years later, the nation looked very different, and much had changed in commemorative organization itself. But American commemoration organizers still stressed the revolutionary period when they tried to imagine shared history, despite the fact that a wide variety of more local and vernacular histories were newly available for inclusion in national commemoration (Kammen 1991). So, in a typical story of the event, planners told in their newsletter of how "New Jersey and Pennsylvania are preparing to focus on George Washington's daring midnight crossing of the semi-frozen Delaware River in the last major reenactment commemorating the nation's Bicentennial" (ARBA 1977: 389). The *Bicentennial Times* stressed revolutionary history much more than other available memories: for instance, they told of a new National Guard Heritage Gallery showing displays "with emphasis on the role of the militia in the Revolutionary War" and reported that the Henry Ford Museum presented artifacts and firsthand accounts of "life at the time of the Revolution" (ibid.: 347). Issues of inclusion were mediated through founding-moment history: for instance, organizers told stories of the "Lesser-Known Women of the Revolution Brought to the Fore by the Bicentennial" (ibid.: 376). Even immigrants from India could "at least be proud that their ancestors helped the colonies in America by dividing the strengths and resources of the British during the Revolution" (ibid.: 417). In main-stream American collective memory, the "founding moment" remained a robust symbol grounding claims about national identity, as significant in 1976 as it had been in 1876. Of course, interpretations and emphases in contemporary understanding of the period were different, but the important point here is that interpretations of national history focused on this period rather than others.

Aspects of history and elements of collective memory apart from the revolutionary period were, on the whole, less significant to those who spoke of the nation in both commemorations. During the centennial, the national century was sometimes framed as one of progress, especially among commercial and industrial elites focusing on economic change (Rydell 1984), but this theme seemed surprisingly rare among other groups. During the bicentennial, progress made an even less compelling framework for discussing history since the Revolution, although local communities and groups, if not central organizers, did commemorate other aspects of the nation's past in particularistic ways. The founding moment of the Revolution was not the only historical period or event mentioned, of course, in either national commemoration; but it was so much more salient and central than other collective memories that these events provide strong support for other observations that the Revolution is often treated as "the end of history" (Bodnar 1992: 234; Spillman 1997: 76–78, 141; Schwartz 1991: 225; Glassberg 1990).

The place of the American Revolution in national collective memory apparently provides ideal-typical evidence of the importance and per-sistence of charismatic constitutive narrative in the founding moments of new nations. The revolutionary period had indeed seen genuinely innova-tive politics, with worldwide consequences, and it had been, among other things, the forging of an identity in conflict. It thus seems quite natural that the Americans developed a "thick description" of their shared identity in a founding historical moment. In many ways, though, discourse about history during the Australian centennial of British invasion and convict settlement in 1888 makes an even stronger case for the constitutive im-portance of founding moments in the collective memory of new nations. In Australia, as in the United States, in the late nineteenth century, the founding moment was important in national identity, not merely the excuse or occasion for celebration. Founding moments took on about equal weight and salience in each centennial.

All the Australians had to claim was a disreputable event in which, as Australians, they took no part. The Australian "founding moment" was inglorious, the beginnings of a penal colony and a life remote from anything Europeans valued. In contemporary thinking, that the first settlers were convicts was still thought to be a humiliating subject (e.g., Roe 1989). Yet, counterintuitively, centennial Australians made constant references to the "founding moment" of British settlement in almost all of the official and unofficial records they left of Australia's centennial year. It was part of what national identity meant, accumulating a density of meaning beyond any necessary reference to the occasion.

The Australian founding moment was often told as an episode of heroic settlement, with the details glossed over. In this narrative, a land of "perpetual solitude" was claimed for British freedom and "pastoral pioneers" (Plummer 1887: 3; Allen 1890: 195). Surprisingly frequently, the founding was characterized as the visit of Captain Cook to Australia 18 years before convict settlement. Thus, for instance, Australia's Centennial International Exhibition in Melbourne included "a tableau of Captain Cook landing at Botany Bay, and many interesting relics of the great navigator," but no apparent reference to the convict settlement that was the occasion of commemoration (Centennial International Exhibition Commission 1890: 213). In one melodramatic verse play from a girls' school, "immortal Cook, that sets my heart aflame" was imagined as a rescuing hero "where lone Australia in silence sleeps, / Or waking, still her desolation weeps" (Celebration in Commemoration 1888: 9, 7). Vague stories of heroic settlement typically ignored aborigines and the European occupation's impact on them. But vagueness was due to embarrassment about convict settlement not invasion (cf. Griffiths 1987). Despite the strong reasons to ignore the founding, though, a founding-moment vision was a significant part of national collective memory in Australia in 1888. Imprecise but heroic stories of the founding as discovery and settlement were meaningful themes to white Australians.

Where the weight of the historical record and the demands of the genre of discourse precluded vagueness, Australians spoke of their founding as a benchmark of progress. Recognizing that "the first period of our history

presents many painful details," they could glory in the myriad achievements of the century: one sermon noted "how marvelous is the transformation" and claimed that it was "impossible to exaggerate the importance
of the first settlement in Australia in 1788, whether regarded in a religious, scientific, commercial, or utilitarian point of view, or to estimate
the influence which that event is destined to exercise on the world at
large" (Woolls 1888: 4–5). Hopelessness, insecurity, and oppression in
the founding were elaborated in order to emphasize national progress:
"Had the adventurous spirit of Phillip a prophetic side, what reconciliation to hard reality might he have extracted from . . . [seeing] a short
century ahead . . . his dispirited little band of exiles replaced by the wealth
and strength of a nation grown to lusty manhood" (Morrison 1888: 214).
Australian collective memory in 1888 often emphasized the century's
progress, but this progress was measured from the founding moment.

The American founding moment has been a compelling and persistent element of collective memory for more than two centuries. Why?
Is this only natural? Arguably, the charisma of the historical moment itself
constrains subsequent memory and explains persistence: the events and
personalities of the 1770s impose themselves as necessary foundations
for any subsequent social construction work. The comparison with the
Australian centennial challenges this explanation, though, because in that
case an elaborate discourse about a founding moment that memory entrepreneurs found embarrassing was endowed with charisma: it appeared to
impose itself in collective memory on thin grounds.

These three commemorations taken together suggest more support
for an explanation of persistent collective memory based on functional
imperatives: the national group is necessarily distinguished by a temporal
order with a beginning, and that beginning is perceived as constituting
the imagined community. Even an embarrassing founding moment can
be interpreted in such a way as to constitute the group. But the case of the
Australian bicentennial challenges explanations of persistence based on
functional imperatives, too. For Australians in 1988, the counterintuitive
power of 1888 founding-moment formulations had evaporated, and most
historical references by Australian bicentennial organizers appealed instead to the 200 years since the first British settlement. Even where British invasion was mentioned, there was a quick transition to a more diffuse
historical review. Australian organizers introduced historical allusions

only casually; for them, the reference to history seemed just a part of the cultural task of the celebration, whereas for Americans, it was independently salient.[11] Although many grounds for claims about the imagined community of the nation were mobilized, collective memories did not provide the most significant grounds for such claims. Where history was remembered, memories were particular, not integrated in a larger national narrative. In the aggregate, the absence of a national metanarrative gave the many particular references to history in the Australian bicentennial the disorganized quality Halbwachs (1992 [1925]: 41–42) attributes to the asocial memory of individual dreams. This was also evident in the postmodern style of an important national traveling exhibition in 1988 (Cochrane and Goodman 1988). There seemed to be little functional necessity for the nation to be imagined as a group with an overarching temporal order, much less as a group constituted in a founding. The reasons for this absence in the Australian repertoire of symbols of national identity suggest a better account of why the American founding moment has remained a robust element of national collective memory for centuries.

CRITICS AND COLLECTIVE MEMORIES

Australian bicentennial organizers avoided talk of the first settlement they were commemorating because they feared opposition from aboriginal activists and their supporters, who pointed out that "40,000 years don't make a Bicentennial" (Hutchinson 1992: 17). Aborigines unsuccessfully demanded the treaty that had not been made in 1788 (Treaty 88 Campaign 1988; Bennett 1989: 155–56). At the beginning of bicentennial planning the Australian government asked that "special attention be given to the concerns of . . . aboriginals" (ABA 1983: 7; cf. Warhurst 1987; Pettman 1988). The Australian Bicentennial Authority emphasized that their project was "much more than a commemoration of the arrival of the First Fleet" (ABA 1981: 6).

Bicentennial plans continued to be influenced by this oppositional politics. A reenactment of the first fleet's voyage was not officially sponsored due to fears of extensive aboriginal protest (Spearritt 1988). Organizers aimed to develop "a programme to foster recognition of the contribution of the aboriginal people . . . achieved through close consultation with aboriginal representatives and . . . developed and implemented by aboriginals" (ABA 1983: 6), and special funding was allocated to such projects as aboriginal community centers and publications (ABA 1989: 1: 39–45). Most bicentennial historiography and regional programs also tried to include aboriginal perspectives and activities. Despite all the attempts to preempt or mute aboriginal protest, Australia's bicentennial year saw boycotts, continued activism, and increased discussion of aboriginal issues. So contemporary critics gave Australians good reason not to mention their founding moment. If more had been said about 1788, claims about the imagined community of the nation would have attracted even more dissent.

By contrast, founding moments were robust to contemporary criticism in the three other commemorations. In the Australian centennial, aborigines had been considered far beyond the relevant public sphere of Australian centennial organizers, and they were almost entirely ignored (although an occasional sentence of sentimental pastoral nostalgia deplored their losses). But those who wished to celebrate the Australian centennial in 1888 were compelled to address several more demanding critiques. First, of course, nobody believed that convict settlement itself was anything but problematic as national history. The most vocal critics, among populist, republican, and labor groups, challenged the legitimacy of the founding moment in collective memory as representing British oppression and an "event rather intimately connected with the gallows." Of a statue of the first governor, they warned, "Unveil it not, lest future ages say / What men were those who stamped their sins in clay?" (Bulletin 1888: 5). Another problem for those who celebrated the centennial was colonial integration: the first settlement had been in New South Wales, one of six British colonies in what people were imagining as the Australian nation, and critics in other colonies could argue that it was not national. Ultimately, though, mainstream founding-moment history was constructed in ways that addressed these problems and suggested common ground with the critics. Vague characterization of 1788 as "heroic settlement" or specific characterization as a "benchmark of progress" allowed potential critics symbolic space to identify with the founding moment as constituting their imagined community, even if they belonged to other colonies. Collective memory of the Australian founding moment was robust to significant contemporary critics in 1888, if not in 1988.

There was no charismatic necessity that Australia's founding moment remain an important part of national memory. There was, however, some functional value in having such a narrative of origins, as its construction in 1888 seems to suggest. The year 1788 proved multivalent enough for constructions that avoided the taboos and prohibitions imposed by contemporary critics (see Olick and Levy 1997). To potential critics a century later, however, that history did not prove susceptible to satisfactory interpretation, and it lost most of its importance as an element of public collective memory. This suggests that the multivalence of historical moments (and persons) encourages their persistence: the more they can be interpreted in different ways to transcend criticism, the longer they will last.

If founding-moment charisma and function do not account for the vicissitudes of collective memory in Australia, do they do so in the more favorable American case? The Australian centennial shows that charisma is in the eye of the interpreter: the Australian bicentennial shows that there is no need to talk about founding moments much at all (other symbols may ground claims about imagined community). The question must be reformulated: why has the revolutionary period preserved its charismatic meaning and its constitutive function in American national memory for two centuries? The comparison suggests looking at the framing of collective memory by critics, and the responses these critics evoked from mainstream memory entrepreneurs. And indeed, though contentious issues themselves were very different in 1876 and 1976, American critics 100 years apart made very similar sorts of uses of national collective memory. The revolutionary period provided important grounds for their critical claims. In the language of critics, 1776 could sound even more charismatic than in mainstream collective memory, and it could be even more functional as a constitutive narrative of the imagined community of the nation.[12]

The commemoration of 1876 evoked dissent from a variety of sources, notably, but not only, from southerners and feminists. Groups of critics themselves had little in common. But challenges often shared the same rhetoric: critical claims were grounded and elaborated with symbols drawn from the founding moment of Revolution. A critic of centennial funding pointed out with some historical detail that "jealousy of centralizing power was the key note of our Revolution" (Tucker 1876: 4), and a centennial magazine argued for fiscal reform by appealing to the "True Independence" of the founding moment, noting that "a false commercial system imposed by foreign rule caused the war of the Revolution" (Centennial Eagle 1876: 162). Feminists interrupted solemn Fourth of July proceedings in Philadelphia to distribute and read a Declaration of Rights for Women (Randel 1969: 314–15; Andres 1976–77; Greenhalgh 1988). During the American centennial, critical groups themselves found the revolutionary founding moment rich grounds for the legitimacy of their challenges, thus its appeal was strengthened as a shared element of collective memory. And organizers and supporters frequently appealed to collective memory of the Revolution in their attempts to mobilize commemoration across salient social differences: "If we stand upon the wise, good and sure foundation which Washington and his compatriots laid, the United States need fear no foe from without or within" (International Order of Odd-fellows 1876: 57).

A hundred years later, though the commemoration did not follow civil war, the oppositional politics of the 1960s and early 1970s still led organizers to express a strong fear of failure. They made early efforts to preempt dissent from youth activists, feminists, and ethnic and racial minorities (like their Australian equivalents facing aboriginal critique). But whereas Australian organizers quickly abandoned a founding-moment vision of history in the face of critical claims, American organizers stressed the founding moment as unifying even in the face of dissent. Official collective memory of the 1770s became newly inclusionary: bicentennial organizers often referred to stories like those of "Vails Gate where 100s of Black soldiers of the Revolution were quartered" and of a tavern owned by a black merchant in New York that was "scene of Washington's farewell to the Continental Army" (ARBA 1977: 417).

Their most vocal critics also emphasized the founding moment in their oppositional visions of the nation's history. Indeed, perhaps the most compelling evidence of the use and power of the American founding moment in national collective memory is the language of bicentennial critics. Critical groups of the 1976 bicentennial appealed as much to founding-moment history as organizers did. In this, publicly imagined collective memory in the American bicentennial was very similar to collective memory in the 1876 centennial. The short-lived Afro-American Bicentennial Corporation argued that "the bicentennial commemoration be viewed as a timely and appropriate vehicle for revitalizing America's continuing revolution in line with the philosophy and aspirations of such early American revolutionaries as Jefferson, Paine, and Sam Adams" (Congressional Record 1973: 13352). Other critics argued that "what we need in this country is a new patriotic movement to restore the same kind of spirit that our Founding Fathers employed 200 years ago against the wealthy aristocracy, against the privileged families and wealthy institutions" (ARBA 1975: 34). Publications and events produced by the alternative People's Bicentennial Commission (PBC) relied extensively on founding-moment symbols to make their critical claims: the PBC urged the nation to reclaim these national symbols, "to challenge the official Bicentennial observance . . . with the words and deeds of the American revolutionary patriots" (Brody 1977: 134). Their alternative guide to bicentennial celebration gave elaborate recognition to founding-moment symbols, arguing that the Fourth of July might be a "truly revolutionary holiday," and also recommended celebrating Tom Paine's birthday, the Boston Massacre, Patrick Henry's "Give me liberty or give me death" speech, Thomas Jefferson's birthday, the battles of Lexington and Concord, the Declaration of Independence, Sam Adams's birthday, and the Boston Tea Party, as well as "days when something of historical importance happened in your community" (People's Bicentennial Commission 1974: 181). Critics appealed as much to founding-moment history as did the organizers of the 1976 celebration (Rifkin 1975).

CONCLUSION

What makes some collective memories robust and persistent? I have addressed this question in a similar case comparison of the place of founding moments in national collective memories in the United States and Australia. National founding moments provide good grounds for arguing both that past events constrain present memories and that memories are malleable according to contemporary concerns.

Founding-moment history was important in grounding claims about the nation in large-scale centennial commemorations in both countries in the late nineteenth century. The founding events of the 1770s remained equally compelling in the American bicentennial, but the Australian founding was no longer significant in the discourse of the Australian bicentenary. Because of the similarity of the cases, general conditions of memory production like availability of records, historiography, institutionalized holidays, and material memorials do not account for the different twentieth-century "outcomes" in collective memory. Historical institutions made founding moments equally available for integration in national collective memory in each country.

Similarly, there is much evidence of the ongoing social construction of collective memory in all four commemorations. But a general theory of the malleability of collective memory does not account well for the survival of American national memories of the revolutionary period over two centuries or for the differential persistence of founding-moment memories in the United States and Australia.

The American founding moment of revolution is often understood as an inherently meaningful and charismatic constitutive narrative grounding claims about nationality. On this view, the question I have pursued in this essay is counterintuitive. The intrinsic meaning of the past events imposes a pattern on later collective memories and constrains memory entrepreneurs: persistent collective memories are robust because they are charismatically meaningful. But talk of the disreputable Australian founding as heroic pattern or benchmark of progress in the late nineteenth century suggests that the attribution of charisma itself requires an account.

Founding moments may also be important in collective memory because they are functional: the beginning of a temporal order may be shared by members of an "imagined community" and differentiate it from others. That this imperative has some force is suggested by the continuing importance of appeals to the revolutionary period in American collective memory, and even more by the appeal to an otherwise inglorious founding moment by Australians in their centennial. But the absence of founding-moment appeals (or, indeed, any national metanarratives) in the Australian bicentennial shows that function alone cannot account for the persistence of founding-moment history in American collective memory.

The factor that best accounts for the different salience of founding moments in national collective memories in these cases is their meaning in oppositional politics. Even the Australian founding moment allowed variant interpretations that addressed the challenges of nineteenth-century critics. But in comparison to the American Revolution, it did not have enough symbolic power to resist critical claims by 1988. Founding-moment claims could not be mobilized by Australian bicentennial organizers in 1988 because, in contrast to the American bicentennial in 1976, these claims could no longer mediate official and oppositional views and hence fell to aboriginal critique.

The period of the American Revolution offered national symbols almost impervious to the vicissitudes of critical discussion. In both 1876 and 1976, the revolutionary period provided rich grounds for the arguments of commemoration critics: at the same time, commemoration planners were often careful to appeal to the "shared" founding moment in order to transcend salient differences. Across the century, the specific concerns of critics and the problems faced by memory entrepreneurs could differ enormously. But the American founding moment remained a robust element of national collective memory because it offered multiple interpretive possibilities in a variety of contexts.

Debates about the fixity or flexibility of the past in collective memory ultimately turn on the extent to which the past carries intrinsic meanings that constrain later interpretation. The cases here suggest that intrinsic meanings of past events are consequential, but in a paradoxical way: the more semiotic flexibility they offer, the more robust those events will be in collective memories. Symbolic power is a function of those past events. At the same time, constraint or possibility offered by past events is expressed in active processes of memory construction by groups and individuals responding to contemporary sensibilities and interests.

NOTES

Parts of this article were presented at the Annual Meeting of the American Sociological Association, New York, August 1996, and the Annual Meeting of the Social Science History Association, Washington, D.C., October 1997. The author would like to thank Diane Barthels, Russell Faeges, Nancy Hanrahan, Steve Hochstadt, Catherine Preston, Jeff Olick, Edith Raphael, Barry Schwartz, Neil Smelser, Ann Swidler, and anonymous reviewers for their various helpful comments and contributions.

1. For many purposes, accounts of collective memories in terms of the politics of cultural production may seem adequate. But as I note later, such accounts become more implausible for collective memories that persist across a number of generations spanning very different political contexts. Indeed, over the long term such accounts are potentially self-contradictory if they assume both that collective memories are shaped by

contemporary concerns and that historical moments such as the American Revolution will be significant to new generations because of earlier ideological mobilizations. One way of avoiding any contradiction is to assert that regardless of labels, what looks like a reference to or memory of the same historical object is not, because contemporary context endows it with entirely different meanings. Since interpretations of such historical events as the Revolution change, any continuous memory of the Revolution is purely a formality. On this view, the problem I am addressing here is the problem of how it is possible that some of the same *labels* persist for collective memories that are, properly understood, entirely different. My argument applies at this level of thin persistence, too. In my view, though, this sort of radical constructionist interpretation weakens theories of malleability by ignoring the concerns of critics who emphasize continuity.

2. Schwartz (1991: 232) also suggests, along the lines of the argument here, that "the Washington image handed down from one generation to the next was not a unitary one. Tradition conveyed contradictory ideas of the man, and by reiterating this duality the debates about 'the real Washington' preserved it."

3. Mircea Eliade (1959 [1954]: 32) argued that in traditional societies, "all important acts of life were revealed *ab origine* by gods or heroes. Men only repeat these exemplary and paradigmatic gestures ad infinitum." While such an ahistorical sacrality would not be attributed to modern societies even on Eliade's view, there is arguably a sense in which symbolically charged appeals to founding moments in national collective memory, like the Philadelphia mayor's welcome, do resonate with Eliade's point (Schwartz 1982: 375–76).

4. This section is drawn from and summarizes evidence and analysis presented in Spillman 1997, which also elaborates other dimensions of national collective memory and other aspects of national identity besides collective memory.

5. On exhibitions see, for example, Rydell 1984 and 1993, Greenhalgh 1988, Breckinridge 1984, Mitchell 1984, Benedict 1983, Davison 1988b, and Niquette and Buxton 1997.

6. Thus, the evidence grounding the following analysis is drawn from unofficial as well as official sources of various sorts, from many different groups, and includes documents from commercial sources and documents from critics. It also includes a substantial number of sources that were not produced for or directly related to the Philadelphia exhibition. However, official sources and records of Philadelphia events do dominate the documents remaining from 1876.

7. Nevertheless, U.S. government contributions to the exhibition were significant in their own right: see Rydell 1984 and Miner 1972.

8. However, see Rydell 1984: 32–33 on discussion and programs concerned with providing opportunities for workers to see the exhibition.

9. On the American bicentennial see Bodnar 1992: 226–44; for further brief comparisons of 1876 and 1976, see Schlereth 1980: 14–41 and Zelinsky 1988: 83–84. On the Australian bicentenary, see, e.g., Warhurst 1987; Janson and MacIntyre 1988; and Bennett et al. 1992. For one comparative overview of the two bicentennials, along with the Canadian centenary of 1967, see Hutchinson 1992.

10. Major exhibitions were held until World War II. Rydell (1993) has shown that they both continued and altered ideological and political trends evident in Victorian exhibitions; see also Greenhalgh 1988 and Bennett 1988. By the time of the bicentennials, issues like costs and overcentralization meant that exhibitions were rejected or not seriously considered as national showpieces (Bodnar 1992: 231; Craik 1992; Davison 1988b). However, more regionally oriented exhibitions associated with bicentennials were held in Spokane in 1974 and in Brisbane in 1988.

11. In samples of stories from bicentennial newsletters of American and Australian commemoration organizers, the difference between countries in percentage of themes stressing founding-moment history was statistically significant at the 0.5 level (Fisher Exact Test) (Spillman 1997: 113–14; cf. Murphy 1988).

12. Schroyer (1982: 81) calls this "cultural surplus," in which "traditional cultural symbols . . . retain their capacity to anticipate utopian alternatives to existing realities."

REFERENCES

ABA. *See* Australian Bicentennial Authority.

Allen, W. 1890. "Centennial Cantata." In *Centennial International Exhibition Commission (1890)*.

American Revolution Bicentennial Administration. 1975. *National Bicentennial Ethnic and Racial Council Conference Report*, Washington, D.C., January 20–22. Washington, D.C.: GPO.

——. 1977. *Bicentennial Times: Commemorative Reprints*. Washington, D.C.: GPO.

Anderson, B. 1991. *Imagined Communities: Reflections on the Origin and Spread of Nationalism*. 2d ed. London: Verso.

Andres, W. D. 1976–77. "Women and the Fairs of 1876 and 1893." *Hayes Historical Journal* 1: 173–83.

ARBA. *See* American Revolution Bicentennial Administration.

Australian Bicentennial Authority. 1981. *First Annual Report on Activities to 30 June 1981*. Sydney: Australian Bicentennial Authority.

——. 1983. *Third Annual Report on Activities to 30 June 1983*. Sydney: Australian Bicentennial Authority.

——. 1989. *Ninth Annual Report 1989: On Activities to 30 June 1988*. 2 vols. Edited by Bruce Pollock. Sydney: Australian Bicentennial Authority.

Benedict, B. 1983. "The Anthropology of World's Fairs." In B. Benedict, ed., *The Anthropology of World's Fairs: San Francisco's Panama Pacific International Exposition of 1915*. London: Lowie Museum of Anthropology in association with Scolar Press.

Bennett, S. 1989. *Aborigines and Political Power*. Sydney: Allen and Unwin.

Bennett, T. 1992. "The Shaping of Things to Come: Expo 88." In T. Bennett, P. Buckridge, D. Carter, and C. Mercer, eds., *Celebrating the Nation: A Critical Study of Australia's Bicentenary*. St. Leonards: Allen and Unwin.

Bennett, T., P. Buckridge, D. Carter, and C. Mercer, eds. 1992. *Celebrating the Nation: A Critical Study of Australia's Bicentenary*. St. Leonards: Allen and Unwin.

Benson, S. P., S. Brier, and R. Rosenzeig, eds. 1986. *Presenting the Past: Essays on History and the Public*. Philadelphia: Temple University Press.

Bodnar, J. 1992. *Remaking America: Public Memory, Commemoration, and Patriotism in the Twentieth Century*. Princeton, N.J.: Princeton University Press.

Breckinridge, C. A. 1984. "The Aesthetics and Politics of Colonial Collecting: India at World Fairs." *Comparative Studies in Society and History* 31: 195–216.

Brody, M. K. 1977. "Sociological Theories of Symbolic Activity: A Case Study Application to the Bicentennial Observance." Ph.D. diss., University of Iowa.

Brotherhead, W. (c.) 1872. *The Centennial Book of the Signers of the Declaration of Independence*. Philadelphia: J. M. Stoddart.

Brown, D. 1966. *The Year of the Century: 1876*. New York: Charles Scribner's Sons.

Bulletin (Sydney). 1888. 4 August.

Campbell, J. W. (c.) 1980. *America in Her Centennial Year, 1876*. Washington: University Press of America.

Celebration in Commemoration of the Centennial of Australia and the Jubilee Year of the Foundation of the Order of the Sisters of Charity in Australia, St. Vincent's Convent. 1888. Sydney: J. G. O'Connor, Nation Office. Held in National Library of Australia, Canberra.

Centennial Board of Finance. 1875. *Celebration of the Ninety-Ninth Anniversary of American Independence in Fairmount Park, Philadelphia, July 5*. Philadelphia: Centennial Board of Finance.

Centennial Eagle. 1876. *The Centennial Eagle. In Twelve Numbers, July–September. An Illustrated Descriptive History of the Centennial Exhibition*. Philadelphia: Centennial Eagle Company.

Centennial International Exhibition Commission. 1890. *Official Record . . . Melbourne, 1888–1889, Containing a Sketch of the Industrial and Economic Progress of the Australasian Colonies during the First Century of Their Existence: and of the Exhibition Held in Melbourne, Victoria, to Commemorate the Close of That Period*. Melbourne: Sands and McDougall Limited, Printers.

Cerulo, K. 1995. *Identity Designs: The Sights and Sounds of a Nation*. ASA Rose Book Series. New Brunswick, N.J.: Rutgers University Press.

Clarke, W. F. 1876. *Centennial Discourse. Delivered July 4, 1876, in St. Joseph's Church, Philadelphia, by Rev. Wm. F. Clarke, S.J., of Baltimore, Md*. Philadelphia: P. F. Cunningham and Son.

Cochrane, P., and D. Goodman. 1988. "The Great Australian Journey: Cultural Logic and Nationalism in the Postmodern Era." In S. Janson and S. MacIntyre, eds., *Making the Bicentenary*. Special issue. *Australian Historical Studies* 23: 21–44.

Congressional Record. 1973. 93rd Cong., 1st sess., vol. 119, pt. 11.

Craik, J. 1992. "Expo 88: Fashions of Sight and Politics of Site," in T. Bennett, P. Buckridge, D. Carter, and C. Mercer, eds., *Celebrating the Nation: A Critical Study of Australia's Bicentenary*. St. Leonards: Allen and Unwin.

Davison, G. 1988a. "Centennial Celebrations," in G. Davison, J. W. McCarty, and A. McLeary, eds., *Australians 1888*. Sydney: Fairfax, Syme and Weldon.

——. 1988b. "Festivals of Nationhood: The International Exhibitions." In S. L. Goldberg and F. B. Smith, eds., *Australian Cultural History*. Cambridge: Cambridge University Press.

Eliade, M. 1959 [1954]. *Cosmos and History: The Myth of the Eternal Return*. Trans. Willard R. Trask. New York: Harper and Brothers.

Evarts, W. M. 1876. "Oration, July 4th 1876, Philadelphia," in *His Royal Highness Prince Oscar at the National Celebration of the Centennial Anniversary of American Independence Held in Philadelphia, U.S.A., July 4, 1876*. Boston: Printed at the Riverside Press for Private Distribution.

Fabre, G., and R. O'Meally, eds. 1994. *History and Memory in African-American Culture*. New York: Oxford University Press.

Foner, P. S. 1976. "Black Participation in the Centennial of 1876." *Negro History Bulletin* 39: 532–38.

Gillis, J. R., ed. 1994. *Commemorations: The Politics of National Identity*. Princeton, N.J.: Princeton University Press.

Glassberg, D. 1990. *American Historical Pageantry: The Uses of Tradition in the Early Twentieth Century*. Chapel Hill: University of North Carolina Press.

Greenhalgh, P. 1988. *Ephemeral Vistas: The Expositions Universelles, Great Exhibitions, and World's Fairs, 1851–1939*. Manchester: Manchester University Press.

Griffiths, T. 1987. "Past Silences: Aborigines and Convicts in Our History-making." *Australian Cultural History* 6: 18–32.

Halbwachs, M. 1992 [1925]. "The Social Frameworks of Memory." In L. Coser, ed., *On Collective Memory*. Chicago: University of Chicago Press.

Hobsbawm, E., and T. Ranger, eds. 1984. *The Invention of Tradition*. Cambridge: Cambridge University Press.

Hutchinson, J. 1992. "State Festivals, Foundation Myths and Cultural Politics in Immigrant Nations." In T. Bennett, P. Buckridge, D. Carter, and C. Mercer, eds., *Celebrating the Nation: A Critical Study of Australia's Bicentenary*. Sydney: Allen and Unwin.

International Order of Oddfellows, Sovereign General Lodge. 1876. *Centennial Celebration in Honor of the Anniversary of American Independence. September 1876*. Philadelphia: Burk and Caldwell, Printers.

Janson, S., and S. MacIntyre, eds. 1988. *Making the Bicentenary*. Special issue. *Australian Historical Studies* 23 (91).

Kammen, M. 1978. *A Season of Youth: The American Revolution and the Historical Imagination*. New York: Oxford University Press.

——. 1991. *Mystic Chords of Memory: The Transformation of Tradition in American Culture*. New York: Knopf.

Kertzer, D. 1989. *Rituals, Politics, and Power*. New Haven, Conn.: Yale University Press.

Ladies' Centennial Committee of Rhode Island. 1875. *Herald of the Centennial*.

Lipset, S. M. 1979. *The First New Nation: The United States in Comparative and Historical Perspective*. New York: Norton.

Litwak, L. 1989. "Trouble in Mind: The Bicentennial and the Afro-American Experience." *Journal of American History* 74: 315–37.

Maines, D. R., N. M. Sugrue, and M. A. Katovich. 1983. "The Sociological Import of G. H. Mead's Theory of the Past." *American Sociological Review* 48: 161–73.

Middleton, D., and D. Edwards. 1990. "Conversational Remembering: A Social Psychological Approach." In D. Middleton and D. Edwards, eds., *Collective Remembering.* Newbury Park, Calif.: Sage.

Miner, H. C. 1972. "The United States Government Building at the Centennial Exhibition, 1874–77." *Prologue* 4: 203–18.

Mitchell, T. 1984. "The World As Exhibition." *Comparative Studies in Society and History* 31: 217–36.

Moore, J. S. 1888. *Memorials of the Celebration of the Australasian Centenary in New South Wales, 1888.* Sydney: Charles Potter, Government Printer.

Morrison, W. F. 1888. *Aldine Centennial History of New South Wales.* Vol. 1. Sydney: n.p.

Murphy, J. 1988. "Conscripting the Past: The Bicentenary and Everyday Life," in S. Janson and S. MacIntyre, eds., *Making the Bicentenary.* Special issue. *Australian Historical Studies* 23: 45–54.

New Jersey State Centennial Board. 1877. *Report of the New Jersey Commissioners on the Centennial Exhibition.* Trenton, N.J.: Naar, Day, and Naar, Printers.

Niquette, M., and W. J. Buxton. 1997. "Meet Me at the Fair: Sociability and Reflexivity in Nineteenth-century World Expositions." *Canadian Journal of Communication* 22: 81–113.

Olick, J. K., and D. Levy. 1997. "Collective Memory and Cultural Constraint: Holocaust Myth and Rationality in German Politics." *American Sociological Review* 62: 921–36.

People's Bicentennial Commission. 1974. *America's Birthday: A Planning and Activities Guide for Citizens' Participation during the Bicentennial Year.* New York: Simon and Schuster.

Peterson, R. 1994. "Cultural Studies through the Production Perspective: Progress and Prospects." In D. Crane, ed., *The Sociology of Culture: Emerging Theoretical Perspectives.* Oxford: Blackwell: 163–89.

Pettman, J. 1988. "Learning about Power and Powerlessness: Aborigines and White Australia's Bicentenary." *Race and Class* 29: 69–85.

Plummer, J. 1887. *Choral Parts of the Centennial Ode. Music by Hugo Alpen.* Sydney: John Sands, General Printer.

Randel, W. P. 1969. *Centennial: American Life in 1876.* Philadelphia and New York: Chilton Book Co.

Rifkin, J. 1975. *Commonsense II: The Case against Corporate Tyranny.* Boston: People's Bicentennial Commission.

Roe, M. 1989. "Vandiemenism Debated: The Filming of 'His Natural Life,' 1926–27." *Journal of Australian Studies* 24: 35–51.

Rydell, R. 1984. *All the World's a Fair: Visions of Empire at American International Expositions, 1876–1916.* Chicago: University of Chicago Press.

———. 1993. *World of Fairs: The Century of Progress Exhibitions.* Chicago: University of Chicago Press.

Schlereth, T. J. 1980. "The 1876 Centennial: A Model for Comparative American Studies." In *Artifacts and the American Past.* Nashville, Tenn.: American Association for State and Local History.

Schroyer, T. 1982. "Cultural Surplus in America." *New German Critique* 26: 81–117.

Schudson, M. 1989. "The Present in the Past Versus the Past in the Present." *Communication* 11: 105–13.

———. 1992. *Watergate in American Memory: How We Remember, Forget, and Reconstruct the Past.* New York: Basic Books.

———. 1994. "Culture and the Integration of National Societies." In D. Crane, ed., *The Sociology of Culture: Emerging Theoretical Perspectives.* Oxford: Blackwell: 21–43.

Schultz, A. 1991. " 'The Pride of Race had been Touched': Norse-American Immigration Centennial and Ethnic Identity." *Journal of American History* 77: 1265–95.

Schuman, H., and J. Scott. 1989. "Generations and Collective Memories." *American Sociological Review* 54: 359–81.

Schwartz, B. 1982. "The Social Context of Commemoration: A Study in Collective Memory." *Social Forces* 61: 372–402.

———. 1987. *George Washington: The Making of an American Symbol.* Ithaca, N.Y.: Cornell University Press.

———. 1990. "The Reconstruction of Abraham Lincoln." In D. Middleton and D. Edwards, eds., *Collective Remembering.* Newbury Park, Calif.: Sage.

———. 1991. "Social Change and Collective Memory: The Democratization of George Washington." *American Sociological Review* 56: 221–36.

Shils, E. 1965. "Charisma, Order, and Status." *American Sociological Review* 30: 199–213.

———. 1981. *Tradition.* Chicago: University of Chicago Press.

———. 1988. "Center and Periphery: An Idea and Its Career, 1935–1987." In L. Greenfeld and M. Martin, eds., *Center: Ideas and Institutions.* Chicago: University of Chicago Press.

Smelser, N. 1976. *Comparative Methods in the Social Sciences.* Englewood Cliffs, N.J.: Prentice-Hall.

Spearritt, P. 1988. "Celebration of a Nation: The Triumph of Spectacle." In S. Janson and S. MacIntyre, eds., *Making the Bicentenary.* Special issue. *Australian Historical Studies* 23: 3–20.

Spillman, L. 1997. *Nation and Commemoration: Creating National Identities in the United States and Australia.* Cambridge: Cambridge University Press.

Swidler, A., and J. Ardit. 1994. "The New Sociology of Knowledge." *Annual Review of Sociology* 20: 305–29.

Thelen, D., ed. 1990. *Memory and American History.* Bloomington: Indiana University Press.

Treaty 88 Campaign. 1988. "Aboriginal Sovereignty—Never Ceded." In S. Janson and

S. MacIntyre, eds., *Making the Bicentenary.* Special issue. *Australian Historical Studies* 23: 1–2.

Trennert, R. A. 1974. "A Grand Failure: The Centennial Indian Exhibition of 1876." *Prologue* 6: 118–29.

Trouillot, M.-R. 1990. "Good Day Columbus: Silences, Power, and Public History (1492–1892)." *Public Culture* 3: 1–24.

Tucker, J. R. 1876. *Centennial Celebration of American Independence. Speech of Hon. John Randolph Tucker, of Virginia, in the H.R. 19 January 1876.* Washington, D.C.: GPO.

United States Centennial Commission. 1873. *The National Celebration of the Centennial Anniversary of the Independence of the United States by an International Universal Exhibition, to be held in Philadelphia in the Year 1876. Accompanied by a Classified Compilation of the Journal of the Proceedings of the Commission and Other Papers.* Compiled and arranged by H. D. Pratt. Washington, D.C.: GPO.

USCC. *See* United States Centennial Commission.

Warhurst, J. 1987. "The Politics and Management of Australia's Bicentenary Year." *Politics* 22: 8–18.

Warner, W. L. 1959. *The Living and the Dead: A Study of the Symbolic Life of Americans.* New Haven, Conn.: Yale University Press.

Williams, R. 1973. "Base and Superstructure in Marxist Cultural Theory." *New Left Review* 82: 3–16.

Woolls, Rev. Dr. 1888. *A Sermon on the Centenary of the Colony Preached in St. Luke's, Burwood, on Sunday, January 22nd, 1888 by the Rev. Dr. Woolls (A Colonist of 56 Years Standing).* Sydney: Geo. Loxton and C., Printers. Held in Dixson Library, Sydney.

Zelinsky, W. 1988. *Nation into State: The Shifting Symbolic Foundations of American Nationalism.* Chapel Hill: University of North Carolina Press.

Zerubavel, E. 1981. *Hidden Rhythms: Schedules and Calendars in Social Life.* Chicago: University of Chicago Press.

Legacies and Liabilities of an

Insurgent Past: Remembering

Martin Luther King Jr. on the

House and Senate Floor

◄ ◄ ◄ ◄ ◄ ◄ ◄ ◄ ◄ ◄ ◄   FRANCESCA POLLETTA

At a ceremony held in 1986 to install a bust of Martin Luther King Jr.
alongside those of other national heroes in the U.S. Capitol, former King
Associate Vincent Harding reminded the audience that King himself
probably would have joined the demonstrators outside the Capitol protest-
ing American policy in Central America (Thelen 1987: 436). Harding's
comment captures the tension between commemoration and dissent, or,
better, between state-sponsored remembrance and state-targeted opposition that is the subject of this essay.

Certainly, states have good reason to commemorate social protest. Nations reforge the bonds of citizenship by celebrating their revolutionary
origins. Current political regimes may warrant themselves as veterans or
legatees of earlier opposition to an unjust regime (Kertzer 1988). Commemoration may underscore and reinforce the *pastness* of dissent, since,
as David Lowenthal (1985: 323) observes, "the memorial act implies termination," thus minimizing dissent's political import for the present and
reestablishing a narrative of harmony and stability. Protest may be commemorated to celebrate its failure, a threat to the nation averted (Greenblatt 1983).

But this enterprise also carries risks. Publicizing the injustices against which insurgents once struggled may suggest continuities with the present state of things. Commemoration may make immediate rather than remote, may remind and inspire rather than distance. Celebrating victory over internal enemies may lead to a subversive identification with the vanquished. There are other risks. Government officials who are self-proclaimed bearers of an insurgent legacy may open themselves to charges of hypocrisy for their current moderation. Since movements rarely fulfill their aims before they fade into obscurity, putative legatees can legitimately be asked what they have done lately with respect to those goals. And commemorants not tarred by allies with the brush of accommodation may be charged by opponents with the opposite transgression, that of undermining political authority by supporting ("celebrating") extra-institutional protest.

States are not monolithic entities; rather, they comprise numerous actors with overlapping, competing, and changing constituencies. For that reason alone, the political stakes in the commemoration of protest are rarely transparent. Indeed, the process of establishing memorials is often marked by strange alliances, surprising reversals, and unwitting ironies. For example, it was Ronald Reagan, rather than Jimmy Carter, who in 1983 signed the legislation making the birthday of Martin Luther King Jr. a federal holiday. The signing came less than three weeks after Reagan had assured an opponent of the legislation that sentiment for the holiday was "based on an image not a reality"; in the interim he decided that "the symbolism of that day is important enough" to sign the legislation. (He also apologized to Coretta Scott King for publicly questioning King's patriotism. Having smoothed ruffled feathers, he left for a golfing weekend at an all-white country club.) If Reagan saw King as "symbolic of what was a very real crisis in our history," Howard Baker, a key Republican supporter of the bill, saw it as symbolic of unity—or symbolic of symbolic unity ("I have seldom approached a moment in this chamber when I thought the action we are about to take has greater potential for good and a greater symbolism for unity").[1] In an earlier, unsuccessful attempt to forestall the legislation, Jesse Helms began a filibuster, the technique made famous by fellow southerners to block civil rights legislation in the 1950s; Bill Bradley, speaking for the importance of commemorating the civil rights past, accused Helms of "speak[ing] for a past that the vast majority of Americans have overcome."[2] Members of the Black Congressional Caucus, meanwhile, lobbied vigorously for the legislation but at the same time opposed plans for a reenactment of the 1963 March on Washington, the occasion of King's famous "I have a dream" speech (Reed 1986).

Of course, one can read each of these political moves, countermoves, and turnarounds as bids for black and white votes at a time when electoral campaigns were getting under way. However, the consequences of positioning oneself vis-à-vis the past are difficult to anticipate. Jesse Helms's staff, for example, admitted that they didn't know whether Helms's intemperate remarks about King's alleged communist sympathies and sexual promiscuity had served to drum up disaffected whites' votes or alienate moderates. And as I will show in this essay, for black legislators, there has been much more at stake in their representations of Dr. King and the movement than a straightforward appeal to constituents. Simultaneously insiders and outsiders, members of the political establishment and yet minority members, they must negotiate complex and competitive relations not only with white political elites but also with black *protest* elites (Reed 1986; Marable 1995; Smith 1996; Swain 1993; Lusane 1994). Collective memory has become a critical terrain for these relations: successfully "representing" King and the movement has become a way to warrant their status as authentic representatives of African American interests. Black elected officials thus have a different relationship to, and stake in preserving, an oppositional past than do white officials, on one hand, and extra-instititional black activists, on the other.

At minimum, then, an instrumentalist approach to collective memory, with memory deployed and molded to further current interests, must be expanded to take into account the conflicting and changing interests among groups often characterized as unitary: "officials" (Bodnar 1992), "subordinates" (Merelman 1992: 248), or "African Americans" (Zerubavel 1996). But even a variegated instrumentalist approach may miss the ways in which representations of the past shape and, indeed, *constitute* interests and identities (Olick 1993; Olick and Levy 1997; Schwartz 1991). If accepted modes of public remembering generate political resources, they also impose real constraints on how the past can be used. To return to my example: When, in debate about passage of the King holiday, Senator Helms complained about the likely revenue loss from giving federal employees a day off, his sentiments were echoed by Democratic and Republican colleagues. When Helms cited King's "action-oriented Marxism" to argue his inappropriateness for national veneration, many senators were forced to change sides, one acknowledging that "the symbolism has just become too heavy." And when Helms argued that since John and Robert Kennedy had authorized wiretaps on King, Edward Kennedy's argument with Helms was really "with his dead brother[s]," he lost almost all his allies. Explained one Republican consultant, "You don't talk about JFK yet here in dirty terms."[3] By the time the King holiday next spurred Senate debate, one didn't talk about King in dirty terms either: Helms's arguments against continued government funding for the federal commission established to promote the holiday were limited to the commission's excessive cost to taxpayers (at $500,000 per year, one of the smaller congressional appropriations).[4]

Identifying *what cannot be said* is a way to get at the constraints imposed by a given representation or representational structure—a collective memory or a way of remembering. The King holiday debate shows in rather stark fashion the contours of the sayable. But collective memories are enacted in more frequently occurring, less overtly conflictual contexts, and in smaller-scale ritual forms than a monument or holiday. Speeches by political leaders are also public rituals—stylized, regularized, performed in "sacred" spaces thought to be separate both from the trivial concerns of civilian life and from the backroom politics of purely sectional interests. They, too, are prime ground for constructing, using, and contesting collective memories. Through a content analysis of the *Congressional Record* (the official transcript of House and Senate floor activity) between 1 January 1993 and 31 May 1997, I parse the structure of representatives' invocations of Dr. King. I identify patterns in who invokes King, when and how they do so, in relation to what issues and people, and with what effect.[5] In the following, I'll sketch brief answers to those questions, but my main interest is in how, when, and why African American legislators refer to King. How, and how successfully, do they use the past to overcome difficulties posed by their congressional role as at once insiders and outsiders?

Much of the floor activity is transcribed for and directed to constituents. One can therefore interpret floor speeches as not only justifying a position on a particular issue but reinforcing the speaker's own credibility and the legislative institution generally. Analysis of floor discourse reveals that legitimation at work: I argue that congressional representations of King assimilate him into a pluralist framework by representing community service and institutional politics as the proper legacy of his activism. Elected officials and community volunteers, not extra-institutional activists, in this scenario, are the bearers of King's dream. So far, my argument is an instrumentalist one. African American officials commemorate King in a way that legitimates their own role as advocates for black interests. But a second feature of their invocations of King points up the limitations of an instrumentalist analysis. It shows black legislators rhetorically *struggling* to represent the purpose of memorializing King and the movement, to retell the past in a way that neither deprecates the movement's accomplishments nor claims that its aims have been fulfilled. The awkwardness of legislators' attempts to do this, in contrast to their customary eloquence, suggests the power of the progress and unity narratives that are built into American commemorative discourse. It also suggests the genre problem that black legislators face. Epideictic rhetoric, considered appropriate to commemorative occasions, invokes the past, but to affirm rather than change the present; it is traditionally distinguished from the deliberative, pragmatic, and policy-oriented argument seen as characteristic of legislative decision making. In the context of a widespread public perception that floor debate has become window dressing for backroom politics on one hand and constituent popularity contests on the other, there may be strong institutional pressures on congressional representatives to keep the two genres separate. But acceptance of that separation surrenders a valuable critical tool: King is used to challenge the present state of things, but mainly on commemorative occasions that are seen as without impact on the legislative process.

If we define protest as organized, extra-institutional efforts to change society (Tilly 1978; McAdam 1982), then a paradox of contemporary commemoration becomes clear: Memorializing protest reinforces the current political system by legitimating institutional political actors as protest's proper heirs and by vouching for the substantive character of formal political debate in its very absence from such debate.

The *Congressional Record* is the official record of floor activity in the House and Senate and is published daily.[6] It includes not only proposals for and debate about new legislation but also "one-minute speeches" on topics of national or district concern delivered by House members at the start of the day's business, and "special orders": five-minute speeches in the Senate and prearranged, 60-minute sessions in the House, usually at the end of the day's business (Tiefer 1989). The *Record* is not a verbatim record of legislators' speech. Speakers may edit their remarks, insert longer statements from which they draw only selectively in their floor speeches, and, with permission, insert previously published reports, articles, and op-ed pieces. For my purposes, this means that speakers have had an opportunity to cast their remarks in what they see as a coherent form. When I refer to awkward formulations, therefore, it is less likely that these are a function simply of the messiness of spoken speech than of the problems generated by the content and context of the utterance.

For each congressional session, I scanned all documents that referred at least once to "Martin Luther King" or "Dr. King"—in total, 843. For the purposes of this analysis, however, I discarded speeches in which the King reference was to an institution, place, or event named after him and those in which King's name appeared only in the title of proposed legislation, as well as *Record* documents that consisted solely of the text of a proposed resolution or bill, a list of sponsors, or other purely procedural material. I also eliminated any statement citing or quoting King that was not made by the legislator who introduced it (for example, newspaper editorials inserted in the *Record*). This left a total of 305 entries over the four-and-a-half-year period in which King was referred to at least once, and a total of 420 speeches.[7]

Are 420 speeches mentioning King over a four-and-a-half-year period a lot? There are a total of 612 entries in which "Abraham Lincoln" or "President Lincoln" is invoked at least once during the same period, less than the 843 for King (but presumably there are fewer events, awards, and places named *Abraham* Lincoln, rather than say, "Lincoln High School"). The comparison with King's civil rights contemporaries is more striking. Roy Wilkins, head of the NAACP; Whitney Young, head of the National Urban League; and James Farmer, head of the Congress of Racial Equality (CORE)—who, together with King and John Lewis (now a congressman) of the Student Nonviolent Coordinating Committee (SNCC), led the major movement organizations of the 1960s—are barely mentioned. Wilkins appears 9 times in four and a half years, Young 4 times, and Farmer 5 times. A. Philip Randolph, head of the Brotherhood of Sleeping Car Porters and organizer of the 1963 March on Washington (and its threatened 1941 predecessor), is mentioned 12 times.

Who invokes King? Overwhelmingly, Democrats. One hundred and twenty-two Democrats, that is, 33 percent of the 370 Democrats who have served in both chambers between 1993 and 1997, made speeches referring to King; Democrats accounted for 344 of the 420 King speeches, or 84 percent. By contrast, only 34 Republicans, or 10 percent of the 333 Republican representatives, made King speeches (as did both Independents). Thirty-five or 71 percent of the 49 African American representatives made speeches invoking King,[8] as did 8 or 42 percent of the 18 Hispanic representatives and 3 of the 7 Asians and Pacific Islanders. By contrast, only 17 percent of the 641 white representatives referred to King in their speeches. African Americans made 182 of the 420 King speeches, or 43 percent. Georgia congressman John Lewis invoked King most frequently—in 24 speeches over the four-and-a-half-year period. Nine other congresspeople, all but one of whom were African American, made seven or more references to King.[9]

In what discursive contexts are references to King made? The largest group comprises tributes to other people, 151 in total, 112 of which note the individual's relationship to King (others simply quote or paraphrase him). Recipients of such tributes are former civil rights activists from the legislator's district (a lawyer who represented activists, a local minister who marched with King), or nationally known former activists (Rosa Parks, James Farmer, Thurgood Marshall, Cesar Chavez, and the archbishop of the Greek Orthodox Church). They are also often people little known outside the legislator's district who were "inspired by Dr. King," "shared Dr. King's goals," or worked "in the spirit of Martin Luther King." References in the second largest group—93—come in speeches honoring historical events: Freedom Summer, the Selma to Montgomery March, King's birthday and assassination, and Black History Month. Fifty-one speeches citing King are commentaries delivered by a representative on a

Table 1. Context of references to Martin Luther King Jr., by race and party

	White Dems.		White Rpubs.		White Ind.	Black Dems.		Black Rpubs.	Other*	Total	
	NO.	%	NO.	%	NO.	NO.	%	NO.	NO.	NO.	%
Tribute	64	43	17	23	2	62	34	0	6	151	36
Anniversary	34	23	11	15	0	42	23	1	5	93	22
King law	7	5	3	4	0	21	12	0	0	31	7
Commentary	9	6	14	19	0	27	15	0	1	51	12
Legislation	36	24	28	38	0	28	16	1	1	94	22
Total	150	101	73	99	2	180	100	2	13	420	99

Source: Thomas at www.thomas.loc.gov.
*Hispanic, Asian, Pacific Islander, and Virgin Islander representatives are all Democrats except Lincoln Diaz-Balart, Republican congressman from Florida, and Victor Frazer, Independent delegate from the Virgin Islands.

topic of interest but not pending legislation. Thirty-one speeches are about legislation proposed to extend the federal King Holiday Commission or to commemorate King or the civil rights movement in other ways, for example, memorials, commemorative coins, or congressional resolutions.

The remaining references come in 94 speeches that are part of debates about specific pieces of legislation. Since representatives speak to issues of policy concern in extensions of remarks, one-minute speeches, special orders, and resolutions that are not part of debate over specific legislation, I have combined "commentary" speeches with "legislative" ones when the commentary spoke to a politically salient issue (see Table 2). Multiple references to King were made in calls for federal legislation to assist in prosecution of church arsonists in the South (17 King speeches), in debates over legislation to toughen penalties against pro-life protests at abortion clinics (11 King speeches, both pro and con), in support of affirmative action policies (11 King speeches), and in opposition to the withdrawal of U.S. troops from Haiti (6 King speeches).

What is the substance of the references to King? How is King viewed in these speeches? Congressional speakers style him as orator and moral leader, not shrewd political strategist. He is remembered for his rhetorical eloquence, for his "dream" of racial harmony, and for his "message," "lesson," "principle," and "spirit" of nonviolence. The dream is rarely

Table 2. References to King made in speeches on legislative and policy issues, by party and race of speaker

Legislative issue	White Dems.	White Rpubs.	Black Dems.	Black Rpubs.	Total
Church arson federal response	6	3	7	1	17
Budget cuts					
For (Balanced Budget Amendment)	0	1	0	0	1
Against (9 domestic, 1 international)	2	0	8	0	10
Abortion Clinic Access Bill					
For	4	0	0	0	4
Against	0	7	0	0	7
Affirmative Action					
For	3	3	5	0	11
Withdrawal of U.S. troops from Haiti					
For	0	1	0	0	1
Against	1	0	5	0	6
Gun control					
For	4	1	0	0	5
Electoral redistricting					
For	0	0	5	0	5
D.C. statehood					
For	0	0	5	0	5
Resolution against Nation of Islam speaker					
For	0	2	0	0	2
Against	1	0	1	0	2
Campaign and lobby reform					
For	3	1	0	0	4
Ban on gays in the military					
For	0	1	0	0	1
Against	2	0	0	0	2
Other*	14	13	8	0	35
Total	40	33	44	1	118

Source: Thomas at www.thomas.loc.gov.
Note: Speeches citing King occurred in debates about bills, concurrent resolutions, and joint resolutions, in one-minute and five-minute speeches, and in special orders. Includes some speeches labeled Commentary in Table 1.
*One or two references to Employment Nondiscrimination Act; Bosnian arms embargo; release of Chinese dissident; human rights enforcement in India; Religious Freedom Restoration Act; constitutional amendment protecting flag; armed forces appropriations; congressional civility pledge; Defense of Marriage Act; army spying; funding for the preservation of historically black colleges and universities; U.S. involvement in multinational miltary forces; Working Families Flexibility Act; release of records on FBI surveillance of King; school voucher program; NAFTA; National Service Bill; support for Nelson Mandela; teenage pregnancy; Workplace Fairness Act; hate crimes; habeas corpus reform; Educate America Act; Violent Crime and Control Act; nomination of NEH head; Republican filibustering.

specified and is sometimes conflated with an American dream of individual success ("One of Dr. King's philosophies revolves around the promise that every individual can achieve his or her dream in America" [McCarthy, House, 11 January 1995]).[10] Neither the movement's protagonists nor its antagonists—those with whom and against whom King fought—are clearly identified in congressional speeches. Instead, King is represented as bringing about change by "inspiring" and by "raising the consciousness" of the nation. Usually it is "America" that changes, and it does so through public acclamation. The only references to the illegality of King's actions come in Republican representatives' opposition to a bill that toughened penalties for harrassment at abortion clinics; opponents of the bill maintained that it violated pro-life demonstrators' freedom of speech and that it would quash the kind of civil disobedience on which King and his supporters had relied.

It is overwhelmingly the "early King" who appears on the House and Senate floor, the King who called for "a society where people will be judged not by the color of their skin but by the content of their character"—an excerpt from his 1963 "I have a dream" speech. This is by far the most often quoted of King's speeches and writings. The excerpt alone is quoted 30 times, the speech 48 times.[11] King's "Letter from a Birmingham Jail," written the same year, is also prominent in congresspeople's speeches, quoted 24 times, and his Nobel Prize acceptance speech, delivered in 1964, is quoted 3 times. Only 5 (or 4 percent) of the 119 quoted excerpts whose source I was able to identify come from speeches delivered between 1965 and King's death in 1968; 3 of those come from his last speech (and are introduced that way). The Dr. King who apprears in congressional speeches is not the one who opposed U.S. militarism, who called for a massive federal financial commitment to the poor, and who questioned a capitalist society's capacity to make that commitment.

Yet he is not so obviously the "harmless black icon" that Vincent Harding (1996) found in official and popular memory, either. He is not an unambiguous symbol of progress and unity or the raceless "American" hero that observers have seen in children's textbooks (Kohl 1995), public oratory about the King holiday (Naveh 1990; Harding 1996; Sandage 1993), and television coverage of the holiday (Campbell 1995). In congressional discourse, King is more likely to be grouped with *black* "he-

roes," "firsts," "greats," or "leaders" than with white ones: Frederick
Douglass, Sojourner Truth, W. E. B. DuBois, Harriet Tubman, civil rights
activists Rosa Parks and Fannie Lou Hamer, baseball player Jackie Robin-
son, and former congresswomen Shirley Chisolm and Barbara Jordan.
Current or recent congressional representatives and federal officials are
often included: Representatives Maxine Waters and John Lewis, Commerce Secretary Ron Brown, Energy Secretary Hazel O'Leary.[12] This suggests not an assimilationist, melting-pot model of ethnic politics, in which
American heroes are stripped of positional identities, honored rather for
their individual talents and claimed universally, but rather an ethnic
group, pluralist model, in which leaders represent the aspirations and
accomplishments of their respective groups (King for African Americans,
Cesar Chavez for Mexican Americans, etc.; on the two models, see Omi
and Winant 1986).

With respect to the unity and progress frames that observers have seen
in public representations of King, analysis of congressional discourse
shows interesting differences between black and white speakers. White
speakers tend to imply Americans' universal appreciation for King's message, using "we" and "us" to refer to Americans black and white. "We
marvel at the courage of Martin Luther King. We are humbled by the
eloquence of Barbara Jordan" (Boyd, House, 11 February 1997). They also
sometimes suggest universal appreciation for King *during his lifetime:* "Let
us recommit to the goals with which Martin Luther King, Jr., inspired us
all over a quarter century ago" (Gilman, Extension of Remarks, 7 January
1997); "It really was not until the late 1950s that we began to rally in
support of the work of Martin Luther King, by businessmen, by laborers,
by church leaders, *by all Americans,* and said 'let's finally get serious and
free ourselves from discrimination'" (Kennedy, Senate, 10 September
1996; my emphasis). The last statement, in addition, represents white
Americans as the ones doing the liberating (of themselves). At least one
speaker implied that racial unity preceded the movement, describing the
"great dream of King's that blacks and whites *can once again* walk together
in this country blessed by God in a land of freedom" (McIntosh, House,
104th; my emphasis).[13] White speakers occasionally indicate that King's
dream has been realized, his battle won. Thus, one described recent
church burnings as "hearken[ing] back to a time when to paraphrase Dr.
King, people were judged not on the content of their character but on the

color of their skin," implying that this is no longer the case (Biden, Senate, 26 June 1996). Another described King's struggle and concluded that "in the end, the American ideal of equality won, and hate lost" (Reed, House, 18 June 1996). More often, however, white speakers rely on a "there are still problems, but we've made great progress" frame. "Progress, not enough, has been made" (Kopetski, House, 24 February 1993); "we have a long way to go in making our Constitutional principles realities for everyone, but we have accomplished very significant progress" (Frank, House, 21 June 1994). The formulaic quality of the statement undercuts its force. Since the comments preceding it emphasize the accomplishments of the movement, and the comments following it rarely give equal emphasis to the problems remaining, the message is one of measured success and of continuing advance.

Black speakers also tend to rely on the "we've made progress but . . ." formulation, while emphasizing the "but . . ." clause. One speaker's comment that King had "moved to correct the evil, to shed not only light but to bring those evils to the forefront and to terminate them and eradicate them from our society" but that "during his lifetime he [King] was only partially successful in doing this" (Hilliard, House, 15 March 1994) is one of two quasi-failure formulations that I found. Most formulations claim success but with qualifications: "Martin would want us to raise our sights to the work yet to be done" (the focus on what King would have wanted, or on the responsibility incurred by his legacy); "Dr. King would find it a scandal that so many young people are still born into poverty, still receive an inadequate education, and still have no chance of achieving the American dream" (Moseley-Braun, Senate, 23 May 1994). The American "dream" of individual success is invoked here to remind listeners of its continued elusiveness for young black people. One speaker asked rhetorically, "If we stop and reflect on where we have gone since the marches and the sit-ins and boycotts of the 1960s, have we really gone far?" (Jackson-Lee, House, 11 February 1997). And another insisted that although "times have changed, we have not reached the promised land" (Clay, House, 23 February 1994).

While they accept the progress frame less readily than their white colleagues do, black representatives are nowhere near as critical of the contemporary state of race relations as were the local celebrations of King Day, mainly directed to black audiences, that Richard Merelman studied.

The most frequent substantive theme of the celebrations was "the continuing and pervasive practice by whites of discrimination against blacks" (1995: 87). "The ceremonies generally agree that the civil rights revolution remains unfinished, and likely to cause conflict in the future," Merelman continues. "References to the distance blacks still must go are four times more frequent than references to the distance blacks have come. Indeed, the ceremonies devote very little attention at all to past accomplishments. In nine of the ceremonies observed, I noted only four explicit references to past successes. By contrast, in these same ceremonies there were seventeen explicit mentions of how far blacks still had to travel" (ibid.: 89). Celebrants emphasized conflict rather than unity and continued inequality rather than progress in eradicating it.

These contrasts suggest that in order to understand how King is represented on the House and Senate floors, and to understand the dynamics of collective remembering more broadly, we cannot treat "congressional interests" monolithically in particular constructions of the past. In the following, I attribute patterns in how African American legislators invoke King to their distinctive political position. In a majority white Congress, their ability to deliver to constituents depends on persuading conservative and/or centrist forces to approve substantial government intervention (Swain 1993). Yet, from the point of view of black protest elites, they are often too close to the halls of institutional power. They are never invulnerable to activists' claims to better represent African American interests. How black congresspeople represent their relationship to the movement—how they define King's "legacy" and their role in furthering it—is important to their own credibility and that of their agenda. At the same time, however, their efforts to use King's memory to call for broadly redistributive policies are constrained by the institutional context in which they operate. The fact that they memorialize King in *Congress* rather than, say, at a King Day celebration in a predominantly black church, limits what they can say and when they can say it.

PROTEST, POLITICS, AND KING'S HEIRS

The passage of the Voting Rights Act in 1965 began what Bayard Rustin (1965) celebrated as a shift "from protest to politics." While in many areas of the South, white citizens and authorities kept up a reign of terror and, in the case of Mississippi, legislated a series of vote-dilution measures to minimize black electoral gains (Parker 1990), the number of black officials at local and state levels of government began to grow. There were 1,100 black elected officials nationwide by 1969, 3,600 by 1983, and 8,000 by 1993 (Marable 1995: 145). Championed as evidence of the civil rights movement's success, entry into electoral politics has not fulfilled the highest aspirations of the activists who fought for it. Those who made the shift from protest to politics were quickly disillusioned by their inability to effect substantive change. A member of the first Washington, D.C., city council under home rule remembers some of his colleagues— activists turned officials—"still damning the power structure and the system. I had to remind them that they *were* the power structure and the system."[14] Meanwhile, civil rights movement veterans and protest organizations like the NAACP, the Southern Christian Leadership Conference (SCLC), and Jesse Jackson's Operation PUSH found themselves not only relatively powerless against an erosion of civil rights gains under two Republican administrations but increasingly marginalized by the black officialdom they had fought to create. The postmovement era has accordingly been marked by persistent tensions between protest and electoral elites (Reed 1986; Smith 1996; Swain 1993; Lusane 1994; Clay 1992) and by skirmishes over guardianship of the movement past.

Thus, Adolph Reed Jr. (1986: 8) describes black elected officials' initial coolness to Jesse Jackson's 1984 campaign as reflecting a "turf dispute" between electoral and protest elites. Jackson "should continue to preach," said Detroit mayor Coleman Young bluntly after Jackson threw his hat in the ring. "As a politician, he's out of his league."[15] That most black elected officials came around to supporting Jackson had to do in part with his success in "legitimiz[ing himself] by projecting images of association with King and the civil rights movement" (ibid.: 28)—or, as an envious strategist for Walter Mondale put it, Jackson's ability to "equat[e] this presidential crusade with the civil rights movement."[16] Manning Marable (1995) likewise sees the 1993 March on Washington as an effort by remnants of the civil rights elite both to publicize Clinton's failures on health care, jobs, and the promotion of black progressives within his administration *and* to regain the mantle of black political leadership from black elected officials. The latter was evidenced in march organizer Joseph Lowery's declaration that the march was intended to "spark a renaissance in social activism and pass the torch so the struggle will continue" (ibid.: 145), and it was underscored by the march planning committee's failure to invite any voting members of Congress to serve among its cochairs.

Congressional invocations of King, like these higher-profile commemorations, reflect the tensions between black aspirations and a centrist political regime *and* between institutional and extra-institutional elites' claims to black leadership. Insofar as black legislators in the 103rd, 104th, and 105th Congresses saw themselves as advancing self-identified "black interests," they represented a constituency 70 percent of whom favored "more laws to reduce discrimination" (barely a third of whites polled agreed), and 51 percent of whom believed that "the USA is moving toward two separate and unequal societies—one black, one white" (one-third of whites agreed) (ibid.: 146). As minority representatives, black congressional legislators have a mandate to secure far-reaching change from an often intransigent political establishment, a task made more difficult by their perennial outsider status. Yet in the eyes of black activists, they are consummate *insiders*, always in danger of giving up an agenda of progressive change in favor of personal ambitions and political comfort. Their status as insider outsiders (or outsider insiders) poses tricky, eminently practical problems. They seek legitimacy as bearers of black interests, in potential or actual competition with civil rights activists. At the same time, they seek a program of progressive legislative change, in competition with those representing majoritarian or "white" interests. I argue that African American legislators use King references to further both tasks but that they are more successful in the first than in the second.

ASSIMILATING KING

Congressional speakers frequently assert their own relationship to King, whether direct ("I feel privileged to have known King personally" [Payne, House, 15 March 1994]; "I met a man who was a preacher from Montgomery" [Hilliard, House, 15 March 1994]; "I remember Fannie Lou Hamer, Martin Luther King, and Mary McCloud Bethune" [Meek, House, 28 February 1996]; "I was privileged to be with [King] on that march from Selma to Montgomery" [Rangel, House, 15 September 1993]), or indirect ("My own story is a testament to King's dream" [Moseley-Braun, Senate, 3 April 1993]; "it is doubtful I would be here today in this Congress if many people in this country who were offended in the 1960s by the remarks of Martin Luther King Jr. had been able to silence him" [Mfume, House, 23 February 1994]). The latter formulations are interesting because they not only vouch for the speaker's commitment to the same goals as King but cast him or her as fruit of the movement. This claim is often explicit: "I along with many of my colleagues am here today as a direct result of the struggles of the sixties" (Thompson, House, 21 June 1994). Congressional representatives are both witness to and evidence of racial advancement: "I have seen progress. . . . I have seen a poor black man, denied the right to vote, become a Member of Congress" (Lewis, House, 11 February 1997); "had Dr. King and many others not made that historic and dangerous walk from Selma to Montgomery, perhaps I would not be standing before this body today" (Collins, House, 14 May 1996).

Speakers are becomingly humble in acknowledging that their own careers were made possible by the travails of an earlier generation of movement activists. But they also style themselves—qua institutional actors—as legitimate heirs to that earlier activism. Their own careers become the next stage in a saga of African American struggle. "I was born, as a matter of African American history," Jesse Jackson Jr. related, "on March 11, 1965. On March 7, 1965, in our history, it is known as bloody Sunday. It is the Sunday that the gentleman from Georgia [John Lewis], Martin Luther King, and Jesse Jackson and many others in our history walked across the Edmund Pettus Bridge for the right to vote. Because of the struggle that they engaged in in 1965, I now stand here as the 91st African American to ever have the privilege of serving in the U.S. Congress" (Jackson, House, 11 February 1997). Another speaker aligned himself with King by appropriating a portion of King's last speech to describe his own situation: "It is a far from perfect situation which exists in Alabama, or in America, but if we realize this fact, and continue to progress and grow, we will reach Dr. King's promised land. And just like Dr. King, I may not be with you when you get there, but if this day comes after my work on earth is done, I assure you that I will be there in spirit" (Hilliard, House, 10 June 1996). Speakers' frequent grouping of King with recent and current congressional representatives has a similar effect. Thus, one representative described former congresswoman Barbara Jordan "in the tradition of Frederick Douglass, Martin Luther King, and Thurgood Marshall" (Jackson-Lee, House, 24 January 1996); another praised Congressman Lewis for "making it possible for me to serve in the U.S. House of Representatives" (Jackson, House, 11 February 1997). Representative Sheila Jackson-Lee cited her African American colleague Harold Ford's leadership in investigating the King and Kennedy assassinations (House, 26 September 1996). The message is one of continuity between a movement past and current institutional politics.

Representatives do not claim exclusive guardianship of the movement's legacy. They share it, they say, with people who are working in "the tradition of King," who are "shining examples of his legacy," the "unsung heroes" of the movement. Who are these co-legatees? Rarely activists, if the term is used to describe organized actors using extra-institutional means to bid for a redistribution of power (Tilly 1978; McAdam 1982). Rather, they are teachers, ministers, the founder of a homeless shelter, two leaders of a boys' club, the president of a city growth association, the director of a family care center, a local high school coach. "Great African American local leaders" are "teachers, parents, elected officials, the caring neighbor" (Velazquez, House, 24 February 1993). King's legacy is service rather than insurgency. This is striking in speeches made as part of special orders commemorating Black History Month in 1994 and 1997, under the rubrics of "Empowering Afro-American Organizations: Present and Future" and "Civil Rights Organizations in History: A Reappraisal," respectively. The organizations honored by legislators both years—many of them citing or quoting King in their remarks—were civil rights organizations of the 1960s (the NAACP, SCLC, and Urban League) and *civic* organizations today: after-school facilities, rehabilitation centers, a police officers' league, a historical preservationist group. Describing black America as "under siege," and quoting from A. Philip Randolph as well as King, Representative Eddie Bernice Johnson called for "work at the grassroots level to protect the hard fought gains of the civil rights movement." She went on to describe a sorority, a fund-raising group for civic causes, and Jack and Jill (a group promoting education and self-esteem among black students) (House, 23 February 1994). Grassroots "mobilizing" thus referred to community service rather than extra-institutional challenge through petitions, boycotts, strikes, or demonstrations.

The association of an earlier era of protest with volunteer efforts today is also evident in speeches urging continued funding for the federal King Holiday Commission. Although the commission established in 1984 to promote the holiday was intended to be privately funded, difficulties in raising adequate sums led to congressional annual appropriations of $300,000 after 1990. In 1994, Harris Wofford and Carol Moseley-Braun in the Senate and Ralph Regula and John Lewis in the House proposed legislation to extend appropriations for five years. In hearings and Senate debate, Wofford gave numerous versions of the following rationale:

> Nothing would have ticked Martin off more than people supposedly honoring him by sitting on their duffs watching the tube or sleeping late. The King holiday should be a day on, not a day off. A day of action, not apathy. A day of responding to community needs, not a day of rest and recreation. So my old civil rights colleague of the Selma march, Congressman John Lewis, and I have introduced legislation designed to remember Martin the way he would have liked: a day that reflects his proposition that "everybody can be great because everybody can serve." . . . Fixing parks, tutoring children, rebuilding schools, feeding the hungry, immunizing children, housing the homeless. (Wofford, Senate, 3 April 1993)

What King "would have liked" is "action," meaning "service." Senator Carol Moseley-Braun noted that "the day could be used to donate blood or volunteer at a hospital, to clean up a park or plant flowers in an inner-city neighborhood, to volunteer for the Boy Scouts or Girl Scouts or the Special Olympics, to tutor children or to work with those who have AIDS" (Senate, 23 May 1994). Wofford's and Moseley-Braun's brief for the legislation is echoed in remarks by other bill supporters. Certainly service is a worthy endeavor with potential for far-reaching change. However, its assimilation to King's extra-institutional activism is a rhetorical accomplishment rather than an obvious historical fact.

In some of these statements, King's commitment to nonviolence is restyled as a commitment to ending violence, especially among youth. Thus, one representative stated: "One needs only listen to the daily news and read the headlines to know that we need this Commission, now more than ever. Our young people are dying in great numbers on the streets, in their classrooms, and in their homes, Mr. Speaker. That is a fact. And the most frightening thing about that fact is—our children are killing each other. The King Holiday Commission is dedicated to teaching the tenets of nonviolence, and the value of community service to our young people"

(Clayton, House, 15 March 1994). "If there is no other reason for this Commission, it is that we can provide to young people precisely that kind of epiphany that says to them that nonviolence is important because it is predicated on a respect for the humanity of another person" (Moseley-Braun, Senate, 23 May 1994). When Coretta Scott King, who had tirelessly lobbied Congress for the holiday and the commission, appeared before a congressional hearing on the bill, she was quizzed on strategies to end teenage crime.[17] Certainly, for a commission under attack, piggybacking on the Clinton administration's volunteerism initiative made strategic sense—even if it meant playing to a belief that the black community's preeminent problem was teen violence. That no one objected to that characterization or offered an alternative one, and that it appears in the *Record* before and after the debate, suggests its general acceptance among congressional representatives.[18]

In congressional discourse, then, the movement with which King was associated has been effectively recast in terms of conventional pluralism. Change, in the pluralist scheme, is effected incrementally through electoral political channels and intermediate organizations, for example civic associations, social clubs, self-help groups, not through extra-institutional, disruptive, collective action, which is unnecessary given the existence of multiple avenues for reform (Gamson 1990; McAdam 1982). Congressional black representatives never denigrate extra-institutional activism and activists—they are, as they repeatedly acknowledge, the beneficiaries of past insurgency. However, by representing King's activism as part of an earlier phase of struggle, as *past*, they represent their own careers as its proper successor. References to King thus warrant black legislators' claim to represent black interests better than contemporary protest elites can.

KING AS CHALLENGE

Yet black congresspeople aim to do more than justify their own existence, and for that reason, they have a real stake in *not* representing the past as past. This is what makes their role, and how they commemorate King, tricky. As representatives of a constituency whose aspirations were voiced but not realized by the 1960s civil rights movement, they must convince their congressional colleagues that there is much more to be done. They must warrant a vision of change, not as unfolding inevitably but as federally enacted and as urgent. If, as Michael Kammen (1991) suggests, collective remembering in the United States is bound to powerful narratives of unity and progress, then African American legislators face peculiar dilemmas in commemorating extra-institutional activism. How to convey not the accomplishments, the steps taken, the threat averted, but the promises not made good on, the unresolved, the incomplete? How to celebrate change achieved through conflict? And how to tie remembering to change *now*? These dilemmas are evident in how congressional speakers represent representation—how they explain commemoration's purpose.

Black congressional speakers repeatedly assert that retelling the African American past—collective struggle, individual accomplishments, and national benefits—is essential to changing the present. But other, and sometimes conflicting, rationales for remembering are also offered.[19] On one, King's contributions are obvious and unforgettable—"Dr. King's stamp upon American history is profound and indelible" (Dixon, House, 7 April 1993); "his perseverance and leadership is indelibly etched in the minds of all Americans" (Stokes, House, 24 February 1993). Commemoration celebrates rather than preserves his memory. On another, it is natural forgetfulness that threatens King's legacy—"the moment of civil rights triumph may be a distant memory to some" (Lewis, House, 24 April 1997)—or African Americans' forgetfulness: "Too many black Americans don't realize the importance and significance of recalling past struggles and achievements and relating those efforts to present day conditions" (Clay, House, 3 February 1994). On still another rationale, it is young people, for whom the movement "has become ancient history" (Moseley-Braun, Senate, 23 May 1994), who are most in need of commemorative efforts; they must be shown that "they have a responsibility . . . to not just glorify Dr. King as a hero but learn and practice his teachings and beliefs" (Collins, 24 February 1993).

Commemoration is necessary to "close a chapter" of the past; by remembering, however, we "make sure that the clock is not turned back . . . make sure that we do not repeat that period of our history" (Clyburn, House, 22 February 1995). For "if we forget the tragic lessons of our history we are doomed to repeat them" (Moseley-Braun, Senate, 23 May 1994). The task is "to revel in our history" and, contrarily, to "draw back from our history . . . to not have some of the unfortunate consequences of our social development repeated" (Tucker, House, 23 February 1994). After one congressman concluded his remarks on the 1960 student sit-ins by urging that "the more we can come to grips with that, the more we can put this, parts of history like the sit-ins, behind us, and we can all become indivisible, under God, with liberty and justice for all," another speaker corrected him: "I thank the gentleman. I hope we will never put the spirit of the sit-ins behind us" (Watt and Owens, House, 11 February 1997). The tensions black commemorants face are evident: commemoration must relive the past without forgetting the present, must honor the movement's leaders without omitting the "unsung heroes," must recognize individual fortitude in the face of adversity without minimizing the oppressiveness of past conditions, and must expose past (and present) suffering without thereby inflaming those who have suffered.

Pervasive in speakers' comments is anxiety, above all, that memory not become nostalgia, that it inspire government action, not substitute for it. *Merely* remembering is as dangerous as forgetting. "We must do more than keep a memory of a great man," Representative Kweisi Mfume insisted. "We must push further ahead past the pain, the hate, and most of all, the complacency that settles when we forget there is more to be done" (House, 7 April 1993). "It is not a day just to remember him but is a day to be joyful that a man of his caliber came along and set the record straight and changed America" (Hilliard, House, 15 March 1994); "we should remember not for memory's sake, or for the sake of nostalgia" (Norton, House, 21 June 1994); "we are not nostalgic about the past but there are some parts of the past that I would like to recall" (Lewis, House, 24 April 1997): these excerpts show speakers trying to make of commemoration something more than, or a special kind of, remembering. One speaker introduced his co-celebrants as those who would "participate in this special order in memory, not just in memory, but in commemoration, I guess, in celebration, of what happened in that little town of Selma" (Lewis, House, 7 March 1995). Another argued that "this is a history that we cannot forget; lest we forget, we will surely allow those enemies of democracy who want to restrict the American people's right to vote to wane" (McKinney, House, 24 May 1995); and another, "let us not ever be so brazen, so commonplace that we forget the struggle" (Watt, House, 7 March 1995). The rhetorical awkwardness of these usually eloquent speakers betrays their struggle to make remembering more than celebration and reveals the limits of the commemorative form with which they must work.

Like their white colleagues, African American representatives are apparently reluctant to specify the protagonists, antagonists, and stakes of the movement in anything but vague terms. They too describe America's conscience stirred, its imagination captured, its commitments honored, and praise King's "message," "teachings," "wisdom." They too assert unity over conflict. "[King's] life was dedicated to fighting for justice and equality not just for African Americans or the poor, but for all Americans" (Moseley-Braun, Senate, 23 May 1994); "the civil rights movement was not a struggle for black Americans alone. It was a struggle to ensure equality of opportunity for all Americans" (Sawyer, House, 26 January 1993); "during his lifetime, Dr. King's faith, perseverance, and determination served as a symbol of the hope for equality for all Americans" (Stokes, House, 11 February 1997). Describing King's impact in terms of his "contributions" and "achievements," common phrases in the speeches, also suggests change through influence rather than struggle.

COMMEMORATIVE OCCASIONS

Even if the King they invoke is less than radical, black congressional speakers do often forcefully describe a society marked by racial inequality and injustice. But the solution to such conditions is *more* storytelling, more commemoration. I noted earlier the speaker who asked, "If we stop and reflect on where we have gone since the marches and the sit-ins and boycotts of the 1960s, have we really gone far?" Her answer was to call for "daily efforts to correct the history that is taught to our children" (Jackson-Lee, House, 11 February 1997). The speaker who pointed out that although "times have changed, we have not reached the promised land" urged that "[we] constantly remind ourselves and others of the great contributions blacks have made and continue to make to this nation" (Clay, House, 23 February 1994). It is "forgetfulness" about "the lessons [King's] life taught us" that has "contributed to the widening gap that remains between the salaries of white and African American workers, the increasing gap between the incomes of middle and lower income African Americans, the continuing segregation of our cities' schools and communities, and the violence among our youth which has reached heights unimaginable even a few years ago," Senator Carol Moseley-Braun argued (3 April 1993). If forgetting has had such debilitating consequences, then remembering should have equally transformative effect. Legislation to commemorate the 1965 Selma to Montgomery March, one speaker promised, "will mark a turning point in the history of this country's struggle for civil rights" (Jackson-Lee, House, 14 May 1996). Another described movement commemorative activities in a project aimed at reducing teenage pregnancy as essential to building "self-esteem" and, thence, responsible behavior (Waters, House, 12 March 1996).

Since most of these statements come in commemorative contexts (Black History Month, King's birthday, the anniversary of the Voting Rights Act) or in discussions of provisions for official commemoration (for example, the extension of the King Holiday Commission), it is unsurprising that they conclude with calls for commemoration. But *the majority of King references are made in such contexts*. I noted earlier that the largest number of King speeches were delivered as part of tributes and on commemorative occasions; in combination with speeches advocating government sponsorship of commemorative activities, they accounted for 275 or 65 percent of the 420 speeches. Is this simply because tributes dominate congressional speech making? The *Congressional Record* database does not provide the overall number of tribute entries relative to legislative discussion entries in a congressional session. So I chose a two-day period on which the number of overall entries was close to the average (267 entries for 15 and 16 March 1994) and, after discarding procedural entries of the kind discussed earlier, coded the remaining speeches. Of the 266 speeches, 53 or 20 percent were tributes, 9 (3 percent) anniversary speeches, 43 (16 percent) commentaries, 5 (2 percent) speeches calling for commemorative legislation, and 156 (59 percent) speeches about pending egislation. Thus, whereas 65 percent of the speeches referring to King were delivered on commemorative occasions, only 25 percent of all speeches were delivered on such occasions. Table 1 shows, moreover, that African American representatives did not invoke King more often in legislative debates than did white Democrats or Republicans during the 1993 to 1997 period and that a smaller proportion of African American representatives' King speeches were delivered in legislative contexts relative to commemorative ones than were those of white representatives. Table 2 shows that the largest number of King speeches in a legislative context called for federal response to the wave of church burnings in the South, a measure that enjoyed bipartisan support. The second largest number came in debate related to abortion and were more likely to be made by Republicans espousing pro-life positions than by Democrats, white or black. The *Congressional Record* reveals, then, an interesting bifurcation: even as African American congressional representatives assert the importance of remembering in order to bring about tangible change, they do not often invoke the past in substantive legislative discussions.

Why not? Black representatives confront a powerful genre problem, I argue: that of using *epideictic* rhetoric in *deliberative* situations. Epideictic rhetoric "praises or blames on ceremonial occasions, invites the audience to evaluate the speaker's performance, recalls the past and speculates about the future while focusing on the present, employs a noble, dignified literary style, and amplifies or rehearses admitted facts" (Campbell and Jamieson 1990: 14). It relies on "*memoria*, or recollection of a shared past" (ibid.: 15) and is primarily contemplative. As Harry Caplan puts it, the speaker tries "to impress his ideas upon them [the audience], without action as a goal" (1954: 173n). Karlyn Kohrs Campbell and Kathleen Hall Jamieson argue that such rhetoric is appropriate to commemorative speeches like presidential inaugural addresses, which seek to affirm unity, communal values, the institution of the presidency, and the president's recognition of the obligations of the office. Thus, genre follows institutional function. Epideictic rhetoric can be contrasted with the deliberative argument that is characteristic of policy making. "Deliberative argument pivots on the issue of expediency, specifically, which policy is best able to address identified problems, which policy will produce more beneficial than evil consequences, and which is most practical, given available resources" (Campbell and Jamieson 1990: 29). Classically, deliberative rhetoric was intended "to persuade the assembly to take a definite course of action, such as going to war or not going to war" (O'Malley 1979: 39). Occasionally, speakers have been able to combine elements of the two genres, and Campbell and Jamieson (1990: 29) cite Lincoln's first inaugural address for its "unusual" rhetorical strategy of using deliberative arguments (against southern secession) for epideictic purposes (unifying the nation and reaffirming communal values). Yet in today's Congress there are strong and distinctive pressures operating to keep the genres separated.

Whether anything gets done on the floor of Congress has always been the topic of dispute. Charges that floor debate is "mere" talk have sharpened in the context of two developments. One is representatives' increased attentiveness to constituents, partly a result of the media's expanded coverage of congressional activities (Bacon et al. 1995: 400). For example, until 1979, commemorative legislation (naming public buildings, for example, or designating special days) accounted for 1 to 10 percent of all legislation. In the 96th Congress, commemorative legislation increased by more than 70 percent and continued to rise thereafter, accounting for more than one-third of all bills signed into law by 1985. Attacked for its diversion of money and attention from substantive to purely symbolic concerns, this increase has been attributed to representatives' orientation to constituents (ibid.).

A second feature of contemporary congressional decision making is the dominant and, according to some, ever expanding role of congressional committees and subcommittees (ibid.: 412; Denton and Woodward 1990: 301). Already in the early nineteenth century, Josiah Quincy of Boston complained that the House "acts, and reasons, and votes and performs all the operations of an animated being, and yet, judging from my own perceptions, I cannot refrain from concluding that all great political questions are settled elsewhere than on this floor" (quoted in Weatherford 1981: 173). Committee rooms were once seen as the actual site of decision making, but, according to J. McIver Weatherford (ibid.: 185), once they were opened to the public in the late 1970s, "the real process of legislation once again escaped beyond the klieg lights" further into the back rooms of politics. Committee hearings became opportunities for the enactment of ritual dramas, and the congressional floor was reduced to an "empty shell." Weatherford's judgment is especially harsh but not too dissimilar from that of other political observers. "The business of the House is dominated by its committees, and with few exceptions oratory has little discernible impact in the process of proposing, drafting, and voting upon legislation," one writer concludes (Bacon et al. 1995: 612). In fact, committees' autonomy has been formally circumscribed in the last two decades, and floor amending activity has increased (ibid.: 420), but "conventional wisdom holds that floor debate does not change minds" (Bessette 1994: 166). Instead, legislation is widely perceived to be made through the vote trading, deal making, and interest-group lobbying that takes place behind closed doors.

An important consequence of these developments may be pressure among congressional representatives to *demarcate* legislative floor debate from both backroom maneuvering and constituent-driven pomp. Establishing symbolic boundaries—spatial, temporal, rhetorical—prevents the "pollution" of legislative functions by activities deemed less legitimate.[20] Limiting the duration of "one-minute speeches," scheduling them in the morning and at the discretion of the Speaker, and relegating special orders to the end of the day, when they will not "interfere" with legislative business, are formal mechanisms for insulating legislative debate from these other forms of talk. But there may also be less explicit pressure to keep epideictic and deliberative rhetorical genres separate, that is, to not memorialize during the "real work" of legislative policy making. Of course, deliberative discourse has always invoked historical precedent, hallowed tradition, and heroic figures. However, the vulnerability of congressional floor discourse to charges that it involves scarce deliberation at all, that it is ritual drama rather than substantive debate, may make representatives anxious to distinguish making history from memorializing it.

I am arguing that the operation of genre boundaries may constrain congressional representatives' ability to use King to criticize rather than to affirm. On legislative occasions, memorializing is at odds with a deliberative rhetorical style, making it difficult to invoke King in debates about substantive policy issues. And on commemorative occasions, memorializing in order not merely to contemplate but to legislate—that is, to take action—is at odds with the conventional requirements of epideictic discourse. Thus, if the first set of constraints that I discussed stems from the commemorative form and the narratives of progress and unity embedded in it, the second stems from the commemorative occasion. The context of their speeches—Martin Luther King Day rather than a debate about the budget, say—encourages speakers to call for more commemoration rather than for new legislation, more appropriations, better enforcement of existing laws, or an otherwise interventionist federal stance. And in those discussions of health care, welfare, toxic waste cleanup, campaign and governmental reform, military defense, crime, education, foreign policy, and telecommunications which took place during the 1993–97 period, the movement, King, and his lessons are not prominent.

Paradoxically, then, the conventions surrounding the memory of insurgency strengthen institutional politics in two ways. Memorializing dissent enables politicians to legitimate themselves as heirs of an activist past. And if the ideological work of commemoration is restricted to special occasions—occasions on which anyone can be honored, from Martin Luther King Jr. to the constituent whose claim to fame is her stamp collection—then what goes on the rest of the time must be driven by national interests rather than partisan ones and must have tangible rather than symbolic consequence. King memorials end up reproducing the legislative institution by their very marginality.

CONCLUSION

Numerous writers have addressed the difficulties nations face in commemorating "difficult" pasts: for example, the Vietnam War (Wagner-Pacifici and Schwartz 1991), the Holocaust (Maier 1988; Olick and Levy 1997), and the atomic bombing of Japan (Linenthal and Engelhardt 1996). I argue that social movements are a special kind of difficult past, with distinctive risks. For African American legislators, commemorating the civil rights movement and its martyred leader risks emphasizing their own position within the political establishment, potentially viewed as cozy rather than transformative, and potentially framed that way by civil rights leaders vying for the mantle of black leadership. Accordingly, black congressional speakers commemorate King in a way that casts electoral politics and community service *rather than* extra-institutional activism (the latter remarkable by its absence from their commemorative speeches) as the legitimate heirs of King and his movement. As representatives of an unequal minority, however, black representatives resist commemorating King in a way that accepts the present state of governmental action vis-à-vis black Americans. Their effort to mold King discourse to point up the unfinished work of the movement is less successful than their effort to legitimate themselves as spokespersons. Using collective memory to do more than memorialize is difficult, not only on account of the progress and unity narratives embedded in the commemorative form but also on account of remembering's restriction to commemorative, rather than legislative, occasions.

What are the implications of this case? For students of social movements, battles over the legacy of protest, the kind of activism it warrants, and the truest spokespeople for its aspirations, point up an important dynamic in the institutionalization of protest. The incorporation of members of an insurgent group into government offices does not signal a definitive shift in leadership from protest to electoral elites. Collective memory and, specifically, the stewardship of an insurgent past can be a crucial terrain for fighting out continuing leadership claims between these two groups. The question is how much winning the battle over memory counts in gaining recognition from governmental elites, potential allies, and constituents as an accepted broker of a group's putative interests. And what counts as winning? Comparison with other groups that have ostensibly made the shift "from protest to politics"—Green Party members in European parliaments, African National Congress members in South Africa, and Irish elected officials associated with Sinn Fein come to mind—would be important in answering these questions. The dominance of the Republican and Democratic Parties and the absence of movement parties in the United States (Rucht 1996) might generate more, or potentially more debilitating, battles between protest elites and their electoral counterparts over who best represents the movement's aspirations and accomplishments. On the other hand, these structural features of the American political system may be counterbalanced by cultural ones, for example, what Michael Kammen (1991) sees as an American tendency to depoliticize the past, resulting in a kind of agnostic support for multiple traditions. One mode of depoliticizing the past, I have argued, may be to bring it up only on formally commemorative occasions.

For students of collective memory, the case attests to the multiple and conflicting projects withing groups often represented as unitary—officials and African Americans, to name two. Counterpoising the commemorative interests of "political structures and ordinary people" (Bodnar 1992: 18), "dominants and subordinates" (Merelman 1992: 248), or "official" and "popular" memory (Scott 1996: 388), even if the focus is on their interrelations, doesn't do justice to the multiple, competitive, and changing relationships *among* elites inside and outside the government, and within subordinated groups. The broader point, of course, is that instrumental interests exist only in relationship. One cannot specify a group's stakes in a particular issue without understanding its position vis-à-vis groups defined as allies, antagonists, competitors, and constituents.

How people represent and seek to use the past can help us to illuminate those alliances and fissures.

The case also points up the inadequacy of an instrumentalist approach, however, by identifying constraints on speakers' instrumental deployment of representations of the past. It isn't what "actually happened"—the past in some pristine, unreconstructed sense—that limits what speakers can do with it. Rather, cultural conventions of commemoration, that is, accepted ways of publicly remembering, shape *what* one can do with the past (the rhetorical form of commemoration) and *when* one can do it (the occasions on which commemoration is acceptable). Accepted ways of doing things, of course, are neither unchanging nor universal. With respect to the latter, this case contributes to locating culture within the institutions it reflects, shapes, and reproduces. Black legislators *use* King remembrances, but they do so in forms and at times that are generally acceptable to the legislative body. The result, though not their intention, is that the commemoration of dissent reproduces a view of Congress's policy deliberations as substantive rather than "merely" symbolic, since the symbolic work of commemoration takes place on occasions reserved for it, and only on those occasions.

Shortly before King's death, his associate Rabbi Abraham J. Heschel said that "the whole future of America depends upon the impact and influence of Dr. King" (Harding 1996: ix). On the floor of Congress, at least, that impact seems to have been largely confined to the realm of memory.

NOTES

Research for this article was supported by a Columbia University Social Sciences Faculty Grant. The author thanks Jeff Olick, Manning Marable, Paula Baker, and an anonymous reviewer for *Social Science History* for generous and insightful comments, and Linda Catalano for research assistance.
1. Francis X. Clines, "Reagan's Doubts on Dr. King Disclosed," *New York Times*, 22 October 1983; "King Holiday—New Law's Effect," *U.S. News and World Report*, 31 October 1983; *Congressional Quarterly Almanac* 1983: 601.
2. *Congressional Quarterly Almanac* 1983: 601.
3. David Alpern, "Behind the King Debate," *Newsweek*, 31 October 1983; "Impact of Helms's Attacks Studied by His Constituents," *New York Times*, 26 October 1983.
4. *Congressional Quarterly Almanac* 1994: 157; *Congressional Record*, Senate, 23 May 1994.

5. I study invocations of King rather than of the civil rights movement because the latter are so few in number. This in itself says something important about the status of the movement in official memory. I will say more on that below.

6. An initiative by Representative Newt Gingrich made the last four and a half years of the *Record* (covering the 103rd, 104th, and 105th Congresses) available via an Internet linkage entitled Thomas; this is the source I used, in conjunction with published transcripts of congressional hearings, some text from earlier, printed issues of the *Congressional Record*, and newspaper accounts and analyses.

7. Entries in the *Congressional Record* may consist of a single speech, an extension of remarks by one representative, or an extended debate. By "speech," I mean a statement that is either a single entry or part of one (but I count numerous speaking turns by one representative in the entry as a single speech). When I refer to the number of "references to King," I mean the number of speeches in which King was mentioned at least once.

8. This includes the nonvoting representative from the District of Columbia but not the delegates from the Virgin Islands.

9. J. C. Watts of Oklahoma, one of the two African American Republican representatives, made two speeches referring to King (his term began in 1995); the other, Gary Franks of Connecticut, made no speeches citing King during his two terms of office (although he was one of the members of the King Holiday Commission).

10. Material in brackets refers to the speaker, forum (House, Senate, Extension of Remarks), and date. See White 1997 and Rosenthal and Schram 1997 on presidential, congressional, and popular constructions of the "American dream."

11. Republicans and Democrats use the phrase in different ways: Democrats interpret it as calling for the creation of an egalitarian society, Republicans as an injunction to treat people in the here and now on the basis of the content of their character. For example, a special order commemorating Black History Month contains this statement: "If we are to move forward as the world's most diverse and successful multicultural nation, we must stop defining each other by the color of our skin, and strive to judge one another by the content of our character" (Martini, House, 28 February 1995). The fact that 1993 was the 30th anniversary of the speech may account in part for its high profile in the 103rd congressional session, when it appeared in 26 speeches by congressional representatives. In the next two-year period, it appeared in 13 speeches. However, it appeared in 9 speeches between January and May 1997, which is only one quarter of the 105th Congress. It would be useful to compare usage of the speech in congressional sessions before 1993.

12. King is also grouped with people characterized by their moral and/or spiritual leadership—Jesus, Moses, Gandhi, Cesar Chavez (although the latter two were political leaders). The only white with whom King is grouped more than three times is Robert Kennedy; all references are to the assassination of both men in 1968. He is linked with Abraham Lincoln three times, George Washington twice, and Thomas Jefferson once. One reference to Lincoln and Washington claimed King's historical importance on the grounds that he was the only other American to have a holiday in his honor; one speech by a white Republican urged that King and Thurgood Marshall be celebrated as *Americans*—as American as Amelia Earhart and George Washington—rather than as African Americans.

13. The importance of the unity narrative for white commemorants may explain why Ronald Reagan, who saw the King holiday as "symbolic of crisis," was reluctant to sign the legislation, while Howard Baker, who saw it as "symbolic for unity," avidly supported it. Alternatively, Reagan's opposition to the legislation may explain why he represented it as "symbolic of crisis"—depending on whether one views representations of the past as shaping policy or legitimating it, that is, as rules or resources.

14. Eric Pianin, "The March and the Dream," *Washington Post*, 27 August 1983.

15. Martin Schram and Dan Balz, "Jackson's Run Poses Dilemma for Black Leaders," *Washington Post*, 27 November 1983, 1.

16. Ibid.

17. See U.S. Senate 1995.

18. Campbell (1995) describes a similar framing in news media's coverage of the King holiday in 1993. The King Holiday Commission's fate is intriguing. After winning authorization for $2 million over five years (*Congressional Quarterly Almanac* 1994: 157), the commission voted *itself* out of existence after only two years; its director explained that they could no longer justify the financial burden on taxpayers. However, transcripts of a closed meeting of the commission's executive committee, along with an earlier memo sent by Coretta Scott King to the commission instructing it to cease using King's name or likeness in its fund-raising efforts, suggest that King and her son Dexter (newly installed as director of the King Center for Nonviolent Social Change) saw the commission's fund-raising efforts as competing with those of the King Center. In 1993, the latter was facing a deficit of $600,000. Commission members acknowledged that a prohibition on using King's name or likeness would cripple their fund-raising efforts and decided, accordingly, to disband. "Adjusting the King Vision," *Atlanta Journal and Constitution*, 7 February 1995; Robert A. Jordan, "King Family Feud Doesn't Deserve Olympic Stature," *Boston Globe*, 5 February 1995.

19. In his study of Civil War monuments, Kirk Savage (1994: 129–30) found that movement sponsors offered several rationales for such monuments, "occasionally advancing the argument that people are forgetful and need their social memory bolstered by powerful mnemonic aids; sometimes arguing instead that memory is safe in the present but monuments are needed to transmit it across generations; yet frequently invoking a startling counterargument—that the memory of heroism is undying and will outlast even monuments, which are therefore built simply as proof of memory's reality and strength." I found the same rationales, and additional ones, in African American legislators' arguments for commemoration.

20. Sociologists and anthropologists since Emile Durkheim have explored the social functions of symbolic boundaries separating the pure from the impure and the sacred from the profane. See especially Douglas 1966 and Alexander and Smith 1993.

Alexander, J., and P. Smith. 1993. "The Discourse of American Civil Society: A New Proposal for Cultural Studies." *Theory and Society* 22: 151–207.

Bacon, D. C., R. H. Davidson, and M. Keller. 1995. *Encyclopedia of the United States Congress.* New York: Simon and Schuster.

Bessette, J. M. 1994. *The Mild Voice of Reason.* Chicago: University of Chicago Press.

Bodnar, J. 1992. *Remaking America.* Princeton, N.J.: Princeton University Press.

Campbell, C. P. 1995. *Race, Myth, and the News.* Thousand Oaks, Calif.: Sage.

Campbell, K. K., and K. H. Jamieson. 1990. *Deeds Done in Words: Presidential Rhetoric and the Genres of Governance.* Chicago: University of Chicago Press.

Caplan, H. 1954. *Rhetorica ad Herennium.* Cambridge: Harvard University Press.

Clay, W. L. 1992. *Just Permanent Interests: Black Americans in Congress, 1870–1991.* New York: Amistad.

Connerton, P. 1989. *How Societies Remember.* Cambridge: Cambridge University Press.

Denton, R. E. Jr., and G. C. Woodward. 1990. *Political Communication in America.* 2d ed. New York: Praeger.

Douglas, M. 1966. *Purity and Danger.* London: Penguin.

Gamson, W. 1990. *The Strategy of Social Protest.* 2d ed. Belmont, Calif.: Wadsworth.

Garrow, D. 1988. *Bearing the Cross.* New York: Vintage.

Greenblatt, S. 1983. "Murdering Peasants: Status, Genre, and the Representation of Rebellion." *Representations* 1: 1–29.

Harding, V. 1996. *Martin Luther King, the Inconvenient Hero.* Maryknoll, N.Y.: Orbis.

Kammen, M. 1991. *Mystic Chords of Memory: The Transformation of Tradition in American Culture.* New York: Knopf.

Kertzer, D. I. 1988. *Ritual, Politics, and Power.* New Haven, Conn.: Yale University Press.

Kohl, H. 1995. *Should We Burn Babar?: Essays on Children's Literature and the Power of Stories.* New York: New Press.

Linenthal, E. T., and T. Engelhart. 1996. *History Wars: The Enola Gay and Other Battles for the American Past.* New York: Henry Holt.

Lowenthal, D. 1985. *The Past Is a Foreign Country.* Cambridge: Cambridge University Press.

Lusane, C. 1994. *African Americans at the Crossroads: The Restructuring of Black Leadership and the 1992 Elections.* Boston: South End Press.

Maier, C. S. 1988. *The Unmasterable Past: History, Holocaust, and German National Identity.* Cambridge: Harvard University Press.

Marable, M. 1995. *Beyond Black and White: Transforming African American Politics.* London: Verso.

McAdam, D. 1982. *Political Process and the Development of Black Insurgency, 1930–1970.* Chicago: University of Chicago Press.

Merelman, R. M. 1992. "Challenge and Resistance: Two Cases of Cultural Conflict in the United States." In Merelman, ed., *Language, Symbolism, and Politics.* Boulder, Colo.: Westview.

——. 1995. *Representing Black Culture*. New York: Routledge.

Naveh, E. J. 1990. *Crown of Thorns: Political Martyrdom in America from Abraham Lincoln to Martin Luther King, Jr.* New York: New York University Press.

Olick, J. 1993. "The Sins of the Fathers: The Third Reich and German Legitimation." Ph.D. diss., Yale University.

Olick, J., and D. Levy. 1997. "Collective Memory and Cultural Constraint: Holocaust Myth and Rationality in West German Politics." *American Sociological Review* 62: 921–36.

O'Malley, J. W. 1979. *Praise and Blame in Renaissance Rome*. Durham, N.C.: Duke University Press.

Omi, M., and H. Winant. 1986. *Racial Formation in the United States: From the 1960s to the 1980s*. London and New York: Routledge.

Parker, F. R. 1990. *Black Votes Count: Political Empowerment in Mississippi after 1965*. Chapel Hill: University of North Carolina Press.

Reed, A., Jr. 1986. *The Jesse Jackson Phenomenon*. New Haven, Conn.: Yale University Press.

Rosenthal, M. B., and S. F. Schram. 1997. "Pluralizing the American Dream." In S. F. Schram and P. T. Neisser, eds., *Tales of the State: Narrative in Contemporary U.S. Politics and Public Policy*. Lanham, Md.: Rowman and Littlefield.

Rucht, D. 1996. "The Impact of National Contexts on Social Movement Structures." In D. McAdam, J. D. McCarthy, and M. N. Zald, eds., *Comparative Perspectives on Social Movements*. New York: Cambridge University Press.

Rustin, B. 1965. "From Protest to Politics: The Future of the Civil Rights Movement." *Commentary* 39: 25–31.

Sandage, S. 1993. "A Marble House Divided: The Lincoln Memorial, the Civil Rights Movement, and the Politics of Memory, 1939–1963." *Journal of American History* 80: 135–67.

Savage, K. 1994. "The Politics of Memory: Black Emancipation and the Civil War Monument." In J. R. Gillis, ed., *Commemorations: The Politics of National Identity*. Princeton, N.J.: Princeton University Press.

Schwartz, B. 1991. "Social Change and Collective Memory: The Democratization of George Washington." *American Sociological Review* 56: 221–36.

Scott, S. 1996. "Dead Work: The Construction and Reconstruction of the Harlan Miners Memorial." *Qualitative Sociology* 19 (3): 365–93.

Smith, R. C. 1996. *We Have No Leaders*. Albany: State University of New York.

Swain, C. M. 1993. *Black Faces, Black Interests*. Cambridge: Harvard University Press.

Thelen, D. 1987. "A Round Table: Martin Luther King, Jr." *Journal of American History* 74: 436–37.

Tiefer, C. 1989. *Congressional Practice and Procedure: A Reference, Research, and Legislative Guide*. Westport, Conn.: Greenwood Press.

Tilly, C. 1978. *From Mobilization to Revolution*. Reading, Mass.: Addison-Wesley.

U.S. Senate. 1995. *King Holiday and Service Act of 1993: Hearing before the Committee on the Judiciary, U.S. Senate, April 13, 1994*. Washington: GPO.

Wagner-Pacifici, R., and B. Schwartz. 1991. "The Vietnam Veterans Memorial: Commemorating a difficult past." *American Journal of Sociology* 97: 376–420.

Weatherford, J. M. 1981. *Tribes on the Hill*. New York: Rawson, Wade.

White, J. K. 1997. "The Storyteller in Chief: Why Presidents Like to Tell Tales." In S. F. Schram and P. T. Neisser, eds., *Tales of the State: Narrative in Contemporary U.S. Politics and Public Policy*. Lanham, Md.: Rowman and Littlefield: 53–62.

Zerubavel, E. 1996. "Social memories." *Qualitative Sociology* 19: 283–300.

Postnationalist Pasts:

The Case of Israel

◀ ◀ ◀ ◀ ◀ ◀ ◀ ◀ ◀ ◀ ◀   U R I   R A M

National identity is hegemonic among the population of Jewish descent in
Israel. Zionism, modern Jewish nationalism, originated in eastern Europe in the last quarter of the nineteenth century. A national movement
without a territory, Zionism naturally adopted the ethnic, or integrative,
type of nationalism that prevailed in the region (for a basic typology of
nationalism see Smith 1986: 79–84). In Palestine the diasporic Jewish
nationalism turned into a settler-colonial nationalism. The state of Israel
inherited the ethnic principle of membership and never adopted the alternative liberal-territorial principle. To this day the dominant ethos of the
state is Zionist, that is, Jewish nationalist. Though Israeli citizenship is de
jure equal to Jews and Arabs, a de facto distinction is easily discernible
between the dominated minority and the dominant majority and its state.[1]

The Zionist movement, the Jewish community in Palestine, and later
the state of Israel had been most successful in the dissemination and
internalization of national faith among the population of Jewish descent.
Two historical experiences have had a formative impact on contemporary
Israeli-Jewish identity: the annihilation of Jews in the Holocaust and the
protracted state of war between Israel and the Arab states (Oron 1993).

These powerful traumas have amplified and fortified the already given sense of ethnic national identity.

The newly established nation of Israel, which was born out of diaspora Judaism, had to reimagine itself (Anderson 1983 [1991]), reinvent a tradition (Hobsbawm and Ranger 1983), and renarrate a historical identity (Bhabha 1990). The social and political project of Jewish immigration to Palestine, the settlement and colonization of the land, and the construction of a Jewish community and state there, all against Arab opposition and hostility, were rendered culturally in terms of national "revival," territorial "repatriation," and historical "redemption."

Historians, together with authors, poets, painters, sculptors, journalists, teachers, and other intellectuals, artists, and persons of letters—and, at a later stage, social scientists as well—took an active, and even leading, part in the composition and propagation of the national narrative. Far from being a remote academic arbiter, Israeli academia was part and parcel of the national endeavor (Ram 1996). Academic disciplines, especially the ones we are concerned with here, history and sociology, had been shaped under the spell of national ideology. Until quite recently the dominant historical paradigm has been underpinned by premises furnished by the national-revival school, led by Ben Zion Dinur and others (Ram 1995; Barnai 1995), and the dominant sociological paradigm has been underpinned by premises furnished by the nation-building school, led by S. N. Eisenstadt and others (Ram 1993, 1995). The history and sociology written in Israel until the last 10 to 15 years conferred an ostensible scientific aura and academic legitimization upon the collective memory and collective ideology required by the crystallizing national identity. The affinity between power and knowledge has been indeed tight in Israel. It would not be a gross exaggeration to suggest that until recently "the nation" has studied itself, rather than being properly studied.

Recently, this situation has been radically changed, at least in part. The carriers of the change on the intellectual terrain are scholars labeled "critical sociologists" and "New historians," who charge the scholars they consider "mainstream sociologists" and "Old historians" with being apologetic toward their topic. The historians' debate that erupted in the late 1980s became exuberant in the mid-1990s. It gained extensive coverage in the mass media, became the axis of quite a few academic conferences held in the country, and was the leading topic in issues of several scholarly journals. Some of its key terms, such as "the New History" and "post-Zionism," have become common in cultural and even daily parlance in Israel. The current study analyzes both the content and context of the historians' debate (with only a brief allusion to the sociologists' debate; for a full analysis of that issue, see Ram 1995).

DISSENTING BODIES OF KNOWLEDGE

What are Israeli historians (and sociologists) debating? For the sake of lucidity, the multiple issues raised in the debate may be classified into three major thematic categories: the Israeli-Arab national conflict; the social policies of the Labor movement; and Hebrew-Zionist culture.

The Israeli-Arab national conflict is the special area of the core group of the New Historians. These historians have challenged the conventional view of the foreign and security policy of Israel, especially (so far) regarding the 1940s and 1950s. In the conventional view Israel is considered to have always been peace seeking and prone to compromise, while the Arab states are portrayed as stubborn aggressors. The New Historians argue, among other things, that the state of Israel declined opportunities for negotiations with Arab states (Flapan 1987; Slater 1995) but on the other hand concluded an unwritten pact with the Jordanian Kingdom to parcel out between the two of them the territory known as the West Bank, in order to prevent the establishment of a Palestinian state there (Pappe 1992; Shlaim 1988).

Furthermore, New Historians argue that Israel bears a large—in certain versions, a major—responsibility for the creation of the Palestinian refugee problem, to use the title of Benny Morris's extensive study of the topic (Morris 1991). It is argued that during Israel's War of Independence of 1948, senior Israeli military commanders, encouraged implicitly by Israel's highest authority of the time, Prime Minister David Ben Gurion, evicted hundreds of thousands of Palestinians from their villages and expelled them beyond the state's borders. In addition, Israel exercised (and still exercises) a tough "no return" policy toward the refugees. Until these revelations scandalized academia and public opinion, professional historians simply avoided these unpleasant aspects of the war, while popular histories and school textbooks tended to refer to it briefly as an Arab "mass escape," sometimes airing the theory that this escape was ordered by Arab leadership. Today, under the force of evidence amassed mainly by Morris, matters of fact are hardly disputed (but see Tevet 1989), though issues of the circumstances and imperatives involved are still very much in question (e.g., Kadish 1989).

In addition, Israel's border security policy of the 1950s—retaliation in kind for terrorist attacks on its citizens—has been discerned as overblown and adventurous. It is claimed that this policy finally provoked an unnecessary war, in 1956. As a potential alternative to Prime Minister Ben Gurion's "activist" hard line, a reconsideration is given to the relative "moderate" line of Moshe Sharet, foreign minister and for a short period prime minister (Morris 1993; Kafkafi 1994; Pappe 1986).

Critical sociologists who researched the early stages of Jewish settlement in Palestine, at the end of the nineteenth century and early decades of the twentieth, have applied an analogous analysis, only in more structural terms. They presented the Zionist settlement as a colonial project involving acquisition of lands, closure of labor markets, and displacement of native Arab peasants (Shafir 1989, 1993; Kimmerling 1983; Ehrlich 1987). This new critical sociology evidently offset mainstream Israeli sociology, which offered a "dualistic" concept of Israeli-Arab relations, according to which the two societies had developed side by side, each according to its own inherent modernizing impetus (Eisenstadt 1967; Horowitz 1977). Furthermore, critical sociologists determined that a military culture has emerged in Israeli society and has significantly contributed to the reproduction of the national conflict (Kimmerling 1993; Ben-Eliezer 1995).

The second category of dispute is that of the social policies of the Labor movement, which was dominant in Israeli society from the 1930s to the 1970s. Mainstream sociology and history used to depict the founders of the movement as idealist pioneers and used to adulate their particular blend of national development and social(ist) construction, captured by the formula of "socialist constructivism" (Eisenstadt 1967; Shapira 1980; Gorni 1973). In sharp contradistinction, New Historians argue that the Jewish Labor movement had been conspicuously nationalist, modeled after the most integrative kind of East European nationalism of the time; that its ideology of equality was no more than a mobilization ruse; and that nothing was farther from its mind than the construction of a model socialist society (Sternhell 1995).

Since the 1970s, a barrage of critical sociologists had expressed coinciding views. They highlighted the power-driven, organizational, manipulative nature of the Labor elite (Shapiro 1975, 1993; Grinberg 1993); they exposed the discriminatory policies exercised by the movement and its governments toward the Arab citizens of Israel in areas such as housing, education, employment, and welfare (Rosenfeld 1978; Rosenhak 1995; Shalev 1992; Yiftachel 1992; Al-Haj 1995); and they disclosed the methods of domination and control over this population by way of second-rate de facto citizenship and an ethnically dominated democratic system (Smooha 1990; Lustick 1988; Peled 1993; Bishara 1993).

A particular target of harsh critique was the pattern of integration of the wave of Jewish immigration from Muslim countries during the 1950s and early 1960s, which almost doubled the population of the state and radically transformed its ethnic complexion. Mainstream sociology had analyzed this issue in its "nation-building" framework in terms of "absorption," a process in which the newcomers are "desocialized" from their former traditional identity and "resocialized" into modern Israeli culture (Eisenstadt 1967; Bar Yosef 1980 [1969]). Critical sociology, again in contradistinction, analyzed the same process in terms of the construction of classes in a capitalist division of labor or in terms of an unequal distribution of power (Smooha 1978). It argued that the Labor movement, and more specifically the leading party, Mapai, initiated labor-intensive industrialization, directed the immigrants to dependent peripheral locations, and placed them in proletarian and marginal positions (Swirski 1981, 1993). The other side of this process of "underdevelopment" of the new Mizrachi population was the "development" of the veteran Ashkenazi population (Jews of European descent) into a "new bourgeoisie," a state-sponsored managerial class (Rosenfeld and Carmi 1976; Carmi and Rosenfeld 1989). Still later, the second generation of these same Jewish immigrants from Muslim countries were channeled into education and military-service conduits that reproduced the initial social inequality (Swirski 1990, 1995; Nahon 1993), and the Jewish-Arab culture of the immigrants was utterly curbed and quelled (Alkalai 1993; Shohat 1989; Piterberg 1995). Another aspect of the Labor movement's self-image to be exposed as a myth was gender equality (Bernstein 1987, 1992; Fogel-Bijaui 1991; Herzog 1994). In addition to what is considered a leftist-radical critique, a bourgeois-liberal version of Israeli history has lately begun to emerge. In this version the role of the Labor movement in the process of nation building is depreciated, and the role of the "private sector" entrepreneurial class is inflated. The latter is presented as the "real" constructor of the economic infrastructure of the Jewish community, and collectivist ideology is presented as having been an hindrance to the further investment and development of this community. In this version of history the first and fourth waves of Jewish immigrants, petit bourgeois farmers and urban merchants, gain a place in a narrative that hitherto considered them failures and that crowned as a success story the second and third waves of Jewish immigrants, who formulated the collectivist ethos and established the collective institutions of the Labor movement (Giladi 1973, 1994; Katz 1989, 1993).

The third area under dispute in the historians' debate is Zionist-Hebrew culture. A major thesis in this regard is that the cornerstone for the construction of a new "positive" Israeli identity in Eretz-Israel was the contrast drawn between it and a contrived "negative" identity of diaspora Jews (Raz-Krakotzkin 1994). In this view the major creed of Hebrew culture was the "negation of diaspora." The pioneers who settled Palestine and their Sabra (native-born) descendants were depicted as physically agile and spiritually brazen biblical peasant-fighters, and diaspora Jews were depicted as the antithetical "others" of the Zionist self. Furthermore, the Jewish past was condensed into a single linear metanarrative of the path "from dispersal to redemption," in which Zionism emerged as the telos of all Jewish history (Firer 1985; Ram 1995).

Others charge that the cultural hiatus erected between Zionist settlers and diaspora Jews is responsible for the tragic fact that during the disastrous times of the Holocaust the leadership of the Yishuv (the prestate Jewish community in Palestine) did not go out of its way to rescue persecuted Jews from Nazi claws (Beit Zvi 1977; Grodzinsky 1994; Segev 1991). This charge is disavowed by mainstream historians, who allude to the frailty and helplessness that paralyzed this leadership in the inconceivable circumstances of those days (Eshkoli-Wagman 1994; Bauer 1993, 1994; Tevet 1994a, 1994b; Weitz 1994; Michman 1994; Porat 1986, 1990). Still others argue that regardless of what was actually done or could have been done to rescue Jews, the memory of the Holocaust is being "nationalized" in Israel and utilized for political purposes, while the universal lessons from the tragedy and a bare sympathy for its victims are grossly omitted (Wasserman 1986; Diner 1988; Firer 1989; Zukerman 1993; Zertal 1994, 1996). Specifically ferocious in its attacks on the Zionist conduct during the Holocaust is the anti-Zionist religious-Orthodox version (see Asaf 1995; Porat 1995).

In every respect, whether the argument relates to Palestinian Arabs, Mizrachi immigrants, or European Jewry, the conventional Zionist "story" is harshly shattered, and its "truths" severely challenged. Zionist idiomatic currencies, such as "a country with no people, to a people with no country" (referring to the Jewish settlement in Palestine), or "there is nobody to talk with" (referring to the claimed absence of Arab partners for peace), or "all of Israel guarantee each other" (referring to Jewish solidarity), are rebuffed or questioned. Beyond specifics, such arguments thwart the Zionist objective of being considered the sole delegate of the interests of Jews in all times and places, the genuine representative of Jewish culture in its variety, and the necessary culmination of Jewish history (Firer 1985; Evron 1988; Barnai 1995; Libes 1992). On a most general plateau, claims such as those raised by the New Historians and critical sociologists deconstruct the Zionist national grand narrative and expose its contradictions and instabilities, omissions and lapses, that have marginalized and repressed others.

CROSS-CUTTING IMAGES OF KNOWLEDGE

On top of the controversies over substantial historical issues historians disagree over matters of historical method, though sometimes the lines of difference cut through the "old" and "new" camps; thus, each camp is divided into "objectivists" and "relativists." By and large, though, in Israel as elsewhere, institutionalized academicians tend to adopt the former position, while young(er) and (more) radical historians tend to the latter. Historical objectivists consider "written history" a textual retrieval of "historical reality." Relativists maintain that the same "piece" of historical reality can be rendered in more than one way. Objectivists consider written history a report on past events; relativists consider written history a narration of past events. The language of report is represented as analytical; the language of a narrative is literary. Objectivists aim toward the ideal of a final and total history; relativists expose the horizonlike evasiveness of this ideal. For objectivists, a historical text is either accurate or fallacious;

for relativists, the historical text always must have a context. Objectivists regard the "logic of discovery" as an unfortunate hindrance, to be cleaned off as much as possible; relativists regard it as an unavoidable constitutive dimension of the "logic of explanation."

Interestingly enough, one of the harbingers of the New History, Benny Morris, is committed to the positivist ideal of historiography. He frequently declares that "there is truth," that "objectivity is possible," and that "the historian of the Israeli-Arab conflict should make an effort to write on this conflict as if he was writing on the war between Carthage and Rome, or as if he just now landed from Mars, and he observes the situation with no connections or commitments" (Morris 1994: 40). His view of his craft is evidently "archivist"—"the tendency of the historian to think that the most important relation is not with the readers, the times, or the questions but with the archives—with what the historian misleadingly calls 'the sources' of history" (Megill 1987).

Yet the more radical contingent of the New Historians in Israel is beginning to absorb relativist positions, inspired by either sociology of knowledge, narrativist approaches to history, or poststructuralist cultural critique and multicultural positions. Ilan Pappe (1994), the most outspoken representative of the New Historians in Israel, poignantly expresses the stakes from this point of view: "Historians today do not profess objectivity. They display cynicism towards the historical narrative woven by past and present political elites, and endeavor to shed light on all those who were delegated to the shades by nationalism, religiosity, racism, and male-chauvinism." (This translation and all others in the essay are my own.)

One can summarize the major positions articulated in the historians' debate in a two-by-two matrix, generated by (a) difference over "body of knowledge" matters, where "apologetic" versus "critical" positions are discernible; and (b) difference over "images of knowledge" matters, where "objectivist" versus "relativist" positions are discernible (for the body/image of knowledge terminology see Elkana 1978). Table 1 thus defines the intellectual space of the historians' debate in Israel, illustrating its division among four major positions.

Some (myself included) consider a more dialectical perspective. In this view the essential philosophical tension between objectivism and relativism is unresolvable. On the one hand, historical research is, and should

Table 1. The major positions regarding nationalist history (body of knowledge) and historical knowledge (image of knowledge) in the historians' debate in Israel

	Body of knowledge	
Image of knowledge	APOLOGETIC	CRITICAL
OBJECTIVIST	"National historiography is objective"	"National historiography is biased"
RELATIVIST	"National historiography is as relative as any other"	"National historiography silences other narratives"

be, directed heuristically toward "the *truth*"; yet on the other hand, historical research is strongly embedded in historical memory, and *"the* truth" is a chimera. Israeli historians of ideas Amos Funkenstein and Shaul Friedlander thus propose that "historical consciousness" should be viewed as a mental-intellectual spectrum that contains both scholarly research and collective memory in an interrelated way (Friedlander 1993; Funkenstein 1991).

The emergent notion in Israeli academe of the dialectical relations between "history" and "memory" is adeptly demonstrated in historical psychologist Dan Bar On's work on the process of transference and articulation of Holocaust memories in Israeli families. Rather than looking positivistically for the validity or accuracy of the memories of his interviewees, Bar On looks hermeneutically for the meaning and repercussions of these memories in the subjects' life. In the process he expounds the sense of historical narration in general: "There are unlimited numbers of alternative life-stories one can tell on oneself. Any given story is always a process of selection among various options: on what to expand? where to contract? what to tell, to omit, to describe? What should be debatable? At what point does the 'no story' becomes a roaring silence on the background of the biographical facts, and at what point is it trivial?" (Bar On 1994: 275).

The changing answers to these questions, he argues, should be regarded not as an approach toward a fixed truth but rather as a continuous dialogue between the present and its past, as "[the] ability to move freely, to and fro, between the there and then and the here and now, namely the ability to live with the memory" (ibid: 275). Biography consists not of bare facts but of the narrative construction of facts into a "self." What Bar On observes here at the individual level is exponentially valid at the collective level. No less than individuals, if not more so, collectivities are engaged in such a constant "process of selection among various options," and they do ask themselves (or some members of them do) "on what to expand? where to contract? what to tell, to omit, to describe? What should be debatable? At what point does the 'no story' becomes a roaring silence on the background of the biographical facts, and at what point is it trivial?" The historians' debate, as outlined above, makes sense only if read against this sort of conceptualization of historical narrative.

Yet more testimony of the radical transformation taking place in the self-understanding of the historical craft in Israel emerges from the examination of the editorial policy of the Hebrew historical periodical *Zmanim* (Times). Its editor attests that between the establishment of the journal in 1979 and mid-1995, it has exchanged a positivistic approach, focused on the textual reconstruction of past events, for a reflective attitude, focused on the critique and deconstruction of the historical composition itself: "Today self-conscious historians are constantly concerned with the questions related to their own work: what is the relation between the object of their inquiry and their own subjectivity? Does the object of inquiry as given out there, as an objective entity, awaited to be discovered, or does its existence depend on the interpretation and significance attributed to it by the historian? They ask questions about, for instance, myth and memory, the representation of historical events, historical narration, myth and history" (Zertal 1995).

The essence of these new sensibilities is a heightened reflectivity—awareness to the historian's self—and a heightened perspectivism—awareness to the historian's positioning. We may thus conclude that in the recent period the notion of historical knowledge in Israel has been radically transformed. Knowledge is conceived now, much more than in any time in the past, as a practice where "power" and "truth" constantly grapple with one another. Historical research and historical memory—in combination, historical consciousness—change in tandem and dialogically. Both are generated by deep undercurrents in the political culture in Israel, to which we now turn.

What sociohistorical circumstances brought about the transformation of historical consciousness in Israel? The transformation is attributable to recent changes in the Israeli sense of identity. The high tide of nationalist identity came in the wake of the establishment of the state in 1948. In the prestate Jewish community this identity was primarily expressed by the "pioneering" "civil religion" of the Labor movement. In the era of the state the ethos of "pioneering" (*haluziyut*) was transmuted into that of "statism" (*mamlachtiut*). Throughout this period there also persisted secondary versions of the national identity: the religious-national, the liberal-civic, and the rightist-nationalist (Liebman and Eliezer 1983). In the second half of the 1960s nationalist identification subsided somewhat, but a chain of unpredictable events, which started with the 1967 war, mixed the cards again and again.

The occupation of the West Bank and other territories in that war reanimated the old creed (predominantly of the right wing) of the Greater Israel; a new social stratum, hitherto marginalized, of religious-national Yeshiva graduates, mobilized since 1974 by the Block of Faithful (Gush Emunim), exploited the opportunity to appropriate and renew the early century's pioneering ethos. In addition, this territorial expansion spurred unprecedented economic growth and, with it, the emergence of newly acquired riches; simultaneously, however, this development incited the outburst of a protest of the second generation of the impoverished Mizrachi population. Back in the 1970s the protest was stirred by a handful of Black Panthers, but by and large it channeled mass support for the Likud, planting the seeds of the future fall of the Labor movement and its ethos. The fall came 10 years after the 1967 war and after another war, the 1973 October War. In that war Israel barely survived a massive Egyptian-Syrian surprise attack. The governing party suffered widespread denunciation, and in 1977 it lost in the elections for the first time in decades.

The rise to power of the right-wing Likud party accelerated the three processes mentioned above: the expansion and deepening of the Jewish settlement in the occupied territories and the general strengthening of religious-national influence on Israeli politics; augmentation of the Mizrachi protest and elevation of the status of Mizrachi culture and its symbols; and the expansion of the range of activity of business corporations and of neoliberal market-oriented stratum of entrepreneurs and managers. The year 1979 marked a big boost for the Likud government and its leader, Menachem Begin, following the first peace treaty signed between Israel and an Arab state—Egypt. In 1981 Likud won the elections again, in one of Israel's most malicious ethnic electoral campaigns. Yet the 1980s proceeded in a different tune. In the first half of that decade Israel was up to its knees in triple-digit inflation, generated by uncontrollable monetary liberalization, and in a bloody entanglement in Lebanon (following its 1982 invasion there). This war became extraordinarily important in the development of Israeli political culture. It was the first war to be deeply contested in Israeli public opinion (Helman 1993; Barzilai 1996). All previous wars were widely perceived as "no choice," defensive wars; this one was openly declared by the prime minister to be a "war of choice," a war initiated by Israel to reach a political end (the destruction of the Palestine Liberation Organization [PLO], then seated in southern Lebanon). The opposition to it marks the genesis of an autonomous civil society in Israel, where state and society had usually been intimately meshed.

The entry of Labor into a "national unity government," following the 1984 elections, facilitated the curb of inflation and the withdrawal of the troops from Lebanon (though a "security zone" and an Israeli-sponsored local militia were left behind). In the socioeconomic arena, the liberalization policy continued to intensify with every successive government. Since the mid-1980s Israel has witnessed its first "bourgeois revolution," in which the collectivist institutions founded by the Labor movement crumbled, and the "privatization" ethos led by a now robust bourgeois class took total precedence. This process reached a symbolic peak in 1994, when the Labor movement lost its historical command over the Histadrut, the large Federation of Labor. In 1987 another deeply contested war began—the Intifada, a Palestinian popular resistance to the Israeli occupation—and it augmented the "Vietnam effect" of the Lebanese war. In 1991 Israeli self-confidence was dealt another blow when its civil rear was exposed to ballistic threat, and its dependency on the United States was clearly underscored. In 1992 Labor won the elections (by a meager majority), and in September 1993 the Oslo accord was signed between Israel and the PLO. Later a peace treaty with Jordan was signed, and negotiations with Syria were conducted.

In November 1995 the prime minister of Israel, Yitshak Rabin, was assassinated. His murderer, a student at Bar Ilan, a religious-nationalist university, was a neo-Zionist zealot. This event consummated two decades of growing malevolence between the two major political blocs that had emerged in Israel since the 1970s. Though almost the entire population of Jewish descent in Israel confesses allegiance to Zionism, the boundaries of Zionist discourse have been significantly transgressed between the 1970s and the 1990s, from both right and left. I label "neo-Zionism" and "post-Zionism" the respective right-wing and left-wing transgressions of classical Zionism. Arguably, while neither one is a majoritarian trend, both redefine the contours of Israeli collective identity in a very significant way. The historical revision and debate in Israel is a manifestation of the decline of the classical Zionist ethos and the renewed contest over Israeli identity. Through this debate, the lines of public discourse are redelineated.

Neo-Zionism emerged in the 1970s. Its constituency consists largely of the Jewish settlers in the territories and their many supporters in the so-called national camp throughout the country. It is represented by a variety of extreme right-wing parties, including core parts of the national-religious party (Mafdal) and the Likud Party (Sprinzak 1991; Peri 1989). This trend regards "the biblical Land of Israel" (identified with all areas under Israeli military control) as more fundamental to Israeli identity than the state of Israel (a smaller territory identified with the 1948 "green-line" borders). The motherland is conceived as a superior end, the state as an instrument for its control. The culture of neo-Zionism is an admixture of Zionist and Jewish ingredients; but while classical Zionism was characterized by discord between nationalism and religion, in neo-Zionism secular nationalism is conceived as a stage in an immanent religious revival (Ravitsky 1996). The political allegiance of neo-Zionism is to an ostensible "Jewish people," conceived as a unique spiritual-ethnic community, rather than to Israeli nationality, in its down-to-earth senses of a political community defined by common citizenship. Legal (and practical) affiliation in the collectivity is considered secondary to the ostensible ascriptive national brotherhood. Neo-Zionism is thus an exclusionary, nationalist (even racist), and antidemocratic political-cultural trend, striving to heighten the fence encasing Israeli identity. It is fed by, and in turn feeds, a high level of regional conflict and a low level of global integration. Conflict vindicates its alarming messages, and global integration has loosened its grip on the national mind.

Post-Zionism started to emerge in the 1980s. Its constituency is composed mainly of the extensive "new" middle classes, typically concentrated in the country's coastal area, especially in the city of Tel Aviv and its vicinities (where a quarter of the population resides). This trend grants more esteem to individual rights than to collective glory. In blunt contrast to neo-Zionism, it considers the collectivity as a tool to serve the welfare of the individual. In its historical horizon the present ("quality of life") is much more important than the past ("history"), and the near future (children) is more meaningful than the remote past (ancestors). One political avant-garde of post-Zionism is the Yesh-Gvul (literally: "There is a border / limit") movement, which surfaced in response to the 1982 war. It consists of reserve soldiers and officers who refuse to serve in the occupation forces in Lebanon and the Palestinian territories, arguing that the role of the military is defense, not repression. Though the movement is rather small, the principles of civil disobedience it represents have gained recognition by a larger sector of the population, which is committed to civil rights rather than to ethnic nationalism. Post-Zionism is, then, a trend of libertarianism and openness, which strives to lower the boundaries of Israeli identity and to include in it all relevant "others." It is fed by, and in turn it feeds, a lower level of regional conflict and a higher level of global integration of Israel. Conflict mobilizes nationalistic feelings and thus disables it; global integration draws people to cosmopolitan consumerism and thus is suitable to it. Table 2 depicts the major orientations of neo- and post-Zionism.

It should be emphasized that the traits of both neo-Zionism and post-Zionism are not entirely foreign to "classical" Zionism. In fact, these are two diametrical accentuations of Zionist traits. Their novelty consists precisely in their one-sided accentuation. Neo-Zionism accentuates Zionism's messianic and particularistic dimensions, while post-Zionism accentuates its normalizing and universalistic dimensions. In their opposing ways both trends indicate the transition toward a postnationalist Israeli collective identity. The nationalist stage was an imperative of the

Table 2. Major orientations of neo-Zionism and post-Zionism (ideal types)

	Neo-Zionism	Post-Zionism
Concept of membership	Ethnic	Civic
Self-identity	Jewish	Israeli
Normative identity	Collectivist	Individualistic
Spatial identification	Land of Israel (biblical land)	State of Israel ("green-line")
Temporal identification	Ancient times and far future ("our ancestors")	Present and near future ("our kids")
Cultural orientation	Particularistic ("chosen people")	Universalistic ("normalization")
Political culture	Fundamentalist-messianic	Utilitarian-pragmatic
Political manifestation	Gush Emunim	Yesh-Gvul

Source: Based in part on Kimmerling 1985.

era of territorial colonization, nation building, and state formation. Tens of years later, a variety of internal and external pressures have worn nationalism thin and enhanced the emergence of postnational alternatives. Neo-Zionism and post-Zionism are "labels" for these dawning alternatives. Neo-Zionism elevates to an exclusive (and exclusionary) status the ethnic dimension of Israeli nationalism; post-Zionism elevates to an exclusive (and in this case inclusive) status the civic dimension of Israeli statehood.

It is this fundamental shaking of the dominant nationalist ethos, Zionism, that generates the historical revision and debate in Israel. What we witness is the scrambling of the unilinear and teleological national metanarrative by a variety of supranarratives (post-Zionist cosmopolitanism), subnarratives (empowered, marginalized, or excluded groups: women, Palestinians, Mizrachi Jews, Orthodox Jews), backlash narratives (neo-Zionist ethnicity), and subsidiary narratives (bourgeois-liberal). Diverse social categories whose voices had until recently been silenced take a stand in the public arena, articulate their own versions of history, and retell it. Their "truths" diverge naturally—or, to put it more correctly, historically—from the hegemonic "truth." Just as in the end of the nineteenth century and the first half of the twentieth century Zionism was busy inventing for itself a tradition and composing for itself a historical narrative, so today in the postnationalist era, a variety of groups in Israel

Table 3. Major controversial axis in the Israeli historical consciousness

Hegemonic	Contestants
National	Cosmopolitan
Collectivist	Individualist
Zionist	Palestinian
Israeli	Jewish
Labor movement	Right-wing
" "	Liberal
" "	Leftist
Ashkenazi	Mizrahi
(European descent)	(Middle-Eastern descent)
Secular	Religious (Orthodox)
Male	Female

are busy deconstructing that particular version of history and constructing their own histories.

The new politics of identity and memory drastically refurbishes the tissue of the historical consciousness in Israel. In place of a unilinear teleological national history, there are now a variety of contestant lines. All of them are critical of the nationalist and socialist master narrative, some more toward the nationalist dimension, others more toward the socialist dimension. This new situation is depicted in table 3.

Yet this tabular depiction is too simplistic. The new situation should be depicted by a more sophisticated graphic presentation, but that would have to be multidimensional and mobile. First, the table is not exhaustive; more categories and subcategories could have been added (such as, for instance, heterosexual-homosexual; cf. Schwarz 1994). In addition, the table presentation does not distinguish among different levels of narrative maturity; for instance, at this point the Palestinian narrative is more fully developed than the female narrative, and so on. But most of all, the table does not display the many dissections and intersections among the various narratives. Identity is not a closed and fixed entity but rather an intersection of a variety of affiliations and influences. Thus, for instance, there is no one comprehensive "female narrative"—there is the female narrative of Labor movement women pioneers, of urban bourgeois women, of Palestinian women, and so forth. In short, if the essay would have allowed it, a multidimensional and mobile presentation would have been required in order to map the contemporary historical consciousness in Israel. It is likely that in the future the historical consciousness in Israel will be, on the one hand, more multivocal and, on the other hand, orchestrated in a more sophisticated way. If an architectural metaphor is allowed, the hegemonic historical consciousness in Israel is comparable to the geometrically shaped white-painted housing buildings that were constructed in Israel under the inspiration of a modernist Bauhaus "international style" from the 1930s to the 1960s. The new historical consciousness may be compared, in this vein, to the colorful and eclectically shaped buildings of Antonio Gaudí.[2]

FROM A CASE TO A PHENOMENON:
POSTHISTORICISM IN THE GLOCAL ERA

The Israeli historical revision and debate is not unique, of course. Having studied it in some detail, we may now observe a larger historiographical terrain. In the 1980s and 1990s historical revisions and debates resounded with much echo in Germany (cf. Berger 1995; Maier 1988; Volkov 1991), France (cf. Rousso 1991; Gildea 1994; Revel and Hunt 1995), and the United States (cf. Foner 1990; Appleby et al. 1994, 1995), to name just some well-publicized cases. In fact, historical revisions, often borrowing theoretical novelties of neighboring disciplines or adopting artistic and literary sensitivities, have become a worldwide phenomenon, exciting public opinion from Japan and Australia (Curthoys 1993; Gibson 1992; Gunew 1990), through India (Chatterjee 1993; Guha and Spivak 1988; Prakash 1994), Africa (Cooper 1994; Feierman 1995), Europe (Karakasidou 1994; Hertzberger 1995), Latin America (Mallon 1994), and Canada (Palmer 1994). In the 1980s and 1990s questions of collective memory and of historiography have emerged as a major preoccupation of literary figures and intellectuals worldwide, especially—though not exclusively—after the lead of "minority" scholars. This is vindicated by the flood of publications, which deters any complete listing here, on topics for which just a few years ago it was quite difficult to compile a decent bibliography. Today one can speak of a postmodern revolution in historiography (Jenkins 1997). Why this phenomenon? Why now?

"History" has a history of its own, closely knitted with that of "nations" and nationalism. The answer to the above queries should therefore be sought in the ambience of crisis that nowadays affects "national identities" almost everywhere. In the last two centuries nationalism has been to modernity what Christianity had been to feudalism in the preceding centuries: that is, it furnished the era with a pertinent cosmology. In the rapidly disenchanting, capitalizing, and bureaucratizing world, where "all that is solid melts into the air," where, on the one hand, the market adjourns all ties and meanings and, on the other hand, the state commands all affiliations, nationalism had become a substitute "religion for the masses," giving them a sense of collective cohesion and existential purpose. As Anthony Smith (1986: 176–77) put it so well, nationalism assumed the role of "a 'surrogate' religion which aims to overcome the sense of futility engendered by the removal of any vision of an existence after death, by linking individuals to persisting communities whose generations form indissoluble links in a chain of memories and identities." Yet nationalism in itself could not cope with the expansion of secularism and its anxieties. All that was left to fill the existential void was "memory and hope, history and destiny" (ibid.). "History" has been the worldly counterpart of the divine "Providence."

Nationalism has thus purchased the warrant for its lowercase (mundane) history in an uppercase (teleological) History. In the modern world, asserts Smith (ibid.: 179), "history has become both a moral teacher and a temporal and terrestrial drama of salvation." Historians, in particular, have assumed the role of the nation's teachers and preachers. Their task has been "to fit the many pieces of [the historical] jigsaw together into a clear and harmonious pattern" and to "translate the idealized images of the ethnic past into tactile realities, according to modern canons of knowledge" (ibid.: 180). Scholars and historians bent on rediscovering or reconstituting a national past, as Smith (ibid.: 182) so tellingly put it, "have felt no compunction about pressing the latest techniques or scientific methods into the service of an unashamedly romantic venture. They have used 'science' to systematize and 'verify' poetic metaphors of collective life, and construct images and mythologies of a dramatic and inspiring past."

Thus, uppercase "History" has extracted from "history" national origins and ancestry, legendary heroes and exemplary persons, dramatic events and golden epochs, immemorial lineages and durable traditions (cf. ibid.: 191–200). National historiographies had been quintessentially *historicist* in the sense of having "a predilection for interpreting individual and social phenomena as the product of sequences of events which unfold the identity of laws of growth of those phenomena" and in the sense of aiming toward "establish[ing], through detailed historical investigation, the origins, growth and purpose of particular entities, or classes of entity" (Smith 1981: 88).

What we witness in the recent period, in the form of manifold historical revisions and historians' debates, is a turn of the historiographical tide. We witness the transition from one dominant historiographical paradigm to another, namely, a transition from a historicist to a posthistoricist era in historiography. In the era of the ascent of nationalism, historicist historiography functioned as a major progenitor of constructed collective identities, or of the uniting of nations. In the era of the ascent of the global social formation and postmodern culture, posthistoricist historiography functions as a progenitor of the deconstruction, the dissolution and the fragmentation of collective identities, or of the disuniting of nations (to follow the title of an Arthur Schlesinger book [1991] that laments this process).

The emerging posthistoricist paradigm may be designated by contrasting it with the historicist one, as described above. The posthistoricist paradigm is suspicious of historicism's predilection to compress individual and social phenomena into "identities" and "laws of growth." From its perspective, such compression forces a cascade of dispersed and blurred events into unified, fixed, essential entities. It deconstructs historical "identities," exposing them as artifacts, and deconstructs historical "laws," exposing the contingencies underlying them. Rather than historical laws, it aims at deciphering the historical *practices* by which ostensible "origins, growth, and purpose" camouflage actual manipulations, exploitations, and exclusions.

Thus, while historicist historiographies construct nations, posthistoricist historiographies *deconstruct* them. They outstrip collectivities and states of their transcendental, uppercase History signification, "disenchant" their ostensible primordialities, and open them up for democratic communication and negotiation based on modern associational membership. To put it in the terminology of Jürgen Habermas, historicist historiography may be considered a counterpart of conventional identity and morality, while posthistoricist historiography may be considered a counterpart of postconventional identity and morality (Habermas 1994, 1984/ 1987).

Construction and deconstruction of collective identities are not entirely separable, of course. Just as in the past the construction of modern national identities involved the deconstruction, or outright destruction, of former traditional identities—tribal, regional, ethnic, religious—today the deconstruction of national identities involves the reconstruction of lost identities or, in many cases, the outright invention of new ones. "History," in other words, is a major cultural arena where national "stories" are contrived at one point (typically from the last decades of the nineteenth century to the 1950s, with some predecessors, such as the English, French, and German), and disentangled at another (typically in the last decades of the twentieth century).

Contemporary historical revisions and debates should be interpreted, then, against the backdrop of specific crises of national identities, and accumulatively as indications of the crisis of national identity as such in our era. In these occasions the constructed past transforms from a unifying fold into a contested terrain, in which social categories hitherto persisting on the margins of the grand national narrative, or entirely outcast from it, gain a voice and launch a struggle for the acceptability of their own bigger (globalist) or smaller (localist) narratives, and through it for their cultural legitimacy and social status. This is why historical revisions and debates shed light on the present no less, if not more, than on the past, paradoxical as it may sound. To understand the current historians' debate is thus to understand the current transformation of national collective identities. In the past such identities served as vehicles for political and economic modernization. Today they experience decline, induced by the pressure of globalization, the vehicles of which are postmodern identities. As Scott Lash and John Urry (1994: 313) put it succinctly, "Mobile objects and reflexive subjects produce disorganized capitalism which involves the dissipation of the national fate community."

Yet globalization should not be conflated with homogenization. As Ronald Robertson (1987: 21) put it, globalization may lead toward "global valorization of particular identities" (Featherstone 1995; Arnason 1990). One of the offshoots of globalization, and dialectically one of its potential obstructions, is the backlash, or defensive reaction, of what may be termed local identities. The formerly "united" nations are today "disunited" by forces that undermine them simultaneously from "above" and "below." Two trends work in parallel: one toward supranational political and economic globalization, and the other toward infranational culture and identity localization (Hobsbawm 1990; Castells 1997). In combination, globalization and localization originate what was recently labeled "glocalization" (Axford 1995: 156). In this process formerly solidified nations do fragment, but some of their components consolidate separably in an attempt to arrest the threatening flood of universal facelessness, or what some term "consumerist cultural imperialism." The thaw of nationalist cores facilitates a consolidation of the peripheral components. It spurs the surface of formerly suppressed minorities (sometimes demographic majorities) and licenses the formulation of new "local politics" and new identities centered around distinctive ideal interests (human rights, environmental concerns), lifestyles (sexual orientations), and so forth. On the other end of the spectrum, the dissolution of the center provokes socially marginal groups (usually from the declining lower middle class) to mobilize for the "protection" of the nation (white supremacy and Christian fundamentalism in the United States; neofascist and extreme nationalist right-wing groups in France and Germany, etc.).

The scissors movement of globalization and localization, the aforementioned glocalization, undermines the sovereignty and autonomy of nation-states both from "above" and from "below." From above, nation-states are worn down by supranational vibrating financial and communicative networks, immense continent-wide commercial and monetary blocs, and potent multinational corporations. From below, nation-states are worn down by subnational regional, ethnic, popular, and individualistic activated fragments (Ross 1990; Bienfeld 1994; Dunn 1994; Muller and Wright 1994; Cable 1995; Schmidt 1995; Soysal 1994; Crawford 1993; Castells 1997).

What happens to the nation-state can perhaps be illustrated by the analogy of the neighborhood grocery store. In the 1950s the neighborhood grocery store was still the major foodstuff retail outlet. It was later surpassed (in advanced industrial societies) in this role by big supermarket chain stores ("Fordist standardization," in a neo-Marxist analysis of globalization; cf. Harvey 1989); still later, the supermarkets were supplemented by "delicatessen" and "gourmet" stores, catering to particular tastes, based on ethnic edibles, special staples or qualities, or distinct orientations (vegetarian, organic, etc.; "post-Fordist specialization," in a neo-Marxist analysis). Now all this does not mean that the grocery store disappears overnight, especially in the impoverished neighborhoods and peripheries, but it does mean that it is no longer the major retail outlet of foodstuffs, and certainly not the cutting edge. Its role has been eroded due to pressures from above—the supermarket chain stores—and from below—the delicatessen and gourmet stores. Something of this sort is happening to the romantic cafés of Paris, where reportedly "for every fast-food branch opening in a certain street, three coffee places are closed," and something of this sort is also happening to the cozy bookstores of Manhattan, where reportedly book marketing is being taken over by "megastore" and "superstore" chains, and the only viability left for small bookstores is specialization.[3]

Not surprisingly, something of this sort is happening to the nation-state in the last decades of the twentieth century, the era of globalization, localization, and postmodernization. Like the grocery stores, the romantic cafés, and the cozy bookstores, nationhood and nation-states are not about to disappear overnight. Yet, as Eric Hobsbawm (1990) and Ernest Gellner (1983) argue, they cannot be considered any more as the actors who shape the era (but see the counterarguments of Smith [1995]). The issue is not the outright disappearance of the nation-state and of national identities but rather the proliferation of other identities alongside the nation-state. Thus, the age is characterized as one of boundary-crossing and hybridity. As Jan Nederveen Pieterse (1995: 63) put it, "State power remains extremely strategic, but it is no longer the only game in town." John Bodnar (1991: 252) has ended his study of collective memory in the United States on an appropriate note: "In this postmodern era various interests and cultures mix more freely in the public sphere—nationalism, internationalism, consumerism, ethnicity, race, gender, private feelings, and official concerns."

Something of this sort is happening to the nation-state in Israel, though this case, like any other, has its historical particularities and non-structural contingencies, to which we attended above. In Israel, in the pace and the circumstances particular to it, one can detect in the last 15 years or so the decline of the homogeneous national narrative and the emergence of a plurality of alternatives, or complementary narratives (including the ultranationalist backlash—which is not the focus of this study [cf. Lustick 1988; Sprinzak 1991]). In Israel, as in so many other places, at least in those social circles exposed to the global tradition-shredding and meaning-evaporating postmodern culture, no simple "story" can be accepted innocently anymore, neither the story of scientific objectivity nor that of national unity. As in the United States and other places, in Israel too "the idea of historical objectivity is perceived as problematic more than in any time in the past" (Novick 1988: 17); "certainty has been replaced by doubt and the present is no longer seen as something that emerged neatly and purposefully from the past, a view that was implicit in the story of nation building" (Bodnar 1991: 252). As argued and demonstrated in this study, a challenge to the stories of objective history and national unity is vigorously pronounced today in Israel by critical sociologists and New Historians (see also Ram 1993, 1995; Pappe 1993; Levi and Peled 1993; Kimmerling 1992; Silberstein 1991).

CONCLUSION: BEYOND PURE KNOWLEDGE AND PURE IDENTITY

In the human and social sciences, text and context are closely bound. This means that in these fields there is no "pure knowledge." No knowledge can be produced, disseminated, and received that is not refracted through the prism of a social standpoint and linguistic rendering. In the last two decades the consciousness of the ties between social positions, social knowledges, and scholarly representations has gained enormous acceptance in academia. Many intellectuals of the present generation regard the politics of knowledge and the politics of identity as closely coupled. Simultaneously, the notion of "pure identity" has been radically criticized. The notion of primordial, fixed, homogeneous identity is widely challenged today by concepts of identity that refer to "otherness," "difference," "hybridity," "diaspora," "migration," and "boundary crossing." Identity is thought of as associative, permeable, unstable, and discursive. From this perspective, signifiers such as "femininity," "nation," or "race" are not considered anymore as direct representations of ostensible "real" signified referents such as biological sex, ethnic group, or physiognomic characteristics, respectively. In this respect, the signifier and the signified themselves lose their "purity" as known identities and instead become discursive relational practices. Identity, then, is today largely considered an unstable social construct or cultural practice rather than a fixed natural given.

In their conjunction, the critiques of pure knowledge and of pure identity have effected a crisis of representation. This crisis, in turn, has invoked a crisis of conventional historiographies and sociographies, that is, of national narratives that are functionalist, consensual, teleological, linear, homogenaic, and triumphal, or, in short, historicist. Instead there emerged narratives that are critical, complementary, or alternative, narratives that allude to other identities, to the otherness of self-identity, and to the fragmentation of the nation. Such narratives connote the experience and the perspective of voices lost, silenced, marginalized, and neglected by the process of nation formation, or even of contestant elites or declining middle classes. Such subnarratives deconstruct the national metanarrative or, in short, as I have argued here, propose posthistoricist histories and sociologies.

It emerges from this study that the historians' debate in Israel should be considered not as a confined academic affair but rather as a milestone in Israel's political-cultural history. The New History and critical sociology challenge one by one Israel's most fundamental ethoses and cherished myths. The emotional charge involved was displayed in a passionate essay published in Israel's most prestigious daily, *Haaretz* (Tel Aviv), by Aharon Meged, a well-known author affiliated with the historical Zionist Labor movement. Meged lamented "all the beautifully formulated idioms in which we used to believe, and on which we were raised for two-three generations,—such as the 'redemption of the land,' the 'conquest of labor,' the 'gathering of diasporas,' self defense and so forth, which are now presented as deceit and hypocrisy." He vehemently denounced the proclamation of the New History, according to which, as he put it, "most of the certainties secured in our consciousness and experience are but lies," and he went so far as to accuse the New Historians of serving the enemies of the State of Israel and to compare them to a contaminating virus that "incrementally eliminates the immunities of our body and weakens our hands" (Meged 1994). In 1995 the historians' debate became an affair of the state when the then minister of culture and education, Amnon Rubinstein (1995), joined the fray and attacked the New Historians, arguing that they aim to "bury" Zionism by "presenting it as an essentially colonialist and racist movement, attributing to it all the evils of darkened nationalism, without displaying towards it the slightest sympathy that the left-wing usually elicits towards national liberation movements; and above all, by considering the very establishment of Israel as an act of villainy and plunder."

While on a plain, *textual* level the historians' debate has been conducted as a professional scholarly disputation, clearly on a more profound, *contextual* level the debate involves much deeper and wider undercurrents, as its publicity and intensity suggest. Though explicitly historians dispute past events, implicitly the disputation is of present sociological significance. On a larger scale, the Israeli debate is just one case within a wider phenomenon of historical revisions and controversies in contemporary nation-states, events that both manifest and articulate crises of national identity related to globalization processes and the postmodernization of culture.

In Israel the debate exhibits the decline of the formerly overriding national Zionist ethos and the emergence of two mutually antagonistic alternative ethoses: a globalist post-Zionist liberal ethos and a localist ethnoreligious neo-Zionist ethos. The eruption of the historians' debate in Israel should thus be understood against the background of both local social changes and global political transformations, as well as against the background of the recent endorsement by dissident scholars in Israeli academia of postmodernist sensibilities and poststructuralist methodologies. A combination of local, global, and cultural influences, then, accounts for the new deconstructive critique and politics of identity, which reshapes Israel's sense of collective identity in general and its historiographical scene in particular.

NOTES

Uri Ram wishes to thank Jeff Olick for encouragement and Dafna Izraeli for comments on a previous version of this work. He also thanks a large number of colleagues who were exposed to his ideas in seminars and conferences and whose comments helped improve the work. In particular, he wishes to thank Deborah Bernstein, Gabi Piterberg, Lev Grinberg, Sarit Helman, Oren Yiftachel, Sammy Smooha, Nathan Szneider, and especially Nava Schrieber.
1. Yoav Peled (1993) categorized the de jure citizenship as "liberal" and the de facto difference as "republican" or communal.

2. On the cultural approaches associated with these architectonic styles, Weingrod 1993 is a miniature illustration of the affiliation between architecture and identity in Israel today.

3. According to a report in the last 30 years the number of coffee places, bistros, and restaurants in Paris shrank from 55,000 to less than 20,000; in France as a whole the respective numbers cited are 220,000 and 65,000 (Lori 1996). According to another report the Barnes and Noble chain store runs 375 book "superstores" and more than 600 smaller stores; it is reported to have opened close to 100 stores last year and to plan the opening of the same number by next year. It constantly drives out of the market smaller competitors (a recent, much-discussed example is the Upper West Side branch of Shakespeare). The chain is reported to employ 40,000 employees, and its yearly revenue is estimated as $3 billion. The cited reasons for the chain's success are superior choice of titles as well as customers' comforts—sofas, air-conditioning, coffee, etc. (Handvaker 1996).

REFERENCES

Al-Haj, M. 1995. *Education, Empowerment, and Control: The Case of Arabs in Israel.* Albany: SUNY Press.

Alkalai, A. 1993. *After Jews and Arabs: Remaking Levantine Culture.* Minneapolis: University of Minnesota Press.

Anderson, B. 1991. *Imagined Communities.* 2d ed. London: Verso.

Appleby, J. O., L. Hunt, and M. Jacobs. 1994. *Telling the Truth about History.* New York: Norton.

Arnason, J. P. 1990. "Nationalism, Globalization, and Modernity." In M. Featherstone, ed., *Global Culture.* New York: Sage.

Asaf, D. 1995. "The Robbers of Memory." *Haaretz,* 17 February.

Axford, B. 1995. *The Global System: Economics, Politics and Culture.* Cambridge, Mass.: Polity Press.

Bernai, J. 1995. *Historiography and Nationalism.* Jerusalem: Magnes [Hebrew].

Bar On, D. 1994. *Fear and Hope.* Kibbutz Lohamei Hegetaot: Ghetto Fighters House [Hebrew].

Bar Yosef, R. 1980 [1969]. "Desocialization and Resocialization: The adjustment process of immigrants." In E. Kraust, ed., *Studies of Israeli Society.* Vol. 1. *Migration, Ethnicity, and Community.* Brunswick, N.J.: Transaction Books.

Barzilai, G. 1996. *Wars, Internal Conflict, and Political Order.* Albany: SUNY Press.

Bauer, Y. 1993. "No 'Tom' and No 'Segev.'" *Iton* 77, 161: 24–28.

——. 1994. "That's What a Jewish State is For." *Haaretz,* 27 September.

Beit Zvi, S. 1977. *Post-Ugandian Zionism in the Crucible of the Holocaust.* Tel Aviv: Bronfman [Hebrew].

Ben-Eliezer, U. 1995. *The Emergence of Israeli Militarism, 1936–1956.* Tel Aviv: Dvir [Hebrew].

Berger, S. 1995. "Historians and Nation-building in Germany after Reunification." *Past and Present* 148: 187–222.

Bernstein, D. 1987. *The Struggle for Equality: Urban Women Workers in Pre-State Israeli Society*. New York: Praeger.

———. 1992. "Human being—or Housewife?: The Status of Women in the Jewish Working class family in Palestine of the 1920s and 1930s." In D. Bernstein, ed., *Pioneers and Homeworks*. Albany: SUNY Press.

Bhabha, H. 1990. *Nation and Narration*. London: Routledge.

Bienfeld, M. 1994. "Capitalism and the Nation-state." *Socialist Register* 30: 94–129.

Bishara, A. 1993. "On the Question of the Palestinian Minority in Israel." In U. Ram, ed., *Israeli Society: Critical Perspectives*. Tel Aviv: Breirot [Hebrew].

Bodnar, J. 1991. *Remaking America: Public Memory, Commemoration, and Patriotism in the Twentieth Century*. Princeton, N.J.: Princeton University Press.

Cable, V. 1995. "The Diminished Nation-state: A Study in the Loss of Economic Power." *Daedalus* 124: 23–53.

Carmi, S., and H. Rosenfeld. 1989. "The Rise of Militaristic Nationalism in Israel." *International Journal of Politics, Culture and Society* 3: 5–49.

Castells, M. 1997. *The Information Age*. Vol. 2. *The Power of Identity*. London: Blackwell.

Chatterjee, P. 1993. *The Nation and Its Fragments: Colonial and Post-colonial Histories*. Princeton, N.J.: Princeton University Press.

Cooper, F. 1994. "Conflict and Connection: Rethinking Colonial African History." *American Historical Review* 99: 1516–45.

Crawford, Y. 1993. *The Rising Tide of Cultural Pluralism: The Nation-State at Bay?* Madison: University of Wisconsin Press.

Curthoys, A. 1993. "Identity Crisis: Colonialism, Nation and Gender in Australian History." *Gender and History* 5: 165–76.

Diner, D. 1988. "The Yishuv in the Face of the Holocaust of European Jewry (review article)." *Haziyonut* 13: 301–8 [Hebrew].

Dunn, J. 1994. "Political Studies: The Crisis of the Nation-state." Special issue. *Political Studies* 42.

Ehrlich, A. 1987. "Israel: Conflict, War and Social Change." In C. a. M. S. Creighton, ed., *The Sociology of War and Peace*. Devonshire: McMillan Press: 121–42.

Eisenstadt, S. N. 1967. *Israeli Society: Background, Development, Problems*. Jerusalem: Magnes [Hebrew].

Elkana, Y. 1978. "Two Tier Thinking: Philosophical Realism and Historical Relativism." *Social Studies of Science* 8: 309–26.

Eshkoli-Wagman, H. 1994. *Silence: Mapai and the Holocaust, 1939–1942*. Jerusalem: Yad Yizhak Ben Zvi.

Evron, B. 1988. *A National Reckoning*. Tel Aviv: Dvir [Hebrew].

Featherstone, M. 1995. *Undoing Culture*. New York: Sage.

Feierman, S. 1995. "Africa in History: The End of Universal Narratives." In G. Prakash, ed., *After Colonialism: Imperial Histories and Postcolonial Displacements*. Princeton, N.J.: Princeton University Press: 40–65.

Firer, R. 1985. *The Agents of Zionist Education*. Kiryat Tivon: Oranim [Hebrew].

——. 1989. *Agents of the Holocaust Lesson*. Tel Aviv: Hakkibbutz Hameuhad [Hebrew].

Flapan, S. 1987. *The Birth of Israel: Myth and Realities*. London: Chroom Helm.

Fogel-Bijaui, S. 1991. "Mothers and Revolution: The Case of Women in the Kibbutz, 1910–1948." *Shorashim* 6: 143–92 [Hebrew].

Foner, E. 1990. *The New American History*. Philadelphia: Temple University Press.

Friedlander, S. 1993. *Memory, History, and the Extermination of the Jews in Europe*. Bloomington: Indiana University Press.

Funkenstein, A. 1991. *Perceptions of Jewish History from Antiquity to the Present*. Tel Aviv: Am Oved [Hebrew].

Gellner, E. 1983. *Nations and Nationalism*. Ithaca, N.Y.: Cornell University Press.

Gibson, R. 1992. *South of the West: Postcolonialism and the Narrative Construction of Australia*. Bloomington: Indiana University Press.

Giladi, D. 1973. *Jewish Palestine during the Fourth Aliya Period (1924–1929)*. Tel Aviv: Am Oved [Hebrew].

——. 1994. *The Return to Our Forefathers' Land: Z. D. Lavontin: A Proponent of a Free Enterprise Approach to Zionism*. Jerusalem: Friends of the Israel Center for Social and Economic Progress [Hebrew].

Gildea, R. 1994. *The Past in French History*. New Haven, Conn.: Yale University Press.

Gorni, Y. 1973. *Achdut Haavoda, 1919–1930*. Tel Aviv: Hakibbutz Hameuhad [Hebrew].

Grinberg, L. 1993. *The Histadrut above All*. Jerusalem: Nevo [Hebrew].

Grodzinsky, Y. 1994. "The Holocaust, the Yishuv, their Leaders and Their Historians (Parts A and B)." *Haaretz*, 8 and 15 April.

Guha, R., and G. C. Spivak, eds. 1988. *Selected Subaltern Studies*. New York: Oxford.

Gunew, S. 1990. "Denaturalizing Cultural Nationalisms: Multicultural Readings of 'Australia.' " In H. Bhabha, ed., *Nation and Narration*. London: Routledge: 99–120.

Habermas, J. 1984/1987. *The Theory of Communicative Action*. Vols. 1 and 2. Cambridge: MIT Press.

——. 1994. "Citizenship and National Identity." In V. S. Bart, ed., *The Condition of Citizenship*. London: Sage.

Handvaker, H. 1996. "Shakespeare Surrenders to the Riggio Brothers." *Haaretz*, 7 July.

Harvey, D. 1989. *The Condition of Post-Modernity*. Oxford: Blackwell.

Helman, S. 1993. "Conscientious Objection to Military Service as an Attempt to Redefine the Contents of Citizenship." Ph.D. diss., Hebrew University [Hebrew], Jerusalem.

Hertzberger, D. 1995. *Narrating the Past: Fiction and History in Post-War Spain*. Durham, N.C.: Duke University Press.

Herzog, H. 1994. "A Forgotten Chapter in the Historiography of the Yishuv: Women's Organizations." *Cathedra* 70: 111–33.

Hobsbawm, E. 1990. *Nations and Nationalism since 1780*. Cambridge: Cambridge University Press.

Hobsbawm, E., and T. Ranger. 1983. *The Invention of Tradition*. Cambridge: Cambridge University Press.

Horowitz, D., and M. Lissak. 1977. *The Origins of the Israeli Polity.* Tel Aviv: Am Oved [Hebrew].

Jenkins, K. 1997. *The Post-Modern History Reader.* London: Routledge.

Kadish, A. 1989. "The Refugees Problem: The History and the Accusation." *Haaretz,* 14 August.

Kafkafi, E. 1994. *An Optional War: To Sinai and Back, 1956–1957.* Ramat Efal: Yad Tabenkin [Hebrew].

Karakasidou, A. N. 1994. "Sacred Scholars, Profane Advocates: Intellectuals Modeling National Consciousness in Greece." *Identities* 1: 35–61.

Katz, Y. 1989. *Hyozma hapratit bebinyan eretz israel betkufat haliya hashniya [The free enterprise's contribution to the build-up of Eretz Israel].* Ramat Gan: Bar Ilan University.

——. 1993. *The Colonization Activity in Palestine of the Zionist Private Companies and Associations.* Jerusalem: Chamul [Hebrew].

Kimmerling, B. 1983. *Zionism and Territory: The Socio-Territorial Dimensions of Zionist Politics.* Berkeley: Institute of International Studies, University of California Press.

——. 1985. "Between the Primordial and the Civil Dimensions of the Collective Identity." In E. C. a. M. L. Uri Almagor, ed., *Comparative Social Dynamics.* Boulder, Colo.: Westview Press.

——. 1992. "Sociology, Ideology and Nation Building: The Palestinians and Their Meaning in Israeli Sociology." *American Sociological Review* 57: 460–66.

——. 1993. "Militarism in Israeli Society." *Theory and Critique* 4: 123–40 [Hebrew].

Lash, S., and J. Urry. 1994. *Economies of Time and Space.* London: Sage.

Levi, Y., and Y. Peled. 1993. "The break that Never Was: Israeli Sociology Reflected through the Six Day War." *Theory and Critique* 3: 115–28.

Libes, Y. 1992. "New Directions in Kabbala Research." *Peamim* 50: 150–70 [Hebrew].

Liebman, C., and D. Y. Eliezer. 1983. *Civil Religion in Israel.* Berkeley: University of California Press.

Lori, A. 1996. "The Battle over the Bank." *Haaretz Supplement,* 2 August.

Lustick, I. 1988. *For the Land and the Lord.* New York: Council on Foreign Relations.

Maier, C. S. 1988. *The Unmasterable Past: History, Holocaust, and German National Identity.* Cambridge: Harvard University Press.

Mallon, F. E. 1994. "The Promise and Dilemma of Subaltern Studies: Perspectives from Latin American History." *American Historical Review* 99: 1491–1515.

Meged, A. 1994. "The Israeli Suicidal Drive." *Haaretz Supplement,* 10 June.

Megill, A. 1987. "The Rhetoric of History." In J. Nelson, A. Megill, and D. McClosky, eds., *The Rhetoric of the Human Sciences.* Madison: University of Wisconsin Press.

Michman, D. 1994. "On History and Charlatanism." *Haaretz,* 6 May.

Morris, B. 1991. *The Birth of the Palestinian Refugees Problem, 1947–1949.* Tel Aviv: Am Oved [Hebrew].

——. 1993. *Israel's Border Wars, 1949–1956.* Oxford: Clarendon Press.

——. 1994. "Objective History." *Haaretz Supplement,* 1 July.

Muller, W. C., and V. Wright. 1994. "The State in Western Europe." In *West European Politics* 17: 3–4. London: Frank Kasse.

Nahon, Y. 1993. "Occupational Status." In M. L. a. Y. N. Eisenstadt S. N., ed., *Ethnic Communities in Israel*. Jerusalem: Jerusalem Institute of Israel Studies [Hebrew].

Novick, P. 1988. *That Noble Dream: The "Objectivity" Question and the American Historical Profession*. Cambridge: Cambridge University Press.

Oron, Y. 1993. *Israeli-Jewish Identity*. Tel Aviv: Siriyat Poalim [Hebrew].

Palmer, B. 1994. "Canadian Controversies." *History Today* 44: 44–49.

Pappe, I. 1986. "Moshe Sharet, David Ben Gurion and the 'Palestinian Option,' 1948–1956." *Zionism* 11: 361–80 [Hebrew].

———. 1992. *The Making of the Israeli-Arab Conflict*. London: I. B. Tauris.

———. 1993. "The New History of the 1948 War." *Theory and Critique* 3: 99–114 [Hebrew].

———. 1994. "The Impact of Zionist Ideology on Israeli Historiography," *Davar*, 15 May.

Peled, Y. 1993. "Strangers in Utopia: The Civic Status of Israel's Palestinian Citizens." *Theory and Critique* 3: 21–38 [Hebrew].

Peri, Y. 1989. "From Political Nationalism to Ethno-nationalism: The Case of Israel." In Y. L. a. A. M. Battah, ed., *The Arab-Israeli Conflict*. Boulder, Colo.: Westview Press: 41–53.

Pieterse, J. N. 1995. "Globalization as Hybridization." In M. F. a. S. Lash, ed., *Global Modernities*. New York: Sage.

Piterberg, G. 1995. "The Nation and its Raconteurs: Orientalism and Nationalist Historiography." *Theory and Critique* 6: 81–104 [Hebrew].

Porat, D. 1986. *An Entangled Leadership: The Yishuv and the Holocaust, 1942–1945*. Tel Aviv: Am Oved [Hebrew].

———. 1990. "Contemporary Historiography of Zionist Efforts During the Holocaust Period." *Yahadut Zemanenu* 6: 117–32 [Hebrew].

———. 1995. "Two Jewish Peoples." *Haaretz*, 17 February.

Prakash, G. 1994. "Subaltern Studies as Postcolonial Criticism." *American Historical Review* 99: 1475–90.

Ram, U. 1993. "Israeli Society: Critical Perspectives." Tel Aviv: Breirot [Hebrew].

———. 1995a. *The Changing Agenda of Israeli Sociology: Theory, Ideology and Identity*. Albany: SUNY Press.

———. 1995b. "Zionist Historiography and the Invention of Modern Jewish Nationhood: The Case of Ben Zion Dinur." *History and Memory* 7: 91–124.

———. 1996. "Historical Consciousness in Israel: Between Zionism and Post-Zionism." *Gesher* 132: 93–97 [Hebrew].

Ravitsky, A. 1996. *Messianism, Zionism, and Jewish Religious Radicalism*. Chicago: University of Chicago Press.

Raz-Krakotzkin, A. 1994. "Exile within Sovereignty: Toward a Critique of the 'Negation of Exile' in Israeli Culture (Parts I and II)." *Theory and Critique* 4 and 5: 6–23, 113–32 [Hebrew].

Revel, J., and L. Hunt. 1995. *Histories: French Constructions of the Past*. New York: New Press.

Robertson, R. 1987. "Globalization Theory and Civilization Analysis." *Comparative Civilizations Review* 17: 20–30.

Rosenfeld, H. 1978. "The Class Situation of the Arab National Minority in Israel." *Comparative Studies in Society and History* 20: 309–26.

Rosenfeld, H., and S. Carmi. 1976. "The Privatization of Public Means, the State made Middle Class, and the Realization of Family Values in Israel." In J. G. Peristiany, ed., *Kinship and Modernization in Mediterranean Society*. Rome: The Center for Mediterranean Studies, American Universities Field Staff.

Rosenhak, Z. 1995. "New Development in the Study of the Palestinian Citizens of Israel: An Analytical Survey." *Megamot* 47: 167–90 [Hebrew].

Ross, Robert J. S. 1990. "The Relative Decline of Relative Economy: Global Capitalism and the Political Economy of State Change." In E. S. G. a. T. M. Mayer, ed., *Changes in the State*. Berkeley: Sage.

Rousso, H. 1991. *The Vichy Syndrome: History and Memory in France since 1944*. Cambridge: Harvard University Press.

Rubinstein, A. 1995. "The Distortion of Zionism." *Haaretz*, 12 September.

Schlesinger, A., Jr. 1991. *The Disuniting of America: Reflections on a Multicultural Society*. New York: Norton.

Schmidt, V. A. 1995. "The New World Order, Incorporated: The Rise of Business and the Decline of the Nation-state." *Daedalus* 124: 75–106.

Schwarz, Y. 1994. "The Hebrew Literature: The 'Post' Era." *Yediot Aharonot: Saturday Supplement*, 29–30.

Segev, T. 1991. *The Seventh Million: The Israelis and the Holocaust*. Jerusalem: Keter [Hebrew].

Shafir, G. 1989. *Land, Labor and the Origins of the Israeli Palestinian Conflict, 1882–1914*. Cambridge: Cambridge University Press.

——. 1993. "Territory, Labor and Population in Zionist Colonization." In U. Ram, ed., *Israeli Society: Critical Perspectives*. Tel Aviv: Breirot.

Shalev, M. 1992. *Labor and the Political Economy of Israel*. Oxford: Oxford University Press.

Shapira, A. 1980. *Berl Katznelson: A Biography*. Tel Aviv: Am Oved [Hebrew].

Shapiro, Y. 1975. *The Organization of Power*. Tel Aviv: Am Oved [Hebrew].

——. 1993. "The Historical Origins of Israeli Democracy." In D. C. a. E. Sprinzak, ed., *Israeli Democracy under Stress*. Boulder, Colo.: Lynne Reinner.

Shlaim, A. 1988. *Collusion across the Jordan: King Abdullah, the Zionist Movement, and the Partition of Palestine*. New York: Columbia University Press.

Shohat, E. 1989. *Israeli Cinema: East/West and the Politics of Representation*. Austin: University of Texas Press.

Silberstein, L. 1991. "New Perspectives on Israeli History." New York: New York University Press.

Slater, J. 1995. "Lost Opportunities for Peace: Reassessing the Arab-Israeli Conflict." *Tikkun* 10: 59–64, 88.

Smith, A. D. 1981. *The Ethnic Revival.* Cambridge: Cambridge University Press.

———. 1986. *The Ethnic Origins of Nation.* Oxford: Oxford University Press.

———. 1995. *Nations and Nationalism in the Global Era.* Cambridge, Mass.: Polity Press.

Smooha, S. 1978. *Israel: Pluralism and Conflict.* Berkeley: University of California Press.

———. 1990. "Minority Status in Ethnic Democracy: The Status of the Arab Minority in Israel." *Ethnic and Racial Studies* 13: 389–413.

Soysal, Y. N. 1994. *Limits of Citizenship: Migrants and Postnational Membership in Europe.* Chicago: University of Chicago Press.

Sprinzak, E. 1991. *The Ascendance of Israel's Radical Right.* New York: Oxford University Press.

Sternhell, Z. 1995. *Nation-Building or New Society?* Tel Aviv: Am Oved.

Swirski, S. 1981. *Orientals and Ashkenazim in Israel.* Haifa: Notebooks for Research and Critique [Hebrew].

———. 1990. *Education in Israel: Schooling for Inequality.* Tel Aviv: Breirot [Hebrew].

———. 1993. "Tomorrow." In U. Ram, ed. *Israeli Society: Critical Perspectives.* Tel Aviv: Breirot [Hebrew]: 351–63.

———. 1995. *Seeds of Inequality.* Tel Aviv: Breirot [Hebrew].

Tevet, S. 1989. "The New Historians." *Haaretz,* 4, 14, 21 April.

———. 1994a. "The Black Hole: Ben Gurion between Holocaust and Revival." *Alpayim* 10: 111–95 [Hebrew].

———. 1994b. "Shock, Ambivalence or Helplessness?" *Haaretz Sfarim,* 30 March, 4–5.

Volkov, S. 1991. "History, Historians and the German Nation-state." *Zmanim* 37: 59–65.

Wasserman, H. 1986. "The Nationalization of the Memory of the Six Million." *Politika* 8: 7–6, 55.

Weingrod, A. 1993. "Changing Israeli Landscapes: Building and the Uses of the Past." *Cultural Anthropology* 8: 370–87.

Weitz, Y. 1994. *Aware But Helpless.* Jerusalem: Yad Yizhak Ben Zvi [Hebrew].

Yiftachel, O. 1992. *Planning a Mixed Region in Israel: The Political Geography of Arab-Jewish Relations in the Galilee.* Aldershot, Hants: Avebury.

Zertal, I. 1994. "The Sacrifice and the Sanctified: The Construction of National Martyrology." *Zmanim* 48: 26–45 [Hebrew].

———. 1995. "On Zmanin." *Haaretz,* 3 December.

———. 1996. *From Catastrophe to Power: Jewish Illegal Immigration to Palestine, 1945–1948.* Tel Aviv: Am Oved [Hebrew].

Zukerman, M. 1993. *Shoah in the Sealed Room.* Tel Aviv: The Author [Hebrew].

What Does It Mean to Normalize

the Past?: Official Memory in

German Politics since 1989

◀ ◀ ◀ ◀ ◀ ◀ ◀ ◀ ◀ ◀ ◀ ◀ ◀   J E F F R E Y   K .   O L I C K

In 1959, Theodor Adorno delivered a lecture whose title and theme played on Immanuel Kant's famous essay "Answering the Question: What Is Enlightenment?" (Beantwortung der Frage: Was ist Aufklärung?). Kant's essay had begun with the statement that enlightenment is humanity's emergence from self-imposed nonage. Called "What Does It Mean to Come to Terms with the Past?" (Was bedeutet: Aufarbeitung der Vergangenheit?), Adorno's lecture takes issue with tendencies in the Federal Republic of Germany to wish away difficult legacies of the Nazi period. Evoking a parallel between Kant's "enlightenment" (*Aufklärung*) and the contemporary expressions "coming to terms" or "working through" (*Aufarbeitung*), Adorno poses a high critical standard for German political culture. According to his diagnosis, the Federal Republic was more concerned with getting beyond the past, with avoiding difficult memory through what Adorno calls "an unconscious and not-so-unconscious defense against guilt," than with the genuine working through that would be required to "break its spell." The latter would demand an act of clear consciousness, a difficult process much like the work of psychoanalysis. According to Adorno, the defensive unwillingness in the Federal Republic to confront the past—at both the personal and official levels—indicated not the persistence of fascist tendencies against democracy (e.g., neo-Nazi groups) but of fascist tendencies *within* democracy. The latter, he argues, are much more insidious.

Adorno's lecture is important in multiple ways. It is a classic of critical theory, combining psychoanalytic, philosophical, and political concepts to diagnose hidden perils in contemporary social forms. It stands against the self-congratulatory tone of an optimistic era, revealing the seamy under-belly of official enthusiasm. The lecture is also an important part of the historical record, emblematic of a growing shift in German political cul-ture: in 1959, the lecture stood at a turning point between the era of the "economic miracle" and the social upheavals of the 1960s. Combined with such events as the publication of *The Diary of Anne Frank*, the 1961 Adolf Eichmann trial, a wave of anti-Semitic vandalism in 1958–59, the erection of the Berlin Wall in 1961, and the grisly Frankfurt Auschwitz Trials of 1963–66, Adorno's analysis formed part of the mood in which a new generation challenged the structures, policies, and attitudes of the early Federal Republic, particularly regarding the memory of the Nazi period; against earlier positions, the new mood emphasized continuities rather than ruptures between the Third Reich and the Federal Republic. For the new generation, Adorno's concern about the persistence of fascist tendencies within democracy was epigrammatic.

Read from our temporal remove, the lecture is an important period piece. Adorno's preference for "working through the past" (Aufarbeitung der Vergangenheit)—which demands a continual self-critical engage-ment—over "mastering the past" (*Vergangenheitsbewältigung*)—which im-plies, to Adorno, silencing it—is an interesting contrast to the discourse of the late 1970s and 1980s. By then, neoconservative critics identified both terms indiscriminately as emblems of everything that was wrong with the New Left of the 1960s. For neoconservatives, Vergangenheitsbewältigung stood for a purported national self-flagellation deriving from New Left interest in the Nazi past, one that constrained Germany's ability to claim a rightfully proud identity and to achieve a power position commensurate with its size and achievements. Vergangenheitsbewältigung was to neo-conservatives the same kind of fighting word that "fascist" had been to the New Left.[1]

In place of a mastering or working through the past in any form, commentators and political leaders in the late 1970s and 1980s called for a "normalization" of the past. Yet exactly what that would involve, and how best to achieve it, has since then been a point of contention both within and outside neoconservative circles. In the spirit of Adorno's lecture, then, this essay asks an analogous question about such demands: "What does it mean to *normalize* the past?" In what different ways have West German leaders pursued such a program, and with what effects? Most important, how have the problems of the German past changed since 1989, when a crucial impediment to Germany's sense of "normalcy" disappeared?

In order to investigate strategies of normalization in West German politics, we can take one further lesson from Adorno's lecture. From our perspective, that lecture demonstrates clearly how much images of the past are tied up with contemporary politics. This has been a perennial theme both of social memory studies generally and of discussions of the German situation in particular. Scholars of social memory, for instance, have consistently pointed out the ways in which social memory is malleable, how the "past" is a cultural construct made in the present and thus subject to the various contemporary interests that bear on it (Hobsbawm and Ranger 1983; Halbwachs 1992; Schwartz et al. 1986). But while some studies have treated the construction of the past as a purely dependent variable, the product of exogenous interests, empirical analysis reveals that this reworking is not merely incidental to those interests: it is a necessary part of their expression and constitution (Schwartz 1991; Olick and Levy 1997). As Michael Stürmer (1987) put it during the German historians' dispute of 1985–86, "the future belongs to those who fill memory, coin concepts, and interpret the past." It is not just new constellations of interests that produce new images of the past, but new images of the past that allow new power positions.

Exactly this observation is at the center of an important article by historian Anson Rabinbach (1988). In an analysis of different images of the past through West German history, Rabinbach argues that every expansion of West German sovereignty was linked to the question of responsibility for the German past. Rabinbach isolated three moments. First, he connected Konrad Adenauer's 1951 call to the Bundestag for West Germany to pay reparations to Israel with an abandonment of hope for reunification and a turn toward Western integration. Second, he argued that the wave of public anti-Semitism in 1959–60 demonstrated the failures of postwar denazification and, connected with the acceptance of NATO by the Social Democratic Party (SPD), prepared the way for a Grand Coalition in 1966–69 and for the opening toward the East known as the new *Ostpolitik*. And third, Rabinbach linked the attempted normalization of the past embodied in the Bitburg ceremony of 1985 to an expanded sense of and claim to German national identity in the mid-1980s.

Of course, we could make an equally strong case for other particular dates. Chancellor Helmut Schmidt's comment in 1981 that German sovereignty should no longer be held hostage to Auschwitz, for instance, evidences an urge to normalization as much as Bitburg does, and this earlier dating raises questions about the usual association of normalization strategies solely with Chancellor Helmut Kohl's conservatives after 1982. The policy of Western integration can be traced as easily to the state's founding in 1948–49 or to debates about rearmament in 1951–52 as it can be to the reparations agreements. And the Eichmann trial and other events of the late 1950s and early 1960s are all at least equally good markers of change as the 1959–60 wave of anti-Semitism was.

Rabinbach's insight that images of the past are associated with the status of sovereignty, however, remains important. Constructing those connections in a somewhat looser fashion, I find the concept of a legitimation profile—comprising a variety of related legitimacy claims, issue cultures, discursive styles, images of the past, *Feindbilder* (enemy images), and the like—to be useful for appreciating the ways in which diverse symbolic elements and issues congeal through time into relatively coherent yet dynamic systems. At different points in West German history, diverse elements have come together in varying ways to form distinct legitimation profiles, profiles in which images of the past played important roles. While particular dates can be more and less important for the structure of political cultures, political cultural change—that is, change in legitimation profiles—usually happens in a more gradual, often piecemeal way; legitimation profiles often overlap, and sometimes compete, though understood holistically they can be useful for characterizing the dominant trend of an epoch.

Elsewhere (Olick 1993; Olick and Levy 1997), I have identified three major legitimation profiles in West German history. The first, what I call the Reliable Nation, runs roughly from the founding of the Federal Republic in 1949 through the early 1960s. In the first few years of West German history, Konrad Adenauer's Christian Democrat–led government sought to resolve institutionally the problems of the past. This involved important legal provisions hammered out during the constitutional convention at Herrenchiemsee in 1948 (including greater federalism than in the Weimar Republic, limitations on presidential powers, and a principle of inviolable human rights in the first paragraph rather than buried later, as it had been in the Weimar constitution), as well as a program of reparations to Israel that was finalized in 1952–53. These institutional changes, combined with a stolid Western orientation, were the basis of Adenauer's claim that West Germany was a reliable nation, one no longer to be associated with its predecessor regime (characterized as a temporary alien presence or criminal seduction).

As part of the generational frisson and Western policy failures of the early 1960s, a new image of Germany as a Moral Nation arose. Unlike the society of the 1950s, the new generation was willing to confront and draw more radical lessons from the past, which were now generalized to world peace and rapprochement with the East. Germany could face up to its responsibilities, though these were now universalized to such an extent that rhetoric often placed West Germany at the avant-garde of progressive morality. In the process, the specificity of German crimes against Jews sank into the background.

By the mid-1970s, following the oil crisis of 1973, a general economic downturn, and the rise of neoconservative ideology, West German leaders (beginning less dramatically with the pragmatist Helmut Schmidt in 1974 and entering a more authentically neoconservative phase with Federal President Walter Scheel in the mid-1970s and Chancellor Helmut Kohl in 1982) portrayed West Germany as a Normal Nation, one with the same problems as other Western states and a history that included "highs as well as lows." The catchword of normalization continued after 1989 as well, though with different effects.

The claim that different moments of confronting the past are associated with different situations of West German sovereignty is an important demonstration of the constructionist theories of memory cited above. But such a historical account of legitimation profiles makes a further important point as well: associated images of the past and legitimacy claims (legitimation profiles) do not follow one another in simple ways but are highly path-dependent. New solutions depend on older ones, providing terms, issues, styles, and expectations as well as points of departure. Older images of the past—like the past itself—are both resources and constraints for the present; no deciphering of interests alone will suffice to account for contemporary versions of the past. More recent work on social memory (see Olick and Robbins 1998) has therefore responded to the constructionists by arguing that images of the past are neither dictated by the past nor wholly invented in the present but result from an ongoing dialogue in which earlier images shape and constrain what can be done with them in successive presents.[2]

The differences between Adorno's challenge of the late 1950s and the desires of the 1980s make clear the importance of both context and history in political cultural profiles. This observation is especially central when asking what normalization can mean because that effort of normalization aims at the past (the Nazi period), at the history of the memory of the past, as well as at the present; each of these requires normalization. My argument in the remainder of this essay is both that the problematic of normalization was shaped decisively by the transformations of 1989 and that the changes of 1989 in Germany were shaped by images of the Nazi past. This is not to say that the West German political culture of the 1980s brought about the fall of the Wall and the demise of the East German regime, although there is an argument to be made about the policy of strength manifested in the "double track" decision of the late 1970s through early 1980s (Herf 1991). But the context in which developments were received certainly did shape the way challenges and opportunities were met.

My major claim is that events since 1989 have involved a more successful "normalization" of the Nazi past than efforts since at least 1982, and arguably since the late 1970s. That success, I argue, depends on a shift in how "normalization" was understood by German politicians.[3] The result has been an altered political cultural landscape, one that represents the past and locates responsibility for it differently than before.

Throughout the 1980s two distinct senses of the world *normalization* were available. The first sense is the one that became famous in the so-called historians' dispute of 1985–86 (Maier 1988; Baldwin 1990) and in the Bitburg ceremony (Hartman 1986) and that pervaded Helmut Kohl's rhetoric through many occasions: that is, normalization as relativization. The German past had its horrors, but so did the pasts of other countries.

The 12 short years of Nazi rule do not exhaust the extent of the German past, which must be "accepted with all its highs and lows." The Nazi past is not particularly special, and the German past contains much more that is beneficial as points of orientation. Germany is thus like other nations, normal in the statistical sense.

Under Helmut Schmidt in the mid-1970s and early 1980s, this meant that West Germany faced the same "normal" problems of other modern welfare states—including rising unemployment, economic downturn, terrorism, loss of faith in endless growth, and so on—in the same "normal" ways. Kohl's style of normalization was more aggressive, embodied in an ideological program for cultural change, which included pride in German history, the celebration of heroes, national museums and monuments, and a distancing of past misdeeds, which now have lost their specificity—all the victims are the same. On this basis, West Germany sought to undertake a greater role in world politics.

The second sense of normalization is that of regularization or ritualization. After forty years of West German history, the commemorative apparatus had become a rather well-oiled machine. Acknowledgments of historical responsibility had become regular features of the political liturgy. Distinctive genres had evolved: there were, for instance, German guilt occasions, including anniversaries of 30 January 1933, 8 May 1945, 1 September 1939, 9 November 1938, *Israelpolitik*, and concentration camp visits; there were celebrations of German suffering, including Memorial Day, and commemorations of the postwar expulsions from Eastern Europe; and there were celebrations of valued German traditions, including the 20 July conspiracy and the *Hambacherfest*, among others. Each of these genres had developed its own appropriate style and language; as time went on, that language, style, and content became increasingly ritualized and regular (Olick 1993). Whether or not the German past was a normal past, it was to a large extent a normal part of West German political ritual. It had been largely domesticated.

But normalization in the 1980s—in both senses—failed as much as it succeeded. Relativization failed not because the idea was new but because it was pursued more openly and aggressively than before and because Kohl insisted that other countries participate. Domestically, it was widely appreciated.[4] The problem was to get the rest of the world to accept the claim that Germany was normal. Bitburg, and Kohl's earlier statements on a 1984 trip to Israel that he was the first German chancellor to be "graced by a late birth," were problematic not because of the claims—which were neither new nor untrue—but because they demanded a change in international and diplomatic attitude toward West Germany. They required the rest of the world's complicity in a process that had been going on for a long time internally. Relativization thus disturbed the delicate ritual strategy that had taken years to construct—one that demanded certain symbolic performances but belied the de facto status quo of German power and position.

Within this climate of heightened sensitivity, however, even standardized atonement rituals could be a relatively delicate matter, requiring substantial symbolic, diplomatic, and even material resources, especially when things did not go according to plan. The Jenninger affair of 1988 is a poignant example of how easy it was to go wrong. The president of the Bundestag, Philipp Jenninger—a highly respected politician and experienced hand at atonement rituals—delivered a speech to a special memorial session of the Bundestag on the 50th anniversary of *Kristallnacht* in which he sought to examine what the world had looked like to Germans in the early 1930s. In laying out how Hitler could have seemed good to the German people, he sounded like he was advocating that interpretation, or at least saying that it was reasonable to have thought so. While a careful reading of the speech makes it clear that this was not what Jenninger had in mind, this was not apparent during the Bundestag reading, and substantial numbers of deputies left the chamber in protest. In the wake of the scandal, Jenninger had little choice but to resign. His mistake did not reside purely in the substance of his comments but in the fact that he violated the entrenched expectations of the occasion. He did not deliver the relatively vapid declaration that ritual definitions required. Normalization as ritualization was thus no more without pitfalls than normalization as relativization. Nevertheless, the fact that this was a failure of ritual rather than of substance evoked a different response from neoconservatives: they accepted Jenninger's resignation with regret but without substantial challenge. The apt comparison is to the intensity with which the Kohl administration defended the Bitburg visit three years earlier.

Have things changed significantly since 1989? My answer is an equivocal yes, equivocal largely because the empirical materials are vast and diverse, deriving from and bearing on a wide array of contexts. It is very difficult, and perhaps dangerous, to generalize about how a whole society through an entire epoch deals with its past: collective memory is a diverse and often contradictory production (Olick and Robbins 1998). And each of the moments and issues I will describe was controversial in its time and context, making clear interpretation difficult. Nonetheless, I think some general patterns are clear, if we remind ourselves that official memory, itself contested, is a very particular kind of remembering that may affect other forms but never dominates them completely. Recognizing this specificity of official memory is important because it was in part the definition of official memory's duties that changed.

The obvious starting point for discussing changes in German memory of the Nazi period since 1989 is the fall of the Berlin Wall and the rush toward unification. West German leaders had always characterized the division of Germany as the result of power politics at Germany's cost. They consistently denied that there was any connection between Germany's crimes during the Nazi period and its postwar division.[5] But rhetorical protestations and the arbitrary realities of Potsdam aside, there is no doubt that some within Germany at least admitted, if not accepted, the association and that many abroad viewed division if not as punishment, then at least as insurance against German militarism in the center of Europe. There is a much quoted remark by a French politician that he liked Germany so much, he was glad there were two of them. It is no surprise, then, that there was significant apprehension in the world about the possibility of German unification.

Two West German moves served to exacerbate that concern. First, Chancellor Kohl moved quickly after 9 November to propose his 10-point strategy for unification. Many commentators abroad felt bulldozed. Indeed, in a high-level discussion, British prime minister Margaret Thatcher is reported to have referred to stereotypically negative German national characteristics as an expression of her distaste for a powerful united Germany in the center of Europe. There was no masking her hesitancy about the whole idea. Historical memories were quite alive through the entire process. Konrad Jarausch (1994: 181) has recently written that "foreign apprehension of the Teutonic threat was slow to disappear because it was focused on the past rather than present." His implication, I think, is that this was not a realistic fear. As we will see next, though, the German government's rhetoric did not unequivocally work toward assuaging those historical concerns. Jarausch was correct, though, when he wrote that "historical anti-German anxieties could complicate but not prevent unity" (181).

The second problem was Chancellor Kohl's refusal to make any clear statement regarding former German territories east of the Oder-Neisse line.[6] Favoring right-wing votes over diplomatic clarity, Kohl worried many observers; this was not because they thought he truly had designs on those territories but, first, because they did not like the choice for domestic votes over international assurances and, second, because they did not like those whom he was domestically assuring and thereby legitimating. This was only the first of many post-Wall moments in which the Kohl government was charged with legitimating right-wing interests. The main point is that throughout the unification process the German official line denied that historical concerns were legitimate in evaluating contemporary positions.

Indeed, even prosaic language caused debate: was Germany unifying or reunifying? If the latter, then what kind of a return was implied? A German national state had been more of a historical oddity than an enduring taken-for-granted in German history. And it was as a nation-state that German militarism created most of its havoc. But without the sense of the nation naturally belonging together (and thus of *reunification*), the whole enterprise might have seemed at risk.

This kind of issue came up again in the debate over where the capital of the new state was to be located: should the German capital remain in the modest Rhineland city of Bonn, with its traditions of stability, peace, and Western integration? Or should it return to the "traditional" capital of Germany, Berlin, with all its historical associations with Prussian militarism, Nazi power, and Central Europe? The debate was vituperative and not necessarily along party lines, and the vote not overwhelming, but nonetheless in favor of Berlin, despite the costs. In the process, however, parliamentarians engaged the difficult issues of Germany's historical and contemporary image (Herles 1991). All sides were heard, but that of German tradition, power, and prestige won out clearly over concerns about historical associations, the advocates of which did not get far enough with pragmatic arguments of cost and contemporary successes. German history was powerful enough to cause a debate but not powerful enough to change its outcome. Commentators have now come to refer (first sometimes facetiously, now without irony) to the new Germany as the Berlin Republic, playing on the terms *Bonn Republic* and *Weimar Republic*.

Even the timing of the Berlin Wall's opening posed significant symbolic difficulties. The day 9 November had been a traditional moment for commemorating German crimes—particularly the pogrom committed on so-called Kristallnacht in 1938. Would the spontaneous euphoria associated with that day in 1989—when the Wall opened—overshadow the established associations of the date? Would collective memory of German national feeling eclipse the acknowledgment of what had been done "in Germany's name"? German leaders, however, were especially careful, particularly after 3 October 1990—the day of official unification—became the date to celebrate. Later, 17 January—the anniversary of the liberation of Auschwitz—was added as a general day of remembrance for the victims of National Socialism (thus, alongside the more specific occasions of 9 November, 20 July [remembrance day for the resistance martyrs], and *Volkstrauertag* [Memorial Day for ordinary German victims of war]). By 1993, after long months of right-wing violence and significant concern in the international press over German xenophobia and neo-Nazi violence, the 55th anniversary of Kristallnacht clearly took precedence in official circles over memory of the Wall. In fact, Bundestag president Rita Süssmuth explicitly avowed the importance of remembering Kristallnacht as a response to presidential candidate Stefan Heitmann, who had recently made remarks to the effect that it was time for Germany to move on from such historical consciousness. (I will say more on Heitmann later.)

Like other new regimes in Central and Eastern Europe, Germany also faced the problem of dealing with leaders of what it considered to be a criminal regime. But unlike the remnant states of the fissiparous Eastern Bloc, Germany had a model for "mastering the past" (Vergangenheitsbewältigung), as it had come to be called. Collective memory—and mythology—about denazification was quite strong in West German political culture, so the second "mastering of the past" was frequently brought into relation to the first. The problem is that concern with the second Vergangenheitsbewältigung displaced the first both historically and rhetorically. Historically, the confrontation with the Nazi past now seemed like ancient history, something that had been accomplished for better or for worse. Events had clearly moved on, and the legacy of Nazism was not considered to be part of the contemporary scene. Rhetorically, the referent

for the word Vergangenheitsbewältigung shifted. It now seemingly referred only to the problem of dismantling and confronting the Stasi
(Staatssicherheit—the East German State Police). Vergangenheitsbewältigung had, like the Nazi past, lost its specificity.

This replacement of the first Vergangenheitsbewältigung by the second served as a potent normalizer. First of all, Germany was now just one
of a number of countries going through the same kinds of problems.
Comparison served the trope of relativization. And second, Germany's
historical problems were now those of communism and police infor-
mants and shoot-to-kill orders for border guards (problems of state violence) and not those of concentration camps and Nazis in the government
(problems of genocide). Indeed, even before 1989, Kohl had referred to
communist "concentration camps"—thus equating the two systems, just
as totalitarian theory had always done; and in a June 1991 wreath-laying
ceremony in Buchenwald, he referred indiscriminately to all the victims
of oppression. The historian Hans-Peter Schwarz expressed a common
desire when he asserted that the communist past would now represent
the main theme of Vergangenheitsbewältigung for future decades, at the
cost of continuing to work through (aufarbeiten) National Socialism. He
argued that this made sense given that the East German regime had lasted
three times as long as the Nazi period (Greiffenhagen and Greiffenhagen
1993: 64). Martin and Sylvia Greiffenhagen have argued that this was an
unrealistic expectation because the direct comparison of the two regimes
is illegitimate. But it may, too, be an unrealistic expectation that the new
Germany will acknowledge that difference. As we are seeing, it does and it
does not.

Rabinbach's claim that changes in West German sovereignty involve
shifts in constructions of the Nazi past seems to apply well to the transition period. One of the first acts of noncommunist East Germany, for
instance, was to acknowledge responsibility for the Nazi past and to promise some form of reparations, though given East Germany's state of fiscal
collapse, there was not much to back up the promise. This gesture, of
course, marked a complete turnaround for the German Democratic Republic, which had always argued that fascism was an outgrowth of capitalism and that a socialist state was thus de facto antifascist.[7] East Germany
argued that it represented the opposition to fascism and thus bore no
responsibility for the crimes of the regime it replaced. The gesture was,

therefore, significant, and it did much to make the transition more palatable to Israel and Jewish groups, who were nonetheless still concerned.

Acknowledgments of Germany's past were also a significant presence in the pomp surrounding unification, though they took the form of general statements about responsibility for the whole of German history and avowals of peaceful intentions. Some Jewish groups objected that the unification treaty itself did not have the desired acknowledgments in its preamble, though statements about responsibility for history were buried later in the document. Acknowledgments of responsibility were there, but by no means front and center.

The new Germany also faced images of the Nazi past in the context of significant world conflicts that arose, and the debates over these images had significant implications for the bearing of the Nazi past on future German power. Debates over the Gulf War, Yugoslavia, and Somalia provided connected occasions for discussing Germany's future role. In the process, the legitimacy of the past as a constraint on German activity was seriously discredited.

The Gulf War could not have been designed as a more complex minefield for Germany. What should Germany's role be? Financial? Military? None at all? Two world wars, forty-five years of superpower troops facing off along the inner German border, and the threat of nuclear destruction had produced a quite strong pacifist presumption in wide segments of the German population. Indeed, pacifism seemed to be the clear lesson of the Nazi experience. But now a concerted world coalition had come together to oppose Saddam Hussein, and Germany's allies demanded a contribution, while German leaders argued that this was Germany's responsibility. And there were further difficulties for Germany: Saddam Hussein threatened the existence of Israel, for whose interests Germany obviously had to be concerned. And participation of German firms in arming Saddam's war machine provided a dicey public relations problem. On top of these issues was the significant cost of the operation at a time when the German government was just beginning to face the real costs of unification.

Usually the world condemned and feared any German military activity. Now they demanded it. The German peace movement opposed participation because of the Nazi past, but now Israeli security was at stake. All signs were reversed, and it was easy to see that there was no correct solution and that no solution for this problem would generalize well to other situations. The ropes twisting around German policy were now clear enough, and the impossibility of correct action in such circumstances made Germany's problems obvious.

A second such moment came in facing the Yugoslavian collapse. After having been criticized for not doing enough in the Gulf War, the Kohl government now sought to lead the pack and pushed for quick European recognition of Croatia. This matter, too, was twisted in the ropes of the German past: a fascist puppet regime in Croatia had worked with the Nazis against the Slavic populations of other regions. German support for Croatian independence was thus connected to the old Nazi-Croatian alliance.

United Nations "humanitarian" missions to protect the Kurds and to feed the Somalis also made the German constitutional prohibition against overseas military action seem like a barrier to fulfilling German responsibilities. The convolutions of these closely packed moments contributed to a general consensus in German government circles that some changes had to be made and that the particular responses to the Nazi past embodied in the German Basic Law had outlived their practicability.[8] Germany was both too big and too powerful, and world events were too complicated, for old formulas. And the apparent schizophrenia of the international community in its expectations of and fears about Germany helped as well.

This long list of issues hardly begins to exhaust the important moments since 1989 for images of the Nazi past. It is necessary to consider two further issue complexes: historical symbolism in the new Germany, and the matter of xenophobia and the New Right.

One major event of German history politics was the return of Friedrich the Great to Sanssouci. The Nazis had moved the German king's body in the last weeks of the war to protect it from Russian troops. Chancellor Kohl saw a procession to Berlin as a major symbolic opportunity for expressing the recovery of German history that accompanied German unity. Critics charged that Friedrich stood for Prussian militarism, nationalism, and obedience. But Kohl's people staged a regal pageant despite the ridicule. Representatives of the German military participated too. At the "final" interment, Kohl intoned that Germans now need "to stand before our entire history." "History," he said, "only contains enlightening insights when we view it as a whole." This had been Kohl's line for years.

But now he was saying it as the chancellor of the largest and most power-ful nation in Europe. The ceremony, however, remained mostly a German matter; it received relatively little attention abroad. Unlike at Bitburg, no international participation was necessary.

Other symbolic moments were more directly concerned with the Nazi period, not just with displacing it from the center of German history. There was, for instance, the matter of the Neue Wache. This was the successor to the East German monument to the unknown soldier from World War II. The unification treaty had included a clause that the Federal Republic would maintain the building as a public monument. In its new incarnation, the monument included a pieta by Käthe Kollwitz and an inscription to all the victims of the Third Reich. The monument thus equalized all the victims, and the irony of the Christian symbolism was apparently missed by the Kohl government.

In addition, there was the matter of the Bomber Harris/Peenemünde complex. The British erected a monument to the designer of the Dresden bombings, Air Marshall Harris. The destruction of Dresden has long stood, for many, as the quintessential demonstration that not all crimes were on the German side. The bombing of Dresden was a major moment in the commemoration of German suffering. Many Germans took sub-stantial umbrage at the idea of a monument to the man who planned the assault, especially when the Queen Mother announced that she would take part in the unveiling. British supporters argued that the destruction of Dresden was a necessary psychological "softening up" of German civil-ians in preparation for the infantry invasion. German opponents argued that it was the celebration of a war criminal considered a hero only be-cause he had been on the winning side. In the process, though, German opponents never acknowledged any connections between the Dresden bombings and German attacks on British civilians.

At about the same time (October 1992), private concerns in Germany proposed and organized a celebration of 50 years of space flight, the birth of which they located in Hitler's secret rocket program at Peenemünde. Eventually, they were forced by criticism and lost government support to cancel the celebration. They had not seen fit to contextualize the event and to acknowledge the motivation behind the rocket program.

Another such symbolic moment, similar to many since the early 1980s, was Chancellor Kohl's March 1992 meeting with Austrian president Kurt Waldheim. Waldheim, of course, had been shunned by most of the diplomatic community because of his apparent involvement, long kept secret, in Nazi crimes in the occupied Balkan territories. Kohl resisted all pressure not to meet with the alleged Nazi, arguing that he would visit whom he wanted, when he wanted, and where he wanted. Kohl would not allow Waldheim's past associations and their relevance for such a meeting to influence his behavior.

Within this context, it may seem rather strange that the government supported the conversion into a museum of the Wannsee villa, in which Nazi leaders had initiated the "final solution." Relativization and ritualization proceeded along their different tracks, producing what Charles Maier (1988) has referred to as a postmodern hodgepodge. At the same time, therefore, the German government also sought to influence the content of the United States Holocaust Museum in Washington, D.C., offering substantial sums of money to the museum to include an exhibit on the democratic achievements of the Federal Republic. The offer was rejected. In another context, the responsible government authority refused to nominate the much acclaimed film *Europa, Europa* (*Hitler Junge Salomon*) for an Academy Award because it did not want Germany to be represented by such a vivid film about that era. Recently, reactions to *Schindler's List* have included the query as to why Germany had not produced such a film.

The major issue complex for images of the Nazi past, however, has clearly been that involving the rise of the New Right, neo-Nazism, violence against foreigners, and the debate about the constitutional right to asylum. In the early 1990s the German and world public were flooded with horrifying images that for many harked back to the 1930s. There has been much speculation about what these new images really mean for German politics and society. Does the potential exist for a revival of National Socialism? Is the apparently anti-Semitic and generally racist violence of large numbers of German youth a serious political matter, or merely one of youth, not entirely specific to Germany? The answers to these questions are that the threat is probably not serious, that it is nonetheless disturbing, and that there is some implication for the German center—if it does not collapse, then it will shift. Indeed, the similarity of the German, French, and Italian New Rights has paradoxically served the trope of relativization, making Germany's problems seem like the same "normal" ones shared by its neighbors.

There are two important aspects to the government reaction to this set of issues. First of all, the Kohl administration has worked hard to frame the problem as one of disaffected youth and ridiculous extremists. The official line has been that acts of vandalism and even murder are a shame and an embarrassment but not a serious indicator of anything but fringe sentiment. This way of framing the issue, of course, has a long history. During the wave of anti-Semitic vandalism in 1959–60, Adenauer's government also worked hard to convince the world that such attitudes were rare and such activities only the work of mischievous teenagers. In 1959, though, the reaction was immediate and significant. In today's Germany, the government has clearly been slow to act. And the response has been anything but seriously concerned: such activities are "a shame for Germany" but more threatening as an international public relations problem than as anything else.

Most of the government reaction can be seen as international damage control. As a number of commentators pointed out with a polemical edge, when neo-Nazis committed arson on the grounds of the Sachsenhausen concentration camp, the federal government sent the foreign minister to protect Germany's reputation rather than criminal investigators to hunt for the perpetrators. Moreover, Kohl has assiduously avoided attending funerals, arguing that this would be "political tourism."

A second aspect of the issue is that debate within the government and public arena has served to legitimate the sentiment, if not the expression. Conservative leaders had for many years been arguing that Germany was being overrun by foreigners. And the numbers have been truly significant. Controlling abuses of the system and the general problem of economic refugees clearly required some attention. Conservatives pushed for a constitutional amendment to limit the handling of asylum seekers. The right to asylum was a constitutional clause that was clearly conceived as a response to Nazi political persecution. Because Germans had committed as well as suffered such persecution during the Third Reich, the constitutional framers saw it as an important feature of West Germany's new rule of law. Conservatives argued that the situation in the 1990s was untenable, while the Social Democrats and others argued that the principle, because of its anti-Nazi context, was inviolable.

The weight of public opinion and the measure of the problem eventually led the opposition to give in. This move is of interest to us for at least two reasons. In the first place, the shift was quite problematic politically because it seemed as if the right-wing violence had worked. It seemed, that is, as if the government had accepted at least part of the xenophobic argument of the violent youths and right-wing leadership. But second, the matter is interesting for the fate of the Nazi past. The number of people seeking asylum in Germany—for whatever reason—was perceived as a strain on resources in a time of economic difficulties (not merely incidentally caused by the costs of unification). One reason the problem was worse for Germany is the legacy of the Nazi past both institutionally and in the political culture. The clear need to manage the problem thus discredited the power of such an anti-Nazi–based argument: the past could no longer legislate in the face of such a problem.[9]

While rather long, this list of issues does not exhaust the moments in which images of the Nazi past played a role or were affected since 1989. Nor has it been possible to delve into the interpretive complexities necessary to a serious study of each of these moments. But constructed images of the Nazi past are clearly strong constitutive presences in German political culture both before and after 1989. In what ways, however, have things changed since 1989? It seems as if relativizing strategies were consistent across the divide; the blurring of victim categories, the historicization of the Nazi years, the search for history "with all its highs and lows," and the argument that the German past should not impinge on the "responsible" exercise of German power were all long-standing and continuing features of neoconservative rhetoric through the 1980s and 1990s. And it is clear that there were plenty of moments other than ordinary speech occasions where the specter of the past loomed potently.

Nonetheless, there has, I think, been a subtle shift—one partly of substance, partly of context. Substantively, new issue complexes have forced certain traditional rhetorical constraints into obsolescence. The examples here are the Gulf War / Croatia / Somalia / Kurd complex and the immigration problem. In both matters, positions based on images of the past became clearly untenable, at least in their convolutions (the Gulf War) and obstinacy (the immigration / asylum issue).

The context, too, has changed. Tough talk from West Germany sounded shrill, even hysterical, while the same language seems more appropriate from the larger new Germany. There is much talk of the new Germany's identity crisis. But I think there is much less of a problem since unification than in the years of division. These are now internal problems. Actual solidarity must arise to fill the space opened by rhetorical gestures, but it surely will. This seems much less worrisome than the German nation in the cultural sky that has caused so much trouble since Hegel and Fichte.

The context of unification also made the historical symbol work propagated by the Kohl government appear somewhat less important. History politics seems more inwardly directed in unified Germany; in West Germany in the 1980s, controversial historical symbolism was played as much for the international audience as for the German public, often making demands on diplomatic partners for acknowledgment. In the West German context of the 1980s, the symbolic politics of history aggressively aimed at changing Germany's status. Now that Germany's status has been changed, the same rhetoric does not seem quite as aggressive.

The government has been careful to make the right noises at the right times, at least enough to make critics appear picky. Symbolism and pomp—historical and otherwise—are to be expected at such a major moment of transition, and no one can be surprised at national celebrations (which otherwise would have seemed out of place), no matter how distasteful one might find even good-willed expressions of German national joy. And I think the Kohl government has gotten somewhat better at the game. They do perform well when they have to, ritually accepting responsibility in the right places; they have learned that the desire for relativization can be fulfilled better by ritualization than by challenge or avoidance.

Indeed, the controversy over Stefan Heitmann was, as a result, not nearly as momentous as it might have been. Heitmann was Helmut Kohl's candidate to replace the popular Richard von Weizsäcker as federal president. Heitmann was dropped quickly after he made comments that he thought it was time to draw a line under the German past, to acknowledge its significance but to move out from under its shadow.[10] Heitmann thus failed an early test of ritual performance. His replacement as Christian Democratic Union candidate—Roman Herzog, president of the Constitutional Court—is probably little different in his views of the German past, but he has performed the ritual well, an important skill for the largely symbolic presidency.

These differences between the 1980s and 1990s were especially clear in the 50th anniversary commemoration of the end of World War II on 8 May 1995. Ten years earlier, events surrounding the 40th anniversary formed a major international controversy—the Bitburg affair. For over a year, public discourse in the Federal Republic was focused on little else. By contrast, the 1995 commemoration went off with only slight difficulties. Polish president Lech Walesa demanded inclusion in what was originally to have been a purely German affair; conservative parliamentarian Alfred Dregger led a campaign against portrayals of 8 May as a day of liberation because such portrayals, he argued, downplayed the innocent suffering of Germans; and a synagogue in Lübeck was firebombed shortly after being newly consecrated. But the government responded briskly and nonconfrontationally to each of these challenges, demonstrating a newfound agility in performing "correctly" in symbolically dangerous waters. It was arranged for the Polish foreign minister to address a special session of the Bundestag as a substitute for Walesa's participating in the official commemorations; the government did not pick up Dregger's challenge in any significant form; and Kohl's cabinet responded to the firebombing briskly and with the appropriate outrage.

Since the paroxysms of 1989, but earlier as well, many nations have confronted the legacies of difficult pasts. As they do so, the German case serves as a powerful substantive and theoretical exemplar. Indeed, the unassimilable memory of the Holocaust has been a powerful determinant of a general politics of regret that has arisen in many places. As early as 1946, the philosopher Karl Jaspers (1987 [1946]) distinguished four notions of guilt: criminal guilt (responsibility for actions that violate clear existing laws, judged by courts); political guilt (responsibility for how we are governed, judged by victors); moral guilt (responsibility for every action we take, including those we take under military or political command, judged by our consciences); and metaphysical guilt (responsibility for all injustice in the world, especially for that of which one is aware or in which one participates, by virtue of a solidarity among human beings). His point was to prevent ordinary citizens from overlooking their complicity in crimes with the defense that they did not actually pull the trigger: responsibility extends far beyond criminal guilt.[11] Such principles of political, moral, and metaphysical guilt have become more potent elsewhere in part because of the German case. Allied denazification and reeducation programs, Nuremberg justice, and arguments about German collective guilt after World War II were rather different than earlier principles of collective responsibility, however much they were resisted or unevenly applied, and these ideas have often been generalized to other cases; they were particularly vibrant during the protest movements of the 1960s and have been an important part of the formation of international institutions. The German case has thus provided much of our contemporary vocabulary for thinking about these issues.

Substantively, the German case shows how difficult it can be to manage collective identity while acknowledging historical burdens. In the German case, we have a catalogue of political, symbolic, psychological, and grammatical mechanisms for facing or avoiding the past. At the official level analyzed here, politicians and commentators from Germany and elsewhere have much to learn from the particular substance of German memory as well as from the Holocaust as civilizational rupture. This has been especially true since 1989, when German leaders began to use the first "mastering of the past" as a model for the second, and other nations began to look to both old and new efforts in Germany as models for their efforts. Both Nuremberg culture and German normalization are potent sources for specific strategies in Germany and elsewhere.

Theoretically, our look at the German case yields important generalizations about how memory works. First, we see how distinct issue complexes pose distinct challenges and yield different solutions. The legacy of the Nazi past, for instance, is somewhat different in the Berlin-Bonn, immigration, and Gulf War debates. Second, we see how solutions to the problems of collective memory are tied up with shifting political situations. Before and after 1989, for instance, the problem of normalization looked different, just as the problem of mastering the past worked differently in the 1950s and in 1960s. And third, we see that solutions are path-dependent, that later versions depend not just on the immediate circumstances but also on the history of earlier formulations. The fate of the German past after 1989, for instance, depends as much on the solutions prior to 1989 as it does on any straightforward expression of ahistorical interests after 1989, just as the solutions of the 1980s responded to those of the 1960s and 1970s.

What does it mean to normalize the past in Germany after 1989? History does not go away, German history in particular. Strategies of normalization as relativization in the 1980s did not work nearly as well as normalization as ritualization in the 1990s. Normalization of the past depends on normalization of the present and future, which could not have happened before the changes of 1989. It thus remains to be seen whether Germany's new past will stand as a living model and warning or whether it will sink into irrelevance. But as long as ritualization assuages the wounds of relativization and interested advocates of distinction become fewer and fewer, normalization of the past, just like that of the present, has more or less been achieved. That, too, is an interesting lesson about how memory works.

POSTSCRIPT: JANUARY 2001

The foregoing essay—first drafted in the fall of 1995—was not foolhardy enough to state any specific predictions for the future. Nevertheless, one could read a general expectation from the analysis presented there: While the Nazi past would not disappear from public discourse in the Federal Republic, its impact would be less significant for the practice of politics, at least as long as ritualization continued to lead relativization as a discursive strategy (as it did between 1989 and 1995) rather than the other way around (as in the 1980s). How well have the intervening years met this expectation? With Goldhagen, Walser-Bubis, *Holocaust-Mahnmal*, and *Leitkultur* making headlines over the last five years (to mention only the most prominent themes), the first impression is that the presence of the past has not changed much at all. Instead of revising the original essay, however, I would like to take this opportunity to reexamine it in two ways. First, I would like to see whether, despite the list I just made, the central claim has not indeed been redeemed. Second, I would like to reflect on the act of interpreting the role of the past in the present at different points in time. For not only do we always read the past from different presents, but we can also read our different readings of the past from different presents.

Has German *Geschichtspolitik* changed significantly in recent years? In my original essay, I suggested that the tone of discourse between the sixties and eighties—in which representations of the Nazi past served as oaths in partisan political debates—had lost some of its potential explosiveness. There were two reasons for this. First, political leaders had suffered the collateral damages of relativization as a discursive strategy for building national identity while ritualization was providing some of the desired benefits by removing memory from the center of political discourse. Whereas actively denying the importance of the past for present policy proved just the opposite (that is, the more one denied the centrality of the past, the clearer it was how central the past was), dutiful performance on segregated occasions and in special places achieved the goal perhaps less dramatically than hoped but, in the end, more effectively. Second, the epic and epochal transformation of world order after 1989 created a new horizon against which to read German politics and the role of German Geschichtspolitik within it. How Germany remembers its past is no longer the biggest question observers ask of it, though paradoxically it is potentially much more important in a world in which Germany once again exercises real power. Nevertheless, as sociological theory teaches us, real power often means more rather than less constraint. Whereas West Germany, one worried, might have been trying to elude the handicaps of historical responsibility, the Berlin Republic has, paradoxically, less room for deviance.

Can one say that ritualization has continued to lead relativization in the past five years? The Walser-Bubis debate seems to suggest the opposite, bringing back strong memories of the *Historikerstreit* of 1985–6. The debate began in October 1998 with writer Martin Walser's speech upon winning the Peace Prize of the German Publishers Association, in which he argued that "the intellectuals who reproach us with . . . our historical burden, our everlasting shame" bogusly see themselves as aligned with the victims; these intellectuals, Walser implied, instrumentalize the past and thus corrupt more genuine forms of memory, which are, in Walser's opinion, private. On this basis, Walser rejected what he saw as the "monumentalization of shame" in the Berlin Holocaust memorial. The Chairman of the Central Council of Jews in Germany, Ignaz Bubis, responded in a speech on the sixtieth anniversary of Kristallnacht by accusing Walser of "spiritual arson," in many ways treating Walser's comments as a replay of the conservative position from the Historikerstreit.

On the face of it, Walser did appear to be another conservative member of the older generation rejecting the burdens of Vergangenheitsbewältigung, seeking to minimize the memory of the Nazi past so as not to unduly restrain German patriotism. In his first responses, Bubis saw a legitimation—or at least an opening to—radical right-wing identity politics and the denial of history. But in further discussions, Bubis and Walser moderated their tones, and Bubis accepted at least some of Walser's position, which was indeed different from that of Nolte or Stürmer in the eighties. Most importantly, Walser had not called for an alternative public memory but rather for memory's privatization, which is a different affair. In this way, Walser's argument was not a mere return to relativization. Walser may not have approved of the form the Berlin memorial was taking, but he was not trying to alter the substantive interpretation of the past: He wanted to change its role in public discourse or its publicness per se. In some ways, Walser's stance could be read as more radical than conventional leftist positions because his rejection of public memory implied a rejection of the complacent ritualization in which the Left has in many ways acquiesced.[1]

In recent commentary, the Walser-Bubis debate is often contrasted directly with that surrounding Daniel Goldhagen's book, *Hitler's Willing Executioners*, in which Goldhagen, a young American political scientist from Harvard, argued that the Holocaust was caused by an "eliminationist" anti-Semitic ideology shared by the vast majority of ordinary Germans. The book quickly became a best seller, and Goldhagen toured Germany, playing everywhere to throngs of young people, many of whom embraced his apparent charges of collective guilt. Whereas Walser called for quiet reflection and was seen by some as just one more older German calling for silence about the past, the Goldhagen reception manifested the enthusiasm of the younger generation for acknowledging German culpability. Walser apparently signaled a decrease in public memory, Goldhagen an increase.

In many ways, however, Walser and Goldhagen manifest the same deep structure of German historical consciousness. The Goldhagen reception, from this perspective, could be seen as exactly the kind of instrumentalization of the past Walser rejected, but one allowed because of the different generational profiles. The young people enthused by Goldhagen, after all, have nothing to lose, particularly since Goldhagen believes in a total break between National Socialism and the Federal Republic, one in which the Federal Republic bears no vestiges of Germany's earlier pathologies. Like their parents in the 1960s, today's university students could reject the world of their grandparents completely because they had no organic connection to it.

But unlike the sixty-eighters, Goldhagen's memory requires no reworking of the Federal Republic. As a result, a great deal of the criticism of Goldhagen came from the Left, which saw itself as the champion of German culpability, rather than from the Right, which often wanted to diminish it. And there's the rub: Goldhagen's penance-free guilt provided exactly the kind of legitimation for the Federal Republic that many conservatives wanted, if without the revival of nineteenth-century rhetoric some may have preferred. Goldhagen offers an almost pleasurable guilt to young Germans because through it they can, exactly as Walser implied, identify with the victims. Goldhagen shows once again that less aggressive strategies of normalization work best: Acknowledge as much guilt as you want, just make sure it is a historical guilt without real connections to the politics of today. Goldhagen's guilt, it seems to me, must be much less threatening to Walser than that of Adorno or Habermas.

Anyone who looks historically at German memory, of course, has a strong feeling of "déjà vu all over again." If Walser-Bubis evokes the Historikerstreit (though falsely, I've just argued) or the Broszat-Friedlaender exchange preceding it, Goldhagen reminds us in some ways of the Fischer controversy (deep origins of German belligerence) and in other ways of the debate over the "Holocaust" TV Miniseries in 1979–80 (empty sympathies born of kitsch—for in many ways Goldhagen's book, with its evocative prose and totalistic argument, is historiographical kitsch—versus serious reflection on historical complexity). Naturally, this can be said about all of the major commemorative debates in the history of the Federal Republic. Each generation has worked through the same issues in its own way, whether it was with Karl Jaspers' *Die Schuldfrage*, Anne Frank's *Tagebuecher*, Peter Weiss' *Die Ermittlung*, "Holocaust," Schindler, or Goldhagen, or any of the other scandals, debates, controversies, and events in the history of German commemoration. The question here is what difference this might make for how we—or, more precisely, how I—read German historical consciousness since 1989 and again since 1995.

For me (born in 1964), my first real engagement with these issues was the Historikerstreit and as such the Historikerstreit remains my benchmark for all German Geschichtspolitik. Of course, as just noted, the Historikerstreit was not without precedent nor was it ever really "concluded," despite some identifications (my own included) of Richard von Weizsäcker's speech to the German Historikertag as a symbolic end. But I do think there was something special about the Historikerstreit that set it apart from all the debates before and after. The conservatives, as Habermas charged, aimed at something of a discursive coup, a real attempt to "normalize" not only the past but also previously taboo positions within debates about it. The goal was to settle the political costs of National Socialism once and for all, as well as to delegitimate anyone who might dissent. Where the Historikerstreit aimed to obliterate the distinctiveness of the German past, Walser aimed only to reduce its political role. Still problematic, but not quite as final.

One quality the Historikerstreit and the Walser-Bubis debate share, however, is that, though public, neither directly involved official statements—unlike many other scandals in the history of German commemoration. And while the Berlin Holocaust Monument required the participation (i.e., money) of the government and was debated by politicians, it was originally a private initiative. This fits well with the pattern I suggested, in which governmental memory sticks closely to a script. The difference between the Historikerstreit and the Walser-Bubis debate in this regard is that official postures were at stake in a somewhat more direct way in the mid-1980s and seemed to be at the center of what German governance was about. The Holocaust remains important, but German governance is now judged, as I already indicated, by more geopolitical concerns. It is only in this context that conservative politicians have advanced a notion of a German Leitkultur without first going directly through images of the Nazi past.

Perhaps part of the problem is with periodization and the "eventful" gaze as such (the focus on particular moments—be they scandals, debates, controversies, or events) and classing them into different groups temporally. The "eventful" gaze of historical sociology leads to a particular kind of narrative framing that notes beginnings, middles, and ends, or imposes them where they do not clearly exist. Here social science shares a phenomenology with journalism as well as with "players" in these contests. All exhibit very short "memories of memory," that is, a focus not only on the history being commemorated or contested but also on the history of that commemoration.[2] We all seem to have an interest in the episodic framing: It allows us to assess, reassess, compare, contrast, and regroup.

In what way, then, is it fair to compare Walser-Bubis to the Historikerstreit and to infer a shift in the referents and strategies of "normalization"? This is where a hermeneutical approach can help, for the "double hermeneutic" calls us to see both interpreter and interpreted as historical beings. A hermeneutical approach helps us avoid bogus judgments and false finalizations. It may well be that the differences I see today between 1985 and 1995, between 1989 and 2001, will, in retrospect, appear very different. But the historiographical question is one of the value of marking epochs at all and my doing so in this particular way.

That German history will never be normal is clear. The question is whether German memory can be. Here I can only say that this is what normalization of the German memory means to me: recognition that the debate is continuous, that there are no final lines, zero-hours, or caesuras in history or in memory, only continual reassessments. These reassessment are beholden to past assessments as well. We cannot reassess the past without reassessing our past assessments, nor can we reassess past assessments without reassessing the past. Until the "players" acknowledge this, German memory will never, in my opinion, be normal. That doesn't mean it hasn't changed.

NOTES

Earlier versions of this article were presented at the Ninth International Conference of Europeanists, April 1994, Chicago, Illinois, and the conference "In Memory: Remembering Nazi Atrocities in Post–Cold War Europe," June 1995, Arezzo, Italy. The author thanks Christhard Hoffman, Daniel Levy, and Guenther Roth for helpful comments.

1. One prominent conservative critic even titled a book about Vergangenheitsbewältigung "The Nose Ring" (Mohler 1991).

2. Michael Schudson (1989), for instance, points out that "the past is in some respects, and under some circumstances, highly resistant to efforts to make it over." He argues that the structures of available pasts, of individual choice, and of social conflict limit our abilities to alter images of the past in the present. Others, like Barry Schwartz (1991) and me (1999), describe mechanisms of ongoing mediation between old images and new contexts.

3. This essay deals with official images of the past. Though there are important relations among official memory, public memory, and private memory, each of these remains distinct both conceptually and substantively. Indeed, one result of "normalization" in official memory has been a ceding of responsibility for commemoration to nonofficial initiatives. Whereas Chancellor Kohl sought to control the politics of history in the 1980s through plans for two new historical museums and through the official ceremonies at Bitburg, later plans for a Holocaust memorial in Berlin were the initiative of private forces. One implication of the analysis I will present here is that while the normalization strategies of the 1980s derived from, and had important repercussions for, official business in the Federal Republic, strategies of the 1990s largely insulated the government from the disturbances of history politics.

4. The relationship between official images of the past and popular memory is obviously a complex one. A liberal view of the state tends to see official versions as expressions of popular sentiments; a cynical view, by contrast, sees official culture as propaganda. Neither of these depictions is accurate. As already indicated in the previous note, memory produced in different social fields operates according to different rules for different purposes. Indeed, differences need not be seen as contradictions: we often have distinct expectations for symbolism in particular fields. Moreover, hegemony theorists and the like (Scott 1990) have pointed out that even when the state takes a leading role in the production of cultural images, there remain spaces for resistance. On the other hand, oral historians and others (Thompson 1988) interested in giving voice to repressed experiences of the disenfranchised often romanticize "vernacular" memory as "authentic." My analytical goal here is to produce an accurate description of official images in their own terms rather than to explain (or, as is sometimes the case, explain away) those images. For a more detailed account of the interplay between official and vernacular, public and private, see Olick 1993 and Olick and Levy 1997.

5. These official positions were matched in public opinion. As recently as 1989, 72 percent of respondents to a West German opinion poll disagreed with the statement that division was a deserved punishment for the crimes of the Third Reich (Noelle-Neumann 1991: 68).

6. This is the border between Germany and Poland established at the Potsdam conference, cutting off Germany from formerly German territories. As a result of the Potsdam accords, millions of German residents of the eastern territories were expelled. Organization of these expellees and their descendants formed a powerful political lobby in the Federal Republic of Germany all the way through the 1980s, though with a more potent humanitarian claim in the 1950s. While always associated with nationalistic positions, these groups were even more revanchist in the 1980s.

7. For more nuanced accounts of East German history politics, based on research in East German archives, see Herf 1997 and Wolffsohn 1995.

8. Of course, this was not the first time that international crises raised complex issues for German policy, nor was it the first time West German leaders and commentators complained about strictures raised by memory. In the Yom Kippur war of 1973, West Germany debated whether or not to allow American supply planes headed to Israel to refuel at bases in Germany; the fear was that doing so would anger Arab countries. In 1982, on a trip to Saudi Arabia to negotiate sale of Leopard 2 tanks to the Saudis, Chancellor Helmut Schmidt was quoted as saying that West Germany foreign policy should no longer "be held hostage to Auschwitz." But it was perhaps the first time that there was little consensus among Germany's Western allies on what the right solution was.

9. One especially problematic move was an agreement Germany negotiated with Romania. In return for monetary and other incentives, Romania agreed to accept deported Sinti and Roma refugees without procedural hassle. The mass deportation of Gypsies clearly raised difficult associations with Nazi persecutions.

10. Heitmann also made disparaging comments about mothers who work outside the home. His comments about the past were thus placed with others to demonstrate a general unsuitability rather than a particular problem of history politics.

11. Of course, one implication of Jaspers's argument is that the prevalent forms of guilt for the Third Reich are not criminal and thus are not punishable.

NOTES TO POSTSCRIPT

1. Here I should not be misunderstood as supporting Walser, whose position I find deeply problematic. Walser called for a privatization of memory to avoid what he saw as the instrumentalization of public memory by the advocates of Vergangenheitsbewältigung, but in doing so he employed questionable notions of *Innerlichkeit*, among others. Overall, there was something disingenuous about this response, particularly in its posed naïveté about how significant a statement it would be.

2. I develop this concept in a recent paper: Jeffrey K. Olick, "Genre Memories and Memory Genres: A Dialogical Analysis of May 8, 1945 Commemorations in the Federal Republic of Germany," *American Sociological Review* 64 (June 1999): 381–402.

REFERENCES

Adorno, T. 1986 [1959]. "What Does Coming to Terms with the Past Mean?" In Geoffrey Hartman, ed., *Bitburg in Moral and Political Perspective*. Bloomington: Indiana University Press.

Baldwin, P., ed. 1990. *Reworking the Past: Hitler, the Holocaust, and the Historians' Debate*. Boston: Beacon Press.

Greiffenhagen, M., and S. Greiffenhagen. 1993. *Ein schwieriges Vaterland: Zur politischen Kultur im vereinigten Deutschland*. Munich: List.

Halbwachs, M. 1992. *On Collective Memory*, ed. Lewis Coser. Chicago: University of Chicago Press.

Hartman, G., ed. 1986. *Bitburg in Moral and Political Perspective*. Bloomington: Indiana University Press.

Herf, J. 1991. *War by Other Means: Soviet Power, West German Resistance, and the Battle of the Euromissiles*. New York: Free Press.

———. 1997. *Divided Memory: The Nazi Past in the Two Germanys*. Cambridge: Harvard University Press.

Herles, H., ed. 1991. *Die Hauptstadt Debatte*. Bonn: Bouvier.

Hobsbawm, E., and T. Ranger, eds. 1983. *The Invention of Tradition*. New York: Cambridge University Press.

Jarausch, K. H. 1994. *The Rush to German Unity*. New York: Oxford University Press.

Jaspers, K. 1987 [1946]. *Die Schuldfrage: Zur politischen Haftung Deutschlands*. Munich: Piper.

Maier, C. 1988. *The Unmasterable Past: History, Holocaust, and German National Identity*. Cambridge: Harvard University Press.

Mohler, A. 1991. *Der Nasenring: Die vergangenheitsbewältigung vor und nach dem Full der Mauer*. Munich: Langen Müller.

Noelle-Neumann, E. 1991. *Demoskopische Geschichtsstunde: Vom Wartesaal der Geschichte zun Deutschen Einheit*. Oshabrück: A. Fromm.

Olick, J. K. 1993. "The Sins of the Fathers: The Third Reich and West German Legitimation, 1949–1989." Ph.D. diss., Yale University.

——. 1999. "Genre Memories and Memory Genres: A Dialogical Analysis of May 8th, 1945 Commemorations in the Federal Republic of Germany." *American Sociological Review* 64 (June): 381–402.

Olick, J. K., and D. Levy. 1997. "Collective Memory and Cultural Constraint: Holocaust Myth and Rationality in German Politics." *American Sociological Review* 62: 921–36.

Olick, J. K., and J. Robbins. 1998. "Social Memory Studies: From 'Collective Memory' to the Historical Sociology of Mnemonic Practices." *Annual Review of Sociology* 24: 105–40.

Rabinbach, A. 1988. "The Jewish Question in the German Question." *New German Critique* 4: 159–92.

Schudson, M. 1989. "The Present in the Past and the Past in the Present." *Communication* 11: 105–13.

Schwartz, B. 1991. "Social Change and Collective Memory: The Democratization of George Washington." *American Sociological Review* 56: 221–36.

——. 1996. "Memory as a Cultural System: Abraham Lincoln in World War II." *American Sociological Review* 61: 908–27.

Schwartz, B., Y. Zerubavel, and B. Bartlett. 1986. "The Recovery of Masada: A Study in Collective Memory." *Sociological Quarterly* 27 (2): 147–64.

Scott, J. C. 1990. *Domination and the Arts of Resistance*. New Haven, Conn.: Yale University Press.

Stürmer, M. 1987. "Geschichte im geschichtslosem Land." In *Historikerstreit*. Munich: Piper: 36–8.

Thompson, P. 1988. *The Voice of the Past: Oral History*. Oxford: Oxford University Press.

Wolffsohn, M. 1995. *Die Deutschland Akte: Tatsachen und Legenden*. Munich: Ferenczy bei Bruckmann.

The "End" of the

Postwar: Japan at the

Turn of the Millennium

◄ ◄ ◄ ◄ ◄ ◄ ◄ ◄ ◄ ◄ ◄ ◄ ◄ ◄ ◄   CAROL GLUCK

We seem, in the 1990s, to be obsessed with "ends": the end of the cold war, of the postwar, and of the modern, and the much heralded but phantasmic end of history. Such "end-ology" is perhaps even stronger in Japan. There the confluence of what is ubiquitously called the fin de siècle—by which is meant simply the calendrical end of the century—with the 50th anniversary of the end of the war in 1995 (in Japanese, the 50th anniversary of the "postwar") and the impending end of the millennium have produced a seemingly irresistible eschatological surge in contemporary Japanese comment—though without apparent mention of the Second Coming. Francis Fukuyama's *The End of History and the Last Man*, translated in two extremely thick volumes, was nowhere bought by so many, read by so few, and connected with so much public self-promotion as in Japan in the early 1990s. Each of these end-ish phenomena encircled the pivotal perception that Japan's long postwar period was finally drawing to a close.

Before considering Japanese versions of these putative endings, it makes prefatory sense to situate the current usages of "the postwar" in some of their late-twentieth-century settings.

First, the "end of the postwar," which in Western parlance is so often equated with the "end of the cold war" and the presumptive end of social-

ism, is primarily a European—or Euro-American—concept. Originally derived from European history as it unfolded after the Second World War,
the "postwar-equals-cold-war" formula most aptly applies to Europe, even
today. When German chancellor Helmut Kohl declared—not for the first
time—"the end of the postwar era" in September 1993, he was referring to
the withdrawal of Russian troops from a newly reunified Germany. According to that definition, until United States troops depart from the
Japanese archipelago and other Asian points, the postwar era will not end
in Northeast Asia. This is not to mention a divided Korean peninsula,
which was a direct consequence of American actions in 1945, when the
end of the hot war against fascism fused with the beginning of the cold
war against communism, and the continued existence of two Chinas,
which perpetuates a cold-war bifurcation of no small importance. In
this sense the West-generated, globo-extended cold war, which was fought
by proxy hot wars in Korea and Vietnam, is not over in Asia until it is
over. Postwar Northeast Asia remains, in Bruce Cumings's view, "under-
alphabetized," without a horizontally multilateral NATO or CSCE, and
over-Americanized, still vertically dependent for security on continued
American hegemony (Cumings 1995).

In Europe in 1995 the official 50th-anniversary commemorations of
the end of the war were suffused with the dual sense of a final salute to the
personal memory of one generation's past and an international gesture to
political memory in the direction of a common future. The aura of "Euro-
peanness" that accompanied the always relentlessly national perspective
of public memory was partly a product of a half century of shared geopolitics among (Western) European nations. There could be no such counterpart in commemorations of the war in Japan, the two Chinas, or the two
Koreas. These postwar–cold-war geopolitics had divided, not united, the
region, which was only now beginning to recultivate an aura of "Asian-
ness"—and in a context still partly governed by structures of the cold-war
framework.

Second, the postwar was *not* coterminous with the cold war, even in
Europe, and certainly not in many other places in the world. To utterly
conflate the two is to commit the Congress of Vienna fallacy, by which I
mean the textbook periodization that implies that everything in society
obediently rearranged itself according to the chronology of geopolitics.
Such are the perils of instant periodization that it already seems as if the

year 1989 is graven in textbook granite, where it may well remain until the next millennium. The chapter that ends with 1989 is likely to pound history into a flattened cold-war shape that ignores major developments, such as change in the social construction of gender, in the relation between capitalism and information, in the myriad interactions in the domain of daily life and all the rest of mid- to late-twentieth-century social experience. Such changes, which were under way before the cold war began and did not cease when the cold war ended, require a more capacious framework of analysis than allowed for by the bipolar confrontation between two military and ideological empires. However powerful an effect the cold war had on the postwar, as historical phenomena the two were different and should not be equated.

Third, not only was the postwar not the same as the cold war but there were multiple postwars in different countries and even within a single society. Each national history inscribed its postwar in a distinctive fashion, whether as national liberation, social experiment, economic growth, or the like. And each zealously, maintained the specialness of its recent historical experience as part of its national raison d'être. For those disenfranchised or otherwise set aside by the postwar settlement as it was nationally construed, the meaning of the postwar could be different indeed, as it was for ethnic minorities in many places or for Okinawa, whose "postwar" only began with the "reversion" to Japan by the United States in 1972 and whose post-postwar will not commence until Tokyo and Washington stop treating it as a negotiable piece of military real estate. At the same time that there were particular postwars, however, there were also postwars in common. For the legacy of world war, like that of world capitalism and world depression, was the commonalities that it engendered and demanded in very different contexts.

Here I use the case of Japan—in its post–cold war, post-postwar, and *posuto-modan* moment, when it is allegedly after everything and before nothing—to suggest both the multiplicities and the commonalities as they appear in postwar Japanese history.

JAPAN AND ITS MULTIPLE POSTWARS

The word *postwar* (*sengo*) in Japanese is a noun, which gives it the substance to stand alone, as it does in "fifty years of the postwar" (*sengo*

50nen), the term used to denote the fiftieth anniversary of the end of the war in 1995. As an adjective attached to Japan, it is the most common term for present-day Japan and has been so since 1945. "Postwar Japan" is not therefore the chronological equivalent of the *Nachkriegszeit* in German, but rather of "contemporary Germany" taken as a whole. The extension of the "postwar" over five decades of Japanese history derives not from some peculiarity of language but from the particularity of historical consciousness in the period since the war. And because the term is so common, it is overdetermined, inhabited by many meanings. Here, schematically, are five "postwars" in their original form, as they appeared in the first few years after the defeat in 1945 (the truly "postwar" period in the chronological sense), followed by the form they took in the mid-1990s, when the question of "the end of the postwar" was again the issue of the day, fifty years on (Gluck 1993; 1992).

First, there was the *mythistoric postwar*, or the postwar as a new beginning. In this conceit history began anew, quite precisely at noon on 15 August 1945, with the emperor's radio broadcast announcing the surrender. The Japanese version of the German "zero hour," this absolute discontinuity between the wartime past and the postwar present was profoundly felt, even by those who did not know the reason for the abrupt uncoupling of history. Middle school boys were instantaneously transformed from patriotic "military youth" to enthusiastic "democratic youth," a genuine and seemingly effortless metamorphosis often recalled with wonder by members of the wartime generation (Yoshio 1995). For older Japanese it was more a matter of willed discontinuity, an individual and collective urge to be released from the past and start over again. In the face of considerable institutional continuity—the same jobs, the same teachers, the same bureaucrats—Japanese subscribed to the belief in utter rupture. The new beginning became the founding myth of "Japan reborn," as it was often called. The notion of "remaking" Japan in pursuit of the twin goals of peace and democracy was shared across the political spectrum. No matter how different their definitions of what peace and democracy ought to be, large numbers of Japanese agreed with their American occupiers that the task at hand was to fashion a "new Japan" (e.g., Cohen 1987). Thus Japan's mythistoric postwar began as if severed from the past. It was also of course connected to it, not only because of lived continuities, however repressed, but also because the mythic insistence on disconnection kept bringing the past relentlessly to mind.

Japan's second postwar emerged from this imaginary of connection/disconnection. The postwar as the *inversion of the prewar* (*senzen*, also a noun) signified that the postwar present would be made as an anti-past. All that was fascist, imperialist, militarist, oligopolist, landlord-exploitative—the entire "emperor system" (*tennōsei*)—in short, all that had brought Japan to war was declared the negative model for the postwar reforms. This conception of an anti-past constituted the original moment of memory, the first postwar redaction of the history of imperialism and war. It produced what I call the "heroic narrative," with villains and victims clearly defined and a plotline so simple and strong that it was almost cinematic.[1] Such narratives typically arise in the immediate aftermath of radical change, as indeed they did in reunified Germany and Eastern Europe after the fall of the Wall in 1989 (Judt 1992). Precisely because political and moral issues are at their murkiest when history suddenly switches sides, people reach for a clarity that makes both the past and the future seem straightforward, uncomplicated, and unequivocally resolved in matters of good and evil.

In 1945 the immediate resolution of villainy to the militarist leadership and victimhood to the Japanese people was also orchestrated to serve the needs of the Allied occupation. The Allies tried the villains as war criminals in the Tokyo War Crimes Tribunal, purposely excluding the emperor at the behest of the United States, which based its case for postwar reform on the fable that the Japanese people (and their emporor) had been victims of the militarists and could now, with guidance, be turned to the true path of democracy. Japan's social and political system was "feudalistic" (the term the occupation preferred to "fascist") and would be dismantled, sector by sector, to be rearranged into democratic shape. General Douglas MacArthur also altered the wartime past by changing the name of the conflict from the Greater East Asia War to the Pacific War, thereby eliminating the war in China, which had been the reason for Pearl Harbor in the first place. Japanese aggression in China and colonialism in Korea were replaced by a neat moral calculus where the attack on Pearl Harbor was balanced by the atomic bombings of Hiroshima and Nagasaki—of which the Japanese people were again the victims. A remarkable amnesia of empire occurred immediately. If, as one scholar has written, the Germans remembered the Holocaust to forget the Third Reich, it may be said that the Japanese remembered the Bomb to forget Manchuria (Domansky 1992: 63). Japan's displacement not only forged a forgetting of the historical complicities of the 1930s, it also turned victimizers into victims and atomic memory into imperial denial.

The heroic narrative generated by the inversion of the prewar past became the template of postwar reform. The narrative told the war almost entirely as a domestic story, a homologue for the occupation's programmatic ambitions for internal structural change. From land reform to freedom of religion, every measure was taken in the name of undoing the institutions of imperial Japan. And because sufficient numbers of Japanese shared the impulse to put the past behind them, the rapid succession of reforms between 1945 and 1947 suggested to many that they had effectively managed to do so. The apparent emergence of a "new Japan" seemed to validate the heroic narrative, with the result that the chronology of public memory of the war reached unusually early closure. Villains were dealt with, victims redeemed, so that the very existence of the postwar was taken as evidence for the utter disappearance of the prewar. And the war itself remained suspended in frozen memory, its evils early met and early mastered, or so it seemed.

The sense of early mastery was deepened by Japan's third postwar, which was the *cold war postwar*, or Japan in the American imperium. Although the Japanese shared this experience with many nations, the U.S. presence was arguably more profound and more direct in Japan than in many cold-war-affected societies. The postwar reforms were, in effect, occupation reforms. Although many of them had been preconceived before the war by Japanese critics and were supported and implemented after the war by Japanese officials, the fact was that under the occupation the Japanese had little choice in the matter. American influence lay heavy in everything from the heroic narrative of the war to the restructuring of the criminal code and the redirection of postwar foreign policy. The occupiers had as much, or sometimes more, power in the so-called indirect occupation of Japan, which implemented its reforms through the Japanese bureaucracy left in place, than in countries where the military government ruled directly. From 1945 to 1947 the rawness of U.S. power was somewhat obscured by the seeming convergence of the postwar determination to begin again, which was shared by occupiers and occupied alike. But when the cold war came to Japan in 1947, both the apparent convergence and the veiled power were unmasked with a force so strong that the ensuing period came to be known as the "reverse course."

Beginning with MacArthur's ban of the General Strike in February 1947 and the announcement of the Truman Doctrine in March, the occupation undertook what the Japanese Left regarded as a complete rollback of the earlier occupation reforms, from de-democratization to de-purging, all in the name of the economic reconstruction of Japan into a "bulwark against communism in East Asia." The transformation of the reformist postwar into the cold-war postwar culminated in 1952, when the peace treaty that granted Japan independence was conjoined with the Japan-U.S. Security Treaty, which bound Japan to American cold-war military geopolitics. Whether the subsequent rhetoric evoked Japan as Pacific ally, Pacific partner, Pacific rival, or Pacific pal, Japan remained a Pacific client of the United States throughout the cold war years. Sometimes willing, sometimes eager, sometimes resentful, sometimes hostile, for decades Japan remained in the geopolitical relationship that Japanese critics of the peace settlement in 1952 had called "subordinate independence."

The widely ramified consequences of the American imperium included U.S. command over Japan's foreign policy, from euphemistic but steady rearmament during the 1950s to sudden but late recognition of the People's Republic of China in 1972. The so-called separation of politics and economics in international relations enshrined Japan's concentration on economic growth at the center of national policy. This left cold-war politics to the United States at the same time that Japan profited mightily from what Prime Minister Yoshida called the "heaven-sent" gift of the Korean War and, later, from the windfall of the war in Vietnam. But the United States was no less influential in domestic politics, supporting the conservative Liberal Democratic Party (LDP). Indeed, in 1994 documents revealed that the CIA had financed the party for years. Considering that the LDP came to power in 1955—ushering in the "55 system" of conservative dominance that lasted until 1993 and beyond—America's cold war reach into domestic issues proved not only deep but enduring.

In foreign affairs, the long orientation toward the United States, in which Japan functioned as an unofficial Pacific outpost of NATO, meant that Japan spent its postwar with its back turned toward Asia. Thus, cold war geopolitics reinforced the amnesia of empire and postponed the confrontation with Japan's Asian past. Not only was the nation aligned with the West in cold war terms, but also in a regional and cultural sense Japan fashioned its postwar national identity largely without an Asian referent. At the same time, however, Japanese allegiance to the cold war itself remained less fervently ideological than geopolitically practical, so that Japan was both in America's cold war but not of it, at least in the way the United States imagined. Or perhaps it would be better to say that in Japan the emphasis lay more on *America* than on the *cold war*. Any consideration of the world's multiple postwars, and indeed of its multiple "cold war postwars," must take such distinctions seriously.

Fourth was Japan's *progressive postwar*, the postwar conceived, criticized, and tirelessly advocated by the Japanese Left, loosely and broadly defined. The resurgent Left reappeared in the fall of 1945, feeling, in Japan as in many other countries (except for the perennial exception, the United States), that its historical moment had finally arrived. From communists to left-liberals, the progressives epitomized the ideals of Japan's original postwar: a new beginning and radical remaking in the name of democratic revolution. In sync with the times, their powerful vision lent to groups as diverse as the Communist Party, the Socialist Party, labor unions, rural land reformers, and the peace movement an optimistic energy and a determined praxis that characterized the reforms of 1945 to 1947. Even after the occupation reversed course, shattering the appearance of convergence between MacArthur and the progressives, theirs remained the quintessential vision—and conscience—of the "postwar." Progressives dominated intellectual life, including the academy, where scholars combined rich and dynamic Marxist scholarship with political and social activism on behalf of "a better postwar." The long dominance of the progressive intellectuals in a society that gradually became the epitome of status quo conservatism is itself one of the distinctive aspects of Japan's postwar.

With the present (and, I think, unseemly) rush from socialism and the Left in the wake of the end of Soviet-style communism, it seems especially important to stress the role of the progressives in postwar Japanese history and, for that matter, elsewhere as well. The potency of the Japanese progressives, after their initial crest in the 1940s and early 1950s, reached another peak in the anti–security-treaty protests of 1960, which was the

Japanese counterpart of 1968 in France and Germany, later to dwindle in influence over the course of the 1970s until the tides of economic power and nationalism effectively ended their three decades of dominance by the mid-1980s. Eric Hobsbawm once mused about how much more badly twentieth-century capitalism might have behaved if it had not had to confront the specter of communism and had instead been left to its own devices (Hobsbawm 1991: 122). For four decades of conservative one-party rule, Japanese progressives acted as a steadfast surrogate opposition, and it is sobering to imagine what postwar history might have been like without the challenge of their alternative vision.

The fifth postwar experience was the *middle-class postwar*, or the postwar of private life. This encompassed the social enunciation of sameness, middleness, homogeneity that lay at the core of postwar Japanese democracy—a democracy that was construed in the first instance in social, rather than in electoral, parliamentary, or constitutional terms. In brief, it was the idea of democracy as "coequality" in access to material and social goods. And part of its persuasive power derived from the immediate postwar disjunction articulated between what was called public sacrifice and private life. In September of 1945, the Japanese were liberated from the imperial state to *seikatsu* (daily life, livelihood) at the same time that the advent of democracy was announced. Once conjoined, the new two centralities, democracy and private life, were not easily put asunder, especially as prosperity overtook society in the period of high growth during the 1960s.

Of course, the declaration that all Japanese had instantly been middle-class-ified was both ideology and illusion. It was a new postwar way to efface difference, whether of class, region, or ethnicity, which before the war had been effaced by the ideology of all Japanese as imperial subjects who lived and died for the state. Now it was all Japanese as "salarymen" (and their wives as "education mamas"), who lived and worked for their private livelihood, which just happened to add up to the burgeoning gross national product. The middle-class myth reaffirmed and regendered the family, remarginalized minorities, and reestablished a monolithic, homogeneous society of 100 million Japanese as one putative middle class. The old "gourd society," with its small neck and its bulging bottom, was said to have been replaced by a (Japanese) "lantern society," which was all one big bulging middle. The suddenly expanded middle class would coequally bear the burdens and coequally reap the benefits of late capitalism in the context of peace and democracy. In this way the social myths of postwar Japan were early established, under the occupation, and later undergirded by the unprecedented prosperity and change in both economic livelihood and social lifestyle.

These five "postwars," though interrelated and nowhere as distinct in social fact as I have made them seem in interpretive depiction, would nonetheless be immediately recognizable in postwar (read: contemporary) Japan as characteristic of Japan's "postwar" (that is, the period immediately after the end of the war). Less ritually apparent, perhaps, is the point that each of these visceral experiences of the originary postwar moment was reconceived after 1945 in the language and idiom not only of postwar reconstruction but of late modernity as a whole.

MULTIPLE POSTWARS AND LATE MODERNITY

Having a postwar in common characterized the mid-twentieth-century phase of a longer modernity, also held in common. And Japan was not alone in linking its postwar vision to the course of its modern history and to modernity writ large. The early years after the war were widely hailed as a new phase in *Les temps modernes*, as Merleau-Ponty and Sartre named their journal in 1945. Modernity, not itself new, required renewal. Scorched by the flames of totalitarianism and war, the idea of modernity might conceivably have been abandoned in favor of a form of civilization less compromised by history. But instead most of the world reupped in service of a more perfect modern, what I think of as "late modernity" because it revamped but did not reject the outlines of the classical modern as it had evolved since the eighteenth century. In Japan, as in Germany, "thinking" the postwar thus meant "rethinking" the modern. The impulse to get beyond a bad modern past to a better modern future ran very deep.

But the discursive solidity of modernity, of course, was a material mirage. It was material because people knew it when they saw, or said, it, as if it stood before them in the road. To take the Japanese word *taiken* literally, the "bodily experience" of the multiple postwars each manifested its own kinesic inflection of modernity. As often as not left undefined, its definition was nonetheless seldom in doubt. Neither defined nor doubted, the modern shimmered like a mirage, never singular, never stable, always ahead just out of reach on the horizon. People did not have to agree on what it was, only that it was not here, not yet, and that they should move toward it with all deliberate (modern) speed. While modernity everywhere remained "incomplete," in postwar Japan and Germany, the charge of the unfinished, or malformed, modern took on concrete impelling force. Though the conceptual spectra of midcentury modernity looked much the same there as in other places, the need to "become" modern often outweighed the sense of "being" modern that saturated societies less beset by their recent past. Here is a brief sketch of the ways in which Japan's multiple postwars intersected with the fractals of modernity reconceived.

First, the mythistoric new beginning rested on the premise that Japan had fought a wrong and catastrophic war, which resulted not only in military defeat but in a rout by history. The war was taken as a judgment on Japan's entire modern past, and its failure meant—metonymically— that modernity had failed as well, betrayed by fascism and war. Much as in Germany, modern history was subjected to a pathological examination to understand "what went wrong." The early diagnoses were stark and essentialist, half *Chrysanthemum and the Sword* and half Marxist-Leninist, with progressive Japanese accounts no less critical than those of the American occupiers, as the two joined forces in pursuit of "feudalism" and flaws in national and social character. Ōtsuka Hisao declared that since there was nothing in Japan's past to generate a "modern democratic ethos," it was necessary to "create a new human type" for the new Japan (Hisao 1946: 1–19). Incomplete in a Habermasian sense, the project of this modernity, whether limned in Enlightenment or Marxist strokes, was not in doubt; it was the execution that had failed. In the light of reason, everything from village social structure to the Meiji Restoration and the emperor system was faulted for inherent unmodernity. Hence the mythistoric need to break with the past and rectify the distortions in Japan's *Sonderweg* in order, finally, to "get modernity right."

The postwar as inverted prewar followed from the same line of reasoning, in that the postwar reforms were regarded as remedial modernizing. But in contrast to the idea of an utterly new beginning, remediation required some historical basis. There could *not* be *nothing* in Japan's past on which to build, or the task would not be remedial but a start-up effort of daunting magnitude. The corrected postwar modernity had to be connected to earlier development—only not to the immediate prewar past, which had become the negative model by inversion. So it was perhaps not surprising that the late moderns salvaged the Meiji period as Japan's first modernizing moment. The government cited the Charter Oath of 1868 as evidence that the Meiji Emperor had begun the work of modernity, his efforts betrayed by unworthy officials in the prewar period. The early Meiji reforms had been antifeudal in intent, it was said, just like the postwar reforms, which would now complete the modernity that militarism had derailed. Progressives argued that the postwar era was the second era of "opening the country," ending Japan's isolation from Western modernity as the first opening had done in the decades preceding the Meiji Restoration.

At the same time that they were dismantling "feudal" tradition, the occupation and Japanese social commentators wanted to locate a tradition for modernity, especially for democracy. Some found it in political developments like the Freedom and Popular Rights movement of the 1870s and 1880s, others in the currents of Taishō democracy in the 1910s and 1920s. Still others found modern signs in the private lives and livelihood of the people, who had long pursued their social and economic interests apart from the shogunal or imperial state. In this regard conservatives claimed that the emperor stood for the people, not the state, and together with them would bring cultural energy and continuity to the new democratic Japan. In other words, the modernity to be completed in the postwar was equipped with historical precedents that necessarily omitted the inverted prewar (and usually most of imperial Japan) and took refuge in earlier periods, either immediately, or long, before the distorted modern had taken its full shape. The kinesic of this modernity gestured less to the philosophical premises of the classical modern than to structural development in service of the nation-state, "modernization" in its familiarly vulgar form.

The postwar of the American imperium contributed to the conception of modernity in two different ways. The first produced a framing effect, not by virtue of a cold-war animus but because of the haven the United States offered Japan in the postwar world order. A century earlier modernization had been the means by which Japan sought to gain acceptance in the Euro-dominated world order. In the language of the day, the acquisition of "civilization" was to enable Meiji Japan to revise the unequal treaties and "enter the ranks of the powers." Domestic reform, in good part, was impelled by the concern for international stature. The defeat in 1945 aroused a similar response. Domestic reform in pursuit of peace and democracy would enable Japan "to regain the trust of the world." In the embrace of the victor, Japan could both complete its modernity and gain the imprimatur of the supreme democratic power at one and the same time. It later became clear that U.S. dominance over Japanese foreign relations had conferred an additional advantage on postwar Japan by enabling it to avoid the arena of international geopolitics, where it had so recently and so badly failed, and concentrate instead on internal economic development with undeniably conspicuous results.

The internal definition of modernity, too, took a decidedly American turn in the postwar years. As in Europe, only more so, the 1940s and 1950s saw a second period of intensive social and cultural "Americanization." In Japan, where the *Amerikanizumu* of the late 1920s had been closely linked to *modanizumu*, the term *modernism* evoked less the vanguard in art than urban mass consumer culture. As in Europe, the Americanizing phenomenon included Fordism in the factories as well as flappers in the dance halls, although the flappers often received greater social attention. The wartime years interrupted the streams of influence from across the Pacific, but they resumed in a tidal wave when the Americans arrived to occupy Japan. Jeeps, movies, English, and democracy all came together, with the result that the definition of the modern swerved in a material and populist direction simultaneously. With as much stake as the occupation put in electoral politics, American-style pursuit of the good life through consumption overwhelmed town-meeting democracy in the evolving definition of the lifestyle modern. To say that a nation under foreign occupation had little choice about the source of such influence does not belie the evident Japanese enthusiasm for American versions of material modernity in the postwar years.

The progressive postwar despaired of such bourgeois symptomology and trod instead the high road toward the social and political modern. In their dedication to eradicate every vestige of the prewar emperor system, the progressives, too, partook of the mythistoric potion that promised a new postwar beginning. But for them the emperor system represented the deviation from the true course of modernity, which they saw as universal: Western in origin but not in essence. "From premodern to modern," ran their postwar battle cry (Rokurō 1984: 68). Like the guardian gods at a temple, the progressives faced the resurgent evil of the state with fierce visage and vigilant energy. Most wanted a social revolution, some a liberal democracy, but all sought a new (modern) subjectivity that could become the agent of its own political fate (Koschmann 1996). In this, they shared the concerns of postwar intellectuals in Britain or France, but after a brief spring of potency after the war, Japanese progressives had to soldier on without corresponding political power in the parties of the Left, labor, or anywhere in the institutional landscape of establishment politics. Conservative politicians and bureaucrats ran the government, while society forsook the political charge of freedom for the material pursuits of private life. Over time, the progressive inflection of postwar modernity came to be defined again by its absence; the mirage grew more distant as the years of high growth padded the precincts of the middle class with consumer comforts.

American-style material populism found its most comfortable home in this middle-class postwar, with which it was often equated. The democratic-equals-modern family of the sort portrayed in the popular comic strip *Sazae-san*; the democratic-equals-modern woman, newly equipped with voting and civil rights; and the democratic-equals-modern styles of consumption, which measured the middle class by its possession of refrigerators and vacuum cleaners—all constituted postwar modernity collectively defined in terms of society rather than the state, livelihood rather than the nation. Later retrospectives of the postwar period celebrated the march of consumer products, from primitive hand-crank washing machines to self-programming electronic home laundries. In the popular view, postwar history was seen from the kitchen table—everyone's kitchen table. Occupation posters had promised that unlike "feudal" Japan, with its vertical hierarchy of authority—represented by a big stick-figure at the top for the emperor, middle-size figures in the center for the bureaucracy, and little figures at the bottom for the people—in the new democratic Japan everyone would be equal—all the stick-figures all the same size all on one level. This schematic iconography became emblematic of Japanese democracy, socially defined, missing only a color television next to each figure to make the representation complete.

There was nothing particularly postwar or particularly Japanese about the triumph of consumer capitalism. Indeed, the commonalities with other late modern societies overwhelm most of the distinctiveness in which Japanese national identity drapes and swathes itself. But the postwar incarnation of late modernity in Japan cut its own figure in the extreme transposition from public to private. It seemed, on the face of it at least, that modernity, which since the nineteenth century had been so singlemindedly conceived to serve the needs of the nation, now held its promise for the "private lives" of the people. As a reaction to the overwhelming public demands of the wartime state, both democracy and modernity were "privatized" at one and the same time. Livelihood swallowed politics in a single drawn-out postwar gulp, with the consequence—intended on the part of the governing conservative party, which was heir to the state, unintended on the part of the progressive opposition, which set itself against the state—that politics were ideologically removed from the popular realm and left to the politicians, who, as long as the washing machines continued to evolve, could expect to remain in power undisturbed.

In these and other ways the experiences of Japan's multiple postwars rendered different fractal patterns of its late modernity, itself understood as a belated opportunity to remedy the defects of the earlier phases of the process of becoming modern. It was this doubling-up of history, this overlay of the sharply delineated postwar and the solid, shimmering modern, that gave so much power to the concept of the "postwar" in Japan. So when it appeared in the early 1990s that both the postwar and the modern might be reaching their "end" at the same time, the doubled historical voltage generated a powerful sort of "history shock."

THE "END" OF THE POSTWARS

How much of this shock was historically warranted? Are the postwars over? Have they reached their end? A résumé of the state of things in the mid-1990s, 50 years after the end of the war, suggests some provisional answers.

Once again, in order: first, the mythistoric postwar of born-again Japan. Despite the fact that the "end of the postwar" had been announced on numerous occasions since the government's 1956 pronouncement referring to economic recovery, Japanese continued to remain nomenclaturally "postwar." The term, that is, continued to characterize contemporary Japan. What I have called "the long postwar" (or even "the too long postwar") owed its longevity to the reaffirmation of the immediate postwar goals of "peace and democracy," which had morphed by the 1970s into "peace and prosperity," as democracy came to be defined in ever more material terms. This "lifestyle revolution" [*seikatsu kakumei*], as Irokawa Daikichi called it, brought with it a socioeconomic existentialism that confirmed the differentness of the present and with it the assertion of a new beginning in 1945 (Daikichi 1991: 82–136).

Nonetheless, in the course of the 1980s certain adjustments occurred in the mythistory. Continuities with the prewar period, for example, gained increasing acknowledgment. Commentators argued the importance of the wartime period (1931 to 1945) for postwar developments, recognizing the effects of what John Dower once termed "the useful war" (Dower 1994: 9–32).[2] This transwar heresy, which not only bridged the chasm of 1945 but suggested positive legacies from the imperial past, emerged in the context of the feel-good conservatism of national economic power. But it did not quite dislodge the hallowed postwar new beginning. Instead the attention shifted again to the question of its ending. In 1989 the death of the wartime emperor, Hirohito, and the end of the Shōwa era coincided, by sheer chance, with the end of the cold war, suggesting to many that the postwar period had met its end as well. Others demurred until the economic "bubble burst" in the early 1990s, signaling, they said, the end of "the Japanese employment system" and of the long postwar prosperity as well. Still others responded instead to the fall of the LDP in 1993, declaring that the collapse of the "55 system" meant the end of the politics that had supported the postwar socioeconomic status quo.

And yet on New Year's Day 1995, a poll published in the *Asahi* newspaper carried the headline, "Postwar Japan, 84% Affirm" [*Sengo Nihon, kōteiha 84%*]. Fifty years after it began, the "postwar" received a higher "approval rating" than any elected politician dared to hope for. Even to pose the question in this way suggested the curious staying power of the postwar. With a straight face the pollsters queried, "As a whole do you think the course of Japan's postwar was good, rather good, not good, or rather not good?" How about "awful"? Not an option, but more important, asking for a blanket response to the postwar "as a whole" seemed a perfectly reasonable question even in 1995. The poll also revealed that half the respondents credited the "peace constitution" and "war experience" as the reasons for Japan's half century of peace. More than half believed that democracy had established itself in postwar Japan. In short, when it came to the idea of a new beginning of a successfully sustained postwar experience, it seemed that mythistorically at least, the postwar was not over even now. All historical indications to the contrary—for these surely suggested that a new name was required to describe present-day Japan—the status quo was ideologically reaffirmed. Hence the rhetorical device that had Japan commemorating "50 years of the *postwar*" in 1995 rather than the anniversary of the end of World War II.

In this sense, too, the postwar as an inversion of the prewar remained largely undisturbed, since the new Japan was judged to have thoroughly replaced the old. When it came to the heroic narrative of the war in public memory, the situation was somewhat different. After its early closure in the early postwar years, the villains-and-victims story remained frozen memory for decades. In a chronology parallel to similar phenomena in West Germany, incidents of neonationalist revisionism occurred with increasing frequency during the 1980s, but they did not change the received story. Only after the Shōwa era and the cold war ended together in 1989 did the issues of memory begin to surface in a new way. This surprised many observers, myself included, since it had come to seem as if Japan's official refusal to confront its aggression in Asia had been steadfast for so long—fifty years—that the time for any meaningful cracks in the frozen memory of the war had long since passed. Instead, a series of conjunctural reasons, including changes in international geopolitics and particularly in the relationship between Japan and Asia, combined to bring issues like the "comfort women" and biological experimentation by the military into public discussion. The use of another name, the Asia-Pacific War, at last recognized the place and the nature of the conflict, and the first two post-LDP prime ministers embarked on "apology tours" to the capitals of Asia.

Open discussion did not mean open acknowledgment of responsibility for the aggression and atrocities committed during the Asian parts of the wartime past. In the fiftieth-anniversary year elements of the LDP continued to hold memory hostage to domestic politics, blocking an outright apology in the antiwar resolution in the Diet and preventing the planned special commemoration on 15 August from taking place at all—although the socialist prime minister did manage to offer his own personal apology on that date. In December 1994 a poll of college and secondary students showed that while 60 percent knew that the defeat had occurred on 15 August, only 10 percent could date Pearl Harbor, and the majority still listed the government and the military as having caused the war. These data combined with the new signs of reflection led one national newspaper to editorialize on the anniversary of Pearl Harbor that "the postwar period has finally begun."[3] And it was true that public opinion in 1995 strongly favored the antiwar resolution, and polls showed that more than 60 percent of the people (70 percent of those in their twenties) thought that Japan had not done enough in the way of "war compensation."[4]

In a chronological irony, it appeared that at about the same time that a newly unified Germany was suspending controversy in the early 1990s for the sake of reconciling two irreconcilable narratives of the war (one on either side of the Berlin Wall), the glaciated memory of Japan's heroic narrative was finally beginning to break up. In this regard it might indeed be true that in the case of Japanese memory, the postwar period, rather than being over, had only recently begun.

The cold-war postwar gave many signs that it was over, some of them misleading. The blend of "Japamerika," or "Amerinippon," had five decades of history behind it, making the two difficult to disentangle even after the American imperium had radically altered. Early in 1995 one progressive critic made the sarcastic suggestion of a merger between the two countries, which would at least remove trade frictions and give Japanese the chance to vote in U.S. presidential elections.[5] But general sentiment ran mostly in the other direction, in favor of a turn away from America, perceived not only as longtime hegemon but also as a power in decline. (Indeed, Paul Kennedy's *Rise and Fall of the Great Powers*, also in two thick volumes of translation, preceded Fukuyama's book on Japanese bestseller lists.) This turn was soon embodied in the rhetoric of "Asianization," which reversed the old Meiji slogan and called instead for Japan to "escape from the West and enter Asia" [*datsuō nyūa*]. The new Asian regionalism, like that of the EU and NAFTA, owed its origins to economics, but in Japan's case it was both something more and something less. Asia was seen as offering an *alternative* to the United States, as if the geopolitical choice were neatly divisible into "either/or." In fact, of course, it was not. But Japan's rhetorical Asianization derived as much, or perhaps more, from Japan's reaction against America as from its pull toward Asia.

And Asia itself was both desirous of and ambivalent toward Japan's leadership in the region. War memories still ran strong, or, as Lee Kwan Yew of Singapore bluntly put it, "Japan is not a normal normal country."

Japan, too, had not lost its ambivalence toward the United States, wanting it gone and wanting it there at the same time. "The idea of reluctantly putting up with what one dislikes is what the Japan-U.S. relationship is all about," commented one conservative historian (Shin'ichi 1992: 104–19). And it was not only a matter of U.S. military bases or security agreements, which most Japanese did not wish to see entirely removed. The deep embeddedness of the United States in Japan's postwar went beyond the cold-war hardware that had made Japanese pacifism possible. It included the "Peace Constitution," which the Americans had written in 1946, its renunciation of war in Article 9 now judged by many Japanese to have been responsible for decades of peace. Even as conservatives published a draft of a revised constitution in 1994, polls showed that only a small minority of the population favored wholesale revision and that support for Article 9 had reached a high of 79 percent.[6] This ambivalence toward the presence of the United States, in both real and symbolic terms, related to the larger problem of Japan and the world, which the postwar American alliance had effectively removed from the screen for so long. Not only had the cold war relationship with the United States practically suspended Japan's relations with Asia, but it had enabled Japan to avoid the thick of the international military and political arena, which had caused such difficulty before in modern Japanese history. With the end of the cold war and the rise in economic power, the time had come, it was said, for Japan to make an "international contribution." But the first test proved a trauma, when the 1991 Gulf War made an issue of Japanese participation in peacekeeping operations (PKO, as it is called in Japan), followed by Cambodia and then the former Yugoslavia. At that point popular support for a Japanese seat on the Security Council pivoted on whether Japan would be required to send uniformed troops abroad. If for Japan the end of the cold war did not bring the end of the cold-war postwar, it was not only because of the continued American military presence but also, and perhaps even more important, because the habits of peace and prosperity formed during the long period of "subordinate independence" had become so comfortably entrenched.

The progressive postwar, however, *was* over. Its potency had begun to

wane long before 1989, most notably during Japan's version of the contemporaneous German "turn" toward conservatism of the 1970s. As
Japan established itself among the advanced capitalist countries in the
mid-1970s, became the world's creditor in the mid-1980s, and paraded in
the neonationalist ranks of the Nakasone-Reagan-Thatcher-Kohl years,
the progressives saw their own hopes for peace and democracy betrayed
by big-power posturing and self-absorbed economism. The lifestyle democracy that the polls reported to have taken root was not the authentic
democracy envisioned by the progressives. Like the writer Ōe Kenzaburō,
who represented the very epitome of the "postwar" progressive vision,
most progressives had come to think that genuine democracy did not exist
in Japan and that the promise of the original postwar had been betrayed by
economic affluence and political venality. As for the parties of the Left, in
1994 the first socialist prime minister since 1947 took office. No sooner
had he donned the obligatory frockcoat and been sworn in than he re-
nounced nearly every hallowed socialist position, most of them held for
decades against the conservative tide. Quite like Europe, Japanese party
politics of the early 1990s had no place for socialism as it was once
understood.

After the collapse of the "55 system" in 1993, the political scene was
repeatedly judged to have fallen into chaos. "Once we had a government
so stable that the rest of Asia admired us," bemoaned a senior bureaucrat
in early 1994. "Now we look like a banana republic."[7] His hyperbole
notwithstanding, the current political scene seemed to resemble what one
observer called "*karaoke* democracy": the melody was played, the words
ran along at the bottom, and anyone could sing along. But not the progressives, whose politics seemed finally to have been eliminated from contention altogether.[8] One conservative critic likened their eclipse to the fall of
Japan's Berlin Wall: now that the Left-Right conflict had collapsed, he said,
Japan was no longer a divided country (Masakazu 1994). Progressive
intellectuals found themselves in a quandary, their postwar paradigms
lost with little hope of politics regained.

In a sense the progressive postwar had constituted the "real" postwar,
meaning the years from 1945 to 1947 and the spirit of political reform that
electrified them. When the progressives became ghosts, their postwar
turned spectral as well. And because of that once apparent convergence
between their vision and the occupation's policies of political democrati-

zation, the demise of the progressives could also be said to signal the final disappearance of democracy in its early, often radical occupation form. Of course, in the longer, five-decade run of the postwar, the progressive fade-out did not take place in the political confusion of the 1990s. The Japanese version of "the end of socialism" had in fact already occurred in the 1970s, a casualty less of politics than of prosperity.

Prosperity carried the middle-class postwar from the peak of high growth in the 1960s through the oil shocks of the 1970s to the Gucci capitalism of the 1980s. By that time, in a reckoning that defied both mathematics and reality, 98 percent of the population perceived themselves as middle class. The post-bubble recession of the early 1990s threatened that perception, bringing record unemployment and the dawning sense that the earlier growth rates were never to resume. Official rhetoric responded, over the tenures of four different prime ministers, with a reassertion of the postwar celebration of private life. Japan henceforth would dedicate itself to being a "lifestyle nation" [*seikatsu kokka*], a "gentle nation," a "lifestyle great power." This softened GNP-ism did not affect the material fact of the downsizing of the middle class, the increase in social stratification, or the sense of "rich Japan, poor Japanese" felt by so many. A special issue of a conservative magazine in January 1995 entitled "Have fifty years of the postwar made Japan happy?" posed a new question, as if to suggest the glimmerings of a post-postwar sensibility in search of happiness as a substitute for the criterion of livelihood.[9]

Shifts in the material basis of the middle class were accompanied by social changes in the family, such as the perceived increase in the reluctance of young women to marry, bear children, and spend the rest of their lives educating them. In these issues it was less a matter of how many women felt this way than the threat that even a small number seemed to pose to the ideology of the middle-class family. The new presence of foreign workers and the strengthened assertiveness of long-standing minorities like the Koreans posed a similar challenge to the postwar myth of social homogeneity. The middle-class postwar had been based on the denial of difference, so that it had coped with "the Other within" not by recognizing but by colonizing it. This middle-class postwar was by no means over, although it was changing. But since social change comes slower in Japan than economic or even political change, and since the middle class constitutes the ideological core of the status quo, its postwar—barring some economic cataclysm—was not likely to end suddenly in any case.

If by the mid-1990s, despite their apparent rhetorical, ideological, and psychological tenacity, the various historical "postwars" were slowly "overing" or "ending," what did this mean for the "modern"? The postwar had been cast in the mold of modernity in its different inflections, and now the postwar itself (or part of it) was becoming history. Just as in the time after the Meiji Restoration, when the Edo period had been invented as "tradition" for Meiji's modernity, in the time after the war, prewar Japan had been conceived as modernity betrayed, finally now to be redeemed. Out of this trope of modernity gone awry came "the tale of the postwar."

By the mid-1990s two things had happened to this tale. First, neoconservatives gave it a triumphalist ring, with the postwar judged to have achieved the completion of modernity. No longer deferred to the future, now the mirage was real. In the account of the triumphal modern, the 15-year war, once the end point, became an episode between the Meiji and the postwar reforms, the former having produced the nation-state, the latter peace, democracy, and prosperity. Now there were said to be no more models to emulate: Japan had "caught up with and overtaken" the West and was itself a model for Asia, what with its Confucian capitalism and its capitalist-development state. In some versions this new telling of "the tale of the modern" uncoupled modernity from the West in a de-Europeanizing move that appeared to be post-postwar in that it admitted *no* universals. In other, more nationalistic forms like the new theories of civilization (*bunmeiron*), the distinctive Japanese road to the modern was proposed as a new universal. In this vein it was said, quite seriously, that "the world is Edo-izing," that is, learning to live in peace in a small space as Japanese did during the Tokugawa period (Gluck 1998). Here the postwar was absorbed in the triumphal modern, and this post-postwar variant of "overcoming the (Western) modern" amounted to the revenge of the periphery, the periphery having now become the core.

At the same time, in the face of a future that seemed more and more uncertain, the tale of the postwar completion of the modern increasingly stressed continuity rather than rupture and evolutionary rather than transformative change. Every one of the new political parties that proliferated after 1993 adorned itself in the language of novelty—Renovation,

Reform, Renaissance, New party, Harbinger party, New Frontier party—and yet the real message of the political day was better found in one politician's remark to the effect that the goal was "tearing out the most rotted pillars of one-party government and rebuilding the temple, without disturbing the Buddha inside."[10] The Buddha—and it was a fat one—was the postwar status quo, defined as before in economic and social terms. One reason why the 1995 subway gassing incident in Tokyo so upset the collective mental equilibrium of people all over the country was the menace it seemed to pose to the social order whose stability had been the cornerstone of the middle-class postwar. Again, Japan is not the only place suffering the anxiety of the disappearing modern defined in this particular postwar way: so goes the American dream, the French good life, the German welfare state, and so on, all with nasty political side effects for the Others within.

And the domestic scene seemed stability itself compared with the looming uncertainty on the international stage. Wavering rhetorically between Asia and the West, hovering militarily out of harm's way, attached to its so-called one-country pacifism, Japan could not easily weave international affairs into the tale of the postwar/modern as either triumph or trepidation. With no successful precedent in recent history to refer to, the tale often turned to the more remote past, in particular to the safe haven of *sakoku*, the seclusion of the Edo period, when Japan was "closed off" from the world. The "closed-off country" was one of the favored metaphors of the early 1990s, and it was perhaps no accident that the Edo period was declared to have been "already modern," indeed presciently *posuto-modan* before Western-style modernity had even appeared. Evocations of an "Edo renaissance" and a "happy feudalism" infused the period before the modern with a postmodern aura, making of the past a refuge from an uncertain future. By the mid-1990s, vernacular talk of the postmodern had noticeably receded, perhaps because anxieties were now focused on the possible loss of the postwar and with it the loss of modernity itself.

MILLENNIAL MODERNITIES

The loss, or "end," of the modern was a concern not confined to Japan. Japan's "postwar" had in common with that of other "advanced" countries (a point too often missed) not so much its cold-war aspects as its relation to modernity, or late modernity. A strong nation-state, late capitalist economic development, participation in the West-North international dominance, political atrophy, social change related to the Others within, whether women or minorities—these and other attributes were familiar enough among these countries. But think of the former Third World, or rather the current two-thirds world, and it is immediately apparent why Francis Fukuyama was so inhuman and wrong when he wrote that now that history has ended, "it matters very little what strange thoughts occur to people in Albania or Burkina Faso" (Fukuyama 1989: 9). Clearly it *does* matter, and because it does, there is no end to history—and no end to the modern either. The history of the nineteenth and twentieth century, around the world, is the history of modernity, as it is differently, unevenly, often inhumanly inflected. Although Eric Hobsbawm wrote of "the short twentieth century," from 1914 to 1991, the century may yet turn out instead to be quite long (Hobsbawm 1994). And it remains fractally modern, for at the moment there is nothing else.

As the postwar finally "ends," the task in Japan and elsewhere is therefore to reconceive the modern, which is less an idea than an episteme, less a concept than a condition. In this respect it may be said that an additional attribute held in common is that we all seem to suffer from a kind of conceptual insufficiency, in that we are facing the twenty-first century armed with the notions of the nineteenth. We are still moderns, which explains our obsession with "ends" and the caesura of 1989, but ours is a "nontopia": we are without a vision of the future. The millennial challenge therefore is less a question of ends or of overcoming the modern than to avoid being overcome *by* the modern and drifting visionless into the next millennium.[11] And this problem is not Japan's alone, but all of ours.

NOTES

1. "Heroic narrative" is from Butterfield 1951, 10–17.
2. Also in Gluck and Graubard, 1993: 49–70.
3. " 'Sengo' ga yatto hajimatta," *Asahi shinbun*, 7 December 1994.
4. "Sengo Nihon, koteiha 84%," *Asahi shinbun*, 1 January 1995.

5. K. Shūichi. "50nenme ni tou sengo," dialogue with Ōe Kenzaburō, *Asahi shinbun,* 1 January 1995.

6. *Mainichi shinbun,* 19 August 1994. The *Yomiuri shinbun* draft was released on 3 November 1994.

7. *New York Times,* 26 January 1994.

8. I. Takashi, "Rekishi ninshiki o tou, kokusai seiji no shiten kara," *Asahi shinbun,* 16 November 1994.

9. "Sengo 50nen wa Nihon o shiawase ni shita ka," *Asuteion,* (January 1995).

10. *New York Times,* 18 July 1993.

11. "Overcome by the modern" is Harry Harootunian's felicitous phrase.

REFERENCES

Butterfield, H. 1951. *History and Human Relations.* London: Collins.

Cohen, T. 1987. *Remaking Japan.* New York: Free Press.

Cumings, B. 1995. "Grand Beginnings and Imagined Endings: Northeast Asian Security after the Cold War." Paper presented at the conference "The United States and Japan on the Eve of the 21st Century," Hakone, Japan, August 1.

Daikichi, I. 1991. *Shōwashi to tennō.* Tokyo: Iwanami shoten. Translated as *The Age of Hirohito: In Search of Modern Japan.* 1995. New York: Free Press.

Domansky, Elisabeth, 1992. "'Kristallnacht,' the Holocaust and German Unity: The Meaning of November 9 as an Anniversary in Germany." *History and Memory* 4, no. 1 (spring/summer).

Dower, J. 1994. "The Useful War." In *Japan in War and Peace: Selected Essays.* New York: New Press.

Fukuyama, F. 1989. "The End of History?" *National Interest* (summer).

Gluck, C. 1992. "The Idea of Shōwa." In Carol Gluck and Stephen R. Graubard, eds., *Shōwa: The Japan of Hirohito.* New York: Norton.

——. 1993. "The Past in the Present." In Andrew Gordon, ed., *Postwar Japan as History.* Berkeley: University of California Press.

——. 1998. "The Invention of Edo." In Stephen Vlastos, ed., *Mirror of Modernity: The Invention of Traditions in Modern Japan.* Berkeley: University of California Press.

Hobsbawm, E. 1991. "Goodbye to All That." In Robin Blackburn, ed., *After the Fall: The Failure of Communism and the Future of Socialism.* London: Verso.

——. 1994. *Age of Extremes: The Short Twentieth Century.* London: Michael Joseph.

Hisao, Ō. 1968. "Kindaiteki ningen ruikei no sōshutsu: seijiteki shutai no minshūteki kiban no mondai" (April 1946). In *Kindaika no ningenteki kiso.* Chikuma shobō.

Judt, T. 1992. "The Past Is Another Country: Myth and Memory in Postwar Europe." *Daedalus* 121, no. 4 (fall): 83–118.

Koschmann, J. 1996. *Revolution and Subjectivity in Postwar Japan.* Chicago: University of Chicago Press.

Masukazu, Y. 1994. " 'Bundan kokka' Nihon no gojūnen." *This is Yomiuri* (September): 138–59.

Rokurō, H. 1984. *The Price of Affluence: Dilemmas of Contemporary Japan*. Tokyo: Kōdansha.

Shin'ichi, K. 1992. "Naze Nihon wa 'sengo' o dakkyaku dekinai no ka." *This Is Yomiuri* (September).

Yoshio, Y. 1995. *Sekao*. November, 22.

Calendars and History:

A Comparative Study of the Social

Organization of National Memory

◀ ◀ ◀ ◀ ◀ ◀ ◀ ◀ ◀ ◀ ◀ ◀   E V I A T A R   Z E R U B A V E L

Human memory is inherently selective. Out of the numerous events that occurred throughout history, only a few are actually preserved in our minds. As far as social memories are concerned, certain parts of our collective past are in the spotlight while others remain in the dark. Those are the figures we come to collectively remember against the backdrop of all the rest of history, which basically recedes and is usually forgotten.

As I have shown elsewhere, time often functions as a semiotic system of periodically alternating "marked" and unmarked blocks signifying fundamental cultural contrasts between marked and unmarked chunks of social reality (Zerubavel 1989 [1985]: 113–20).[1] Along somewhat similar lines, the general shape of our collective memory is a product of a mental process of differentiating marked historical periods during which a lot seems to have happened, from essentially unmarked lulls that seem relatively uneventful. Our collective memory, in other words, telescopically amplifies what appears to us historically momentous while compressing or even entirely ignoring what we consider uneventful. The "history" we collectively remember thus typically consists of small pockets of highly eventful periods interspersed among long stretches of seemingly empty ones (Sorokin 1943: 212; Lévi-Strauss 1966 [1962]: 257–59; Glassie 1982:

621–22, 652–54). Indeed, it is the mental act of differentiating eventful (marked) chunks of the past from uneventful (unmarked) ones that allows us to assign them social significance: "In so far as history aspires to meaning, it is doomed to select [certain historical periods] . . . and to make them stand out, as discontinuous figures, against a continuity . . . used as a backdrop" (Levi-Strauss 1966 [1962]: 257).

Since collective memory is more than just an aggregate of individuals' personal memories (Frisch 1989; Zerubavel 1997: 95–96), one cannot study the social marking of the past by looking at how individuals draw their own personal timelines of history (e.g., Herbert 1986). In order to produce a sociology of memory, one needs to examine the unmistakably social timelines constructed by entire mnemonic communities.[2]

One of the distinctive features of human memory is that we usually remember far more than just what we have personally experienced through our own senses (Zerubavel 1997: 89–95). Indeed, being social presupposes the ability to experience things that happened to groups long before we joined them as if they were part of our own past. Such fusion of our own biography with the history of the nation, profession, or religious community to which we belong is an indispensable part of our national, professional, or religious identity.

Given its highly impersonal nature, collective memory is clearly not stored only in individuals' minds but also in history textbooks, television footage, archives, museums, war memorials, and other unmistakably social "sites" of memory (Nora 1989). Furthermore, since the socially marked (or "sacred") is often manifested in ritual displays of collective sentiments (Durkheim 1995 [1912]: 303–417) we also need to look at the way past events are ritually commemorated. By carving socially marked events out of essentially unmarked stretches of history, ritual commemoration helps articulate what groups collectively consider eventful. In other words, it "lifts from an ordinary historical sequence those extraordinary events which embody our deepest and most fundamental values. Commemoration . . . is in this sense a register of sacred history" (Schwartz 1982: 377). Hence the value of studying commemorative rituals as major sites of collective memory (Zerubavel 1995; Connerton 1989).

Perhaps the most spectacular site of collective memory in this regard is the calendar. As a cycle of holidays specifically designed to commemorate socially marked events, the calendar year often encapsulates the conventional master narratives constructed by mnemonic communities from their history. By examining which historical events are commemorated on holidays, we can identify the most sacred periods in a group's collective past.

Although calendars also serve to articulate social commitment to various transhistorical ideas such as nature (Arbor Day), family (Mother's Day), and work (Labor Day), they usually help mnemonic communities (including couples celebrating their wedding anniversary every year) preserve their collective memories. Through the institutionalization of commemorative holidays, they help establish an annual cycle of remembrance designed to ensure that several times every year members will recall certain "sacred" moments from their collective past.[3] Like a perpetual film loop that keeps replaying the group's sacred history for its members, such a cycle can, in theory, run to the end of time. When a new leader designates the day when he seized power as a national holiday, he is essentially making a conscious effort to preserve that memory *forever*.

Commemorative holidays play a critical role in our "mnemonic socialization" (Zerubavel 1997: 87–89, 96). As Yael Zerubavel (1995: 217) has noted, before being introduced to our nation's collective past in history classes we already become acquainted with it by observing national holidays. Long before American children are formally introduced to the English colonization of North America through the social studies curriculum in school, for example, they already learn, through their annual observance of Thanksgiving, about the early-seventeenth-century pilgrims who settled New England.

As institutionalized occasions for remembering, holidays remind us that our social environment affects not only what we remember but also when we remember it. Furthermore, they enhance the social coordination of individuals' memories. After all, recalling the historical events associated with those holidays is an act that is typically performed by group members together. On the very same day, an entire mnemonic community focuses its historical attention on the very same moment in the past. Through such "mnemonic synchronization" (Zerubavel 1997: 97), a remarkable sociocognitive feat that no other species can possibly accomplish, the calendar ensures that the remembering will indeed be done collectively, at the level of the entire community. In other words, it helps make the holiday truly commemorative.

CALENDARS AND NATIONAL MEMORY

Defining any historical moment as memorable, of course, is a matter of memory rather than actual history and thus inevitably retrospective. In fact, events we now consider historic watersheds may not have even attracted a lot of public attention when they actually occurred. When one considers the shoot-out between South African troops and some South West African rebels at Omgulumbashe on 26 August 1966, for example, or the demonstration against the establishment of Urdu as the official language of East Pakistan on 21 February 1952, one realizes that only in retrospect have the events publicly commemorated today on Namibia's Heroes' Day and Bangladesh's National Mourning Day come to be seen as historically significant turning points. By the same token, only with hindsight can one narratologically construct a failed guerrilla attack on 26 July 1953 as the beginning of what would six years later come to be known as the great revolution celebrated today by Cuba on Revolution Day (Bernstein 1994; Zerubavel 1995: 221–28).

In a somewhat similar vein, one can never fully predict how long any such historic landmark will remain memorable. Commemorating a group's sacred history calendrically involves an active decision to introduce particular holidays in the first place, as well as a tacit decision repeatedly made every year to keep observing them. Thus, aside from a mnemonic community's explicit initial decision to commemorate a particular historical event by establishing a new holiday, it also makes every single year an implicit decision to *keep* commemorating it by keeping that holiday on its calendar. It is a tacit decision of which we normally become aware only when such days are explicitly deleted from the group's public memory by being removed from its calendar.

Unlike actual history, memory is essentially fluid. As a group keeps changing, its public memory also keeps changing (e.g., FitzGerald 1980; Schwartz 1990; Zerubavel 1995), and it is not unusual for new events from the past to be added to its calendar and for some others to be removed from it. Soon after President Siyad Barre was overthrown in 1991, for example, Somalia stopped commemorating the coup that had brought him to power in 1969. By the same token, as soon as its Communist regime collapsed, Hungary stopped celebrating its liberation by the Soviet army in 1945. And since Nelson Mandela's 1994 victory, a new South Africa no longer seems to feel any need to keep commemorating its former "founding father," Paul Kruger.

Calendars generally tend to reflect the collective identities of those who use them (e.g., Zerubavel 1985 [1981]: 70–100; 1982a), and by commemorating on holidays certain past events groups implicitly articulate their visions of their present social essence. By examining what they consider memorable, we can thus gain better access to who they believe they are.

The present essay follows some earlier efforts made by David Cressy, Paul Connerton, and Yael Zerubavel to study the commemorative function of the calendar and highlight its critical role in the social organization of memory (Cressy 1989; Connerton 1989: 41–71; Zerubavel 1995: 138–44, 216–21). Focusing on the way in which past events are preserved in our collective memory through traditional association with annually recurring "holy days," it is an attempt to examine the unmistakably social logic underlying the choice of the particular slices of history conventionally commemorated in calendars. Essentially viewing the calendar as a social artifact that reflects as well as shapes our collective visions of the past, it tries to explore what those visions are.

The particular type of social group I examine here is the nation, the specific historic form of which is currently represented by the nation-state. As such, I focus specifically on *national* commemorative holidays, thereby confining my study to calendars of nation-states and ignoring those of cities, regional provinces, or religious communities. Thus, I do not examine, for example, the traditional Parsi celebration of the birth of Zoroaster on Khordad Sal, the annual celebration of the founding of Kyoto on Jidai Matsuri, or the commemoration of the English colonization of Maryland on Founder's Day. Being specifically interested in commemorative holidays that are part of the state ritual, I also confine my analysis to official public holidays and therefore do not examine, for example, Denmark's commemoration of King Valdemar II's victory over the Estonians on Flag Day, South Korea's celebration of the invention of the Korean alphabet on Han'gul Day, or lovers' traditional commemoration of the martyrdom of Saint Valentine on Valentine's Day.

The 191-country national holiday data set on which I draw here is based on information I gathered from *The Europa World Year Book 1997*, *The Traveler's Handbook* (Haines 1997), the *Holidays, Festivals, and Celebrations of the World Dictionary* (Henderson and Thompson 1997), Robert Weaver's *International Holidays* (1995), Ruth Gregory's *Anniversaries and Holidays* (1983), *Chase's 1997 Calendar of Events*, the *World Calendar of Holidays 1981*, and various country-specific travel guides. In order to identify the specific historical moments that these holidays are designed to evoke, I used William Langer's *Encyclopedia of World History* (1968), international news updates such as the weekly *Facts on File* and the monthly *Keesing's Record of World Events*, as well as numerous country-specific history books and historical dictionaries. I also consulted the *Scott 1999 Standard Postage Stamp Catalogue*, since issuing stamps on specific dates is one of the main official commemorative rituals marking anniversaries of major historical events in many countries.

My main goal here is to identify various generic patterns of calendrical commemoration. Through an essentially comparative, cross-national analysis of national calendars, I try to show that even what may at first glance seem nation-specific is usually but an exemplar of some transnational commemorative pattern. Thus, although each of the 191 countries examined here selects the particular slices of history it tries to preserve in its calendar quite independently from other countries, we can nonetheless see certain generic affinities among those hundreds of seemingly unique decisions and thereby identify some truly transnational patterns of calendrical commemoration.

A comparative approach to calendrical commemoration that ignores nation-specific mnemonic idiosyncrasies has two major methodological implications. First, it requires detaching one's findings from the specific national context within which one finds them. After all, whether a particular holiday I use in my analysis happens to be Turkish or Bolivian is secondary to my interest in the generic features of national memory. Second, it entails ignoring change, which typically tends to be nation-specific. As groups undergo major cultural or political transformations, their recollections of their past also keep changing,[4] yet only by ignoring such changes can we discern certain transnational generic patterns that a more diachronic approach would most likely prevent us from noticing.

Thus, despite the inevitable cost involved in doing a strictly synchronic analysis of national memory, I believe the potential intellectual benefit it entails is well worth the effort.

ROOTS AND WATERSHEDS

The first category of events typically commemorated on national holidays are historic watersheds marking major changes in nations' political (the abolition of monarchy in Brazil), cultural (the introduction of Christianity to Ireland), or moral (the abolition of slavery in the Bahamas) identity. Particularly common, in this regard, are calendrical commemorations of key moments in nations' political history, such as the end of the Italian occupation of Albania in 1944 (Liberation Day), the overthrow of Sudan's President Jaafar al-Numeiry in 1985 (Uprising Day), or the French Revolution (Bastille Day). Such moments often involve the adoption of a new constitution, and thirty-one countries indeed celebrate a Constitution Day, the most explicit symbolic expression of a dramatic transformation of a nation's internal political nature.

Watersheds basically punctuate the histories of the mnemonic communities observing the holidays associated with them. Commemorating such symbolic landmarks, in other words, helps nations flesh out their conventional systems of historical periodization (Zerubavel 1993 [1991]: 18–20).

A perfect example of such historical punctuation marks are "founding moments" marking various conventional beginnings (Zerubavel 1993: 457–58). Some nation-states, for example, set aside special days to commemorate the historic points that mark their symbolic "birth" as single entities following the political merger of several smaller entities, as in Switzerland in 1291 (Confederation Day), Canada in 1867 (Canada Day), Romania in 1918 (National Day), Somalia in 1960 (Union Day), or the United Arab Emirates in 1971 (National Day). Others likewise commemorate various other symbolic beginnings involving "discovery" (Columbus Day) (Zerubavel 1998: 320–24), settlement (Australia's Foundation Day), or immigration (Trinidad and Tobago's Indian Arrival Day). Some countries also design special commemorative holidays to help current leaders establish lines of symbolic descent "connecting" them to some momentous historic event such as the founding of the ruling dynasty (Japan's

National Foundation Day) or political party (Tanzania's Saba Saba Day) or the inception of the current form of government (Laos's Republic Day).

The most spectacular conventional historical "beginning" engraved on national calendars in the form of commemorative holidays, however, is nations' symbolic birth as sovereign polities. Out of the 191 countries examined here, 139 actually celebrate a national "birthday" commemorating the historic moment at which they became independent. From a strictly calendro-commemorative standpoint, the birth of a nation is clearly the most significant political event preserved in its collective memory.

Yet independence days are not the only days specifically designed by nations to commemorate their sovereignty. Some countries, for example, also commemorate other tokens of political sovereignty, such as the expansion of its territorial scope (Costa Rica's annexation of the Guanacaste province in 1824, Morocco's 1975 invasion of Spanish Sahara) or its defense (the lifting of the Ottoman siege of Malta in 1565, Ethiopia's 1896 victory over Italy at the battle of Aduwa). Some also set aside special days to commemorate their "founding fathers" (Argentina's José de San Martín, North Korea's Kim Il Sung) or the introduction of their national flag (Swaziland) or anthem (Panama). Others commemorate various symbolic equivalents of political sovereignty, such as the achievement of military, economic, or cultural autonomy. Consider, in this regard, the commemorations of the French evacuation of a Tunisian naval base in 1963, the nationalization of Iran's oil industry in 1951, or the rejection of Russian as Moldova's official language in 1989.

Such events constitute a considerable bulk of the collective memories preserved by some nations in their calendars. Thus, for example, in Angola, six of the seven national holidays designed to commemorate historical events (Armed Struggle Day, Pioneers' Day, Armed Forces Day, Independence Day, Victory Day, and Heroes' Day) basically revolve around the country's struggle for independence from Portugal. In a somewhat similar manner, Ecuador sets aside five days every year (Quito Independence Day, Cuenca Independence Day, Anniversary of the Independence of Guayaquil, Independence Battle Day, and Bolívar Day) to commemorate its national struggle for independence from Spain. Multiple annual commemorations of the "births" of Panama (Martyrs' Day, National Anthem Day, Independence from Colombia Day, Flag Day, First Cry of Independence Day, and Independence from Spain Day) and Haiti (Independence Day, Heroes of Independence Day, Flag Day, Vertières Day, and National Sovereignty Day) likewise underscore the almost obsessive calendrical preoccupation of some nations with their sovereignty.

That the earliest historical event calendrically commemorated by Mozambique is the 1964 outbreak of its struggle for independence (Liberation Day) suggests that it may not even see itself as having been a distinct national entity before that. Note the conspicuous absence of any event more recent than the martyrdom of Saint Stephen or the "assumption" of the Virgin Mary in the first century on Liechtenstein's national calendar,[5] and on Ireland's national calendar, history practically "ends" more than fifteen centuries ago with Saint Patrick. Unlike Panama or Angola, which are so preoccupied with the memories of their birth as nations, these countries take their nationhood for granted and do not seem to experience any fundamental existential insecurity that might call for a commemorative reaffirmation of who they are. Thus, they feel quite comfortable commemorating only their distant religious "roots" and do not seem to need to keep reminding their members that they have not always been around.

One of the most remarkable findings of this study is the pervasive presence of religion in modern national calendars. Out of the 191 countries examined here, 176 officially commemorate their spiritual origins on religious holidays. In fact, on ten of the eleven days designated on their national calendar as commemorative holidays (Feast of the Immaculate Conception, Christmas, Feast of the Epiphany, Easter Monday, Ascension Day, Corpus Christi, Whit Monday, Saint Stephen's Day, Feast of the Assumption of the Blessed Virgin Mary, and All Saints' Day), Austrians basically celebrate their common Christian "roots." The situation is quite similar in India (where fourteen of the country's seventeen official commemorative holidays are specifically designed to celebrate Indians' Hindu, Buddhist, Jainist, Christian, Muslim, and Sikh origins), Spain (ten of twelve such days), Ethiopia (nine of eleven), Italy (seven of nine), Senegal (eleven of thirteen), Indonesia (eight of nine), and Liechtenstein (all fourteen). Long before they actually take their first formal history class in school, children in such countries already become quite familiar with some major parts of their collective past through the annual public celebration of religious holidays.

We have already seen that although each nation basically organizes its calendar quite independently from other nations, there are nonetheless some fundamental consistencies in the content of what nations choose to remember on holidays. By the same token, however, we can also identify some generic schematic patterns in the *structure* of national memories as manifested in the way nations' histories are conventionally "narrated" through their annual holiday cycles.

The social organization of memory involves a particular way of experiencing time that is altogether different from the conventional mathematical manner in which we normally process it in our minds. Essentially nonmetric, it basically rests on the perceived qualitative heterogeneity of mathematically identical durations (e.g., Bergson 1960 [1889]; Hubert 1909 [1905]: 197–210; Sorokin 1943: 158–225; Flaherty 1999). As Henri Hubert first pointed out upon noting the social foundations of such experience of temporality, mathematically equal time intervals are often made socially unequal (Hubert 1909 [1905]: 207–8; Sorokin 1943: 184; Zerubavel 1979: 113–17).

Such "qualitative" phenomenology of time also entails an essentially nonmetric approach to chronology whereby mathematically identical historical stretches often vary in their perceived "amplitude." We thus often distinguish "pregnant periods packed with eventfulness" from "empty" stretches during which nothing of major significance seems to have happened (Sorokin 1943: 212). Such tendency to remember certain historical periods much more intensely than others has been well noted by Claude Lévi-Strauss:

> We use a large number of dates to code some periods of history; and fewer for others. This variable quantity of dates applied to periods of equal duration are [*sic*] a gauge of what might be called the pressure of history: there are 'hot' chronologies which are those of periods where . . . numerous events appear as differential elements; others, on the contrary, where . . . very little or nothing took place. . . . Historical knowledge thus proceeds in the same way as a wireless with frequency modulation: like a nerve, it codes a continuous quantity . . . by frequencies of impulses proportional to its variations. (1966 [1962]: 259)

Such a nonmetric view of chronology is quite evident in communal commemorative rituals. As W. Lloyd Warner, for example, first noted upon examining the historical contents of a commemorative procession representing the first 300 years of a New England town's collective past, the events mnemonic communities typically come to regard as their history are unevenly distributed chronologically:

> The forty-three floats of the Procession . . . were spread throughout the three hundred years being officially celebrated. . . . Further inspection demonstrates that chronologically they are not spread equally throughout the three centuries. There are sharp divergencies between the social time of the Procession and the chronology of objective time. . . . Since three hundred years were being celebrated, if only the statistical probability of pure chance were at work each century would receive a third of the scenes displayed and each half- and quarter-century be given its proportion of symbolic events. The criteria of objective time and "probability" would both be served. But in fact, one brief period of little more than a decade received as much attention as the previous hundred years. One full quarter-century was not represented at all. (Warner 1959: 129–30)

In an accompanying chart explicitly contrasting mathematical "chronology" with essentially nonmetric "social time," Warner specifically referred to uneven chronological distribution patterns such as having the 25-year interval from 1780 to 1805 represented by nine floats yet the mathematically identical interval from 1705 to 1730 by practically none (ibid.: 133).

The same fundamental commemorative pattern was further confirmed by Barry Schwartz in a somewhat similar examination of the chronological distribution of the historical events publicly commemorated through the art objects exhibited in the U.S. Capitol's art collection in Washington, D.C. One only needs to contrast the public American commemoration of the highly eventful 1770s and the virtually barren 1760s, for example, to appreciate the fundamental difference between "sacred" and "profane" stretches of the past (Schwartz 1982: 381–83).

Such intense commemoration of brief yet highly eventful periods in nations' collective pasts is quite evident in their calendars. Consider, for example, the dense chronological clustering of the historical events commemorated on Libya's Revolution Day (the overthrow of King Idris by Muammar Qaddafi), British Bases Evacuation Day (the closing of the military bases at el-Adem and Tobruk), American Bases Evacuation Day (the closing of the Wheelus Air Force Base), and Evacuation of Fascist Settlers Day (the expulsion of Italians from Libya)—all four of which occurred within the brief, thirteen-month period between 1 September 1969 and 7 October 1970. Or the five days (Victory Day, Armed Forces Day, Heroes' Day, Independence Day, and MPLA Foundation Day) set aside by Angola to commemorate the relatively brief period between the resumption of its struggle for independence from Portugal in 1974 and the restructuring of the Popular Movement for the Liberation of Angola as a political party in 1977. Consider Turkey's obvious mnemonic preoccupation with the four-year period leading to the proclamation of the Turkish Republic in 1923, which it commemorates on four national holidays (National Sovereignty Day, Youth and Sports Day, Victory Day, and Republic Day). Or the brief yet highly eventful periods from 1803 to 1805 in Haiti, 1825 to 1828 in Uruguay, 1896 to 1898 in the Philippines, and 1990 to 1991 in Azerbaijan, each of which is publicly commemorated on at least three separate national holidays.

Like heart attacks and earthquakes, such highly "loaded" periods are obviously difficult for nations to forget. Indeed, as annual cycles of "holy" days, national calendars come to embody tacit cardiogram- and seismogram-like narratives that encapsulate nations' collective histories as strings of sacred peaks sporadically protruding from wide, commemoratively barren valleys of profane time (Lévi-Strauss 1966 [1962]: 259; Glassie 1982: 621–22).[6] By highlighting the varying "amplitude" of socially memorable and immemorable stretches of history, such *commemograms* certainly underscore the sociological value of studying the chronological distribution of the "sacred" historical events commemorated on national holidays.

The typical commemorative profile emerging from a cross-national examination of 191 such commemograms consists of two chronologically dense, commemoratively "hot" periods standing out against a backdrop of long, mnemonically "empty" stretches of history. The most common national calendro-commemorative pattern, in other words, is bipolar, with most national holidays essentially commemorating historical events that

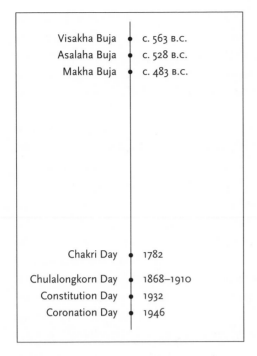

Visakha Buja	c. 563 B.C.
Asalaha Buja	c. 528 B.C.
Makha Buja	c. 483 B.C.
Chakri Day	1782
Chulalongkorn Day	1868–1910
Constitution Day	1932
Coronation Day	1946

Figure 1. Thailand's
National Commemogram

happened either in the very distant past or in relatively recent memory (Vansina 1985: 23–24, 168–69).

The generic structure of national memory that seems to emerge is thus fairly clear. The historical events nations usually commemorate on holidays are typically organized chronologically in two clusters. Those clusters normally consist of a set of religiously significant events that occurred in the very distant past and another set of politically significant events that occurred in the last two hundred years. They are typically separated from each other by long stretches of commemoratively unmarked, "empty" history.

Consider, for example, the commemorative review of history officially encapsulated in Thailand's national calendar. It begins with three major events in the life of Buddha—his birth around 563 B.C. (Visakha Buja), his first sermon around 528 B.C. (Asalaha Buja), and the announcement of his imminent death around 483 B.C. (Makha Buja). This rather "dense" 83-year period is followed by a practically barren 2,265-year historical lull that is associated with virtually no national holiday and ends only with the foundation of the current royal dynasty by King Rama I in 1782 (Chakri Day). Thailand's three remaining "historical" holidays commemorate the reign of King Rama V from 1868 to 1910 (Chulalongkorn Day), the country's transition to constitutional monarchy in 1932 (Constitution Day), and the accession of its current ruler, King Bhumibol, in 1946 (Coronation Day).

A rather similar "two-act" commemogram is embodied in Morocco's national calendar. With the single exception of Abraham's willingness to sacrifice his son Ishmael (Eid el-Kebir), a mythical event essentially associated with some "prehistoric" past (Zerubavel 1998: 318–24), Moroccans' calendrically commemorated history basically consists of two chronologically dense periods separated from each other by a seemingly uneventful 1,275-year historical lull. As in Thailand, the country's first cluster of commemorative holidays is associated with its spiritual origins and essentially covers the birth of Mohammed around 570 (Birthday of Prophet), the period around 610 when he received divine revelations (Ramadan), and the martyrdom of the Shi'ite saint Hussein in 680 (Ashoura). By the same token, the second cluster is designed to commemorate four relatively recent political events, namely, Morocco's independence from France in 1955 (Independence Day), King Hassan II's accession in 1961 (Festival of the Throne), the invasion of the former Spanish Sahara in 1975 (Anniversary of the Green March), and its formal annexation in 1979 (Oued ed-Dahab Day).

When a nation acknowledges more than just one religion as a major source of its spiritual heritage, its calendar often embodies a somewhat modified, "*three*-act" commemogram, as in Burkina Faso, for example. Like Morocco, the former Upper Volta also commemorates Abraham's willingness to sacrifice Ishmael (Tabaski), an essentially mythical, prehistoric moment chronologically followed by two separate clusters of historical events associated with Christianity and Islam, respectively. The first cluster consists of Jesus's birth around 4 B.C. (Christmas), his ascension to heaven around A.D. 30 (Ascension Day), and his mother's assumption sometime after that (Feast of the Assumption of the Blessed Virgin Mary), followed by the thematically related yet chronologically vaguer period traditionally associated with All Saints' Day. The second cluster essentially covers Mohammed's birth around 570 (Birth of Prophet) and the period around 610 when he received divine revelations (Ramadan). Then, follow-

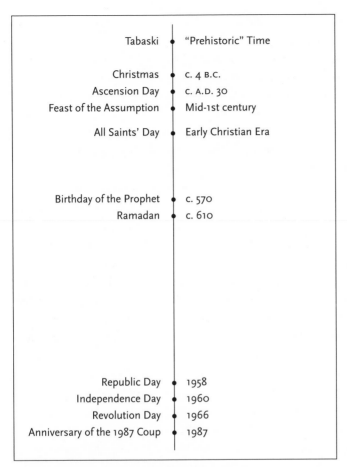

Tabaski	"Prehistoric" Time
Christmas	c. 4 B.C.
Ascension Day	c. A.D. 30
Feast of the Assumption	Mid-1st century
All Saints' Day	Early Christian Era
Birthday of the Prophet	c. 570
Ramadan	c. 610
Republic Day	1958
Independence Day	1960
Revolution Day	1966
Anniversary of the 1987 Coup	1987

Figure 2. Burkina Faso's National Commemogram

ing a seemingly uneventful 1,348-year historical lull associated with practically no national holiday, comes a third cluster of four relatively recent
political events, namely, Upper Volta's decision to become an independent
republic in 1958 (Republic Day), its actual independence from France in
1960 (Independence Day), and the military overthrows of Presidents
Maurice Yaméogo and Thomas Sankara by Sangoulé Lamizana in 1966
(Revolution Day) and Blaise Compaoré in 1987 (Anniversary of the 1987
Coup).

A most striking feature of such commemograms are the long historical
stretches that remain practically empty in nations' collective memories.
Thus, throughout the Muslim world, there is a thirteen-century calendro-

commemorative gap stretching from around 620 (Mohammed's night journey to heaven) or 680 (the martyrdom of Hussein) to this century. Even more spectacular is the similar 18- or 19-century gap that exists throughout much of the Christian world—a commemorative blackout that usually begins right after the assumption of the Virgin Mary in the middle of the first century and is interrupted only by the glow of early-modern mnemonic beacons such as the British settlement of Australia in 1788, the proclamation of Poland's first constitution in 1791, and the American Revolution.

Of the 191 countries examined here, only 22 try to invoke through their calendars the memory of any historical event (other than the European "discovery" of America in 1492) that occurred during the seemingly un-eventful 11-century period between the martyrdom of the Shi'ite saint Hussein in 680 and the American Revolution. Furthermore, in 13 of those countries, those events occurred only in the 16th or 17th centuries. In other words, around the entire world, only nine countries actually commemorate on their national holidays historical events that occurred between 680 and 1492—Bulgaria (the invention of the Cyrillic alphabet in 855), the Czech Republic (the birth of Slavonic culture around 860 and the martyrdom of Jan Hus in 1415), Slovakia (the birth of Slavonic culture around 860), Spain (the alleged discovery of Saint James's body in Compostela in 899), Hungary (the reign of King Stephen I from 1001 to 1038), Lithuania (the coronation of Grand Duke Mindaugas around 1240), Andorra (the joint suzerainty agreement between France and the Bishop of Urgel in 1278), Switzerland (the establishment of the Swiss confederation in 1291), and India (the birth of Guru Nanak, the founder of Sikhism, around 1469). Which also means that, from a strictly calendro-commemorative standpoint, the eighth, tenth, twelfth, and fourteenth centuries are considered practically "empty" worldwide!

THE WEB OF MNEMONIC AFFILIATIONS

National holidays also remind us that the layering of our social recollections is far more complex than may appear to us at first glance (Halbwachs 1992 [1925]). Since modern identities entail multiple social affiliations (Simmel 1964 [1998]: 127–95), the modern individual is actually a member of several rather distinct mnemonic communities (Zerubavel

1997: 17–18). While it is basically as Venezuelans that people commemorate their country's independence from Spain on Battle of Carabobo Day, it is essentially as Christians that they remember the Crucifixion on Good Friday and as members of the Pan-American community that they recall Christopher Columbus's historic landing in the Bahamas on Columbus Day (Zerubavel 1992: 28–29).

As we have seen, national calendars encompass a curious blend of national and religious elements. While nationalism is undoubtedly an extremely powerful collective sentiment, modern nation-states evidently feel the need to further bolster it with some traditional religious sentiments.[7] As evident from their calendars, most nations today try to maintain a delicate balance between their members' national and religious attachments, thereby preserving side-by-side multiple histories reflecting the inevitable structural complexity of their collective identity.

Such complexity stems from the conjunction of national and religious sentiments. Many nation-states regard themselves as home to more than just a single religious community, and the various calendrical solutions it generates certainly reflect countries' differing approaches to cultural (and particularly religious) pluralism. Thus, on the one hand, one sees countries that officially observe holidays of two (Chad, Albania), three (Suriname, Indonesia), four (Singapore, Bangladesh), and even six (India) different religions, thereby commemorating side by side several different histories that often have very little to do with one another. At the same time, in some parts of the United States, one also sees the unofficial integration of Christmas and Hanukkah into a single "holiday season" (Zerubavel 1982a: 288), while Fiji is even considering merging the Hindu and Muslim celebrations of Diwali and Mohammed's birth into a single holiday, Girmit (*Europa World Year Book 1997*: 1244).

Yet commemorative holidays are also observed by mnemonic communities that are larger than the nation-state. One can see such mnemonic communion among countries that were once parts of a single political entity, such as Guatemala and Nicaragua, both of which still commemorate on 15 September their joint independence from Spain 178 years ago, or North and South Korea, which still celebrate on 15 August the end of the Japanese occupation of the Korean peninsula in 1945, despite having been bitter enemies for the past 50 years. It is also evident at the continental level, as exemplified by the commemorations of the foundation of the Organization for African Unity across Africa (such as in Zambia, Mali, and Equatorial Guinea), the end of World War II across Europe (such as in Holland, Slovakia, and the Ukraine), and the European "discovery" of the Western Hemisphere across America (such as in Chile, the United States, and Belize).

Even more remarkable, in this regard, are the essentially international holidays associated with the great world religions. Long before there was any economic evidence of the process of globalization, it had already manifested itself calendrically through the spread of both Christianity and Islam. To appreciate the extent of such calendrical globalization (Zerubavel 1985 [1981]: 96–100; 1982b: 12–17; 1989 [1985]: 24–26; 1997: 104, 109), consider, for example, the mnemonic status of Mohammed, the events of whose life are officially commemorated by sixty-two countries. An even greater international calendrical star is Jesus. Not only does most of the world today use a conventional chronological dating framework essentially revolving around his birth, 149 of the 191 countries examined here officially celebrate Christmas, while 133 (including prominently Muslim countries such as Syria, Indonesia, and Pakistan) also observe Easter.

Observing such international holidays involves some remarkable mnemonic synchronization on a global scale. After all, on Good Friday, people in Finland, Slovenia, and Madagascar come to recall the Crucifixion essentially *together*, as a single mnemonic community. On the same day, the birth of Mohammed is *jointly* remembered in Guyana, Malaysia, and Sudan, thereby giving an altogether new meaning to the modern image of the world as a single "global village."

"IN THOSE DAYS AT THIS TIME"

The relation between calendars and history is essentially a semiotic one. As a cycle of national holidays, the calendar year is basically designed to represent a nation's collective past (Zerubavel 1995: 216). Yet the association of particular calendrical signifiers with particular historical signifieds is only symbolic,[8] and we should therefore not expect national holidays to literally embody the actual temporal profiles of the historical events they are designed to commemorate.

Thus, for example, Americans routinely celebrate Independence Day and Thanksgiving Day less than five months apart from each other despite the obvious fact that the actual historical events they are designed to commemorate (the European colonization of New England and the American Revolution) occurred more than a century and a half apart. Moreover, that the event commemorated in July occurred *after* the one commemorated in November does not even strike anybody as odd (Zerubavel 1995: 216–17).

By the same token, we should also not expect a perfect fit between the calendar year and a nation's history in terms of the actual durations of national holidays and the historical events they are designed to commemorate. In fact, through symbolic compression, a single calendar day may come to represent several years of actual history. Thus, on Martin Luther King Jr. Day, Americans commemorate not only King's actual birth but the entire battle for civil rights during the 1950s and 1960s.

Furthermore, a single national holiday is sometimes designed to commemorate several different historical events. Thus, on Constitution Day, for example, Mexico commemorates both its 1857 and 1917 constitutions, while Denmark celebrates the abolition of absolute monarchy in 1849 as well as the parliamentary reforms of 1953. Such efforts to commemoratively lump several related historical occurrences in a single calendrical observance are clearly inspired by the sanctity attached to holy days. Such sanctity must have played a major role in Saddam Hussein's decision in 1979 to assume absolute power on the anniversary of the 17 July coup that brought Iraq's Ba'ath party to power in 1968, as well as in Hungary's decision in 1989 to proclaim its new republic on the anniversary of its 23 October uprising against the Soviet Union in 1956.[9]

Despite all this, however, nations normally do aim for a perfect temporal fit between holidays and the historical events they are designed to commemorate. Indeed, holidays are usually designed to evoke the memory of particular days in nations' history, such as 30 May 1991 (the decision to secede from Yugoslavia) in the case of Croatia or 7 August 1819 (Simón Bolívar's victory over Spain at the battle of Boyacá) in the case of Colombia.

Such perfect symmetry between calendars and history (most spectacularly epitomized by the Church's bold attempt to have the three months from Ash Wednesday to Whit Monday "represent" three corresponding historical months some 20 centuries ago [Warner 1961: 345–

62]) is clearly inspired by the traditionalistic urge to do away with the very distinction between past and present. After all, when Jews bless God on Hannukah for the miracles he performed "in those days at this time" (*ba-yamim ha-hem ba-zman ha-ze*), they basically associate the holiday with a particular time in history as well as a particular nonhistorical time of year at the same time (Zerubavel 1989 [1985]: 84).

Such remarkable simultaneity of past and present (likewise attempted through traditionalistic reenactment rituals like Christmas and Thanksgiving pageants) is what nations aim for when they try to organize time to flow isochronally at the levels of both the calendar and history (Eliade 1959 [1957]: 68–113; Connerton 1989: 41–71). It all rests on our ability to symbolically condense thousands of years of history into a single annual cycle of holidays—arguably one of the most spectacular cultural arrangements that help transform people into nations.

NOTES

I would like to thank Yael Zerubavel, Jeffrey Olick, Dan Ryan, Christena Nippert-Eng, John Gillis, Barry Schwartz, Ruth Simpson, John Martin, Ian Watson, and William Smith for their very helpful comments on an earlier version of this paper.

1. See also Hubert 1909 [1905]; Leach 1961; Foster 1996. On the social marking of reality, see also Brekhus 1996; 1998.

2. On such communities, see Zerubavel 1997: 90.

3. For some similar cycles of remembrance, consider, e.g., the Christian weekly cycle designed to commemorate the Resurrection (Zerubavel 1989 [1985]: 20–21), as well as centennial anniversary cycles (Spillman 1997).

4. See, for example, Lewis 1975: 30–41, 70–87; FitzGerald 1980; Zerubavel 1982a; Schwartz 1990; Zerubavel 1995: 147–85, 197–213, 221–28; Assmann 1997; Olick 1999; Olick unpublished. A similar revision of memory is evident among individuals undergoing significant identity crises around conversion or divorce. See Berger 1963: 54–65.

5. I do not distinguish here historical events from mythical ones and am therefore not concerned whether any given event actually happened as long as it is conventionally located for commemorative purposes in some commonly shared past.

6. On sacred and profane time, see also Zerubavel 1985 [1981]: 101–37.

7. On the heavy price paid by nations who tried to calendrically dispense with their traditional religious roots, see, e.g., Zerubavel 1977: 875; 1989 [1985]: 33–35, 42–43.

8. Unlike commemorative stamps or statues, calendars do not even rely on iconic representation.

9. Consider the days currently celebrated in Russia (7 November) and South Africa

(16 December) as Day of Reconciliation. As their name suggests, the collective sentiments they are designed to evoke today are quite different from the ones they were
traditionally expected to evoke as the annual anniversaries of the 1917 Bolshevik Revolution and the 1838 Boer victory over the Zulu at the battle of Blood River. That they are
still observed on the same dates, however, clearly underscores the sanctity attached to
those dates. See Olick, 1999.

REFERENCES

Assmann, J. 1997. *Moses the Egyptian: The Memory of Egypt in Western Monotheism.*
    Cambridge, Mass.: Harvard University Press.
Berger, P. L. 1963. *Invitation to Sociology: A Humanistic Perspective.* Garden City, N.Y.:
    Doubleday Anchor.
Bergson, H. 1960 [1889]. *Time and Free Will: An Essay on the Immediate Data of Con-
    sciousness.* New York: Harper and Row.
Bernstein, M. A. 1994. *Foregone Conclusions: Against Apocalyptic History.* Berkeley: Uni-
    versity of California Press.
Brekhus, Wayne. 1996. "Social Marking and the Mental Coloring of Identity: Sexual
    Identity Construction and Maintenance in the United States." *Sociological Forum* 11:
    497–522.
———. 1998. "A Sociology of the Unmarked: Redirecting Our Focus." *Sociological Theory*
    16: 45–62.
Chase's 1997 Calendar of Events. 1996. Chicago: Contemporary.
Connerton, P. 1989. *How Societies Remember.* Cambridge: Cambridge University Press.
Cressy, D. 1989. *Bonfires and Bells: National Memory and the Protestant Calendar in
    Elizabethan and Stuart England.* Berkeley: University of California Press.
Durkheim, E. 1995 [1912]. *The Elementary Forms of Religious Life.* New York: Free Press.
Eliade, M. 1959 [1957]. *The Sacred and the Profane: The Nature of Religion.* New York:
    Harcourt, Brace & World.
Europa World Year Book 1997. London: Europa Publications.
FitzGerald, F. 1980. *America Revised: History Schoolbooks in the Twentieth Century.* New
    York: Vintage.
Flaherty, M. G. 1999. *A Watched Pot: How We Experience Time.* New York: New York
    University Press.
Foster, J. 1996. "Menstrual Time: The Sociocognitive Mapping of 'The Menstrual Cy-
    cle.'" *Sociological Forum* 11: 523–47.
Frisch, M. 1989. "American History and the Structures of Collective Memory: A Mod-
    est Exercise in Empirical Iconography." *Journal of American History* 75: 1130–55.
Glassie, H. 1982. *Passing the Time in Ballymenone: Culture and History of an Ulster
    Community.* Philadelphia: University of Pennsylvania Press.
Gregory, R. W. 1983. *Anniversaries and Holidays.* 4th ed. Chicago: American Library
    Association.

Haines, M., ed. 1997. *The Traveler's Handbook.* 7th ed. London: Wexas.

Halbwachs, M. 1992 [1925]. *The Social Frameworks of Memory.* In Lewis A. Coser, ed., *Maurice Halbwachs on Collective Memory.* Chicago: University of Chicago Press.

Henderson, H., and S. E. Thompson, eds. 1997. *Holidays, Festivals, and Celebrations of the World Dictionary.* 2d ed. Detroit: Omnigraphics Inc.

Herbert, U. 1986. "Good Times, Bad Times." *History Today* 36 (February): 42–48.

Hubert, H. 1909 [1905]. "Etude Sommaire de la Représentation du Temps dans la Religion et la Magie." In Henri Hubert and Marcel Mauss, eds., *Mélanges d'Histoire des Religions.* Paris: Félix Alcan and Guillaumin: 189–229.

Langer, W. L., ed. 1968. *An Encyclopedia of World History: Ancient, Medieval, and Modern Chronologically Arranged.* 4th ed. Boston: Houghton Mifflin.

Leach, E. 1961. "Two Essays Concerning the Symbolic Representation of Time." In *Rethinking Anthropology.* London: Athlone.

Lévi-Strauss, C. 1966 [1962]. *The Savage Mind.* Chicago: University of Chicago Press.

Lewis, B. 1975. *History: Remembered, Recovered, Invented.* Princeton, N.J.: Princeton University Press.

Nora, P. 1989. "Between Memory and History: Les Lieux de Mémoire." *Representations* 26: 7–25.

Olick, J. K. 1999. "Genre Memories and Memory Games: A Dialogical Analysis of May 8th, 1945 Commemorations in the Federal Republic of Germany." *American Sociological Review* 64 (June): 381–402.

——. Unpublished. "Figurations of Memory: A Process-Relational Methodology, Illustrated on the German Case."

Schwartz, B. 1982. "The Social Context of Commemoration: A Study in Collective Memory." *Social Forces* 61: 374–96.

——. 1990. "The Reconstruction of Abraham Lincoln." In David Middleton and Derek Edwards, eds., *Collective Remembering.* London: Sage: 81–107.

Scott 1999 Standard Postage Stamp Catalogue. 1998. 6 vols. Sidney, Ohio: Scott Publishing Co.

Simmel, G. 1964 [1908]. "The Web of Group Affiliations." In *Conflict and the Web of Group Affiliations.* New York: Free Press.

Sorokin, P. A. 1943. *Sociocultural Causality, Space, Time: A Study of Referential Principles of Sociology and Social Science.* Durham, N.C.: Duke University Press.

Spillman, L. 1997. *Nation and Commemoration: Creating National Identities in the United States and Australia.* Cambridge: Cambridge University Press.

Vansina, J. 1985. *Oral Tradition as History.* Madison: University of Wisconsin Press.

Warner, W. L. 1959. *The Living and the Dead.* New Haven, Conn.: Yale University Press.

——. 1961. *The Family of God.* New Haven, Conn.: Yale University Press.

Weaver, R. S. 1995. *International Holidays: 204 Countries from 1994 through 2015.* Jefferson, N.C.: McFarland.

World Calendar of Holidays 1981. 1980. New York: Morgan Guaranty Trust Co.

Zerubavel, E. 1977. "The French Republican Calendar: A Case Study in the Sociology of Time." *American Sociological Review* 42: 868–77.

——. 1979. *Patterns of Time in Hospital Life: A Sociological Perspective*. Chicago: University of Chicago Press.

——. 1982a. "Easter and Passover: On Calendars and Group Identity." *American Sociological Review* 47: 284–89.

——. 1982b. "The Standardization of Time: A Sociohistorical Perspective." *American Journal of Sociology* 88: 1–23.

——. 1985 [1981]. *Hidden Rhythms: Schedules and Calendars in Social Life*. Berkeley: University of California Press.

——. 1989 [1985]. *The Seven-Day Circle: The History and Meaning of the Week*. Chicago: University of Chicago Press.

——. 1992. *Terra Cognita: The Mental Discovery of America*. New Brunswick, N.J.: Rutgers University Press.

——. 1993 [1991]. *The Fine Line: Making Distinctions in Everyday Life*. Chicago: University of Chicago Press.

——. 1993. "In the Beginning: Notes on the Social Construction of Historical Discontinuity." *Sociological Inquiry* 63: 457–59.

——. 1997. *Social Mindscapes: An Invitation to Cognitive Sociology*. Cambridge, Mass.: Harvard University Press.

——. 1998. "Language and Memory: 'Pre-Columbian' America and the Social Logic of Periodization." *Social Research* 65: 315–30.

Zerubavel, Y. 1995. *Recovered Roots: Collective Memory and the Making of Israeli National Tradition*. Chicago: University of Chicago Press.

Afterword: Borges and Brass

◂ ◂ ◂ ◂ ◂ ◂ ◂ ◂ ◂ ◂ ◂ ◂ ◂ ◂   CHARLES TILLY

"*Pienso en las cosas,*" wrote Jorge Luis Borges in *Historia de la Noche*, "*que pudieron ser y no fueron*" (I reflect on things that could have been but never were [Borges 1977: 91]). His poem mentions the treatise on Saxon mythology that chronicler Bede never wrote, history without Helen of Troy's face, the American Confederacy's victory at Gettysburg, the unicorn's other horn, and more. Without obvious effort, Borges's poetry vivifies anagrams, nursery rhymes, shopping lists, and descriptions of ordinary objects—trivia, one might wrongly say. Wrongly, because things that never happened are profoundly important.

We could add to Borges's list a Mongol empire that conquered the rest of the 12th-century world, surgeons condemned to their academic cousins' genteel poverty, cities without wheels, households in control of their own armies, fertility decline in the absence of mortality decline, money bereft of commodities. This roster differs from Borges's: All these things have actually half-happened somewhere. The Mongols did conquer, however temporarily, much of their known world. Surgeons in Mexico or Cuba occupy economic positions more similar to professors than they do in the United States, cities of the Ottoman Empire before 1900 existed in the near-absence of wheeled vehicles, and so on.

The half-happening of these events provides the rationale of history, at least in its explanatory mode. It also provides the rationale of historically informed social science. Social science is the systematic study of what could happen, what could have happened, what will possibly happen, in human social life, and why. History places that systematic study firmly in time and space, insisting that where and when something happens affects *how* it happens. Both differ from poetry, science fiction, and philosophy by grounding their thought about the nonexistent in verifiable analyses of what so far has been possible, or even has occurred. But it still concerns that which is not, was not, or will not be.

The genius of historical explanation concerns principles of change and variation that show nonexistent conditions to have been possible and, perhaps, still to be possible. Barrington Moore Jr. titles chapter 11 of his book *Injustice* "The Suppression of Historical Alternatives: Germany 1918–1920." The chapter asks under what conditions a durable demo-cratic revolution could have occurred in Germany. If the notion of sup-pressed historical alternatives, he says, "is to be more than a rhetorical device to trigger off suitable moral emotions (e.g. condemnation of all existing social institutions, romantic glorification of any struggle against authority) it ought to be possible to show in some concrete historical situation just what was possible and why. That means marshaling evi-dence, creating and testing an argument, in the same way one goes about explaining any form of human behavior" (Moore 1978: 376). Precisely. In the spirit of Barrington Moore, let us reflect on methodological problems in the actual preparation of historical explanations. In order to take coun-terfactual explanation seriously, we must identify the fields of variation within which the phenomena occur, invoke explanatory principles appro-priate to those fields of variation, then locate the concrete phenomena under examination precisely within those fields, taking into account the effect of time and place on the causal processes involved (see Centeno and López-Alves 2001; Hawthorn 1991; Tetlock and Belkin 1996; Wong 1997). The field of collective memory provides a splendid opportunity for reflection on the proper utilization of suppressed historical alternatives because it concerns the process by which a limited number of competing historical accounts—sometimes only one—come to prevail in place of all the others that might have been and sometimes even were.

To clarify the discussion's stakes, we can return to another Borges text, then contrast the view of memory it suggests with a very different account of memory construction offered by Paul Brass. In a famous story, Borges tells of his encounters with Funes El Memorioso, a prodigy of individual memory, in a small Uruguayan town. Ireneo Funes, who knew no Latin, borrowed two complex Latin texts and a dictionary from the storyteller. Not long after (Borges does not tell us exactly how long), his father's illness suddenly called the storyteller back to Buenos Aires. Before departing, he visited Funes to recover the Latin books. As he arrived, he heard the nineteen-year-old Funes reading Pliny aloud in the original Latin with "obvious delight." When the two began to converse, Funes alternated between Spanish and Latin; in both languages, he recounted prodigious feats of memory described in the books the storyteller had loaned him.

Gradually the storyteller realized that Funes did not simply possess a fabulous memory. He remembered everything:

> We, in a glance, perceive three wine glasses on the table; Funes saw all the shoots, clusters, and grapes of the vine. He remembered the shapes of the clouds in the south at dawn on the 30th of April of 1882, and he could compare them in his recollection with the marbled grain in the design of a leather-bound book which he had seen only once, and with the lines in the spray which an oar raised in the Rio Negro on the eve of the battle of the Quebracho. These recollections were not simple; each visual image was linked to muscular sensations, thermal sensations, etc. He could reconstruct all his dreams, all his fancies. Two or three times he had reconstructed an entire day. He told me: *I have more memories in myself alone than all men have had since the world was a world.* And again: *My dreams are like your vigils.* And again, toward dawn: *My memory, sir, is like a garbage disposal.* (Borges 1962: 112)

Funes went even further: he resisted categories, substituting specific names of objects, substances, or persons for every single numeral he ever used, indeed creating separate niches for different states of what ordinary people would consider the "same" objects, substances, or persons. Funes' memory contained a moving picture of everything he had ever experienced.

Funes represents, then, the terrifying prospect of complete, consistent, concrete memory. Borges's astonished raconteur represents ordinary people. Ordinary people select, simplify, classify, and recast, then retain only the residue. Collective memory, at this extreme, consists simply of the same selection, simplification, classification, recasting, and recollection as carried on by whole populations rather than one person at a time. To what extent the process occurs independently in separate minds or emerges through interaction and socialization, of course, constitutes a serious conundrum for such a strongly cognitive view of collective memory. In attributing coherent, if changing, memories to whole nations, Eviatar Zerubavel comes closer than any of this book's other authors to a strictly cognitive collective process in which interaction and socialization do not figure prominently. But even he treats collective memory as a form of social problem-solving. He does not reach the mind-centered extreme symbolized by Borges' fabulous memorizer.

Near the other extreme stands Paul Brass. Brass, a superbly attentive student of local conflicts in India, has recently worked on how Indians fashion stories about what happened in such conflicts. In particular, he watches how local struggles involving particular interests acquire the reputation of springing from old, categorically based hatreds. "The argument I develop," says Brass,

> is that the publicized versions of many so-called caste and communal riots in India, like many aspects of ethnic identity itself, are constructions upon events that are usually open to a multiplicity of interpretations. When examined at the actual originating sites of ethnic and communal violence, it is often the case that the precipitating incidents arise out of situations that are either not inherently ethnic/communal in nature or are ambiguous in character, that their transformation into caste or communal incidents depends upon the attitudes toward them taken by local politicians and local representatives of state authority, and that their ultimate elevation into grand communal confrontations depends upon their further reinterpretation by the press and extralocal politicians and authorities. (Brass 1997: 6)

In Brass's account, even the participants often dispute what happened, especially when the actions in question lend themselves to competing assignments of motives or responsibility. But officials, politicians, and reporters play important parts in mapping local conflicts into broader categories. They thus serve their own purposes by reproducing the divisions that inform and justify their livelihoods.

Brass devotes particular attention to an episode from which no consensus story emerged. The process of crystallization he analyzes elsewhere began, but stopped halfway, leaving contradictory narratives of what had happened rather than one hegemonic story. In 1975, someone stole an idol from a Jain temple in Madrauna, Uttar Pradesh. In 1983, residents of a nearby village unearthed the idol. Hearing of the discovery, Jains from Madrauna requested the idol's return to them, but the villagers rejected their request. While the Jains were reporting the incident to the police, enlisting help from influential regional politicians, and initiating a lawsuit, villagers were building a small temple on the village road to display the idol. On 26 May 1983, a police officer came to the village for the idol but withdrew after concluding that the villagers would resist. At 1 AM on 29 May, a regional election day, a constabulary force of 90 armed men invaded the village, fought the villagers, seized the disputed idol, and perhaps looted as well. A police captain and an ox died in the incident.

Eventually three clusters of stories competed. Jains commonly said that villagers had stolen the idol, had tried to sell its precious metals, but when detected had built their shrine to cover their tracks and claim possession; they had then resisted the police, according to this story, out of greed. Villagers often argued that the idol had appeared miraculously and that Jains and police had colluded (aided, in some accounts, by bandits) in looting the village. Higher-ranking outsiders provided interpretations in terms of confessionally based political rivalries (Brass 1997: 63–96). Collective memory failed to consolidate. Brass himself scrutinizes each competing account with exquisite care, but ultimately throws up his hands: "When such an incident involves persons of different faiths or castes, the possibilities for intensification of conflict and enlarging of its boundaries increase. In contemporary India, the enlargement of the boundaries of conflict also brings into play the multiplicity of values and discursive formations that pervade society. A local theft then becomes an incident to be placed in a broader context and struggle takes place among the parties involved to capture the incident and place it in one's favored narrative framework" (Brass 1997: 89).

In contrast to the Borges extreme, the Brass interpretation treats collective memory as a negotiated political production. The production of memory, in Brass's rendering, by no means always ends with consensus or clarity. It has nothing in common with photography, whether motion pictures or stills. Radically contradictory stories sometimes compete for priority over long periods, so long as party interests in different versions persist. Among this volume's contributors, Uri Ram's self-styled "dialectical" analysis of dissent among interpreters of the Israeli past comes closest to the Brass extreme.

Filtered record of the past or opportunistic promotion of interest-driven narratives? Let us resist two opposite temptations: to insist on one half of the dichotomy, or to assume that truth must lie halfway between the extremes. Instead of arguing either position, I want to distinguish four questions at issue in the analysis of collective memory. The four overlap but point to somewhat different kinds of answers and modes of inquiry. Each has a descriptive version (what exists?), a normative version (what should exist?), and an explanatory version (what causes it?). Here are the explanatory versions:

(1) What produces the structure and content of shared references to the past that are available in a given population?
(2) Given complex events, how and why do some elements and interpretations of those events (a) become available, (b) survive?
(3) Given the availability of multiple elements and interpretations, what causes some to prevail and others to disappear from general awareness?
(4) When people engage in public contests over the past, how, why, and with what effects do they do so?

Broadly speaking, question 1 dominates inquiries at the Borges extreme, question 4 at the Brass extreme.

Such a sorting out of relevant questions certainly does not provide definitive answers to the big questions authors in this book are pursuing. But it indicates that eventually students of collective memory themselves will have to distinguish which of these questions they are addressing. Questions 1 and 2 call for extremely general accounts of cultural production. Questions 3 and 4 move analysts into the zone of contentious politics. Authors in this book, as I read them, make gestures to questions 1 and 4, but generally concentrate on 2 and 3. In that middle zone, it is somewhat easier to adopt this book's most frequent position: that collective memory results from socially conditioned cultural production.

To be sure, reductionists lurk at either end: some culturalists see all political struggle as a form of cultural production, just as some analysts of power see all cultural production as an outcome of struggles for domination. Short of rank reductionism, however, a fruitful division of labor could emerge. From one side, analysts of stories, identities, and shared memories have much to teach students of contentious politics. From the other, analysts of contentious politics are making serious efforts to learn how stories, identities, and shared memories interact with collective struggle. In collaboration, the two groups of analysts have the capacity to create sound, valuable counterfactuals concerning collective memories that could have existed—or perhaps even did at some point—but never crystallized. *Memory and the Nation* broadens the ground for such a collaboration.

REFERENCES

Borges, J. L. 1962. *Ficciones*. New York: Grove Press.
——. 1977. *Historia de la Noche*. Buenos Aires: Emecé.
Brass, P. R., ed. 1996. *Riots and Pogroms*. New York: New York University Press.
——. 1997. *Theft of an Idol: Text and Context in the Representation of Collective Violence*. Princeton, N.J.: Princeton University Press.
Centeno, M. A. and F. López-Alves, eds. 2001. *The Other Mirror: Grand Theory through the Lens of Latin America*. Princeton, N.J.: Princeton University Press.
Hawthorn, G. 1991. *Plausible Worlds: Possibility and Understanding in History and the Social Sciences*. Cambridge: Cambridge University Press.
Tetlock, P. E. and Aaron Belkin, eds. 1996. *Counterfactual Thought Experiments in World Politics: Logical, Methodological, and Psychological Perspectives*. Princeton, N.J.: Princeton University Press.
Wong, B. 1997. *China Transformed: Historical Change and the Limits of European Experience*. Ithaca, N.Y.: Cornell University Press.

Frederick C. Corney is an assistant professor in the Department of History at the University of Florida. At present he is working on a monograph on the October Revolution as a process of cultural construction in the first decade after October 1917 in Soviet Russia, with special reference to its incorporation as part of collective and individual memory.

Simonetta Falasca Zamponi is an associate professor in the Department of Sociology at the University of California, Santa Barbara. Her areas of research include cultural sociology, political sociology, and Western European studies. Her book *Fascist Spectacle: The Aesthetics of Power in Mussolini's Italy* was awarded the 1998 Pacific Sociological Association Distinguished Scholarship Award.

Matt K. Matsuda is an associate professor teaching Modern European History and Asian and Pacific comparative histories at Rutgers University, New Brunswick. He has published widely on cultural and intellectual history and is the author of *The Memory of the Modern*. His new work, *Until the End of the World: Love, Empire, and History in the Pacific*, is forthcoming.

Tong Zhong is a graduate student in sociology at the University of Georgia.

Barry Schwartz is a professor emeritus of sociology at the University of Georgia. He is author of many books, most recently *Abraham Lincoln and the Forge of American Memory*.

Paloma Aguilar teaches political science at the Universidad Nacional de Educación a Distancia and at the Instituto Universitario Gutiérrez Mellado, both in Madrid. She is a member of the Juan March Institute (Center for Advanced Study in Social Sciences, Madrid). She is author of *Memory and Amnesia: The Role of the Spanish Civil War in the Transition to Democracy* and co-editor of *The Politics of Memory: Transitional Justice in Democratizing Societies*.

Lyn Spillman is a cultural and comparative historical sociologist; she teaches at the University of Notre Dame and is author of *Nation and Commemoration: Creating National Identities in the United States and Australia* and editor of *Cultural Sociology*. Her current research interests include cultural constraints on national collective memories, themes of diversity in American national identity, and the cultural construction of markets.

Francesca Polletta is an associate professor of sociology at Columbia University. She is author of *Freedom is an Endless Meeting: Democracy in American Social Movements* and co-editor of *Passionate Politics: Emotions and Social Movements*.

Uri Ram is a sociology lecturer in the department of Behavioral Sciences at Ben Gurion University, Beer Sheve, Israel. He is author of *The Changing Agenda of Israeli Sociology*.

Jeffrey K. Olick is an associate professor of sociology at Columbia University. He has recently completed *The Sins of the Fathers: Governing Memory in the Federal Republic of Germany* and has published numerous articles on collective memory and German politics, among other topics.

Carol Gluck is George Sansom Professor of History at Columbia University. She is author of *Japan's Modern Myths: Ideology in the Late Meiji Period*, coeditor of *Asia in Western and World History* and *Showa: The Japan of Hirohito*, and is currently working on *Versions of the Past: The Japanese and their Modern History*.

Eviatar Zerubavel is a professor of sociology at Rutgers University. His publications include *Patterns of Time in Hospital Life, Hidden Rhythms, The Seven-Day Circle, The Fine Line, Terra Cognita, Social Mindscapes, The Clockword Muse,* and *Time Maps.* He is currently working on a book on the sociology of denial.

Charles Tilly is Joseph L. Buttenwiser Professor of Social Sciences at Columbia University. His work focuses on large-scale social change and its relationship to contentious politics, especially in Europe since 1500.

Jeffrey K. Olick is Associate Professor of
Sociology at Columbia University.

Library of Congress Cataloging-in-Publication Data
States of memory : continuities, conflicts,
and transformations in national retrospection /
edited by Jeffrey K. Olick.
p. cm. — (Politics, history, and culture)
Includes bibliographical references and index.
ISBN 0-8223-3051-2 (cloth : alk. paper)
ISBN 0-8223-3063-6 (pbk. : alk. paper)
1. Memory—Social aspects. 2. History—
Psychological aspects. 3. Nationalism—Psychological
aspects. I. Olick, Jeffrey K. II. Series.
BF378.S65 S83 2003   153.1′2—dc21   2002153879